BARRON'S

Pass
Key
to the
TOEFL®
iBT

NINTH EDITION

Pamela J. Sharpe, Ph.D.

P9-CLB-488

**To my former students
at home and abroad**

Material in this book was adapted from
Barron's *How to Prepare for the TOEFL*,
14th Ed., by Pamela J. Sharpe, Ph.D. © Copyright 2013
by Barron's Educational Series, Inc.

All inquiries should be addressed to:
Barron's Educational Series, Inc.
250 Wireless Boulevard
Hauppauge, New York 11788
www.barronseduc.com

Library of Congress Control No. 2016938918

ISBN: 978-1-4380-7626-3

PRINTED IN CANADA
9 8 7 6 5 4 3 2 1

ACKNOWLEDGMENTS

With affection and appreciation, I acknowledge my indebtedness to the friends, family, and colleagues who have been part of the TOEFL team for so many years.

Dr. Jayne Harder, former Director of the English Language Institute at the University of Florida for initiating me into the science of linguistics and the art of teaching English as a second language;

Robert and Lillie Sharpe, my parents for their assistance in typing and proofreading previous editions and for their enthusiastic encouragement throughout my career;

The late Dr. Tom Clapp, former Dean of Continuing Education at the University of Toledo for the maturity and confidence that I gained during our marriage because he believed in me;

Carole Berglie, former Editor at Barron's Educational Series, Inc. for her guidance in seeing the first edition of the manuscript through to publication;

Kristen Girardi, Editor at Barron's Educational Series, Inc. for assembling an expert team, providing leadership, and creating an environment that encouraged our best work; as well as for her invaluable insights and wise counsel during every stage of development and production;

Debby Becak, Senior Production Manager at Barron's Educational Series, Inc. for the creative suggestions and designs, large and small, that have improved every chapter;

Bob O'Sullivan, Former Publisher, Test Prep Division at Barron's Educational Series, Inc. for making important decisions at critical times for previous editions;

Peter Mavrikis, Editorial Director, Test Prep Division at Barron's Educational Series, Inc. for a fresh perspective on the TOEFL and key support for the TOEFL team;

John Rockwell, Editor and President of Rockwell Audio Media, for casting and directing the talented voices and bringing the script to life;

Sara Black, Copy Editor for her constructive criticism and helpful corrections throughout the manuscript;

Kathy Telford, Proofreader at Proofreaders Plus for her attention to the important details, her positive approach to errors, and her friendship;

Dennis Oliver, Professor at Estrella Mountain Community College for collaborating on the original version of *Glossary of Campus Vocabulary*;

Robin Fogg, Professor at the Address English Center for key suggestions that made the book much easier for students to use;

John T. Osterman, my husband—a special thank you for the unconditional love and the daily interest in and support for my writing career, as well as for checking my math in the evaluation tables. Each revision of this book is better than the last, and every new and revised year with John is the best year of my life.

SOURCES/CREDITS

TABLE OF CONTENTS

9 RESOURCES 551

TIMETABLE FOR THE TOEFL® iBT

Test Section	Questions	Time
Reading	3–4 passages with 12–14 questions each	60–80 minutes
Listening	2–3 conversations with 5 questions each 2–3 lectures with 6 questions each 2–3 discussions with 6 questions each	60–90 minutes
BREAK		10 minutes
Speaking	2 independent tasks 4 integrated tasks	20 minutes
Writing	1 integrated task 1 independent task	20 minutes 30 minutes

Note: The tests in this book contain three reading passages, three conversations, three lectures and three discussions *or* four reading passages, two conversations, two lectures and two discussions because that is the standard length for an official TOEFL. Every official test includes either reading or listening material that is being field-tested for future use. There is no tutorial on the iBT.

Important Note

There are currently three different packages for *Barron's TOEFL® iBT*. The book is the same in all three packages.

1. *Barron's TOEFL® iBT* Book with 2 MP3 CDs. Prepare using the audio for the practice activities, quizzes, and the 7 model tests in the book. MP3 CDs do NOT show visuals on the computer.*
2. *Barron's TOEFL® iBT* Book with 2 MP3 CDs and 1 CD-ROM. Prepare using the audio for the practice activities and the quizzes. Use the CD-ROM for the 7 model tests in the book as well as for Model Test 8, which is a bonus test on the CD-ROM. The CD-ROM simulates the TOEFL® iBT tests on the computer, including the ability to record and play back responses in the Speaking section and save your essays.
3. *Barron's TOEFL® iBT Superpack* consisting of the *Barron's TOEFL® iBT* book with 2 MP3 CDs and CD-ROM, *Barron's Essential Words for the TOEFL*, *Barron's TOEFL Strategies and Tips* with MP3 CD, and *Barron's Writing for the TOEFL iBT* with MP3 CD.

All of the packages also include four video lessons for academic skills and access to a website that provides interactive pronunciation practice for campus vocabulary.

*If you wish to purchase the CD-ROM separately, please visit *www.barronseduc.com* for details.

1

ORIENTATION

ORIENTATION TO THE TOEFL® iBT

The TOEFL® iBT tests your ability to understand and use English for academic purposes. There are four sections on the TOEFL, with special directions for each section.

READING SECTION

The Reading section tests your ability to understand reading passages like those in college textbooks. There are three passages on the short format and four passages on the long format. After each passage, you will answer 12–14 questions about it.

LISTENING SECTION

The Listening section tests your ability to understand spoken English that is typical of interactions and academic speech on college campuses. During the test, you will listen to conversations, lectures, and discussions, and answer questions about them. There are two conversations, two lectures, and two discussions on the short format and three conversations, three lectures, and three discussions on the long format.

SPEAKING SECTION

The Speaking section tests your ability to communicate in English in an academic setting. During the test, you will be presented with six speaking questions. The questions ask for a response to a single question; a reading passage and a conversation; a reading passage and a lecture; a conversation or a lecture.

WRITING SECTION

The Writing section tests your ability to write essays in English similar to those that you would write in college courses. During the test, you will write one essay about an academic topic and one essay about a familiar topic.

TO THE STUDENT: HOW TO USE THIS BOOK TO SUCCEED

A STUDY PLAN

Welcome to *Barron's Pass Key to the TOEFL® iBT, 9th Edition.* Do you know what a pass key is? A pass key is a master key, a key that opens every door. This book and the audio CDs were designed to help you prepare for the iBT®—the Internet-Based TOEFL. After you have succeeded on the TOEFL, other doors will open for you. But first you need a pass key to unlock the TOEFL.

Barron's Pass Key to the TOEFL® iBT, 9th Edition is the concise version of the classic book, *Barron's TOEFL® iBT, 15th Edition.* Small enough to carry in your backpack, book bag, or even a purse, this convenient book can always be in the right place when you have a few minutes to study—on the bus, while you wait for an appointment, or on break at work or school.

This concise version, *Pass Key to the TOEFL® iBT, 9th Edition*, can be used to prepare for the Internet-Based TOEFL® iBT. To make this book less expensive and more convenient to carry with you, we have included three model tests in the book along with audio for each test. The larger version of this book, *Barron's TOEFL® iBT,*

15th Edition, includes a detailed review of academic skills that you will need to develop, as well as four more model tests for a total of seven model tests. The CDs that supplement the larger book provide the audio for all seven model tests. The CD-ROM that supplements the larger book includes both the audio and the visuals for the seven model tests on computer screens. It also includes a bonus model test.

Ideally, you would use the two versions of this book for two different purposes. You would use this book, *Pass Key to the TOEFL® iBT, 9th Edition*, to take the best advantage of your time while you are away from your computer or when you don't want to carry heavy materials. You would use the larger version of the book, *Barron's TOEFL® iBT, 15th Edition*, and the CD-ROM that supplements it, to study academic skills, practice taking additional model tests, and simulate the experience of taking the TOEFL® iBT on the computer.

Whether you decide to use this book alone or in combination with the larger version, study thoughtfully, and take the TOEFL with confidence. It may well be the most important examination of your academic career. And this book can be a pass key to your success.

STEPS TO SUCCESS

This book is easy to use. More than one million Barron's students have succeeded on the TOEFL. You can be successful too, by following twelve steps.

➤ 1. Inform yourself about the test.

Read the answers to "FAQs—Frequently Asked Questions About the TOEFL® iBT" in this chapter. Then, if you cannot find a copy locally, visit the TOEFL web site at *www.ets.org/toefl* to download a copy of the *TOEFL Information and Registration Bulletin*. Research demonstrates that students who know what to expect will perform better on an examination.

➤ 2. Invest time in your study plan.

Be realistic about how much time you need to prepare for the TOEFL. Choose a syllabus from the choices in this chapter. Use distributed practice—two hours every day for four months will give you better results than twelve hours every day for ten days, even though you will be studying 120 hours for both schedules.

➤ 3. Develop study habits.

The study habits explained at the end of this chapter will help you succeed on the TOEFL and after the TOEFL when you are admitted to a college or university, or when you continue your professional training to keep your licenses current. Successful students understand the value of these habits.

➤ 4. Evaluate your strengths and weaknesses.

Take the Pretest, Model Test 1 in Chapter 4 and check your answers using the Explanatory or Example Answers in Chapter 7. Which sections of the TOEFL were easier for you? Which were more difficult? Plan to spend more time on the sections on which you received lower scores.

➤ 5. Master academic skills.

Chapter 3 contains ten of the academic skills that you will need to complete the tasks on the TOEFL® iBT. Read the strategies, complete the practice activities, and check your answers. If this chapter is difficult for you, it may be a good idea to refer to the larger version of this book, *Barron's TOEFL® iBT, 15th Edition*. The larger version includes forty academic skills.

➤ 6. Improve English proficiency.

Chapter 2 will show you how your English proficiency is tested on the TOEFL. Review important types of questions and identify strategies for the language skill that corresponds to each section—Reading, Listening, Speaking, and Writing. Take the quizzes and check your answers. Although you need to know more English than it is possible to include in one chapter, this review will help you apply the English you know to the test situation. You will improve your English proficiency as measured by the TOEFL.

➤ 7. Understand the directions.

Take the time to read and understand the directions for each question in Chapter 2 and each section on the model tests. If you already understand what to do in order to complete a certain type of question, you will not have to spend as much valuable time reading and analyzing the directions when you take the official TOEFL.

➤ 8. Check your progress.

After you finish the work in Chapters 2 and 3, you will be ready to check your progress. Take the first Progress Test, Model Test 2 in Chapter 5 and check your answers using the Explanatory or Example Answers in Chapter 7. You should begin to see how the academic skills are used on the TOEFL® iBT.

➤ 9. Practice taking model tests.

Students who have an opportunity to take at least one model test will almost always increase their scores significantly on the official TOEFL test. Experience is a great teacher. This book provides you with three model tests for practice. In order to take advantage of these experiences, you should always follow the test directions carefully and time each section. Take each model test without stopping for a break until you finish the Reading and Listening sections. Then take a ten-minute break and work without stopping until you complete the Speaking and Writing sections. By simulating the test conditions, you will become familiar with the way that it feels to take the TOEFL and you will be able to concentrate on the questions instead of trying to figure out what is going to happen next. You will also learn to pace yourself so that you can finish each section within the time limits. Remember, you should not try to memorize the questions on the model tests. You will find similar questions on the official TOEFL, but you will not find exactly the same questions. Try to improve your skills, not your memory.

➤ 10. Estimate your TOEFL score.

Chapter 8 gives you a method for estimating your TOEFL score from scores on the model tests in this book. If you do not have a teacher or a reliable grader to evaluate your speaking and writing sections, you may want to consider using one of the services listed at the end of the chapter. You need to know how your speaking and writing will factor into the total score.

➤ 11. Maintain a positive attitude.

Throughout the book, you will find advice for staying positive and motivated. Most of it can be found under the heading "Advisor's Office." Take the time to read the suggestions and think about them. Other successful students have benefited from the same advice.

➤ 12. Take the test when you are ready.

Some students try to succeed on the TOEFL before they are ready. Be realistic about your study schedule. If you are not scoring very well on the model tests and the estimates of your TOEFL scores are below the minimum for you to achieve your goal, you should reconsider your registration date. Knowing when to take the test is part of a successful study plan. If you give yourself the time you need and if you follow the study plan using this book, you will reach your goal. In the future, you will not be asked whether you took the TOEFL a month earlier or later but you *will* be asked to produce the required score. You can do it! Take the test when you are ready.

TO THE TEACHER: RECOMMENDATIONS AND RESOURCES

PERSPECTIVES

In the Middle Ages, a man approached two stonemasons and asked them what they were doing. The first stonemason replied, "I am laying stones." The other answered, "I am building a cathedral."

I have been teaching TOEFL preparation classes since 1970 and writing TOEFL materials since 1975. As I go into my classes, I ask myself: Am I teaching TOEFL prep or am I helping students achieve their career goals? As I prepare each new edition of my books, I ask myself: Am I writing TOEFL preparation books or am I making tools that will help students succeed on the TOEFL and *after* the TOEFL? It is a very different perspective and inspires in a different way.

Certainly, we have seen many changes in the TOEFL across the decades. Often Educational Testing Service has revised the TOEFL in an effort to keep pace with changes in our ESL/EFL teaching paradigms, and occasionally the revisions in the TOEFL have produced changes in our teaching paradigms in something referred to as a *washback effect*.

This is probably the most challenging time in TOEFL preparation that I have experienced because the Internet-Based TOEFL (iBT) is more than a revision. It is a completely different kind of test, which requires a new approach to learning. Our students will have to demonstrate their ability to integrate the language skills by completing tasks similar to those that they will be expected to accomplish in academic settings. They will have to speak and write at high levels of proficiency.

Eventually, I believe that the changes on the TOEFL® iBT will be beneficial for our students and for us, their teachers. During the initial transition period, however, it could be difficult to plan appropriate lessons and adjust our teaching styles.

TEACHING TIPS

These ideas work for me. I invite you to try some of them in your classes.

➤ 1. Begin with a positive message.

It can be very simple. For instance, "The highest tower is built one brick at a time." If you put a new message in the same place every time—on an overhead or on the board—students will learn to look for it when they come into the room. Music serves the same purpose. It sets a positive mood for the session.

➤ 2. Write three important goals for the class so that students can see them.

Three goals are manageable for one class session. When they are visible, they keep us all on track. At the end of the class, referring to the goals gives everyone a sense of progress and closure for the day.

➤ 3. Arrange for model tests to be taken in a lab or at home on the honor system.

Your time with students is too valuable for you to spend four hours proctoring each model test. That would add up to twelve hours of class time for all of the model tests in this book.

➤ 4. Allow students to grade the Reading and Listening sections of their model tests.

If students take responsibility for grading the objective sections of their model tests, and for referring to the explanatory answers, you will save hours that you would have had to use doing routine clerical tasks. If the students take the model tests on the computer, the scoring for these sections will be done automatically; if they are using the book, the answer key is printed in Chapter 7. This will afford you the time you need to concentrate on answering questions.

➤ 5. Ask your students to send you their questions on email before class.

When students refer to the explanatory answers, many questions are resolved for them without asking the teacher. If students write down their questions, sometimes the answer becomes apparent to them at this stage. The questions that they bring to class are really worth discussion. If you have them on email, you can prepare your answers for the question-and-answer session at the beginning of the next class. You always have the answer!

➤ 6. When several students have the same question, prepare a short presentation.

When the question is repeated, it gives us an indication of what our students need to know. By using their questions for class preparation, we show that we are teaching people, not subjects.

➤ 7. Make slides of test questions and show the students how you choose an answer.

Let the students "listen in" on your thought processes as you decide why answers are incorrect and which answer choice is correct. Use the explanatory answers in the book to help you. For example, you might say, "I know that A is not correct because the professor did not include this research in his lecture. Choice B looks possible, but it is not complete. The choice leaves out the second part of the answer. That means it must be either Choice C or D. I know that D is not correct because the professor said that there were three types, not two. It must be Choice C." Modeling *how* to think helps students *learn* to think when they see similar test items.

➤ 8. Use class time to teach and practice academic skills.

Make slides of material from Chapter 3 and go over it in class. Take the quizzes in class, using "Think, Answer, Compare, Discuss." Students have time to think and respond to each answer independently, and then they compare their answers to the correct answer and discuss why that choice is a good one.

➤ 9. Focus on speaking and writing in class.

Provide many good models of responses to speaking and writing questions in class. Show students how to use the checklists to evaluate speaking and writing.

➤ 10. Assign speaking tasks and writing tasks as homework.

Have students turn in speaking assignments and essays. Students can send sound files to you with one-minute responses to speaking tasks. Spend grading time on these important sections. Bring samples of good work to class—good organization, good openings, good support statements, good closings. Catch your students doing something good and use it as an example.

➤ 11. Provide counseling and encouragement as part of the class routine.

Ideally, one minute at the end of class can be used for a pep talk, a cheer, or a success story about a former student. This is one of my favorite cheers: T-O-E-F-L. We're making progress. We're doing well. T-O-E-F-L. I also like to stand by a poster at the door when students are leaving my class. The last thing they see is the affirmation on the poster: "I know more today than I did yesterday. I am preparing. I will succeed." Some students want a handshake, a high five, or a hug. Others just smile and say good-bye. Some hang by the door, and I know that they need to talk. Every excellent TOEFL prep teacher I know is also a very good counselor. You probably are, too.

RESOURCES

Several resources for teachers are listed in Chapter 9. Four syllabus options are listed in the next section. It is also worthwhile to read the "Steps to Success" for students printed on the previous pages. The most frequently asked questions (FAQs) are answered at the end of this chapter. If I can be of help to you or your students, please contact me at *sharpe@teflprep.com* or by visiting my website at *www.teflprep.com*.

SYLLABUS OPTIONS

A *syllabus* is a "study plan." There are four options from which to choose. The estimated number of hours for each option is the minimum time that is required to complete the plan.

The Standard Syllabus requires 12 weeks and 100 hours of your time. It is the best option because it allows you to study about 8 hours each week, and you can build in some review if you need it.

The Accelerated Syllabus also requires 100 hours, but it is possible to complete it in half the number of weeks by making a commitment to studying 15–20 hours each week. *Accelerated* means "fast." This calendar does not include time for review.

The Abbreviated Syllabus should be chosen only when you cannot find the time in your schedule to follow one of the other calendars. *Abbreviated* means "shorter." This calendar does not allow you to complete all the study materials in the larger book. This concise version, *Barron's Pass Key to the TOEFL® iBT, 9th Edition*, contains only the material in the abbreviated syllabus.

The Individualized Syllabus is often chosen when you have already taken the TOEFL and you are very sure which sections will be most difficult for you when you take it again. This calendar allows you to concentrate on one or two sections without repeating information that you have already mastered on other sections.

Note: For a classroom syllabus instead of a self-study syllabus, teachers can contact Dr. Sharpe at *sharpe@teflprep.com*. The classroom syllabus includes an outline for class, lab, homework, and extra credit.

Standard Syllabus—12 Weeks/100 Hours

Textbook: *Barron's TOEFL® iBT 15th Edition*

Week	Topic	Reference Chapter	Estimate
1	Orientation Model Test 1: Pretest	Chapter 1, Pages 1–25 *Read the Orientation* Chapter 4, Pages 207–252 *Take all four sections of the test* Chapter 5, Pages 580–613 *Study the Explanatory and Example Answers*	8 hours
2	Review of TOEFL Sections	Chapter 2, Pages 27–38, 45–55, 60–76, 80–91 *Read the review of question types for each section* *Take the quiz for each section* Chapter 5, Pages 39–44, 56–59, 77–79, 91–93 *Study the Explanatory and Example Answers*	8 hours
3	Model Test 2: Progress Test	Chapter 4, Pages 253–297 *Take all four sections of the test* Chapter 5, Pages 614–642 *Study the Explanatory and Example Answers*	8 hours
4	Academic Skills	Chapter 3, Pages 95–130 *Study Campus Vocabulary and Taking Notes* *Complete Practice Activities* Chapter 5, Pages 535–545 *Study the Answers and Scripts*	8 hours
5	Academic Skills	Chapter 3, Pages 131–179 *Study Paraphrasing and Summarizing* *Complete Practice Activities* Chapter 5, Pages 545–563 *Study the Answers and Scripts*	8 hours
6	Academic Skills	Chapter 3, Pages 180–206 *Study Synthesizing* *Complete Practice Activities* Chapter 5, Pages 564–579 *Study the Answers and Scripts*	8 hours

Week	Topic	Reference Chapter	Estimate
7	Model Test 3: Progress Test	Chapter 4, Pages 298–342 *Take all four sections of the test* Chapter 5, Pages 643–677 *Study the Explanatory and Example Answers*	8 hours
8	Model Test 4: Progress Test	Chapter 4, Pages 343–384 *Take all four sections of the test* Chapter 5, Pages 678–705 *Study the Explanatory and Example Answers*	8 hours
9	Model Test 5: Progress Test	Chapter 4, Pages 385–427 *Take all four sections of the test* Chapter 5, Pages 706–738 *Study the Explanatory and Example Answers*	8 hours
10	Model Test 6: Progress Test	Chapter 4, Pages 428–473 *Take all four sections of the test* Chapter 5, Pages 739–768 *Study the Explanatory and Example Answers*	8 hours
11	Model Test 7: Progress Test	Chapter 4, Pages 474–518 *Take all four sections of the test* Chapter 5, Pages 769–802 *Study the Explanatory and Example Answers*	8 hours
12	Model Test 8: CD–ROM Test	*Take all four sections of the test on the CD-ROM in Test Mode* *Study the Explanatory and Example Answers in Practice Mode*	12 hours

Accelerated Syllabus: 6 Weeks/100 Hours

Textbook: *Barron's TOEFL® iBT 15th Edition*

Week	Topic	Reference Chapter	Estimate
1	Orientation Model Test 1: Pretest	Chapter 1, Pages 1–25 *Read the Orientation* Chapter 4, Pages 207–252 *Take all four sections of the test* Chapter 5, Pages 580–613 *Study the Explanatory and Example* * Answers*	15 hours
	Review of TOEFL Sections	Chapter 2, Pages 27–38, 45–55, 60–76, 80–91 *Read the review of question types* * for each section* *Take the quiz for each section* Chapter 5, Pages 39–44, 56–59, 77–79, 91–93 *Study the Explanatory and Example* * Answers*	
2	Model Test 2: Progress Test	Chapter 4, Pages 253–297 *Take all four sections of the test* Chapter 5, Pages 614–642 *Study the Explanatory and Example* * Answers*	20 hours
	Academic Skills	Chapter 3, Pages 95–130 *Study Campus Vocabulary and* * Taking Notes* *Complete Practice Activities* Chapter 5, Pages 535–545 *Study the Answers and Scripts*	
3	Academic Skills	Chapter 3, Pages 131–179 *Study Paraphrasing and* * Summarizing* *Complete Practice Activities* Chapter 5, Pages 545–563 *Study the Answers and Scripts* Chapter 3, Pages 180–206 *Study Synthesizing* *Complete Practice Activities* Chapter 5, Pages 564–579 *Study the Answers and Scripts*	20 hours

Week	Topic	Reference Chapter	Estimate
4	Model Test 3: Progress Test	Chapter 4, Pages 298–342 *Take all four sections of the test* Chapter 5, Pages 643–677 *Study the Explanatory and Example Answers*	15 hours
	Model Test 4: Progress Test	Chapter 4, Pages 343–384 *Take all four sections of the test* Chapter 5, Pages 678–705 *Study the Explanatory and Example Answers*	
5	Model Test 5: Progress Test	Chapter 4, Pages 385–427 *Take all four sections of the test* Chapter 5, Pages 706–738 *Study the Explanatory and Example Answers*	15 hours
	Model Test 6: Progress Test	Chapter 4, Pages 428–473 *Take all four sections of the test* Chapter 5, Pages 739–768 *Study the Explanatory and Example Answers*	
6	Model Test 7: Progress Test	Chapter 4, Pages 474–518 *Take all four sections of the test* Chapter 5, Pages 769–802 *Study the Explanatory and Example Answers*	15 hours
	Model Test 8: CD–ROM Test	CD-ROM *Take all four sections of the test on the CD-ROM in Test Mode* *Study the Explanatory and Example Answers in Practice Mode*	

Abbreviated Syllabus: 4 Weeks/50 Hours

Textbook: *Barron's Pass Key to the TOEFL® 9th Edition*

Week	Topic	Reference Chapter	Estimate
1	Orientation Model Test 1: Pretest	Chapter 1, Pages 1–35 *Read the Orientation* Chapter 4, Pages 187–244 *Take all four sections of the test* Chapter 7, Pages 403–450 *Study the Explanatory and Example Answers*	12 hours
	Review of TOEFL Sections	Chapter 2, Pages 37–134 *Read the review of question types for each section and the quiz for each section* *Skim the Explanatory and Example Answers*	
2	Model Test 2: Progress Test	Chapter 5, Pages 245–302 *Take all four sections of the test* Chapter 7, Pages 451–491 *Study the Explanatory and Example Answers*	12 hours
	Academic Skills	Chapter 3, Pages 135–153 *Study Campus Vocabulary and Taking Notes* *Read the Practice Activities* Chapter 7, Pages 380–382 *Skim the Answers and Scripts*	
3	Academic Skills	Chapter 3, Pages 154–170 *Study Paraphrasing and Summarizing* *Read the Practice Activities* Chapter 7, Pages 383–391 *Skim the Answers and Scripts* Chapter 3, Pages 170–186 *Study Synthesizing* *Complete Practice Activities* Chapter 7, Pages 391–402 *Study the Answers and Scripts*	20 hours
4	Model Test 3: Progress Test	Chapter 6, Pages 303–358 *Take all four sections of the test* Chapter 7, Pages 492–540 *Study the Explanatory and Example Answers*	6 hours

Individualized Syllabus: Variable Weeks/Hours

Textbook: *Barron's TOEFL® iBT 15th Edition*

Week	Topic	Reference Chapter	Estimate
1	Orientation Model Test 1: Pretest	Chapter 1, Pages 1–25 *Read the Orientation* Chapter 4, Pages 207–252 *Take all four sections of the test* Chapter 5, Pages 580–613 *Study the Explanatory and Example Answers*	15 hours
	Review of TOEFL Sections	Chapter 2, Pages 27–93 *Read the review of question types for each section and the quiz for each section* *Study the Explanatory and Example Answers*	
2	Group and Individual Assignments	Concentrate on the most challenging sections	As needed

Both *Barron's TOEFL® iBT, 15th Edition* and *Barron's Pass Key to the TOEFL® iBT, 9th Edition,* are designed to support self-study. After analyzing the Pretest, the teacher can assign individualized review by selecting the chapters and pages that focus on the most challenging sections of the test for each student. It is often helpful to divide the class into groups of students who have similar patterns of error on the Pretest. Model tests provide a process for monitoring individual progress and redirecting student effort. Students who are not in a class can determine which sections of the test require the most time for self-study. *Barron's Practice Exercises for the TOEFL®, 8th Edition,* and *Barron's TOEFL Strategies and Tips: Outsmart the TOEFL, 2nd Edition*, are additional resources for individual practice.

FAQs—FREQUENTLY ASKED QUESTIONS ABOUT THE TOEFL® iBT

The TOEFL is the Test of English as a Foreign Language. More than 30 million students from 180 countries have registered to take the TOEFL at 4,500 test centers throughout the world. Some of them do not score well because they do not understand enough English. Others do not score well because they do not understand the examination. The following questions are frequently asked by students as they prepare for the TOEFL.

TOEFL PROGRAMS

➤ What is the purpose of the TOEFL?

Since 1963, the TOEFL has been used by scholarship selection committees of governments, universities, and agencies such as Fulbright, the Agency for International Development, AMIDEAST, and Latin American Scholarship Programs as a standard measure of the English proficiency of their candidates. Some professional licensing and certification agencies also use TOEFL scores to evaluate English proficiency. The admissions committees of more than 9,000 colleges and universities in the United States, Canada, Australia, Great Britain, and 130 other countries worldwide require foreign applicants to submit TOEFL scores along with transcripts and recommendations in order to be considered for admission. In addition, workers applying for visas often use TOEFL scores as part of their applications.

➤ When will the TOEFL® iBT be administered in my country?

The TOEFL® iBT is offered in 180 countries at thousands of sites, and new sites are opened every month. It is now very convenient to take the TOEFL® iBT. The Paper-Based TOEFL (PBT) is still offered in a few remote areas or in locations where the Internet is difficult to access, but 96 percent of all TOEFL administrations are iBT exams. The TOEFL iBT is offered more than 50 times every year. To see a schedule of times and test centers, visit the TOEFL website or check the *TOEFL® iBT Registration and Information Bulletin* on the TOEFL website at *www.ets.org/toefl*. A revised timeline is continuously updated on the TOEFL website.

➤ May I choose the format that I prefer—iBT or PBT?

The official TOEFL is offered in two formats—the Internet-Based TOEFL (iBT) or the Paper-Based TOEFL (PBT). The format that you take depends on the test center location for which you register. Only a 4 percent of the time sites continue to offer the PBT, and it is being phased out.

➤ What is the Institutional TOEFL Program (ITP)?

Many schools, colleges, universities, and private agencies administer the Institutional TOEFL (ITP). The Institutional TOEFL is used for admission, placement, eligibility, or employment only at the school or agency that offers the test. The dates for the Institutional TOEFL usually correspond to the beginning of an academic session on a college or university calendar. The fees are set by the institution administering the test. The format is paper-based. If you plan to use your TOEFL score for a different college, university, or agency, you should not take the Institutional TOEFL at another site. You should register for the official iBT.

➤ Which language skills are tested on the TOEFL?

Institutional TOEFL (ITP)	Internet-Based TOEFL (iBT)
Listening	Listening
Structure	Speaking
Reading	Reading
Optional Essay	Writing

➤ Does the TOEFL have a Speaking section?

The Internet-Based TOEFL (iBT) includes a Speaking section with six questions. No Speaking section is currently planned for the Institutional ITP.

➤ Why was the Structure section removed from the TOEFL® iBT?

Grammar is tested as part of the other sections. It is important to use good grammar in the Speaking and the Writing sections.

➤ Will the TOEFL® iBT writing topics be published?

Not at this time. However, many of the topics that were previously published are similar to the types of topics found on the independent writing task for the iBT.

➤ Which keyboard will be used for the Writing section?

A standard English language QWERTY keyboard will be used for the Writing section on TOEFL® iBT examinations worldwide. QWERTY is the most common keyboard for English-language computers. Its name refers to the first six letters on the top row left. It is a good idea to practice on this type of keyboard when you prepare for the TOEFL, using the model tests in this book.

➤ Is it possible to take the iBT without the Speaking or the Writing sections?

The Speaking section and the Writing section are required on the Internet-Based TOEFL. You must take all sections of the TOEFL in order to receive a score.

➤ Is the Internet-Based TOEFL more difficult than previous TOEFL formats?s

Although the Reading and Listening sections contain longer passages, the questions are not very different from those on previous TOEFL formats. However, most students find the Speaking and Writing sections more challenging. That is why it is a good idea to practice, using this book.

REGISTRATION

➤ How do I register for the TOEFL?

You can register for the Internet-Based TOEFL online, by mail, or by telephone.

Online   *www.ets.org/toefl* for testing worldwide

Phone   1-800-GO-TOEFL (1-800-468-6335) or 1-443-751-4862 for testing in the United States, U.S. territories, and Canada, or call your Regional Registration Center for testing outside the United States and Canada.

Mail   Download a registration form from the TOEFL website and mail it to the closest Regional Registration Center (addresses listed in the *TOEFL® iBT Registration and Information Bulletin* and on the ETS website as well as in the Resources on pages 553–556 of this book).

➤ Where can I find a free TOEFL® iBT Registration and Information Bulletin?

This important bulletin includes the information that you will need to register for the TOEFL. It can be downloaded free from the TOEFL website *www.ets.org/toefl*. In addition, most Regional Registration Centers have paper copies of the bulletin, or it can be found at many libraries, universities, and educational counseling centers around the world.

➤ Where are the TOEFL® iBT Resource Centers?

Resource centers support the test sites and counseling centers in each region. They are listed in the Resources found in Chapter 9 of this book. Remember, TOEFL iBT Resource Centers cannot usually assist with registration or score reporting.

➤ Will my registration be confirmed?

Your registration number can be printed when you register online, and you will also receive your number by email.

➤ When should I register for the TOEFL?

You must register at least seven days before the test date. If there is space, you may register three days before the test date. The late fee for a three-day registration is $40. Because test centers fill rapidly during desirable times, it is a good idea to register three or four months in advance. You will have a chance to see a list of available testing centers before you complete your registration. If you are taking the TOEFL as part of the application process for college or university admission, you should plan to take the test early enough for your score to be received by the admission office before the application deadline.

➤ May I change the date or cancel my registration?

To receive a refund, you must reschedule or cancel three full days before your test date. For example, if your test is on Friday, you must call to cancel your registration on Monday. If you cancel your registration, you will usually receive half of your test fee as a refund. Some countries have additional requirements.

➤ What are the fees for the TOEFL® iBT?

The fee for the test administration, including four score reports depends on the location that your choose. Current fees range from $160 to $250 U.S.

➤ How may I pay the fees?

You may pay by credit card, e-check from bank accounts in the United States and its territories, PayPal, paper checks for accepted currencies, or money orders in U.S. dollars drawn on a bank in the United States, checks in Canadian dollars drawn on a bank in Canada, and euro checks drawn on a bank in the same country as the person writing the check. For a list of centers and resellers in your area, visit the TOEFL website at *www.ets.org/toefl*. Accepted currencies include U.S. dollars, British pounds, Canadian dollars, euros, and Japanese yen.

TEST ADMINISTRATION

➤ How is the TOEFL® iBT administered?

The TOEFL is offered on a schedule of dates in a network of test centers throughout the world. The room in which the TOEFL is administered is usually a computer lab. You will be assigned a seat. If you are late, you will probably not be admitted.

➤ Where can I take the TOEFL?

The TOEFL website at *www.ets.org/toefl* lists test centers and schedules.

➤ When should I arrive at the test center?

You must arrive at least 30 minutes before your test is scheduled to begin so that you can complete the check-in procedure. You should allow plenty of time to travel to the center so that you are not feeling rushed and stressed before you begin your exam.

➤ In what room will the test be offered?

The room may be a computer lab or a language laboratory. It may be a classroom with about fifteen computers at least four feet apart. You will be assigned a seat.

➤ What should I take with me to the test room?

Take your registration confirmation with your registration number on it and your valid identification to the test site. You are not permitted to take anything with you when you enter the test room except your identification. No cell phones, watches, paper, dictionaries, pens, or pencils are allowed. The test supervisor will give you a headset, paper, and pencils. Some of the sites have lockers for you to store your personal items, but some sites do not have secure storage space. You should not take anything to the test site that is too large for a small locker.

➤ What kind of identification is required?

In the United States, only your valid passport will be accepted for admission to the TOEFL. In other countries, your valid passport is still the best identification, but if you do not have a passport, you may refer to the TOEFL website for special directions. Your photograph will be taken at the test center and reproduced on all official score reports, along with your signature. Be sure to use the same spelling and order of your name on your registration materials, the test center log that you will sign when you enter and leave the test area, the forms on the computer screens, and any correspondence that you may have with the TOEFL office. You should also use the same spelling on applications for schools and documents for agencies that will receive your score reports. Even a small difference can cause serious delays or even denial of the applications. You should also take your registration number with you. You will find this number on the confirmation receipt that you are sent when you register. At some centers, thumb prints, hand-held metal detectors, biometric voice identifications, and others forms of technology will be used to verify your identity.

➤ What are the procedures before testing?

You will be asked to copy a paragraph in which you agree not to share information about the test. Then you will have your photograph taken and other security procedures will be performed.

EXAMINATION

➤ How long is the testing session?

The TOEFL® iBT takes about four to four and a half hours to administer, including the time required for giving directions and the break between the Listening and the Speaking sections.

➤ What kinds of questions are found on the TOEFL® iBT?

The majority of the questions on the iBT are multiple choice. Some computer-assisted questions are also on the iBT. These questions have special directions on the screen. You will have many examples of them in the model tests in this book.

➤ Are all of the TOEFL® iBT tests the same?

Unlike some computer-based tests that present questions based on your responses to previous questions, the iBT is a linear test. That means that on the same form, all of the test questions are the same. More than one form may be administered on the same day, however.

➤ Why are some of the Reading and Listening sections longer?

Some of the tests include questions that are being field tested for use in future exams. Test developers include the experimental questions for either the Reading or the Listening section. Your answers to these experimental questions will not be calculated as part of your score, but you must do your best on all the questions because you will not know which questions are experimental and which are test questions that will be scored. For example, you may be taking the iBT with someone who has experimental questions in Reading, but you may have experimental questions in Listening. For this reason, your friend's test may have a longer Reading section, and your test may have a longer Listening section. The experimental questions may be at the beginning, middle, or end of the section.

➤ May I choose the order of the sections on my TOEFL?

You may not choose the order. Reading, Listening, Speaking, and Writing are tested in that order on the TOEFL, with a 10-minute break between the Listening and Speaking.

➤ What kinds of questions are found on the TOEFL® iBT?

Most of the questions are multiple choice, but some questions have special directions on the screen. You will have examples of the most frequently-tested items in Chapter 2 in this book.

➤ May I take notes?

You are permitted to take notes and use them to answer the questions on the iBT. You will be given scratch paper for that purpose when you enter the test room. Your notes will not be graded. They will be collected and shredded after the test.

➤ May I change an answer?

The Reading section is divided into passages. You can change your answer by clicking on a new answer. You can change your answer as many times as you wish, and you can go back to previous answers in the same passage or previous passages. On the Listening section, you can change your answer by clicking on a new answer. You can change your answer as many times as you wish until you click on the **Confirm Answer** (**OK**) button. On the Speaking section, you will be cued with a beep to begin and end speaking. Everything that you say during the recording time will be submitted. You cannot change an answer. On the Writing section, you can revise your essays as much as you wish until the clock indicates that no time is remaining. If you submit your essays before time is up, you cannot return to them. The CD-ROM that supplements the larger version of this book will provide you with practice in choosing and changing answers on the computer screen.

➤ If I am not sure of an answer, should I guess?

If you are not sure of an answer, you should guess. The number of incorrect answers is not subtracted from your score. First, eliminate all the possibilities that you know are NOT correct. Then, if you are almost sure of an answer, guess that one. If you have no idea of the correct answer for a question, choose one letter and use it for your "guess answer" throughout the entire examination. The "guess answer" is especially useful for finishing a section quickly.

➤ What if I cannot hear the audio for the Listening section?

You will receive your own headphones with a microphone attached. Before the test begins, you will have an opportunity to adjust the volume yourself. Be careful to adjust the volume when you are prompted to do so. If there is a problem with your headset, raise your hand, and ask the test supervisor to provide you with another headset.

➤ Will everyone speak at the same time to record the answers for the Speaking section?

Speakers will begin to record their answers at slightly different times. The problem is that you may be disturbed by the noise while you are trying to concentrate on your answers either on the Speaking section or on other sections of the TOEFL. It is a good idea to keep your earphones on during the entire test in order to block out as much of the noise as possible.

➤ What can I do if there is a problem during the test?

If there is a problem with the Internet connection or the power that supplies the computers, and if the test must be discontinued, everyone who is taking the test at that site is entitled to a refund or a free test on another date. This does not happen very often.

➤ What if I have a personal problem during the test?

If you become ill or you are being disturbed by the behavior of another person in the room, raise your hand and tell your test supervisor immediately. If you think that your score may be affected by the problem, ask the supervisor to file a report.

➤ Are breaks scheduled during the TOEFL?

A mandatory 10-minute break is scheduled between the Listening and the Speaking sections. If you need to use the restroom at another time during the test, you may, but the test clock will not stop while you are gone.

➤ How often may I take the TOEFL® iBT?

You may take the TOEFL® iBT as many times as you wish to score to your satisfaction, but only once within 12 days.

➤ If I have already taken the TOEFL, how will the previous scores affect my new score?

TOEFL scores are valid for two years. If you have taken the TOEFL more than once but your first score report is more than two years ago, the first score will not be reported. If you have taken the TOEFL more than once in the past two years, a report will be sent for the test date that you request.

➤ May I keep my test?

You cannot save your test to a disk or send it to an email address. If you try to do so, the TOEFL office may take legal action.

➤ What happens to someone who cheats on the TOEFL® iBT?

Entering the room with false identification, tampering with the computer, using a camera, giving or receiving help, or trying to remove test materials or notes is considered cheating. Do not cheat. In spite of opportunity, knowledge that others are doing it, the desire to help a friend, or fear that you will not make a good score, *do not cheat*. On the TOEFL, cheating is a very serious matter. If you are discovered, you will be dismissed from the room, your score will be canceled, and you may not be able to take the test again on a future date.

SCORE REPORTS

➤ How is the Speaking section scored?

Trained raters listen to each of the speaking responses and assign them a number 0–4. The scores for all six responses are converted to a total section score 0–30. The raters grade the Speaking section using checklists similar to those printed in this book.

➤ How is the Writing section scored?

Trained raters read your essays and assign them a number 0–5. Automated machine scoring called e-rater complements the scores by human raters. If there is disagreement about your score, a team leader will also read your essays. The scores for each essay are combined and converted to a section score 0–30. Raters grade the Writing section using checklists similar to those printed in this book. The combination of human raters for content and meaning and machine scoring for language and mechanics provides a more objective evaluation.

➤ How is the total TOEFL score calculated?

The iBT has converted section scores for each of the four sections. The range for each section score is 0–30. When the scores for the four sections are added together, the total score range is 0–120.

➤ How do I interpret my score?

You cannot pass or fail the TOEFL. Each school or agency will evaluate the scores according to its own requirements. Even at the same university, the requirements may vary for different programs of study, levels of study (graduate or undergraduate), and degrees of responsibility (student or teaching assistant). Many universities are setting minimum requirements for each section. The following range of requirements is typical of admissions policies for North American, European, Australian, and UK colleges and universities. This assumes, of course, that the applicant's documents other than English proficiency are acceptable.

Reading	20–25
Listening	20–25
Speaking	20–25
Writing	20–25
TOTAL	80–100

To be certain of the requirements for your school or agency, contact them directly.

➤ How do the scores compare on the iBT and ITP formats?

The following chart compares TOEFL scores on the two current formats—the Internet-Based TOEFL (iBT) and the Institutional TOEFL Program (ITP). More detailed charts are posted on the website maintained by Educational Testing Service at *www.ets.org*.

iBT	ITP
111–120	640–677
96–110	590–639
79–95	550–589
65–78	513–549
53–64	477–512
41–52	437–476
30–40	397–436
19–29	347–396
6–18	311–346
0–5	310

➤ When can I see my scores?

You will be able to see and download your score report online about 10–13 days after you take the TOEFL. You will receive an email to verify that the score has been posted. Official score reports will be mailed to you and to the schools and agencies that you designate a few days after they have been posted online. You should expect delivery by mail in ten days in the United States and as long as six weeks outside the United States. You are entitled to five copies of your test results, including one copy for you and four official score reports.

➤ What is on the score report?

The score report includes your scores for each section of the test and your total TOEFL score, as well as a statement explaining the typical performance skills of test takers with the same score. The report does not include scores for tests that you have taken previously.

➤ May I cancel my scores?

If you choose to report your scores, you will choose four institutions or agencies to receive score reports. All of this is arranged by responding to questions on the computer screen at the end of the TOEFL exam. If you do not want your scores to be reported, click on **Cancel** when this option appears on the screen.

➤ How can I send additional score reports?

If you need more than four score reports, which are provided as part of your test fee, you may order more at $19 each. Order online or mail in the order form that you will find in your *TOEFL® iBT Registration and Information Bulletin.* You may also fax your order to 1-610-290-8972. Reports are sent in four to seven days when you order them online. Fax orders are mailed two weeks after payment.

➤ How long are my scores valid?

Your scores are valid for two years after the test date.

➤ Is there a direct correspondence between proficiency in English and a TOEFL score?

There is not always a direct correspondence between proficiency in English and a score on the TOEFL. Many students who are proficient in English are not proficient in how to approach the examination. That is why it is important to prepare by using this book.

➤ Can I estimate my TOEFL score before I take the official test?

To estimate your TOEFL score, after you complete each of the model tests, use the score estimates in Chapter 8 of this book. If you complete the model tests on the CD-ROM that supplements the larger version of this book, you will see an estimate of your TOEFL scores on the screen.

➤ Will I succeed on the TOEFL?

You will receive from your study what you give to your study. The information is here. Now, it is up to you to devote the time and the effort. More than one million students have succeeded by using *Barron's TOEFL*. You can be successful, too.

STUDY HABITS

A habit is a pattern of behavior that is acquired through repetition. Research indicates that it takes about twenty-one days to form a habit. The following study habits are characteristic of successful students. Be successful! Form these habits now. They will help you on the TOEFL and after the TOEFL.

➤ Accept responsibility.

Successful students understand that the score on the TOEFL is their responsibility. It doesn't happen because of luck. It is the result of their own efforts. Take responsibility for your TOEFL score. Don't leave it to chance.

- Don't rely on luck.
- Work diligently.

➤ Get organized.

You will need a place to study where you can concentrate. Try to find a place where you can arrange your study materials and leave them until the next study session. If that is not practical, then find a bag that you can use to store all your materials so that you can have everything you need when you go to the library or another place to study. Don't use the bag for anything else. This will save time because you will not be looking for everything in different areas of your house or room, and you will not be trying to find TOEFL preparation material among other things in the bag. You are less likely to lose important notes.

- Find a study area.
- Keep your materials in one place.

➤ Set realistic goals.

Be honest about your preparation. Students who are just beginning to learn English are not prepared to take the TOEFL. Give yourself the time you need to prepare. By setting an unrealistic goal, for example, to finish preparing with this book in one week, you will probably be very disappointed. Even advanced students need time to learn academic skills and review language skills as well as to take model tests.

- Evaluate your English.
- Set a goal that you can achieve.

➤ Make a plan.

It is not enough to have a goal, even a realistic goal. Successful students also have a plan to accomplish a goal. What are you going to do to achieve the goal you have set? You will need to have time and resources. What are they? To help you make your plan, look at the options for a syllabus on pages 12–17.

- Dedicate time and resources.
- Select a syllabus.

➤ Establish priorities.

The pretest on pages 187–244 in this book will be helpful to you when you set priorities. By analyzing your strengths and weaknesses on the test, you will know which sections of the test will be the most difficult and which will be easy for you. You will also know which problems within each section require the most study. By focusing on those sections and problems, you can set priorities and use your time wisely.

- Take the pretest.
- Analyze your strengths and weaknesses.

➤ Manage time.

How do you spend time? Clearly, a certain amount of your time should be spent sleeping or relaxing. That is important to good health.

However, you should think about how much time you spend worrying or procrastinating. That is not a healthy way to spend time. Successful students have a schedule that helps them manage their time. Preparing for the TOEFL is written down on the schedule. TOEFL preparation is planned for on a regular basis just like a standing appointment. If it is written down, it is more probable that you will give it the time necessary to achieve your goal. When you start to worry, use that energy to do something positive. Learn to use time while you are waiting for an appointment or commuting on public transportation to study. Even a five-minute review will help you.

- Schedule study time.
- Use unscheduled time well.

➤ Learn from mistakes.

If you knew everything, you wouldn't need this book. Expect to make mistakes on the quizzes and on the model tests. Read the explanatory answers, and learn from your mistakes. If you do this, you will be less likely to make those mistakes again on the official TOEFL.

- Study the explanatory answers.
- Review your errors.

➤ Stay motivated.

It is easy to begin with enthusiasm, but it is more difficult to maintain your initial commitment. How do you stay motivated? To keep their energy up, some students give themselves some incentives. Without small rewards along the way, it may be more difficult to stay motivated. Just be sure that the reward doesn't take more time than the study. Remember, an incentive is supposed to keep you moving, not slow you down.

- Give yourself small incentives.
- Keep moving.

➤ Choose to be positive.

Your attitude will influence your success on the TOEFL examination. To be successful, you must develop patterns of positive thinking. To help develop a positive attitude, memorize the following sentences and bring them to mind after each study session. Bring them to mind when you begin to have negative thoughts:

I know more today than I did yesterday.
I am preparing.
I will succeed.

Remember, some tension is normal and good. Accept it. Use it constructively. It will motivate you to study. But don't panic or worry. Panic will cause loss of concentration and poor performance. Avoid people who panic and worry. Don't listen to them. They will encourage negative thoughts.

You know more today than you did yesterday.
You are preparing.
You will succeed.

There is more advice for success in the "Advisor's Office" throughout the book. Please read and consider the advice as you continue your TOEFL preparation.

REVIEW OF TOEFL® iBT SECTIONS

READING

OVERVIEW OF THE READING SECTION

The Reading section tests your ability to understand reading passages like those in college textbooks. The reading passages are presented in one complete section, which allows you to move to the next passage and return to a previous passage to change questions or answers that you may have left blank throughout the entire section. The passages are about 700 words in length.

There are two formats for the Reading section. On the short format, you will read three passages. On the long format, you will read four passages. After each passage, you will answer 12–14 questions about it. Only three passages will be graded. The other passage is part of an experimental section for future tests. Because you will not know which passages will be graded, you must try to do your best on all of them. You may take notes while you read, but notes are not graded. You may use your notes to answer the questions. Some passages may include a word or phrase that is underlined in blue. Click on the word or phrase to see a glossary definition or explanation.

Choose the best answer for multiple-choice questions. Follow the directions on the page or on the screen for computer-assisted questions. Most questions are worth 1 point, but the last question in each passage is worth more than 1 point.

Click on **Next** to go to the next question. Click on **Back** to return to previous questions. You may return to previous questions for all of the passages.

You can click on **Review** to see a chart of the questions you have answered and the questions you have not answered. From this screen, you can return to the question you want to answer.

Although you can spend more time on one passage and less time on another passage, you should try to pace yourself so that you are spending about 20 minutes to read each passage and answer the questions for that passage. You will have 60 minutes to complete all of the passages and answer all of the questions on the short format and 80 minutes to read all of the passages and answer all of the questions on the long format. A clock on the screen will show you how much time you have to complete the Reading section.

REVIEW OF PROMPTS AND QUESTIONS

➤ Prompts

A prompt for the Reading section is usually a passage from an undergraduate college textbook in one of the natural sciences, social sciences, humanities, or arts. The length of the passage is from 650 to 800 words. If there are technical words, they are explained in a glossary after the passage. There are either three or four prompts in the Reading section with twelve to fourteen questions after each prompt. When you are presented with three prompts, all three will be graded. When you are presented with four prompts, only three will be graded, and one will be used for experimental purposes. You should do your best on all four prompts because you will not know which of them will be graded. Questions 1–14 in this review refer to the following prompt:

"Producers, Consumers, and Decomposers"

P1 → Organisms that are capable of using carbon dioxide as their sole source of carbon are called *autotrophs* (self-feeders), or **producers**. These are the plants. They chemically fix carbon through photosynthesis. Organisms that depend on producers as their carbon source are called *heterotrophs* (feed on others), or **consumers**. Generally, these are animals. From the producers, which manufacture their own food, energy flows through the system along a circuit called the **food chain**, reaching consumers and eventually *detritivores.* Organisms that share the same basic foods are said to be at the same *trophic* level. Ecosystems generally are structured in a **food web**, a complex network of interconnected food chains. In a food web, consumers participate in several different food chains, comprising both strong interactions and weak interactions between species in the food web.

P2 Primary consumers feed on producers. Ⓐ Because producers are always plants, the primary consumer is called an **herbivore**, or plant eater. A **carnivore** is a secondary consumer and primarily eats meat. Ⓑ A consumer that feeds on both producers (plants) and consumers (meat) is called an **omnivore.** Ⓒ

P3 Detritivores (detritus feeders and decomposers) are the final link in the endless chain. Ⓓ Detritivores renew the entire system by releasing simple inorganic compounds and nutrients with the breaking down of organic materials. Detritus refers to all the dead organic debris—remains, fallen leaves, and wastes—that living processes leave. Detritus feeders—worms, mites, termites, centipedes, snails, crabs, and even vultures, among others—work like an army to consume detritus and excrete nutrients that fuel an ecosystem. **Decomposers** are primarily bacteria and fungi that digest organic debris outside their bodies and absorb and release nutrients in the process. This metabolic work of microbial decomposers produces the rotting that breaks down detritus. Detritus feeders and decomposers, although different in operation, have a similar function in an ecosystem.

P4 → An example of a complex community is the oceanic food web that includes krill, a primary consumer. *Krill* is a shrimplike crustacean that is a major food for an interrelated group of organisms, including whales, fish, seabirds, seals, and squid in the Antarctic region. All of these organisms participate in numerous other food chains as well, some consuming and some being consumed. *Phytoplankton* begin this chain by harvesting solar energy in photosynthesis. *Herbivorous zooplankton* such as krill and other organisms eat Phytoplankton. Consumers eat krill at the next trophic level. Because krill are a protein-rich, plentiful food, increasingly factory ships, such as those from Japan and Russia, seek them out. The annual krill harvest currently surpasses a million tons, principally as feed for chickens and livestock and as protein for human consumption.

Efficiency in a Food Web

P5 Any assessment of world food resources depends on the level of consumer being targeted. Let us use humans as an example. Many people can be fed if wheat is eaten directly. However, if the grain is first fed to cattle (herbivores) and then we eat the beef, the yield of available food energy is cut by 90% (810 kg of grain is reduced to 82 kg of meat); far fewer people can be fed from the same land area.

P6 In terms of energy, only about 10% of the kilocalories (food calories, not heat calories) in plant matter survive from the primary to the secondary trophic level. When humans consume meat instead of grain, there is a further loss of biomass and added inefficiency. More energy is lost to the environment at each progressive step in the food chain. You can see that an omnivorous diet such as that of an average North American and European is quite expensive in terms of biomass and energy.

P7 → Food web concepts are becoming politicized as world food issues grow more critical. Today, approximately half of the cultivated acreage in the United States and Canada is planted for animal consumption—beef and dairy cattle, hogs, chickens, and turkeys. Livestock feed includes approximately 80% of the annual corn and nonexported soybean harvest. In addition, some lands cleared of rain forest in Central and South America were converted to pasture to produce beef for export to restaurants, stores, and fast-food outlets in developed countries. Thus, lifestyle decisions and dietary patterns in North America and Europe are perpetuating inefficient food webs, not to mention the destruction of valuable resources, both here and overseas.

Glossary
phytoplankton: a plant that lives in the sea and produces its own energy source
trophic level: category measured in steps away from the energy input in an ecosystem

➤ Questions

This review presents the types of questions that are most frequently tested on the TOEFL. They will appear randomly after a reading passage. Directions will appear with the questions, but if you already recognize the type of question presented, and you are familiar with the directions, you will save time. The less time you have to spend reading directions, the more time you will have to read the passages and answer the questions. The number of points assigned to each question is based on the evaluation system for the TOEFL. The frequency level for each question is based on the average number of 12–14 questions that are usually included in a reading passage.

Low	0–1
Average	1
High	2–4
Very high	3–5

1: TRUE-FALSE

A *True-False* question asks you to identify the true statement.
Choose from four sentences.
Points—1
Frequency Level—Low

1. According to paragraph 1, which of the following is true about autotrophs?

   ● They use a chemical process to produce their own food.
   Ⓑ They require plant matter in order to survive.
   Ⓒ They need producers to provide them with carbon.
   Ⓓ They do not interact with other organisms in the food chain.

   Paragraph 1 is marked with an arrow [→].

2: VOCABULARY

A *Vocabulary* question asks you to choose a general synonym.
Choose from four words or phrases.
Points—1
Frequency Level—Very high

2. The word sole in the passage is closest in meaning to

   Ⓐ major
   Ⓑ steady
   ● only
   Ⓓ ideal

3: TERMS

A *Terms* question asks you to explain a word that is specific to the reading passage.
Choose from four definitions.
Points—1
Frequency Level—Low

3. Based on the information in paragraph 1, which of the following best explains the term "food web"?

  Ⓐ Energy manufactured by producer organisms in the food chain
  Ⓑ Another term that defines the food chain
  ● An interactive system of food chains
  Ⓓ Primary and secondary consumers in the food chain

  Paragraph 1 is marked with an arrow [→].

4: INFERENCE

An *Inference* question asks you to draw a conclusion based on information in the passage. Choose from four possibilities.
Points—1
Frequency Level—Average

4. It may be concluded that human beings are omnivores because

  Ⓐ people feed on producers for the most part
  Ⓑ people are usually tertiary consumers
  ● people generally eat both producers and consumers
  Ⓓ most people are the top carnivores in the food chain

5: REFERENCE

A *Reference* question asks you to identify a word or phrase in the passage that refers to another word or phrase.
Choose from four words or phrases in the passage.
Points—1
Frequency Level—Low

5. The word others in the passage refers to

   Ⓐ debris
   ● feeders
   Ⓒ processes
   Ⓓ nutrients

6: PURPOSE

A *Purpose* question asks you to understand why the author organizes a passage or explains a concept in a specific way.
Choose from four reasons.
Points—1
Frequency Level—Average

6. Why does the author mention "krill" in paragraph 4?

   Ⓐ To suggest a solution for a problem in the food chain
   Ⓑ To provide evidence that contradicts previously stated opinions
   Ⓒ To present an explanation for the killing of krill
   ● To give an example of a complex food web

Paragraph 4 is marked with an arrow [→].

7: PARAPHRASE

A *Paraphrase* question asks you to choose the best restatement.
Choose from four statements.
Points—1
Frequency Level—Average

7. Which of the sentences below best expresses the information in the highlighted statement in the passage? The other choices change the meaning or leave out important information.

   Ⓐ Part of the one million tons of krill harvested annually is used for protein in animal feed.

   Ⓑ Both livestock and chickens as well as humans eat krill as a main part of their diets.

   Ⓒ The principal use of krill is for animal feed, although some of the one million tons is eaten by people.

   ● More than one million tons of krill is eaten by both animals and humans every year.

8: DETAIL

A *Detail* question asks you to answer a question about a specific point in the passage.
Choose from four possible answers.
Points—1
Frequency Level—Very high

8. According to paragraph 7, how much land is used to grow crops for animal feed?

   Ⓐ 80 percent of the acreage in Europe

   Ⓑ Most of the rain forest in Central America

   ● 50 percent of the farm land in Canada and the United States

   Ⓓ Half of the land in North and South America

Paragraph 7 is marked with an arrow [→].

9: CAUSE

A *Cause* question asks you to explain why something in the passage occurred.
Choose from four reasons.
Points—1
Frequency Level—Average

9. According to paragraph 7, food webs are inefficient because

  ● consumers in developed nations prefer animal protein
  Ⓑ politicians are not paying attention to the issues
  Ⓒ there are not enough acres to grow crops efficiently
  Ⓓ too much of the corn and soybean harvests are exported

  Paragraph 7 is marked with an arrow [→].

10: Opinion

An *Opinion* question asks you to recognize the author's point of view.
Choose from four statements.
Points—1
Frequency Level—Low

10. Which of the following statements most accurately reflects the
    author's opinion about food issues?

  Ⓐ Too much grain is being exported to provide food for
    developed nations.
  Ⓑ More forested land needs to be cleared for food production
    in developing nations.
  ● Food choices in developed nations are very costly in terms
    of the environment.
  Ⓓ More animal protein is needed in the diets of people in
    developing nations.

11: Insert

An *Insert* question asks you to locate a place in the passage to insert
a sentence.
Choose from four options marked with a square.
Points—1
Frequency Level—Average

11. Look at the four squares [■] that show where the following sentence could be inserted in the passage.

   A tertiary consumer eats primary and secondary consumers and is referred to as the "top carnivore" in the food chain.

   Where could the sentence best be added?   B

   Click on a square [■] to insert the sentence in the passage.

12: EXCEPTION

An *Exception* question asks you to select a statement that includes information NOT in the passage.
Choose from four sentences.
Points—1
Frequency Level—Average

12. According to the passage, all of the following characteristics describe producers EXCEPT

   Ⓐ Producers serve as food for consumers.
   Ⓑ Producers make their own food.
   Ⓒ Producers form the first trophic level.
   ● Producers include bacteria and fungi.

13: CLASSIFICATION

A *Classification* question asks you to match phrases with the category to which they refer.
Choose phrases for two or three categories. Two phrases will not be used.

Points—1–4 points for seven choices
1 point for 4 correct answers
2 points for 5 correct answers
3 points for 6 correct answers
4 points for 7 correct answers
Frequency Level—Low

Points—1–3 points for five choices
1 point for 3 correct answers
2 points for 4 correct answers
3 points for 5 correct answers

13. **Directions:** Complete the table by matching the phrases on the left with the headings on the right. Select the appropriate answer choices and drag them to the type of organism to which they relate. TWO of the answer choices will NOT be used. ***This question is worth 3 points.***

To delete an answer choice, click on it. To see the passage, click on **View Text.**

Answer Choices

Ⓐ Depend upon photosynthesis to survive

Ⓑ Has a weak interaction among species

Ⓒ Generally consist of animal life forms

Ⓓ Include both herbivores and carnivores

Ⓔ Eat meat as one of its primary food sources

Ⓕ Are always some variety of plant life

Ⓖ Made exclusively of inorganic materials

Producers

• Ⓐ

• Ⓕ

Consumers

• Ⓒ

• Ⓓ

• Ⓔ

14: SUMMARY

A *Summary* question asks you to complete a summary of the passage. Choose three sentences from six choices. Three sentences will not be used.
Points—1–2
1 point for 2 correct answers
2 points for 3 correct answers
Frequency Level—Average

14. **Directions:** An introduction for a short summary of the passage appears below. Complete the summary by selecting the THREE answer choices that mention the most important points in the passage. Some sentences do not belong in the summary because they express ideas that are not included in the passage or are minor points from the passage. *This question is worth 2 points.*

The food web is comprised of producers, consumers, and decomposers, which interact in endless cycles.

- Ⓐ
- Ⓑ
- Ⓒ

Answer Choices

Ⓐ Consumers, primarily animals, feed on producers, plants which manufacture their own food source through photosynthesis.

Ⓑ Decomposers digest and recycle dead plants and animals, releasing inorganic compounds into the food chain.

Ⓒ Since more energy is depleted into the environment at each level in the food chain, dietary choices affect the efficiency of food webs.

Ⓓ Among consumers, human beings are considered omnivores because they eat not only plants but also animals.

Ⓔ An example of an undersea food web includes phytoplankton, krill, and fish as well as birds, seals, and whales.

Ⓕ Rain forests are being cut down in order to clear pastureland for cattle that can be exported to countries with fast-food restaurants.

READING STRATEGIES

In addition to the academic skills that you will learn in Chapter 3, there are several reading strategies that will help you succeed on the TOEFL and after the TOEFL.

➤ Preview

Research shows that it is easier to understand what you are reading if you begin with a general idea of what the passage is about. Previewing helps you form a general idea of the topic. To preview, first read the title, the headings and subheadings, and any words in bold print or italics. You should do this as quickly as possible. Remember, you are reading not for specific information but for an impression of the topic. Next, read the first sentence of each paragraph and the last sentence of the passage. Again, this should take seconds, not minutes, to complete. This time you are looking for the main idea.

- Look at the title and headings
- Read the first sentence of every paragraph
- Read the last sentence of the passage

➤ Read faster

To read faster, read for meaning. Try to understand sentences or even paragraphs, not individual words. To do this, you should read phrases instead of reading word by word. Practice using the vision that allows you to see on either side of the word you are focusing on with your eyes. This is called *peripheral vision*. When you drive a car or ride a bike, you are looking ahead of you but you are really taking in the traffic situation on both sides. You are using peripheral vision to move forward. This is also important in learning to read faster. Your mind can take in more than one word at the same time. Just think if you stopped every time you wanted to know what was going on in the next lane! You would never get to your destination. To read faster, you have to read for ideas. If you don't know the meaning of a word but you understand the sentence, move on. Don't stop to look up the word in your dictionary. Don't stop your car or your bike.

- Use peripheral vision
- Read for meaning

➤ Use contexts

Before you can use a context, you must understand what a context is. In English, a *context* is the combination of vocabulary and grammar that surrounds a word. Context can be a sentence or a paragraph or a passage. Context helps you make a general prediction about meaning. If you know the general meaning of a sentence, you also know the general meaning of the words in the sentence. Making predictions from contexts is very important when you are reading a foreign language. In this way, you can read and understand the meaning of a passage without stopping to look up every new word in a dictionary. On an examination like the TOEFL, dictionaries are not permitted in the room. Of course, you have to know some of the words in order to have a context for the words that you don't know. That means that you need to work on learning a basic vocabulary, and then you can make an educated guess about the meaning of new words by using the context.

• Learn basic vocabulary
• Guess new words in context

➤ Make inferences

Sometimes you will find a direct statement of fact in a reading passage. Other times, you will not find a direct statement. Then you will need to use the facts as evidence to make an inference. An *inference* is a logical conclusion based on evidence. It can be about the passage itself or about the author's viewpoint. For example, you may begin reading a passage about the Native Americans who lived on the plains. You continue reading and note that they used buffalo for food. Later, you read that they used buffalo for clothing and shelter. From these facts, you can draw the conclusion that the buffalo was very important in the culture of the plains people. The author did not state this fact directly, but the evidence allows you to make an inference.

• Locate the evidence
• Draw conclusions

➤ Skim and scan

To *scan* is to let your eyes travel quickly over a passage in order to find something specific that you are looking for. By scanning, you can find the place in a reading passage where the answer to a question is found. First, read the question and look for a reference. A reference in the TOEFL will identify a paragraph where the answer to the question is found. For example, you may read, *Paragraph 2 is marked with an arrow* [➔]. You know that you need to scan for the arrow at the beginning of paragraph 2 in the passage. The paraphrased sentences and the vocabulary words on the TOEFL are shaded to help you find them.

If a question does not have a reference like an arrow or shading, then you should find the important content words in the question. *Content words* are usually nouns, verbs, or adjectives. They are called content words because they contain the meaning of a sentence. Now scan the passage for the same content words or synonyms of the words in the questions. Finally, read those specific sentences carefully, and choose the answer that corresponds to the meaning of the sentences you have read.

- Refer to arrows and shading
- Locate the details
- Check for exceptions

➤ Make connections

Reading is like having a conversation with the author. Your mind makes connections with the passage. Sometimes this will happen when you are reading and a word or phrase refers back to a previous point in the passage. On the TOEFL, one question requires you to insert a sentence at the most logical place in a passage. In this case, you are connecting a new sentence with the ideas in the passage. Active readers are always thinking about how the next sentence fits in with what they have already read.

- Find references
- Insert sentences

➤ Summarize

A summary includes only the main idea and the major points in a passage. Although a passage may contain many points, only the most important are included in a summary. In English, many writers tend to use a formula with one main idea and three major points. It is customary to find between two and four major points in a short passage.

When you are reading content material in textbooks or on examinations, pause at the end of a section to summarize. First, re-read the title or the section heading. State the main idea. Then, summarize the major points from that section. You can summarize by speaking or writing. The last question on the TOEFL is often a summary of the entire passage.

- State the main idea
- List the major points

APPLYING THE ACADEMIC SKILLS TO THE TOEFL

➤ Campus Vocabulary

This important skill is tested in other sections of the TOEFL® iBT.

➤ Taking Notes

For some people, taking notes while they read the passage is a good strategy. For other people, it is not a good use of their time. They prefer to read once to get a general idea of the passage and then to go back and scan for each question. The way that you use your time is a very personal choice. When you take the model tests in the next chapters, practice by taking notes on some passages and by scanning on other passages. Use the model tests to determine whether you should spend time taking notes on the reading passages.

➤ Paraphrasing

This is the most important academic skill for the Reading section. Many of the questions and answer choices are paraphrases of information from the passage. Your ability to recognize paraphrases will be essential for you to score well on this section.

➤ Summarizing

The last question for every reading passage will require you to summarize the passage either by classifying information or by distinguishing between major points and minor points. Your skill in summarizing will be important because the last question is worth more points than the other questions.

➤ Synthesizing

This important skill is tested in other sections of the TOEFL® iBT.

QUIZ FOR THE READING SECTION

This is a quiz for the Reading section of the TOEFL® iBT. This section tests your ability to understand reading passages like those in college textbooks. During the quiz, you will read one reading passage and respond to 14 questions about it. You will have 20 minutes to read the passage and answer the questions. You may take notes while you read. You may use your notes to answer the questions.

"The Heredity Versus Environment Debate"

P1   The past century has seen heated controversy about whether intelligence, which relates strongly to school achievement, is determined primarily by heredity or by environment. [A] When IQ tests were undergoing rapid development early in the twentieth century, many psychologists believed that intelligence was determined primarily by heredity. [B]

P2   ➔ **Environmentalist view.** By the middle of the twentieth century, numerous studies had counteracted the hereditarian view, and most social scientists took the position that environment is as important as or even more important than heredity in determining intelligence. [C] Social scientists who stress the **environmentalist view of intelligence** generally emphasize the need for continual compensatory programs beginning in infancy. Many also criticize the use of IQ tests on the grounds that these tests are culturally biased. [D]

P3   James Flynn, who collected similar data on other countries, found that "massive" gains in the IQ scores of the population in fourteen nations have occurred during the twentieth century. These improvements, according to Flynn's analysis, largely stemmed not from genetic improvement in the population but from environmental changes that led to gains in the kinds of skills assessed by IQ tests. Torsten Husen and his colleagues also have concluded, after reviewing large amounts of data, that improvements in economic and social conditions, and particularly in the availability of schooling, can produce substantial gains in average IQ from one generation to the next. In general, educators committed to improving the performance of low-achieving students find these studies encouraging.

P4   → **Hereditarian view.** The **hereditarian view of intelligence** underwent a major revival in the 1970s and 1980s, based particularly on the writings of Arthur Jensen, Richard Herrnstein, and a group of researchers conducting the Minnesota Study of Twins. Summarizing previous research as well as their own studies, these researchers identified heredity as the major factor in determining intelligence—accounting for up to 80 percent of the variation in IQ scores.

P5   Jensen published a highly controversial study in the *Harvard Educational Review* in 1969. Pointing out that African-Americans averaged about 15 points below whites on IQ tests, Jensen attributed this gap to a genetic difference between the two races in learning abilities and patterns. Critics countered Jensen's arguments by contending that a host of environmental factors that affect IQ, including malnutrition and prenatal care are difficult to measure and impossible to separate from hereditary factors. IQ tests are biased, they said, and do not necessarily even measure intelligence. After his 1969 article, Jensen continued to cite data that he believed links intelligence primarily to heredity. His critics continue to respond with evidence that environmental factors, and schooling in particular, have a major influence on IQ.

P6   → **Synthesizers' view.** Certain social scientists have taken a middle, or "synthesizing," position in this controversy. The **synthesizers' view of intelligence** holds that both heredity and environment contribute to differences in measured intelligence. For example, Christopher Jencks, after reviewing a large amount of data, concluded that heredity is responsible for 45 percent of the IQ variance, environment accounts for 35 percent, and interaction between the two ("interaction" meaning that particular abilities thrive or wither in specific environments) accounts for 20 percent. Robert Nichols reviewed all these and other data and concluded that the true value for heredity may be anywhere between 0.40 and 0.80 but that the exact value has little importance for policy. In general, Nichols and other synthesizers maintain that heredity determines the fixed limits of a range; within those limits, the interaction between environment and heredity yields the individual's intelligence. In this view, even if interactions between heredity and environment limit our ability to specify exactly how much of a child's intelligence reflects environmental factors, teachers (and parents) should provide each child with a productive environment in which to realize her or his maximum potential.

Glossary
IQ: intelligence quotient; a numerical value for intelligence

1. According to paragraph 2, which of the following is true about environmentalists?

   Ⓐ They had only a few studies to prove their viewpoint.
   Ⓑ They did not agree with the use of IQ tests to measure intelligence.
 ※Ⓒ They did not believe that educational programs could raise IQ scores.
   Ⓓ They were already less popular by the mid twentieth century.

Paragraph 2 is marked with an arrow [→].

2. Which of the sentences below best expresses the information in the highlighted statement in the passage? The other choices change the meaning or leave out important information.

   Ⓐ Changes in the environment rather than genetic progress caused an increase in IQ scores, according to studies by Flynn.
   Ⓑ Flynn's studies were not conclusive in identifying the skills that resulted in improvements on IQ tests.
   Ⓒ IQ test results in research by Flynn did not improve because of genetics and environment.
 ※Ⓓ The reason that gains in IQ tests occurred was because of the changes in skills that were tested.

3. The word data in the passage is closest in meaning to

   Ⓐ experts
   Ⓑ advice
   Ⓒ arguments
 ※Ⓓ information

4. Why does the author mention the "Minnesota Study of Twins" in paragraph 4?

    Ⓐ To argue that environment is more important than heredity
    Ⓑ To prove the importance of heredity in measuring IQ
    Ⓒ To establish the synthesizer's view of intelligence
    Ⓓ To summarize previous research before designing a new study

    Paragraph 4 is marked with an arrow [➜].

5. According to paragraph 4, what can be inferred about the results of the Minnesota Study of Twins?

    Ⓐ Twins brought up in different environments probably had similar IQ scores.
    Ⓑ The environments were more important to IQ than the genetic similarity of twins.
    Ⓒ The study did not support the previous work by Jensen and Herrnstein.
    Ⓓ The IQ scores of twins can vary by as much as 80 percent.

    Paragraph 4 is marked with an arrow [➜].

6. According to Jensen's opponents, why are IQ tests unreliable?

    Ⓐ Heredity is not measured on the current forms of IQ tests.
    Ⓑ It is difficult to determine whether a factor is due to heredity or environment.
    Ⓒ Learning abilities and patterns are different for people of diverse racial heredity.
    Ⓓ They only measure intelligence and not many other important factors.

7. The word these in the passage refers to

    Ⓐ differences in measured intelligence
    Ⓑ a large amount of data
    Ⓒ particular abilities
    Ⓓ specific environments

8. Based on the information in paragraph 6, which of the following best explains the term "synthesizing"?

   Ⓐ A moderate position between the two extremes
   Ⓑ A position for which the evidence is overwhelming
   Ⓒ A controversial position that is hotly debated
   Ⓓ A modern revision of an outdated position

Paragraph 6 is marked with an arrow [➜].

9. According to a synthesizer's view, how does heredity influence intelligence?

   Ⓐ Heredity is very important but not as influential as environment.
   Ⓑ Heredity sets limits on intelligence, but environment can overcome them.
   Ⓒ A productive environment influences intelligence more than any other factor.
   Ⓓ Heredity and environment interact within the limits set at birth.

10. According to the passage, all of the following are true of the hereditarian view EXCEPT

   Ⓐ Studies by Jensen and Herrnstein support this point of view.
   Ⓑ Many psychologists in the early twentieth century were hereditarians.
   Ⓒ Intelligence as measured by IQ tests is a result of genetic predisposition.
   Ⓓ Environmental factors are not able to be separated from heredity.

11. Which of the following statements most accurately reflects the author's opinion about IQ tests?

   Ⓐ The author believes that IQ tests should be used continuously from infancy.
   Ⓑ According to the author, there are too many disadvantages to IQ testing.
   Ⓒ The author maintains a neutral point of view about IQ tests in the discussion.
   Ⓓ IQ tests should be used in research studies but they should not be used in schools.

12. Look at the four squares [■] that show where the following sentence could be inserted in the passage.

   Those who took this *hereditarian* view of intelligence thought that IQ tests and similar instruments measured innate differences present from birth in people's capacity.

   Where could the sentence best be added?

   Click on a square [■] to insert the sentence in the passage.

13. Complete the table by matching the phrases on the left with the headings on the right. Select the appropriate answer choices and drag them to the views of intelligence to which they relate. TWO of the answer choices will NOT be used. *This question is worth 4 points.*

   To delete an answer choice, click on it. To see the passage, click on **View Text**.

   Answer Choices

   Ⓐ Proposed interaction between heredity and environment.

   Ⓑ Attributed lower IQ to malnutrition and lack of health care.

   Ⓒ Suggested an innate range of IQ was influenced by environment.

   Ⓓ Was supported by the Minnesota Twins study in the 1970s.

   Ⓔ Claimed racial composition was a factor in measured IQ.

   Ⓕ Maintained that IQ tests were often biased in favor of the majority culture.

   Ⓖ Cited schooling as a positive consideration in the gains in IQ.

   Ⓗ Stated that social improvements improve performance on IQ tests.

   Ⓘ Advanced this viewpoint when IQ tests were being developed.

   Hereditarian

   • D

   • E

   • F

   Environmentalist

   • B

   • C

   • G

   • H

14. **Directions:** An introduction for a short summary of the passage appears below. Complete the summary by selecting the THREE answer choices that mention the most important points in the passage. Some sentences do not belong in the summary because they express ideas that are not included in the passage or are minor points from the passage. *This question is worth 2 points.*

Historically, psychologists have proposed three viewpoints to explain the influence of heredity and environment on IQ scores.

- F
- C
-

Answer Choices

A Studies by James Flynn verified significant increases in IQ scores among populations in fourteen nations in the last century.

B By the 1970s, psychologists reversed their position, citing heredity as the primary determiner of intelligence as measured by IQ tests.

C Because IQ tests are unfair to minority cultures, the current view is to disregard previous studies that use them as a basis for measurement.

D In the mid 1900s, the popular view was that environment was the more important factor in the development of intelligence.

E Before the development of IQ tests, both heredity and environment were thought to influence the relative intelligence of children.

F Some modern psychologists have proposed a theory that relies on the interaction between heredity and environment to determine IQ.

STOP **This is the end of the Reading Quiz. To check your answers, refer to the Progress Chart for the Reading Quiz, Chapter 7, pages 359–360.**

STUDY PLAN

What did you learn from taking the quiz? What will you do differently when you take the model tests? Take a few minutes to think, and then write a sentence or two to help you revise your study plan.

EXTRA CREDIT

After you have completed this chapter, you may want to continue a review of reading. Here are some suggestions.

Practice reading on a computer screen. Reading on a computer screen is different from reading on a page. First, there is generally less text visible. Second, you must scroll instead of turning pages. Finally, there may be quite a few icons or other distracting visuals surrounding the passage. To become comfortable with reading on a computer screen, you should take advantage of every opportunity you have to practice. If you have a computer, spend time reading on the screen. Everything you read will help you improve this new skill.

Practice reading the kinds of topics that you will find in the Reading section. The reading passages are similar to the information that you will find in textbooks from general courses taught in colleges and universities during the first two years. If you can borrow English language textbooks, read passages from natural sciences, social sciences, the humanities, and the arts. The kinds of passages in encyclopedias are usually at a reading level slightly below that of textbooks, but they offer an inexpensive way to obtain a lot of reading material for different content areas. If you have access to the Internet, free encyclopedias are available online. An encyclopedia on CD-ROM is another option, which you may be able to use at a local library. If you purchase an encyclopedia on CD-ROM, an edition from a previous year will be cheaper and just as useful for your purposes.

ADVISOR'S OFFICE

If your body is relaxed, your mind can relax more easily. During the TOEFL examination, if you find yourself pursing your lips, frowning, and tightening your shoulders, then use a few seconds to stretch. Clasp your hands and put your arms over your head. Then turn your palms up to the ceiling and look up at your fingers. Pull your arms up as high as you can to stretch your muscles. Be sure not to look at anything but your own hands and the ceiling. That way, you won't be suspected of signaling to a friend. Even a two-second stretch can make a difference. Now, yawn or take a deep breath in and out, and you'll be more relaxed and ready to go on.

LISTENING

OVERVIEW OF THE LISTENING SECTION

The Listening section tests your ability to understand spoken English that is typical of interactions and academic speech on college campuses. During the test, you will listen to conversations, lectures, and discussions, and you will answer questions about them.

There are two formats for the Listening section. On the short format, you will listen to two conversations, two lectures, and two discussions. On the long format, you will listen to three conversations, three lectures, and three discussions. After each listening passage, you will answer 5–6 questions about it. Only two conversations, two lectures, and two discussions will be graded. The other passages are part of an experimental section for future tests. Because you will not know which conversations, lectures, and discussions will be graded, you must try to do your best on all of them.

You will hear each passage one time. You may take notes while you listen, but notes are not graded. You may use your notes to answer the questions.

Choose the best answer for multiple-choice questions. Follow the directions on the page or on the screen for computer-assisted questions. Click on **Next** and then on **OK** to go to the next question. You cannot return to previous questions.

Important Note
You will notice that the headphones icon (🎧) appears periodically. This is your cue to put on your headphones and play the track number that is indicated. To study without the audio, use the scripts in the back of the book whenever you see the headphone icon.

The Listening section is divided into sets. Each set includes one conversation, one lecture, and one discussion. You have 20 minutes to answer all of the questions on the short format and 30 minutes to answer all of the questions on the long format. A clock on the screen will show you how much time you have to complete your answers for the section. The clock does NOT count the time you are listening to the conversations, lectures, and discussions.

REVIEW OF PROMPTS AND QUESTIONS

➤ Prompts

A prompt for the Listening section is either a conversation on a college campus or part of a lecture or discussion in a college classroom on one of the natural sciences, social sciences, humanities, or arts. Each conversation, lecture, or discussion is between three and six minutes long. There are either 6 or 9 prompts in the Listening section with 5–6 questions after each prompt. When you are presented with 6 prompts, all 6 will be graded. When you are presented with 9 prompts, only 6 will be graded, and 3 will be used for experimental purposes. You should do your best on all 9 prompts because you will not know which of them will be graded. Questions 1–4 in this review refer to the first prompt. Questions 5–10 refer to the second prompt. The scripts for the prompts in this review chapter have been printed for you to study. On the official TOEFL® iBT, you will not see the prompts, but you will see the questions while you hear them. Model Tests 1, 2, and 3 are like the official TOEFL® iBT. You will not see the scripts while you listen to the prompts for the model tests.

CONVERSATION

Questions 1–4, Conversation, Track 2

Listen to a conversation on campus between two students.

Man:	Wait up. I need to ask you about something.
Woman:	Oh, hi Jack.
Man:	Hi. Listen, I was just wondering whether you understood what Professor Carson was saying about the review session next Monday?
Woman:	Sure. Why?
Man:	Well, the way I get it, it's optional.
Woman:	Right. He said if we didn't have any questions, we should just use the time to study on our own.
Man:	Okay. That's what I thought. Maybe I'll just skip it then.
Woman:	Well, it's up to you, but the thing is . . . sometimes at a review session, someone else will ask a question, and, you know, the way the professor explains it, it's really helpful, I mean, to figure out what he wants on the test.
Man:	Oh I didn't think about it that way, but it makes sense. So, you're going to go then.
Woman:	Absolutely. Um, I've had a couple of other classes with Carson and the review sessions always helped get me organized for the test.
Man:	Oh.
Woman:	And, if you've missed any of the lectures, he usually has extra handouts from all the classes. So . . .
Man:	Well, I haven't missed any of the sessions.
Woman:	Me neither. But I'm still going to be there. Look, uh, if it's like the other review sessions, the first hour he's going to go over the main points for each class, kind of like an outline of the course. Then from five-thirty to six-thirty, he'll take questions. That's the best part. And the last half hour, he'll stay for individual conferences with people who need extra help. I usually don't stay for that.

Man:	Okay. So we just show up at the regular time and place for class?
Woman:	Or not, if you decide to study on your own.
Man:	Right. But, don't you think he'll notice who's there?
Woman:	He said he wasn't going to take attendance.
Man:	Yeah, but still . . .
Woman:	It's a fairly large class.
Man:	But if he's grading your final and he remembers you were at the review, it might make a difference.
Woman:	Maybe. I think the important thing is just to study really hard and do your best. But, the review sessions help me study. I think they're really good.
Man:	Okay. Thanks. I guess I'll go, too.
Woman:	So I'll see you there.
Man:	Yeah, I think I . . . I'd better go.

➤ Questions

This review presents the types of questions that are most frequently tested on the TOEFL. The number of points assigned to each question is based on the evaluation system for the TOEFL. The frequency level for each question is based on the average number of 17 questions that are usually included in a Listening set of three prompts.

Average	1–2
High	3–4
Very high	5+

1: PURPOSE

A *Purpose* question asks you to explain why the speakers are having a conversation or why the professor is presenting the material in a lecture. Choose from four reasons.
Points—1
Frequency Level—Average

1. Why does the man want to talk with the woman?

    Ⓐ To ask her to help him study for the exam
    Ⓑ To get some handouts for a class he has missed
    ● To clarify his understanding of the review session
    Ⓓ To find out her opinion of Professor Carson

2: DETAIL

A *Detail* question asks you to answer a question about a specific point in the conversation or lecture.
Choose from four possible answers.
Points—1
Frequency Level—Very high

2. Why does the woman think that the review session will be helpful?

    Ⓐ Because she has some questions that she wants to ask the professor
    Ⓑ Because Professor Carson will tell them some of the test questions
    ● Because it helps to hear the answers to questions that other people ask
    Ⓓ Because she needs an individual conference with the professor

3: INFERENCE

An *Inference* question asks you to draw a conclusion based on information in the conversation or lecture. Choose from four possible answers.
Points—1
Frequency Level—Very high

3. Why does the man decide to go to the review session?

    Ⓐ Because the review session will make up for absences
    ● Because the woman convinces him that it is a good idea
    Ⓒ Because the professor has recommended the session
    Ⓓ Because he needs help to organize his class notes

4: Pragmatics

A *Pragmatics* question asks you to comprehend the function of language on a level deeper than the surface meaning. You may need to understand the purpose or motivation of the speaker, or you may need to interpret the speaker's attitude or doubt about something in the conversation or lecture. Listen to a replay of the sentence or sentences that you must interpret.
Choose from four possible answers.
Points—1
Frequency Level—Very high

4. Listen again to part of the conversation. Then answer the following question.

> Woman: He said he wasn't going to take attendance.
> Man: Yeah, but still . . .
> Woman: It's a fairly large class.

Why does the man say this: "Yeah, but still . . ."?

- ● He thinks that the professor will notice if a student is absent.
- Ⓑ He agrees with the woman about the attendance policy.
- Ⓒ He wants to change the subject that they are discussing.
- Ⓓ He tries to encourage the woman to explain her opinion.

Lecture

Questions 5–10, Lecture, Track 3
Listen to part of a lecture in a zoology class.

Professor:
As you know from the textbook, mimicry isn't limited to insects, but it's most common among them, and by mimicry I'm referring to the likeness between two insects that aren't closely related but look very much alike. The insects that engage in mimicry are usually very brightly colored. One of the insects, the one that's characterized by an unpleasant taste, a bad smell, a sting or bite, that insect is called

the *model*. The mimic looks like the model but doesn't share the characteristic that protects the model from predators. But, of course, the predators associate the color pattern or some other trait with the unpleasant characteristic and leave both insects alone.

Henry Bates was one of the first naturalists who noticed that some butterflies that closely resembled each other were actually unrelated, so mimicry in which one species copies another is called Batesian mimicry. I have some lab specimens of a few common mimics in the cases here in the front of the room, and I want you to have a chance to look at them before the end of the class. There's a day flying moth with brown and white and yellow markings. And this moth is the model because it has a very unpleasant taste and tends to be avoided by moth eaters. But you'll notice that the swallowtail butterfly mounted beside it has very similar coloration, and actually the swallowtail doesn't have the unpleasant taste at all. Another example is the monarch butterfly, which is probably more familiar to you since they pass through this area when they're migrating. But you may not know that they have a very nasty taste because I seriously doubt that any of you have eaten one. But for the predators who *do* eat butterflies, this orange and black pattern on the monarch is a warning signal not to sample it. So, the viceroy butterfly here is a mimic. Same type of coloring but no nasty taste. Nevertheless, the viceroy isn't bothered by predators either, because it's mistaken for the monarch. So how does a predator know that the day flying moth and the monarch aren't good to eat? Well, a bird only has to eat one to start avoiding them all—models and mimics.

A stinging bumblebee is another model insect. The sting is painful and occasionally even fatal for predators. So there are a large number of mimics. For example, there's a beetle that mimics bumblebees by beating its wings to make noise, and the astonishing thing is that it's able to do this at the same rate as the bumblebee so exactly the same buzzing sound is created. I don't have a specimen of that beetle, but I do have a specimen of the hoverfly, which is a mimic of the honeybee, and it makes a similar buzzing sound, too. When you compare the bee with the fly, you'll notice that the honeybee has two sets of wings, and the hoverfly has only one set of wings, but as you can imagine, the noise and the more or less similar body and color will keep most predators from approaching closely enough to count the wings.

Some insects without stingers have body parts that mimic the sharp stinger of wasps or bees. Although the hawk moth is harmless, it has a bundle of hairs that protrudes from the rear of its body. The actual purpose of these hairs is to spread scent, but to predators, the bundle mimics a stinger closely enough to keep them away, especially if the hawk moth is moving in a threatening way as if it were about to sting. There's a hawk moth here in the case, and to me at least, it doesn't look that much like the wasp mounted beside it, but remember when you're looking at a specimen, it's stationary, and in nature the *movement* is also part of the mimicry.

Oh, here's a specimen of an ant, and this is interesting. Another naturalist, Fritz Muller, hypothesized that similarity among a large number of species could help protect *all* of them. Here's what he meant. After a few battles with a stinging or biting ant, especially when the entire colony comes to the aid of the ant being attacked, a predator will learn to avoid ants, even those that don't sting or bite, because they all look alike and the predator associates the bad experience with the group. And by extension, the predator will also avoid insects that mimic ants, like harmless beetles and spiders.

Look at this.

Ant Spider

I have a drawing of a specimen of a stinging ant beside a specimen of a brownish spider and the front legs of the spider are mounted so they look more like antennae because that's just what the spider does to mimic an ant. That way it appears to have six legs like an ant instead of eight like a spider.

Okay, we have about ten minutes left, and I want you to take this opportunity to look at the specimen cases here in the front of the room. I'll be available for questions if you have them. How about forming two lines on either side of the cases so more of you can see at the same time?

5: MAIN IDEA

A *Main Idea* question asks you to identify the topic of the lecture, that is, what the lecture is mainly about.
Choose from four possible answers.
Points—1
Frequency Level—High

5. What is the lecture mainly about?

- ● An explanation of mimicry among species in the insect world
- Ⓑ A comparison of the features of the viceroy and the monarch butterfly
- Ⓒ A hypothesis to explain why similarity among species protects them all
- Ⓓ A response to questions about the specimens displayed in the cases

6: ORGANIZATION

An *Organization* question asks you recognize the rhetorical structure of a lecture or part of a lecture. For example, chronological order, steps in a sequence, cause and effect, comparison.
Choose from four possible answers.
Points—1
Frequency Level—Average

6. How does the professor organize the lecture?

- ● He shows specimens to demonstrate his points.
- Ⓑ He compares the theories of two naturalists.
- Ⓒ He classifies different types of mimics.
- Ⓓ He puts the ideas in chronological order.

7: DETAILS

A *Details* question asks you to answer a question about a specific point in the conversation or lecture.
Choose two or three answers from four to six possibilities.
Points—1
Frequency Level—Very high

7. According to the lecture, what are some characteristics of a *model*?

Click on 3 answer choices.

A   A pair of wings

■   A foul odor

■   A bad taste

D   A drab color

■   A painful sting

8: TECHNIQUE

A *Technique* question asks you to identify the way that a professor makes a point, for example, by comparing, by providing a definition, by giving an example.
Choose from four possible answers.
Points—1
Frequency Level—Average

8. How does the professor explain Batesian mimicry?

Ⓐ By giving a precise definition
● By providing several examples
Ⓒ By referring to the textbook
Ⓓ By contrasting it with another hypothesis

9: YES-NO

A *Yes-No* question asks you to decide whether statements agree or disagree with information in the lecture.
Mark a list of statements in a chart as either *Yes* or *No*.
Points—1–2
Frequency Level—Low

9. In the lecture, the professor explains Fritz Muller's hypothesis. Indicate whether each of the following supports the hypothesis. Click in the correct box for each choice.

		Yes	No
A	Predators avoid species of insects that have harmed them in the past by stinging or biting them.	✔	
B	Predators may be killed when an entire colony of insects joins forces against them.		✔
C	Predators leave harmless insects alone if they are part of a group that includes stinging insects.	✔	
D	Predators will refrain from attacking harmless insects if they look like insects that have stung them before.	✔	
E	Predators protect themselves from harmful insects by stinging or biting them before they are attacked.		✔

10: CONNECTIONS

A *Connections* question asks you to relate ideas or information in the lecture.

Match answers with categories, list the order of events or steps in a process, and show relationships on a chart.

Points—1–4/Seven choices

     1–3/Five choices

Frequency Level—Low

10. Indicate whether each insect below refers to a model or a mimic. Click in the correct box for each phrase.

Insects		Mimic	Model
A	A viceroy butterfly ⟶		
B	A brown spider ⟶		
C	A hawk moth ⟶		
D	A bumblebee ⟶		
E	A biting ant ⟶		

LISTENING STRATEGIES

In addition to the academic skills that you will learn in Chapter 3, there are several listening strategies that will help you succeed on the TOEFL and after the TOEFL.

➤ Get organized

Before you begin the Listening section on the official TOEFL, you will have an opportunity to adjust the volume on your headset. Be sure to do it before you dismiss the directions and begin the test. After the test has begun, you may not be able to adjust the volume without missing some of the information in the audio. When you practice using the model tests in this book, adjust the volume at the beginning. Learn to get it right without touching the volume button again during practice. Then, prepare to listen. The directions tend to be long and boring, especially if you have experience taking model tests and know what to do. Don't get distracted. Be ready to hear the first word in the introduction to the first listening passage.

• Adjust the volume first
• Prepare to listen

➤ Preview

The introductions for the conversations and lecture contain important information that will help you prepare your mind to listen. For example, the narrator may say, "Now get ready to listen to part of a lecture in a history class." When you hear the introduction, you learn two useful facts. First, you know that you will be listening to a lecture. Second, you know that the lecture will be about history. This is helpful because it is a preview for the listening passage.

- Pay attention to the introductions
- Glance at the photo

➤ Use visuals

The photographs and other visuals are there to provide a context for the conversations and lectures. In general, the pictures of people are for orientation to the conversations and lectures, whereas the visuals of objects, art, specimens, maps, charts, and drawings support the meaning of the conversations and lectures. Do *not* focus on the pictures of people. *Do* focus on the other visuals that appear during the conversations and lectures. They could reappear in a question. When you take the model tests, practice selective attention. Look briefly at the pictures of the professor and the students, but be alert to the other visuals. If you become too involved in looking at the people, you may pay less attention to the audio, and you could miss part of the passage.

- Glance at the photos of people
- Focus on content visuals

➤ Read screen text

During the questions for conversations and lectures, watch the screen carefully. You will hear the questions, and you will also see them as text on the screen. If you find that it is to your advantage to close your eyes or look away from the photo during the short conversations, be sure to give your full attention to the screen again while the questions are being asked and the answer choices are presented. By using the model tests, you will be able to develop a rhythm for interacting with the screen that is best for you.

- Read the questions
- Develop a rhythm

➤ Understand campus context

The conversations and lectures take place in a campus context. A glossary at the end of this book contains a listing of campus vocabulary. These words and phrases will help you understand the conversations between campus personnel, professors, and students. Pragmatic understanding will help you understand the function of a sentence. A few examples of function are an apology, an explanation, or a way to get the listener's attention or to change the topic. Pragmatic understanding will also help you interpret the speaker's attitude and the nature of the information—a fact or an opinion. Studying the glossary is an important strategy for the Listening section. Start now.

- Learn campus vocabulary
- Study pragmatic cues for lectures

➤ Concentrate

Sometimes the environment for the TOEFL is not ideal. If the room is small, you may hear a very low hum from another headset, the scratch of pencils on paper when others are taking notes, or even their spoken responses for questions on the Speaking section. These sounds can be distracting, especially during the Listening section. The earphones on your headset should suppress most of the noise, but it will be helpful if you have some strategies to help you concentrate. Some students press their earphones more tightly to their ears by holding them with their hands during long listening passages, but this may be clumsy for you when you reach for the mouse to answer questions. Other students train themselves to concentrate in a somewhat distracting environment by taking at least one model test in a small room where other people are studying, such as a library or a study lounge in a dormitory. Remember, you may not be able to control the test environment, but you can control your response to it. By keeping your eyes on the screen and the scratch paper and by remaining calm, you will be able to concentrate better. If the test situation is noisy, don't get angry and start negative talk in your mind. Don't let your emotions interfere with your concentration.

- Focus on the test materials
- Stay calm

APPLYING THE ACADEMIC SKILLS TO THE TOEFL

➤ Campus Vocabulary

The first listening passage in each set of three passages is a conversation that takes place on a college or university campus. Your facility to understand campus vocabulary will help you gain valuable points when you respond to the questions about these conversations.

➤ Taking Notes

Taking notes is probably the most important academic skill for the Listening section. When you take notes, you will organize the information into major points and minor points. You will also record information that you can refer to when you answer questions. Your ability to take notes will be critical for you to score well on this section.

➤ Paraphrasing

Many of the answer choices are paraphrases of information from the passage. Your ability to recognize paraphrases will be helpful as you choose your answers.

➤ Summarizing

The first question in each conversation usually requires you to understand the purpose of the conversation, and the first question in each lecture usually requires you to recognize a summary of the main idea. By mastering the academic skill of summarizing, you will be able to respond correctly to the first question in each prompt. You will also be better prepared to relate ideas and make connections.

➤ Synthesizing

This important skill is tested in other sections of the TOEFL® iBT.

QUIZ FOR THE LISTENING SECTION

This is a quiz for the Listening section of the TOEFL® iBT. This section tests your ability to understand campus conversations and academic lectures. During the quiz, you will listen to one conversation and one lecture. [On the official TOEFL] you will hear each conversation or lecture one time and respond to questions about them. You may take notes while you listen. You may use your notes to answer the questions. Once you begin, do not pause the audio. For your reference, the script for this quiz is printed on pages 361–366.

CONVERSATION

Questions 1–4, Conversation, Track 4
Listen to a conversation on campus between a professor and a student.

1. Why does the man go to see his professor?

   Ⓐ To borrow a reference book that he needs
   Ⓑ To ask a question about the material
   Ⓒ To get advice about studying for a test
   Ⓓ To pick up some handouts from the class

2. Why does the student say this:

   Ⓐ To challenge the professor's idea
   Ⓑ To encourage the professor to explain
   Ⓒ To try to change the subject
   Ⓓ To interrupt the professor respectfully

3. How should Jack prepare for the test?

   Ⓐ He should memorize the material in the book.
   Ⓑ He should study the questions before the test.
   Ⓒ He should organize his notes by topic.
   Ⓓ He should not change his usual study plan.

4. Why does the professor give open-book tests?

   Ⓐ Because she believes it helps students with memorization
   Ⓑ Because her tests contain a large number of small facts
   Ⓒ Because her students are more successful with the course
   Ⓓ Because she thinks it provides a better learning experience

LECTURE

🎧 **Questions 5–14, Lecture, Track 4 continued**
Listen to part of a lecture in an economics class.
The professor is talking about *supply side* economics.

5. What is the lecture mainly about?

   Ⓐ Changes in economic systems
   Ⓑ Tax incentives for business
   Ⓒ Supply-side economics
   Ⓓ A favorable balance of trade

6. How does the professor organize the lecture?

   Ⓐ By contrasting several economic systems
   Ⓑ By taking a historical perspective
   Ⓒ By arguing against Friedman and Asmus
   Ⓓ By pointing out the benefits of Reaganomics

7. According to the lecturer, what did Kennedy and Reagan have in common?

Ⓐ They were both honored as Nobel laureates in economics.
Ⓑ They cut taxes to spur the economy during their administrations.
Ⓒ They identified themselves with supply-side economics.
Ⓓ They both taught at the Chicago School of Economics.

8. What would Milton Freidman most likely say about moving a manufacturing plant from the United States to a site abroad?

Ⓐ He would oppose it because it would cause people to lose their jobs.
Ⓑ He would consider it an opportunity for business to cut costs.
Ⓒ He would view it as a natural process in the shift to technology.
Ⓓ He would be concerned about the decrease in productivity.

9. According to Barry Asmus, what are two key ways that consumers contribute to the creation of new jobs?

Click on 2 answer choices.

Ⓐ By investing their tax savings

Ⓑ By purchasing cheaper goods

Ⓒ By moving on to better paying jobs

Ⓓ By spending more money

10. How does the professor explain the shift from manufacturing to technology?

Ⓐ He points to the global economy as the explanation for it.
Ⓑ He disagrees with most economists about the long-term effects.
Ⓒ He compares it with the change from agriculture to manufacturing.
Ⓓ He believes that it is too soon to draw any conclusions about it.

11. Why does the professor mention the General Electric plant?

    Ⓐ Because the plant is a good example of increased productivity
    Ⓑ Because unemployment resulted from company decisions
    Ⓒ Because the company was able to retrain their employees
    Ⓓ Because the plant was down-sized and many jobs were lost

12. Why does the professor say this: 🎧

    Ⓐ He would like the students to answer the question.
    Ⓑ He is joking with the students about the supply-siders.
    Ⓒ He wants the students to follow his logical answer.
    Ⓓ He is impatient because the students aren't paying attention.

13. In the lecture, the professor explains supply-side economics. Indicate whether each of the following strategies supports the theory.
Click in the correct box for each choice.

		Yes	No
A	Reduce tax rates		
B	Cut government spending		
C	Increase productivity		
D	Tolerate temporary unemployment		
E	Discourage consumer spending		

14. Put the following events in the correct order.

    Ⓐ Businesses hire more employees with the tax savings.
    Ⓑ The government works to affect a reduction in taxes.
    Ⓒ The businesses and their employees pay more taxes.
    Ⓓ Profits increase because of the growth in businesses.

STOP **This is the end of the Listening Quiz. To check your answers, refer to the Progress Chart for the Listening Quiz, Chapter 7, pages 367–368.**

STUDY PLAN

What did you learn from taking the quiz? What will you do differently when you take the model tests in the next chapters? Take a few minutes to think, and then write a sentence or two to help you revise your study plan.

EXTRA CREDIT

After you have completed this chapter, you may want to continue a review of listening. Here are some suggestions.

Listen to an international news broadcast in English. Be sure to select a television or radio program that includes reporters from various English-speaking countries, especially Canada, the United States, Australia, and Great Britain. The Listening section of the TOEFL now includes voices that represent a variety of English accents. The purpose of this activity is to understand diverse speech. Don't take notes. Just listen and try to understand as much as you can.

Watch educational television programs. The Learning Channel, Discovery, PBS, BBC, and others provide narrated programming with visuals on subjects that simulate lecture topics on the TOEFL. Take notes while you watch the program. During commercial breaks, mute the program and try to summarize the major points that you have heard, using your notes.

Attend lectures in English. Local colleges and clubs often have free lectures in English. Choose to attend lectures that simulate college classrooms. In addition, several websites offer lectures and talks. Use the resources listed on pages 551–552. Select topics from natural science, social science, humanities, and the arts.

Advisor's Office

There is usually a ten-minute break after the Listening section. What you do during the break is important. If you start to talk in your language with friends who are nervous or negative, you will go back into the Speaking section nervous and negative. If you are permitted to talk, choose a friend who is willing to speak English with you during the break. Use the time to encourage each other with positive talk. If you speak English, you will continue thinking in English, and you will make a smooth transition into the next section of the TOEFL. If you are also thinking positively, you will be ready to do your best. If you are instructed not to talk to others, then prepare some positive phrases in English to repeat in your mind or begin to rehearse some of the phrases that you have prepared for the first two tasks, page 101 and page 104 in this chapter.

SPEAKING

OVERVIEW OF THE SPEAKING SECTION

The Speaking section tests your ability to communicate in English in an academic setting. During the test, you will be presented with six speaking questions. The questions ask for a response to a single question, a conversation, a talk, or a lecture. The prompts and questions are presented only one time.

You may take notes as you listen, but notes are not graded. You may use your notes to answer the questions. Some of the questions ask for a response to a reading passage and a talk or a lecture. The reading passages and the questions are written, but the directions will be spoken.

Your speaking will be evaluated on both the fluency of the language and the accuracy of the content. You will have 15–20 seconds to prepare and 45–60 seconds to respond to each question. Typically, a good response will require all of the response time, and the answer will be complete by the end of the response time.

You will have about 20 minutes to complete the Speaking section. A clock on the screen will show you how much time you have to prepare each of your answers and how much time you have to record each response.

REVIEW OF PROMPTS AND QUESTIONS

➤ Prompts

A prompt for the Speaking section is either spoken or written. For example, a prompt might be a question, a conversation, part of a lecture, a written announcement, or part of a textbook passage. Each question has a slightly different prompt. There are six sets of prompts in the Speaking section with 1 question after each set. Questions 1–6 in this review refer to the kinds of prompts that are typical on the TOEFL® iBT. The scripts for the spoken prompts have been printed for you to study while you listen to them. On the official TOEFL, you will not see the spoken prompts. You will see the written announcements and textbook passages, and you will also see the questions while you hear them. The quiz at the end of this review and the model tests are like the official TOEFL® iBT. You will not see the scripts while you listen to the prompts.

➤ Questions

This review presents the types of questions that are most frequently tested on the TOEFL. The task for each question is explained. Each question appears as one of the 6 tasks included in the Speaking section.

1: EXPERIENCES

In Question 1, you will be asked to speak about a personal experience. This may be a place, a person, a possession, a situation, or an occasion. After you hear the question, you will make a choice from your experience and then explain why you made that choice.

You will have 15 seconds to prepare and 45 seconds to speak.

Task

- Describe your experience
- Explain the reasons for your choice

🎧 Example Question, Track 5

Where would you like to study in the United States?

Example Notes—Answer and Reasons

Washington, D.C.

- Family in the area—advice, help
- International city—food, stores
- Tours—sites, trains to other cities
- Universities—excellent, accepted at 1

🎧 Example Answer, Track 5 continued

I'd like to study at a university in Washington, D.C., because I have family in the area, and . . . and it would be nice to have them close by so I could visit them on holidays and in case I need advice or help. I've been to Washington several times, and I like it there. It's an international city with restaurants and stores where I can buy food and other things from my country while, uh, while I'm living abroad. And Washington is an exciting place. I've gone on several tours, but I still have many places on my list of sites to see. Also, um, there are trains to New York and Florida so I could take advantage of my free time to see other cities. Um, as for the universities, there are several, uh, several excellent schools in Washington and . . . and I'd probably be accepted at one of them.

Checklist 1

✔ The talk answers the topic question.
✔ The point of view or position is clear.
✔ The talk is direct and well-organized.
✔ The sentences are logically connected.
✔ Details and examples support the main idea.
✔ The speaker expresses complete thoughts.
✔ The meaning is easy to comprehend.
✔ A wide range of vocabulary is used.
✔ There are only minor errors in grammar.
✔ The talk is within a range of 125–150 words.

2: PREFERENCES

In Question 2, you will be asked to speak about a personal preference. This may be a situation, an activity, or an event. You may be asked to agree or disagree with a statement. After you hear the question, you will make a choice between two options presented and then explain why you made that choice.

You will have 15 seconds to prepare and 45 seconds to speak.

Task

- Choose between two options
- Explain the reasons for your preference

Example Question, Track 6

Some students live in dormitories on campus. Other students live in apartments off campus. Which living situation do you think is better and why?

Example Notes—Choice and Reasons

Dormitories

- More interaction—practice English, study
- Less responsibility—meals, laundry, cleaning
- Better location—library, recreation, classroom buildings

Example Answer, Track 6 continued

A lot of my friends live off campus, but I think that living in a dormitory is a better situation, uh, especially for the first year at a new college. Dormitories are structured to provide opportunities for interaction and for making friends. As a foreign student, it would be an advantage to be in a dormitory to practice English with other residents and to find study groups in the dormitory. And dorm students have, uh, less responsibility for meals, laundry, and . . . and, uh, cleaning because there are meal plans and services available, uh, as part of the fees. Besides, there's only one check to write so the bookkeeping . . . it's minimal. And the dormitory offers an ideal location near the library and, um, all the recreational facilities, and . . . and the classroom buildings.

Checklist 2

✔ The talk answers the topic question.
✔ The point of view or position is clear.
✔ The talk is direct and well-organized.
✔ The sentences are logically connected.
✔ Details and examples support the main idea.
✔ The speaker expresses complete thoughts.
✔ The meaning is easy to comprehend.
✔ A wide range of vocabulary is used.
✔ There are only minor errors in grammar.
✔ The talk is within a range of 125–150 words.

3: REPORTS

In Question 3, you will be asked to read a short passage and listen to a speaker on the same topic. The topic usually involves a campus situation and the speaker's opinion about it. After you hear the question, you will be asked to report the speaker's opinion and relate it to the reading passage.

You will have 45 seconds to read the passage. After you have listened to the talk, you will have 30 seconds to prepare and 60 seconds to speak.

Task

- Summarize a situation and an opinion about it
- Explain the objections or support
- Connect listening and reading passages

Reading
45 seconds

Announcement concerning a proposal for a branch campus
The university is soliciting state and local funding to build a branch campus on the west side of the city where the I-19 expressway crosses the 201 loop. This location should provide convenient educational opportunities for students who live closer to the new campus as well as for those students who may choose to live on the west side once the campus is established. The city plan for the next ten years indicates that there will be major growth near the proposed site, including housing and a shopping area. By building a branch campus, some of the crowding on the main campus may be resolved.

🎧 **Talk, Track 7**
Now listen to a student who is expressing an opinion about the proposal.

I understand that a branch campus on the city's west side would be convenient for students who live near the proposed site, and it might attract more local students, but I oppose the plan because it will redirect funds from the main campus where several classroom buildings need repair. Hanover Hall for one. And, uh, a lot of the equipment in the chemistry and physics labs should be replaced. In my lab classes, we don't do some of the experiments because we don't have enough equipment. And we need more teachers on the main campus. I'd like to see the branch campus funding allocated for teachers' salaries in order to decrease the student-teacher ratios. Most of the freshman classes are huge, and there's very little interaction with professors. A branch campus would be a good addition, but not until some of the problems on the main campus have been taken care of.

Example Notes—Situation and Opinion

Plans to open a branch campus

- convenient for students near
- might attract more students
- relieve crowding on main campus

But will redirect funds from main campus

- buildings need repair
- equipment should be replaced
- more teachers—smaller classes

Example Question, Track 7 continued

The man expresses his opinion of the proposal in the announcement. Report his opinion and explain the reasons he gives for having that opinion.

Example Answer, Track 7 continued

The man concedes that the branch campus might be advantageous for students living close to the new location, but he's concerned that the funding for a branch campus will affect funding on main campus for . . . for important capital improvements such as classroom buildings that are, uh, in need of repair. Um, and equipment in the science labs is getting old, so it needs to be replaced. And he also points out that more teachers are needed for the main campus in order to reduce student-teacher ratios, which . . . which would improve the quality of the teaching and the amount of interaction in classes. So the man feels that more attention should be given to the main campus and funding should be directed to improve the main campus before a branch campus is considered.

Checklist 3

✔ The talk summarizes the situation and opinion.
✔ The point of view or position is clear.
✔ The talk is direct and well-organized.
✔ The sentences are logically connected.
✔ Details and examples support the opinion.
✔ The speaker expresses complete thoughts.
✔ The meaning is easy to comprehend.
✔ A wide range of vocabulary is used.
✔ Errors in grammar are minor.
✔ The talk is within a range of 125–150 words.

4: EXAMPLES

In Question 4, you will be asked to listen to a speaker and read a short passage on the same topic. The topic usually involves a general concept and a specific example of it. After you hear the question, you will be asked to explain the example and relate it to the concept.

You will have 45 seconds to read the passage. After you have listened to the talk, you will have 30 seconds to prepare and 60 seconds to speak.

Task

- Summarize the concept in the reading
- Explain how the example in the listening supports the concept

Reading
45 seconds

> The telegraphic nature of early sentences in child language is a result of the omission of grammatical words such as the article *the* and auxiliary verbs *is* and *are* as well as word endings such as *-ing, -ed*, or *-s*. By the end of the third year, these grammatical forms begin to appear in the speech of most children. It is evident that a great deal of grammatical knowledge is required before these structures can be used correctly, and errors are commonly observed. The correction of grammatical errors is a feature of the speech of preschoolers four and five years old. The study of the errors in child language is interesting because it demonstrates when and how grammar is acquired.

Lecture, Track 8
Now listen to a lecture on the same topic.

English uses a system of about a dozen word endings to express grammatical meaning—the *-ing* for present time, *-s* for possession and plurality, and, uh, the *-ed* for the past, to mention only a few. But . . . how and when do children learn them? Well, in a classic study by Berko in the 1950s, investigators . . . they elicited a series of forms that required the target endings. For example, a picture was shown of a bird, and . . . and the investigator identified it by saying, "This is a Wug." Then the children were shown two similar birds, to, uh, . . . to elicit the sentence, "There are two___." And if the children completed the sentence by saying "Wugs," well, then it was inferred that they had learned the *-s* ending. Okay. Essential to that study was the use of nonsense words like "Wug," since the manipulation of the endings could have been supported by words that the children had . . . had already heard. In any case, charts were developed to demonstrate the gradual nature of grammatical acquisition. And the performance by children from eighteen months to four years confirmed the basic theory of child language that the . . . the gradual reduction of grammatical errors . . . that these are evidence of language acquisition.

Example Notes—Concept and Example

Word endings—grammatical relationships

- -ed past
- -s plural

Wug experiment—Berko

- Nonsense words—not influenced by familiar
- Manipulated endings
- Data about development

🎧 **Example Question, Track 8 continued**

Describe the Wug experiment and explain why the results supported the basic theory of child language acquisition.

🎧 **Example Answer, Track 8 continued**

In English, there are several important word endings that express grammatical relationships, for example, the *-ed* ending signals that the speaker's talking about the past and the *-s* ending means "more than one," uh, when it's used at the end of a noun. So, when children learn English, they, um, they make errors in these endings, but they gradually refine their use until they master them. In the Wug experiment, Berko created nonsense words to get children to use endings . . . so . . . so the researchers could, uh, follow their development. It was important not to use *real* words because the children might have been influenced by a word they'd heard before. So this experiment provided data about the time it takes and the age when endings are learned. It supported the basic theory of child language that, um, sorting out grammatical errors is a feature of the speech of four-year-olds and a stage in language acquisition.

Checklist 4

✔ The talk relates an example to a concept.
✔ Inaccuracies in the content are minor.
✔ The talk is direct and well-organized.
✔ The sentences are logically connected.
✔ Details and examples support the opinion.
✔ The speaker expresses complete thoughts.
✔ The meaning is easy to comprehend.
✔ A wide range of vocabulary is used.
✔ The speaker paraphrases in his/her own words.
✔ The speaker credits the lecturer with wording.
✔ Errors in grammar are minor.
✔ The talk is within a range of 125–150 words.

5: PROBLEMS

In Question 5, you will be asked to listen to a conversation and explain a problem as well as the solutions that are proposed.

After you have listened to the conversation, you will have 20 seconds to prepare and 60 seconds to speak.

Task

- Summarize the problem discussed in the conversation
- Explain why you think that one solution is better than the other

Conversation, Track 9

Student 1:   Did your scholarship check come yet?
Student 2:   Yeah, it came last week. Didn't yours?
Student 1:   No. That's the problem. And everything's due at the same time—tuition, my dorm fee, and let's not forget about books. I need about four hundred dollars just for books.

Student 2:	Well, do you have any money left from last semester, in your checking account, I mean?
Student 1:	Some, but not nearly enough. The check probably won't be here until the end of the month and I won't get paid at work for two more weeks . . . I don't know what I'm going to do.
Student 2:	How about your credit card? Could you use that?
Student 1:	Maybe, but I'm afraid I'll get the credit card bill before I get the scholarship check and then I'll be in worse trouble because of, you know, the interest rate for the credit card on top of everything else.
Student 2:	I see your point. Still, the check might come before the credit card bill. You might have to gamble, unless . . .
Student 1:	I'm listening.
Student 2:	Well, unless you take out a student loan. A short-term loan. They have them set up at the Student Credit Union. Isn't that where you have your checking account?
Student 1:	Umhum.
Student 2:	So you could take out a short-term loan and pay it off on the day that you get your check. It wouldn't cost that much for interest because it would probably be only a few weeks. That's what I'd do.

Example Notes—Problem and Possible Solutions, Opinion, and Reasons

Problem—not enough money

- Scholarship check late
- Books, tuition, dorm due

Solutions

- Use credit card
- Take out student loan

Opinion—support student loan

- Paid same day
- # not much

Example Question, Track 9 continued

Describe the woman's budgeting problem and the two suggestions that the man makes. What do you think the woman should do and why?

Example Answer, Track 9 continued

The woman doesn't have enough money for her expenses. Um, she has to pay tuition and her dorm fee is due at the same time. Besides that, she needs to buy books. So the problem is everything has to be paid now, and she won't get her scholarship check until the end of the month, and she won't get her paycheck for two weeks. Um, the man suggests that she use her credit card because she won't have to pay it off until the end of the month, but the problem is the interest would be substantial if the scholarship check is delayed. The other idea—to take out a student loan—that seems better because the loan could be paid off on the day the check arrives instead of a fixed date, and it wouldn't cost much to get a short-term loan at the Student Credit Union. So . . . I support applying for a student loan.

Checklist 5

✔ The talk summarizes the problem and recommendations.
✔ The speaker's point of view or position is clear.
✔ The talk is direct and well-organized.
✔ The sentences are logically connected.
✔ Details and examples support the opinion.
✔ The speaker expresses complete thoughts.
✔ The meaning is easy to comprehend.
✔ A wide range of vocabulary is used.
✔ Errors in grammar are minor.
✔ The talk is within a range of 125–150 words.

6: SUMMARIES

In Question 6, you will be asked to listen to part of an academic lecture and to give a summary of it.

After you have listened to the lecture, you will have 20 seconds to prepare and 60 seconds to speak.

Task

- Comprehend part of an academic lecture
- Summarize the main points

🎧 **Lecture, Track 10**

Two types of irrigation methods that are used worldwide are mentioned in your textbook. Flood irrigation—that's been a method in use since ancient times—and we still use it today where water's cheap. Basically, canals connect a water supply like a river or a reservoir to the fields where ditches are constructed with valves that allow farmers to siphon water from the canal, sending it down through the ditches. So that way the field can be totally flooded, or smaller, narrow ditches along the rows can be filled with water to irrigate the crop. But, this method does have quite a few disadvantages. Like I said, it's contingent upon cheap water because it isn't very efficient and the flooding isn't easy to control, I mean, the rows closer to the canal usually receive much more water, and of course, if the field isn't flat, then the water won't be evenly distributed. Not to mention the cost of building canals and ditches and maintaining the system. So let's consider the alternative—the sprinkler system. In this method of irrigation, it's easier to control the water and more efficient since the water's directed only on the plants. But, in hot climates, some of the water can evaporate in the air. Still, the main problem with sprinklers is the expense for installation and maintenance because there's a very complicated pipe system and that usually involves a lot more repair and even replacement of parts, and of course, we have to factor in the labor costs in feasibility studies for sprinklers.

Example Notes—Main Points

Flood

- Not efficient
- Difficult to control—flat fields
- Initial expense to build canals, ditches
- Requires maintenance

Sprinkler

- Complicated pipe system
- Expensive to install, maintain, repair, replace
- Labor cost

Example Question, Track 10 continued

Using examples from the lecture, describe two general types of irrigation systems. Then explain the disadvantages of each type.

Example Answer, Track 10 continued

Two methods of irrigation were discussed in the lecture. First, flood irrigation. It involves the release of water into canals and drainage ditches that flow into the fields. The disadvantages of the flood method, um, well, it isn't very efficient since more water is used in flooding than the crops actually, uh, need, and also it isn't easy to control. Another problem is the initial expense for the construction of the canals and the connecting ditches as well as . . . as maintenance. And besides that, if the fields aren't flat, the water doesn't—I . . . I mean, it isn't distributed evenly. The second method is sprinkler irrigation, which uses less water and provides better control, but there is some evaporation, and the pipe system's complicated and can be expensive to install and maintain. So . . . there's usually a lot more labor cost because the equipment must be repaired and replaced more often than a canal system.

Checklist 6

✔ The talk summarizes a short lecture.
✔ Inaccuracies in the content are minor.
✔ The talk is direct and well-organized.
✔ The sentences are logically connected.
✔ Details and examples support the main idea.
✔ The speaker expresses complete thoughts.
✔ The meaning is easy to comprehend.
✔ A wide range of vocabulary is used.
✔ The speaker paraphrases in his/her own words.
✔ The speaker credits the lecturer with wording.
✔ Errors in grammar are minor.
✔ The talk is within a range of 125–150 words.

SPEAKING STRATEGIES

In addition to the academic skills that you will learn in Chapter 3, there are several speaking strategies that will help you succeed on the TOEFL and after the TOEFL.

➤ Anticipate the first question

You will probably be asked to talk about familiar topics at the beginning of the Speaking section. If you think about some of these topics, you will know how to answer when you hear the questions. A few seconds to prepare does not give you enough time to organize your thoughts unless you have the advantage of prior preparation.

You may be asked to choose a favorite person, place, activity, or item to talk about. To prepare for this question, spend a few minutes thinking about your personal favorites.

- Prepare some answers
- Read them aloud

EXAMPLE

My favorite pastime is
_____*traveling*_____.

1. My favorite teacher is

   _____.

2. My favorite city is

   _____.

3. My favorite class is

   _____.

4. My favorite book is

   _____.

5. My favorite movie is

   _____.

6. My favorite sport is

   _____.

7. My favorite vacation place is

   _____.

8. My favorite holiday is

   _____.

9. My favorite music is

   _____.

10. My favorite person is

   _____.

➤ Support your answers

The directions in speaking questions usually ask you to give examples or reasons to support your answers. Develop the habit of adding the word *because* after your opinions, and provide at least two reasons to support your position. You will become a better thinker and a better speaker. For example, "My favorite pastime is traveling *because* I like to meet people and I enjoy learning about different places." "My favorite city is San Diego *because* the climate is beautiful year round and there are many interesting sights in or near the city."

- Use the word *because*
- Give two or three examples or reasons

➤ Understand the task

You must listen to the question to understand how to organize your answer. If you are being asked to state an opinion, you should state your opinion and argue only one side of the issue. If you are being asked to argue both sides of the issue and take a stand, then the task is very different. In that case, you will have to make a case for both sides before you state your opinion.

- Read the question carefully
- Respond to the topic

➤ Pronounce to communicate

Everyone has an accent in English. People from Australia have an Australian accent. People from the United States have an American accent. People from Britain have a British accent. See what I mean? The important point is that your accent is okay as long as the listener can understand you. It is good to try to improve your pronunciation, but communication is more important for the TOEFL and for your academic and professional life.

- Accept your accent
- Improve communication

➤ Sound confident

If you speak in a very low voice, hesitating and apologizing, the listener makes some negative assumptions. This person is not confident. This person probably doesn't know the answer. Try to speak up and sound assertive without being aggressive. It helps to start with a smile on your face.

- Speak up
- Be assertive

➤ Read 135 words per minute

Yes, this is a speaking strategy. To succeed on the Speaking section, you will be asked to read short passages of about 100 words each, and you will have about 45 seconds in which to complete the reading. This reading speed is not impossibly fast, but you will have to avoid re-reading phrases in order to finish within the time limit. When you take the quiz at the end of this section, you will hear a cue to start reading, and a question at the end of 45 seconds. This will help you time yourself. You probably already read 135 words per minute. If not, work on reading faster, using the reading strategies at the beginning of this chapter.

- Time yourself
- Increase speed to 135

➤ Adapt notes

The system for taking notes that you will learn in Chapter 3 can be made more effective by adapting it for each question. Use the task and the question to anticipate an outline for your notes. Refer to the example notes for Questions 1–6 on pages 87, 88, 91, 94, 96, and 99 for models of adapted notes.

- Use a system for taking notes
- Adapt the format for each question

➤ Pace yourself

There is no time for a long introduction. You have one minute or less to make your point. Start immediately with a direct statement. For example, "The lecturer compares bacteria and viruses." Include the most important points. When you practice speaking, using the model tests in this book, you will hear a prompt to start and a beep to end your speech. On the TOEFL, you must stop when the beep sounds. Always time yourself when you are practicing for the Speaking section. If you are not using the audio timing, then set a kitchen timer for the number of seconds that corresponds to the type of test problem that you are practicing—45 or 60—and then begin speaking. When the bell rings, stop speaking. Did you complete your thought or did you have more to say? Learn to pace yourself. Soon you will develop a sense of timing for the questions and you will know how much you can say in a short answer.

- Start with a direct statement
- Make a few major points
- Set a timer

➤ Prepare key phrases

Some key phrases are useful for each of the problems in the Speaking section.

Question 1: Experiences

My favorite _____ is _____ because _____ .

Question 2: Preferences

Although some people _____ , I prefer _____ because _____ .

Although there are many good reasons why _____, I favor _____ because _____ .

Although a good argument can be made for _____ , my preference is _____ because _____ .

Question 3: Reports

The speaker supports _____ because _____ .

The speaker opposes _____ because _____ .

Question 4: Examples

According to the (reading, lecture) _____ .

_____ is an example of _____ .

Question 5: Problems

The problem is that _____ .

According to _____ , one solution is to _____ .

Another possibility is to _____ .

I think that the best solution is to _____ because _____ .

It seems to me that _____ is the best solution because _____ .

Question 6: Summaries

Definition: According to the lecturer, a _____ is _____ .

Description: According to the lecturer, a _____ has (three) characteristics.

Classification: (Two) types of _____ were discussed in the lecture.

Chronology: The lecturer explained the sequence of events for _____ .

Comparison: The lecturer compared _____ with _____ .

Contrast: The lecturer contrasted _____ with _____ .

**Cause and
Effect:**   The lecturer explains why _____ .

**Problem and
Solution:**   The lecturer presents several solutions for the problem of _____ .

- Study the key phrases
- Practice using them

➤ Use verbal pauses

If you get to a point where you don't know what to say, it is better to use some verbal pauses to think instead of stopping and thinking in silence. Silence on the tape is going to lose points for you. You can say, *Okay, Now, Um, And,* or *Uh.* All of these verbal pauses are very common in the speech of native speakers. Of course, if you use these too often, you will also lose points because they will distract the listener and you won't have enough time to answer the question completely.

- Learn verbal pauses
- Use them when necessary

➤ Correct yourself

How can you correct yourself while you are speaking? First, recognize the difference between mistakes and slips. Most of the time, you *don't know* that you have made a mistake, but you *do know* when you make a slip. Even native speakers make mistakes and slips in grammar. In a very long sentence, we can forget whether the subject was singular or plural, and we can make a mistake. But sometimes we hear our mistake, and we correct slips by backing up and starting over. Some commonly used phrases to correct a previous grammatical slip are *I mean* or *that is*. For example, "The worker bees that take care of the young is called, I mean are called, nurses." These phrases can be used to correct content, too. For example, "Drones are female bees, I mean, male bees." A good rule is to always correct slips in content and correct slips in grammar and word choice if you can do it quickly and move along without interrupting the flow of your speech.

- Correct slips
- Use common phrases

➤ Speak to the criteria for evaluation

There are checklists for each question on the Speaking section. Use these checklists to evaluate your speaking. If you do not know how to use the checklist, get some extra help. For other options to evaluate your speaking, see page 548.

- Keep the checklists in mind
- Take advantage of other options

➤ Stay positive

It is natural to be a little anxious about speaking in a second language, but it is important not to become negative and frightened. Negative thoughts can interfere with your concentration, and you may not hear the questions correctly. Take some deep breaths before each question and say this in your mind: "I am a good speaker. I am ready to speak." If you begin to have negative thoughts during the test, take another deep breath and think "confidence" as you breathe in. Focus on listening to the questions. Focus on taking notes.

- Take deep breaths
- Use positive self-talk

APPLYING THE ACADEMIC SKILLS TO THE TOEFL

➤ Campus Vocabulary

Campus vocabulary is important when you are responding to Questions 3 and 5 on the Speaking section. In Question 3, you will read a campus announcement and listen to a conversation about it. In Question 5, you will listen to a campus conversation. Your ability to understand campus vocabulary will help you understand the announcement and the conversations. If you can use campus vocabulary correctly in your responses to these questions, you will impress the raters.

➤ Taking notes

Taking notes is an important academic skill for the Speaking section because you will use them to organize your talk and you will refer to them while you are speaking. When you take notes, it will help you to adapt to the type of question presented. Use the example notes in this chapter to help you. Your ability to take notes will support your success on every question in the Speaking section.

➤ Paraphrasing

Many of the answer choices are paraphrases of information from the passage. Your ability to recognize paraphrases will be helpful as you choose your answers.

➤ Summarizing

You will be speaking a minute or less in response to each question. You must be brief, but you must also include all of your major points. In other words, you must summarize. The first two questions in the Speaking section require you to talk about familiar topics. In these questions, you can summarize your experiences. The last two questions require you to summarize the information in a conversation and a lecture. Your ability to summarize will be crucial for you to score well on this section.

➤ Synthesizing

This important skill is tested in two questions on the Speaking section. Question 3 requires you to synthesize the information in a talk and in a short reading. Question 4 requires you to synthesize the information in a reading passage and in a lecture. You will receive points not only for speaking well but also for including accurate content. The ability to integrate reading and listening by synthesizing information will be necessary for you to achieve a high score on the Speaking section.

QUIZ FOR THE SPEAKING SECTION

This is a quiz for the Speaking section of the TOEFL® iBT. This section tests your ability to communicate in English in an academic context. During the quiz, you will respond to six speaking questions. You may take notes as you listen. You may use your notes to answer the questions. The reading passages and the questions are written/printed in the book for this quiz, but the directions will be spoken. Once you begin, do not pause the audio.

Quiz for the Speaking Section, Track 11

QUESTION 1

If you were asked to choose one movie that has influenced your thinking, which one would you choose? Why? What was especially impressive about the movie? Use specific reasons and details to explain your choice.

Preparation Time: 15 seconds
Recording Time: 45 seconds

Question 2

Some people think that teachers should be evaluated by the performance of their students on standardized tests at the end of the term. Other people maintain that teachers should be judged by their own performance in the classroom, and not by the scores that their students achieve on tests. Which approach do you think is better and why? Use specific reasons and examples to support your opinion.

Preparation Time: 15 seconds
Recording Time: 45 seconds

Question 3

Reading Time: 45 seconds

Policy for Tuition

In order to qualify for instate tuition, a student must have lived within this state for a period of not less than one year. Furthermore, the instate address must be the permanent residence of the student. College campus addresses may not be used as permanent residences. The student's driver's license and any vehicles must be registered in the state, and the previous year's state tax form must have been submitted to this state. Voter registration and a high school diploma may also be used as evidence of instate status. Spouses and children of military personnel qualify for instate tuition without residence requirements.

The student expresses his opinion of the policy for instate tuition. Report his opinion and explain the reasons that he gives for having that opinion.

Preparation Time: 30 seconds
Recording Time: 60 seconds

QUESTION 4

Reading Time: 45 seconds

Communication with Primates

Early experiments to teach primates to communicate with their voices failed because of the differences in their vocal organs, not their intellectual capacity. Dramatic progress was observed when researchers began to communicate by using American Sign Language. Some chimpanzees were able to learn several hundred signs that they put together to express a number of relationships similar to the initial language acqusition of children. In addition, success was achieved by using plastic symbols on a magnetic board, each of which represented a word. For example, a small blue triangle represented an apple. Chimpanzees were able to respond correctly to basic sequences and even to form some higher-level concepts by using the representative system.

Explain how the example of the Kanzi experiment demonstrates progress in research on primate communication.

Preparation Time: 30 seconds
Recording Time: 60 seconds

QUESTION 5

Describe the woman's problem and the two suggestions that her friend makes about how to handle it. What do you think the woman should do, and why?

Preparation Time: 20 seconds
Recording Time: 60 seconds

QUESTION 6

Using the main points and examples from the lecture, describe the habitable zone, and then explain how the definition has been expanded by modern scientists.

Preparation Time: 20 seconds
Recording Time: 60 seconds

This is the end of the Speaking Quiz. To check your answers, refer to the Progress Chart for the Speaking Quiz, Chapter 7, page 374.
Example answers can be heard on Track 12.

STUDY PLAN

What did you learn from taking the quiz? What will you do differently when you take the model tests in the next chapters? Take a few minutes to think and then write a sentence or two to help you revise your study plan.

EXTRA CREDIT

After you have completed this chapter, you may want to continue a review of speaking. Here are some suggestions.

Listen to good models of speaking in similar situations. Research is clearly on the side of those who advocate listening as a method to improve speaking. This means that one of the best ways to learn to speak well is to listen to good speakers. It is also important to simulate the kind of speaking situation that you will be required to complete. On the TOEFL, you have six questions and six situations. If you ask similar questions to excellent speakers and listen carefully to their responses, you will learn a great deal. That is why this book contains recorded examples of the answers that excellent speakers might provide for the questions in this review chapter and in the Speaking section of each model test. For extra credit and improvement, ask teachers or English-speaking friends to record their answers to the Speaking questions in this book. Don't give them the questions in advance. Use the same presentation and timing that you are using for the model tests. Then listen to their answers.

Practice using the telephone to speak. Call a friend to practice some of the speaking questions by phone. Speak directly into the phone. Ask your friend to confirm that you are speaking at a good volume to be heard clearly and that you sound confident, but not arrogant. If your friend is a native speaker, you can ask some of the Speaking questions and listen to the responses. Most telephones have a recording option. With your friend's permission, you can record the call. Be sure to time the responses.

OPTIONS FOR EVALUATION

It is difficult to evaluate your own speaking. If you are taking an English class, ask your teacher to use the checklists in this chapter to evaluate your speaking. You need to know how you are progressing in relationship to the criteria on the checklists because that is how you will be evaluated on the TOEFL® iBT.

If you do not have good options to have your speaking evaluated without a fee, there is a fee-based option that will provide professional evaluations. See page 546 for details.

ADVISOR'S OFFICE

When you face a challenge, "fake it until you can make it." This means that you should act as though everything were working out well, even when you have doubts. Put a smile on your face, even if it isn't real, and eventually it will be a real smile. Stand up straight with your head high and walk with purpose. You will start to actually feel more confident. If you are acting like a successful person, it may feel strange at first. But the more you practice your role as a successful person, the more comfortable you will be. Soon, when you reach your goals and you are truly successful, you will have practiced the role, and you will be the person you have been playing.

WRITING

OVERVIEW OF THE WRITING SECTION

The Writing section tests your ability to write essays in English similar to those that you would write in college courses. During the test, you will write two essays.

The Integrated Essay. First you will read an academic passage and then you will listen to a lecture on the same topic. You may take notes as you read and listen, but notes are not graded. You may use your notes to write the essay. The reading passage will disappear while you are listening to the lecture, but the passage will return to the screen for reference when you begin to write your essay. You will have 20 minutes to plan, write, and revise your response. Typically, a good essay for the integrated topic will require that you write 150–225 words.

The Independent Essay. You will read a question on the screen. It usually asks for your opinion about a familiar topic. You will have 30 minutes to plan, write, and revise your response. Typically, a good essay for the independent topic will require that you write 300–350 words.

A clock on the screen will show you how much time you have left to complete each essay.

REVIEW OF PROMPTS AND QUESTIONS

➤ Prompts

A prompt for the Writing section is either a question that refers to both a spoken and written text for the integrated essay or a written question for the independent essay. Questions 1 and 2 in this review present the kind of prompts that are typical on the TOEFL. On the official TOEFL® iBT, you will be asked to respond to one integrated question and one independent question. The scripts for the spoken prompts have been printed for you to study while you listen to them. On the official TOEFL® iBT, you will not see the spoken prompt. You will see the written question and the textbook passage.

➤ Questions

This review provides the types of questions that are most frequently tested in the Writing section on the TOEFL. The task for each question is explained here.

1: SYNTHESIS OF OPPOSING IDEAS

In this integrated essay question, you will be asked to read a short passage from a textbook and then listen to part of a short lecture about the same topic. The ideas in the textbook and the lecture will not agree. After you read the question, you write an essay that includes information from both the reading and the lecture.

You will have 20 minutes to plan, write, and revise your essay. Typically, a good response will require that you write 150–225 words.

Task

- Read a short passage and take notes
- Listen to a short lecture and take notes
- Answer a question using information from *both* the reading and the lecture

Reading Passage
Time: 3 minutes

Global warming has become a hotly contested issue. Although they concede that changes will be different from one region to another globally, a consensus of scientists support the theory that greenhouse gases produced by human activities are causing unprecedented changes. According to the Intergovernmental Panel on Climate Change (IPCC), the warming of the climate system is evident from observations of increases in global average air and ocean temperatures, widespread melting of snow and ice, and rising global average sea levels. The panel cites 200 worldwide scientific organizations that hold the same position.

Satellite data also supports the position on climate change. Earth orbiting satellites and other technological advances have enabled scientists to collect information about the planet and climate on a global scale. For example, we know that less CO_2 has been escaping to outer space at the specific wavelengths of greenhouse gases but increased long-wave radiation is measured at the surface of the Earth at the same wavelengths.

Finally, in spite of the fact that the global annual temperature is lower than would have been expected by models of warming, supporters of the global warming model account for the missing heat by postulating that it can be found in the oceans. Variations in ocean temperatures occur on a 15- to 30-year cycle. In the positive phase, El Niño tends to warm the atmosphere. In the negative phase, La Niña brings cold waters up from the depths along the Equator and cools the planet. By inserting this cyclical factor into the climate change model, the lower temperatures fit the general pattern predicted.

Example Notes

Global Warming
Data does not prove model

Consensus of scientists

IPCC observations 200 organizations	1 contradiction refutes Lindzen and Choi study IPCC—clouds Ø simulated

Satellite data

Satellite data supports Less CO_2 escaping/ more long-wave @ surface	NASA w/ U Alabama discrepancy 25 yrs predictions more heat than data

Global average temperatures

Missing heat in oceans El Niño/La Niña cycle	von Shuckmann—problem top cooling No hot spot tropics

Lecture, Track 13
Now listen to a lecture on the same topic as the passage
you have just read.

Although the dominant argument for global warming is that a majority of scientists support the model, well, any scientist would have
to agree that consensus is a false proof of a scientific theory. Why?
Because only one contradictory piece of empirical evidence is sufficient to refute a theory. That is, to quote Richard Feynman, "The
exception proves that the rule is wrong." That's the core of the scientific method. And many scientists with credentials equal to those

of the proponents of global warming have put forward objections to the models that argue the global warming issue. To cite only one example, Lindzen and Choi have measured changes in the outgoing long-wave radiation from the top of the atmosphere during periods of warming, and their findings directly contradicted the global warming model because the increased carbon dioxide didn't block outgoing long-wave radiation. Even the latest IPCC report acknowledges that the models don't simulate clouds well and that's where the main uncertainties lie. So there isn't a consensus, even among the proponents of the global warming models.

Now let's look at the satellite data, that supposedly proves the theory. In a joint study by the University of Alabama with NASA, . . . in their study, they found a huge discrepancy between the forecasts by the United Nations, using computer models and the actual amount of heat that's trapped, especially over the oceans. In fact, the NASA data show that the models put forward for the past 25 years have consistently predicted more heat being trapped than real-world satellite data actually records.

Finally, we must examine the primary explanation for the difference between the climate change in global average temperature that global warming has predicted and the much lower change in global average temperature that we've experienced. Now according to a model by von Shuckmann, the missing heat is in the ocean at depths of about 2000 meters but the problem here is that the top of the ocean is cooling, so how can the bottom be warming? And furthermore, we should see a hot spot close to the tropics because more water should have evaporated to this part of the atmosphere and would have caused rapid warming if the models were accurate, but again this doesn't conform to the scientific data.

Essay Question
Summarize the main points in the lecture, and explain how they cast doubt on the ideas in the reading passage.

Integrated Essay
The lecturer refutes all three arguments for global warming presented in the reading passage. First, she points out that a consensus

does not prove a theory. For scientific proof, all the evidence must support the hypothesis. However, many credible scientists disagree with those who champion the global warming issue. For example, the results of experiments by Lindzen and Choi contradicted the global warming model. Furthermore, the most recent IPCC report recognizes that the model doesn't simulate clouds well, which introduces uncertainty even among those who come down on the side of global warming.

Next, satellite data released by NASA in a joint study with the University of Alabama revealed a major inconsistency between the predictions by the United Nations, using computer models and actual data collected by satellites for the past 25 years. The models projected more heat, especially over the oceans, than the satellite data recorded.

Last, global warming proponents have offered a weak explanation for the lower average temperatures on Earth as compared with the expected temperatures in the model. According to von Schuckmann, for instance, the missing heat can be found in the ocean at depths of about 2000 meters. One flaw in this argument is the inconsistency of cooling on the surface and warming below it. A second problem is the absence of a hot spot near the tropics where more water should have evaporated, causing rapid warming, as predicted in the global warming model.

In short, at this point, many highly regarded experts disagree with the model because the scientific data contradicts it.

Checklist for Integrated Essay

✔ The essay answers the topic question.
✔ Inaccuracies in the content are minor.
✔ The essay is direct and well-organized.
✔ The sentences are logically connected.
✔ Details and examples support the main idea.
✔ The writer expresses complete thoughts.
✔ The meaning is easy to comprehend.
✔ A wide range of vocabulary is used.
✔ The writer paraphrases in his/her own words.
✔ The writer credits the author with wording.
✔ Errors in grammar and idioms are minor.
✔ The academic topic essay is within a range of 150–225 words.

Evaluator's Comments
The essay answers the topic question and the content is accurate. The writer credits the researchers and paraphrases ideas. It is a well-organized essay with logically connected sentences. The meaning is clear.

2: OPINION

In this independent essay question, you will be asked to write an essay about a familiar topic. This may be a place, a person, a possession, a situation, or an occasion. After you read the question, you will state your opinion and then explain why you have that opinion.

You will have 30 minutes to plan, write, and revise your essay. Typically, a good response will require that you write a minimum of 300 words.

Task

- State your opinion
- Explain the reasons for your opinion

Essay Question
Some students apply for admission only to their first-choice school, while others apply to several schools. Which plan do you agree with, and why? Be sure to include details and examples to support your opinion.

Example Notes
Several schools

- application Ø guarantee admission
  competitive standards
  no space
  w/o school 1 semester
  # but saves time

- *learn about options*
  communications
  discover advantages
  assistantships
  negative experience
- *I plan 3 schools*
  1 choice happy
  options open

Independent Essay

Although I understand students who desire to concentrate all of their energy on applications to their first-choice schools, I support making application to several different schools. There are two reasons why I feel this is important. First, application does not guarantee admission, even for a very highly qualified applicant. The school that a student prefers may have very competitive standards for acceptance. In spite excellent academic credentials, high scores on admissions tests such as the SAT and the TOEFL, and exceptional supporting documents, some qualified applicants may be turned away because not enough space to accommodate them. If students apply to their first-choice schools, and they are not accepted for reasons that could not be anticipated, they may find themselves in the position of being without a school for at least a semester while they scramble to apply to the schools they had considered as second or third choices. It is expensive to apply to a large number of schools because of the application fees, but making application to three schools can save time, which is also a valuable commodity.

Another reason to apply to several schools is the opportunity to learn more about each the educational options during the application process. While materials are being submitted and communication is occurring between the student and the school officials, advantages at the second- or third-choice school may be discovered as a result of the information exchanged. Scholarships, grants, and other opportunities may be extended when the committee is reviewing the application at one of the schools. For example, an unpublicized research assistantship may be available because of the prior work experience that an applicant has included on the application form. Conversely, the experience that the student has in applying to the first-choice school may be so negative that another school will be more attractive than the first-choice institution.

When I am ready to study at a university, I plan to apply to three schools—two with very competitive standards, and one with moderate standards. If I am admitted at my first-choice school, I will be happy, but I will leave my options open during the application process just in case I discover some advantages at one of the other schools.

Checklist for Independent Essay

✔ The essay answers the topic question.
✔ The point of view or position is clear.
✔ The essay is direct and well-organized.
✔ The sentences are logically connected.
✔ Details and examples support the main idea.
✔ The writer expresses complete thoughts.
✔ The meaning is easy to comprehend.
✔ A wide range of vocabulary is used.
✔ Various types of sentences are included.
✔ Errors in grammar and idioms are minor.
✔ The essay is within a range of 300–350 words.

Evaluator's Comments

The writing sample is well-organized. It addresses the question and does not digress from the topic. There is a logical progression of ideas, and the writer uses good transitions. Opinions are supported by examples. The writer demonstrates excellent language proficiency, as evidenced by a variety of grammatical structures and acceptable vocabulary. The reader can understand this opinion without re-reading. There are only a few grammatical errors that appear to have occurred because of time constraints. They have been corrected below:

Line 7	in spite of
Line 10	because there is not enough space
Line 19	each of the educational options

WRITING STRATEGIES

In addition to the academic skills that you will learn in Chapter 3, there are several writing strategies that will help you succeed on the TOEFL and after the TOEFL. Some of the strategies are more appropriate for the integrated essay and others are more useful for the independent essay.

Integrated Essay

The integrated question asks for a synthesis of the content in a lecture and a reading passage. It is usually the first essay question.

➤ Report

When you are writing about content, it is important not to offer your opinions. To do this, you must distinguish between content and opinion. Content may include both facts and the ideas of the author or lecturer. Opinion is what *you* think. Your job in an integrated essay is to report the facts and ideas without making judgments and without expressing your opinions.

- State the facts and ideas
- Avoid expressing your opinions

➤ Identify sources

In the question for the integrated essay, you will be directed to the primary source. For example, the question may ask you to summarize content *from the reading* or to summarize the main points *in the lecture*. This is a cue to begin with a summary from the primary source identified in the question—either the reading or the lecture. Then, you will be asked to support or contrast the information in the primary source with the information in the secondary source. Go to the other source after you have completed your summary. Be sure to include information from both sources, but begin with the primary source.

- Begin with the primary source
- Include both sources

➤ Make connections

Supporting Transitions	Opposing Transitions
When the secondary source agrees with the primary source, use supporting transitions.	When the secondary source does not agree with the primary source, use opposing transitions.
Moreover, Furthermore, In addition,	In contrast, On the other hand,

- Establish the relationship between sources
- Choose appropriate transitions

➤ Include a variety of structures

Essays with a variety of sentence structures are more interesting, and they receive higher scores. Complex sentence structures, achieved by combining simple sentences, also improve scores.

- Vary sentence structures
- Combine sentences

➤ Edit your writing

If you use all of your time to write, you won't have enough time to edit your writing. Students who take the time to read what they have written will find some of their own mistakes and can correct them before submitting the final essays. Be sure to edit both the independent essay and the integrated essay. To edit most effectively, use the grading checklist that raters will use to evaluate your writing.

- Re-read your essay
- Edit with the checklist

Independent Essay

The independent question on the TOEFL asks for your opinion. It is usually the second essay question.

➤ Respond to the topic

It is very important to read the question carefully and analyze the topic. If you write on a topic other than the one that you have been assigned, your essay will not be scored.

- Analyze the topic
- Write on the assigned topic

➤ Be direct

When you are asked for your *opinion*, it is appropriate to begin with a direct statement. The following phrases and clauses introduce an opinion:

Introduction	*Opinion*
Introductory phrase,	**Direct statement = Subject + Verb**
In my opinion,	school uniforms are a good idea.
In my view,	
From my point of view,	
From my perspective,	
Introductory Clause	**Direct statement = Subject + Verb**
I agree that	school uniforms are a good idea.
I disagree that	
I think that	
I believe that	
I support the idea that	
I am convinced that	
It is clear to me that	

- Begin with an introductory phrase or clause
- Make a direct statement of opinion

➤ Concede the opposing view

Sometimes you will be offered two choices. When stating a *preference*, it is polite to concede that the opposing view has merit. The following words and phrases express concession: *although, even though, despite,* and *in spite of.* For example:

Concession	Opinion
Concession clause	**Direct statement = Subject + Verb**
Although there are many advantages to living in the city,	I prefer life in a small town.
Even though technology can damage the environment,	I think it causes more good than harm.
Despite the differences among cultures,	I believe that peace is possible.
In spite of the benefits of studying in a group,	I prefer to study alone.

- Begin with a concession clause
- Make a direct statement of opinion

➤ Use an outline sentence

Some books call the second sentence in an essay the *topic sentence,* the *controlling sentence,* the *thesis statement,* or the *organizing sentence.* The purpose of this sentence is to outline the essay for the reader. Here are some examples of outline sentences.

First sentence:
Although there are many advantages to living in the city, I prefer life in a small town.
Outline sentence:
Three personal experiences convince me that small towns provide a better life style.

First sentence:
Despite the differences among cultures, I believe that peace is possible.
Outline sentence:
History provides several encouraging examples.

First sentence:
In spite of the benefits of studying in a group, I prefer to study alone.
Outline sentence:
There are three reasons why I have this preference.

- Outline the essay for the reader
- Write an outline sentence

➤ Think in English

How do English-speaking writers think? According to research by Robert Kaplan, they organize their thoughts in a linear pattern. This means that they think in a straight line. Details and examples must relate to the main points. Digressions are not included.

For essays that require an opinion, the organization would look like this:

Opinion ↓	In my view, school uniforms are a good idea.
Outline Sentence ↓	Three reasons convince me that wearing uniforms will improve the educational experience of students.
Reason 1 ↓	In the first place, uniforms are not as expensive as brand name clothing.
Example/Detail	For example, a new school uniform costs about $30, but designer jeans and a name-brand shirt cost five times that amount. An expensive book would be a better investment.
Reason 2 ↓	Second, it is easier to get ready for school.
Example/Detail	When there are five choices, it requires time and thought to decide what to wear. Uniforms simplify the problem of choosing a shirt to complement a certain pair of pants and, furthermore, selecting socks and shoes to go with them. All of these decisions take time and divert attention from preparing for classes.

Reason 3   Finally, students who wear uniforms identify
↓   themselves with their school.

Example/Detail   Wearing the school colors establishes that
                            each student is part of the group.

Conclusion   In conclusion, I think schools that require
                            uniforms send a positive message to their stu-
                            dents. They communicate that it is more impor-
                            tant to be the best student than it is to have the
                            best clothing.

- Think in a straight line
- Connect each idea with the next

➤ Write a strong conclusion

In TOEFL essays, it is not appropriate to apologize for not having written enough, for not having enough time, or for not using good English skills. An apology will cause you to lose points. In addition, a good conclusion does not add new information. It does not introduce a new idea. A strong conclusion is more like a summary of the ideas in one last sentence.

- Summarize the main idea
- Avoid apologies and new topics

APPLYING THE ACADEMIC SKILLS TO THE TOEFL

➤ Campus Vocabulary

Campus vocabulary is more important to success in other sections of the TOEFL. The essays require more formal, academic English.

➤ Taking Notes

Taking notes is an important academic skill for the Writing section because you will use them to organize your essay. Because you will not be graded on the notes, you should not worry about making them perfect. It is more important for them to be useful to you.

➤ Paraphrasing

In the integrated essay, you must be careful not to use the exact words from the reading or the lecture. Plagiarizing will result in a failing score on the essay. You must use the skills that you learned to paraphrase in your essay.

➤ Summarizing

As you will remember, summarizing is one of the steps in synthesizing. You will often be asked to summarize the primary source before you relate it to the secondary source.

➤ Synthesizing

Part 1 of the Writing section is the integrated essay. It is a synthesis of information from a reading passage and a lecture. Synthesizing is the most important academic skill for the integrated essay.

QUIZ FOR THE WRITING SECTION

This is a quiz for the Writing section of the TOEFL® iBT. This section tests your ability to write essays in English. During the quiz, you will respond to two writing questions. You may take notes as you read academic information. You may use your notes to write the essays. Once you begin, you have 20 minutes to write the first essay and 30 minutes to write the second essay.

QUESTION 1

Reading Passage
Time: 3 minutes

Stonehenge

Stonehenge, located on the Salisbury Plain in England, is a circular arrangement of bluestones and sarsen stones. Each bluestone weighs several tons and each sarsen stone weighs ten tons, or more. The question is, what was the original purpose of this monument?

Many theories have been put forward, the most popular being that ancient astronomers may have used Stonehenge as a solar calendar; however, excavations by researchers from the Stonehenge Riverside Project support a newer hypothesis. Evidence of burials and cremations dating back to 3000 B.C.E. influenced researchers involved in the Riverside Project to conclude that the real purpose of Stonehenge was to serve as a burial site. More than 50,000 cremated bone fragments of 63 individuals were excavated and studied by the team, including about equal numbers of men and women, as well as an infant.

In addition to cremated remains, chalk dust in several holes suggested that fifty-six bluestones once stood in the circular arrangement. According to the lead researcher, Professor Mike Parker Pearson, bluestones have been closely associated with burials from similar time periods, and their presence serves as further support for the burial ground hypothesis.

Finally, although few artifacts have been unearthed at Stonehenge, the head of a stone mace, an object similar to a scepter, supported the assumption that important persons were selected for burial in the site. A small bowl, burned on one side, may have held incense, further suggesting that the dead could have been religious and political leaders and their immediate families. Most prehistorical burials in England involved leaving the dead in the wild for animals to clean or throwing the bodies into the rivers, another indication that the Stonehenge burial site was reserved for leaders. Clearly, a possession like the stone mace would have belonged to someone of high rank and status among those who occupied the site and could have been buried with the body.

Question 1, Lecture, Track 14
Now listen to a lecture on the same topic as the passage you have just read.

Question
Summarize the points in the lecture, and then explain how they cast doubt on the ideas in the reading passage.

Writing Time: 20 minutes
Typical Response: 150–225 words

Question 2
Some people like to communicate by email and voice mail. Other people like to communicate by telephone or face-to-face. Which type of communication do you prefer, and why? Be sure to include details and examples to support your opinion.

Writing Time: 30 minutes
Typical Response: 300–350 words

STOP **This is the end of the Writing Quiz. To check your answers, refer to the Progress Chart for the Writing Quiz, Chapter 7, page 378.**

STUDY PLAN

What did you learn from taking the quiz? What will you do differently when you take the model tests in the next chapters? Take a few minutes to think and then write a sentence or two to help you revise your study plan.

EXTRA CREDIT

After you have completed this chapter, you may want to continue a review of writing. Here are some suggestions.

Become familiar with the independent writing topics. Topics previously used for independent questions on the CBT TOEFL Writing section are listed in the TOEFL® iBT *Information Bulletin* available free from Educational Testing Service. They are also listed on the web site at *www.ets.org.* Read through the questions, and think about how you would respond to each of the topics. Since most of them require you to state an opinion, it is helpful to form a general opinion on each topic.

Read good examples of expository writing. Research confirms that reading is important to the development of writing. This means that one of the best ways to learn to write well is to read good models of writing. By being exposed to good writing, you will acquire good techniques. That is why this book contains examples of the answers that excellent writers might create in response to the questions in this review chapter and in the Writing section of each model test. It is important to read these example answers carefully. Remember that you will be asked to produce expository, not literary essays. For this reason, you should read opinion essays instead of short stories. It is also a good idea to read summaries of content material. Many popular college textbooks in English provide summaries at the end of the chapters. In general, these summaries are good models for you to read.

OPTIONS FOR EVALUATION

It is difficult to evaluate your own writing. If you are taking an English class, ask your teacher to use the checklists in this chapter to evaluate your writing. You need to know how you are progressing in relationship to the criteria on the checklists because that is how you will be evaluated on the TOEFL.

If you do not have good options to have your writing evaluated without a fee, there are fee-based options that will provide professional evaluations. See page 547 for details.

ADVISOR'S OFFICE

Keep your eyes on the destination, not on the road. There are short roads and long roads to the same destination, but the important point is to arrive where you want to be. Of course, there are several reasons why you prefer to achieve a successful score on the TOEFL the first time that you attempt it. It is costly to take the test again, and you are eager to begin your academic studies or professional life. Nevertheless, a goal is seldom destroyed by a delay, so don't destroy your positive attitude, either. If you take the time to prepare, you will probably be able to take the short road, but if you have not studied English very long, you may need more practice. Please don't compare yourself to anyone else. They are on their road, and you are on yours. Just keep going. You will get there.

3

ACADEMIC SKILLS

The TOEFL iBT is a test of academic English. This means that you need more than English language proficiency to succeed. You need academic skills as well. You won't find a chapter like this in any other TOEFL preparation book. Campus Vocabulary, Taking Notes, Paraphrasing, Summarizing, and Synthesizing will help you succeed on the TOEFL and on campus in your college or university program.

CAMPUS VOCABULARY

Many references provide a list of academic vocabulary, which contains words that are commonly found in textbooks and academic journals, but the *Glossary of Campus Vocabulary* at the end of this book is unique. It includes the most common vocabulary that you will hear and use in conversations on campus at English-speaking colleges and universities. There are three problems that you will confront when you are using campus vocabulary on the TOEFL and after the TOEFL when you are on an actual college or university campus.

1. **The meaning of the word is specific to a college or university campus.** This means that you have to understand the glossary meaning of campus vocabulary words.
2. **Intonation might change the meaning of the word.** This means that you also have to understand the meaning that is implied when the word is spoken in a conversation.

3. **You need to be able to pronounce the words so that you are understood.** This means that you have to be able to use campus vocabulary when you respond to some of the speaking tasks on the TOEFL and, afterward, when you are on campus.

This chapter will help you improve your campus vocabulary. You will learn how to

- **Become familiar with the definitions**
- **Recognize patterns of intonation**

How will these strategies help you on the TOEFL? By learning campus vocabulary, you will be able to understand the conversations on the Listening section and respond to questions that refer to them. You will also be able to understand the conversations in Tasks 3 and 5 on the Speaking section and prepare better responses to these tasks. After you are admitted to a college or university program, you will continue to use this important list to help you interact with professors, staff, and other students on campus.

➤ Become familiar with the definitions

PRACTICAL STRATEGY

Using a pronouncing glossary is not like using a traditional dictionary. You can read the words and learn the meanings as you would when you use a dictionary, but you can also learn how the words are pronounced. The *Glossary of Campus Vocabulary* on pages 557–610 is also on a dedicated Internet site, exclusively for those who have purchased this book. The site presents a flash card for each vocabulary entry. Click on the speaker icon beside the word or phrase to hear the correct pronunciation. Then click on the speaker icon beside the example sentence to hear it again in a longer context.

PRACTICE ACTIVITY 1

Did you understand? Listen to the words and example sentences from the *Glossary of Campus Vocabulary*, which you will find by accessing the Barron's web page at:

http://barronsbooks.com/tp/toefl/flashcards/

Identify five entries to practice every day. Repeat the word or phrase after the speaker. Then repeat the example sentence. Do you understand the meanings when you see them? When you hear them? The example in Activity 1 shows you how to interact with the glossary.

EXAMPLE

Go to http://barronsbooks.com/tp/toefl/flashcards/

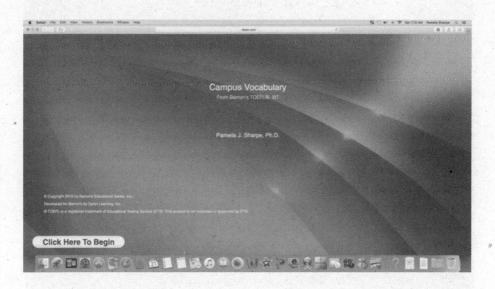

Click on **Click Here To Begin** to see the list of Campus Vocabulary words.

Click on a word to see the flash card.

Click on the **Arrow** button beside the word to hear the pronunciation. You can click more than one time to repeat it.

Click on the **Arrow** button under the Example to hear the word in the context of a sentence.

Click on the **Term Selector** button to see the list of all the Campus Vocabulary words.

Click on the **Previous** button to return to the flash card for the previous word in the alphabetical list.

Click on the **Next** button to progress to the flash card for the next word in the alphabetical list.

PRACTICAL STRATEGY

Use the glossary in the book and online to look up unfamiliar vocabulary as you continue to prepare for the TOEFL with the model tests in the next chapter. Don't stop to search for a word or phrase while you are taking a model test, but when you are using the answer key and the explanatory answers, you can note campus vocabulary that you want to add to your list of five entries to practice every day.

➤ Recognize patterns of intonation

INTERPRET EXPRESSIONS OF SURPRISE

Two ways to express surprise are commonly used in conversation— question statements and emphatic statements.

PRACTICAL STRATEGY

A rising intonation is usually heard at the end of a *question*. When a rising intonation is heard at the end of a *statement*, it shows surprise. The speaker had assumed the opposite.

PRACTICE ACTIVITY 2

Did you understand? Listen to the following sentences from your glossary. Anticipate the rising intonation at the end, which expresses surprise. You may also hear emphasis and a rising intonation in a key word or phrase in the statement. Try to repeat each sentence after the speaker, using the same intonation. Notice that question statements include a question mark at the end.

 Activity 2, Track 15

EXAMPLE

ace
Kathy aced her computer science class?

tuition
1. Tuition at private colleges is more?

prerequisites
2. You took the prerequisites last year?

handout
3. You lost the handouts?

laptop
4. Your laptop crashed?

article
5. You read the articles already?

skip class
6. Ron skipped class yesterday?

review session
7. The review session was productive?

call on
8. You sat in the front of the room and weren't called on?

curve
9. Dr. Graham grades his tests on the curve?

book bag
10. Your brand new book bag fell apart?

PRACTICAL STRATEGY

Sometimes a statement of surprise is introduced by the phrase *You mean*.

PRACTICE ACTIVITY 3

Did you understand? Listen to the following sentences from your glossary. Identify the intonation that signals surprise. Try to repeat each question after the speaker, using the same intonation.

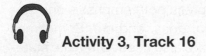 **Activity 3, Track 16**

EXAMPLE

off campus
You mean Carol doesn't want to live off campus?

notes
1. You mean you lent your notes to someone?

audit
2. You mean you're auditing the course?

turn in
3. You mean I could have turned in my paper tomorrow?

cram
4. You mean you crammed for the biology final?

draft
5. You mean you wrote the first draft in one night?

drop
6. You mean you dropped the class because it was too hard?

extension
7. You mean your request for an extension was denied?

lower division
8. You mean all the lower-division classes are full?

plagiarize
9. You mean you know someone who plagiarized?

sophomore
10. You mean Bill is only a sophomore?

PRACTICAL STRATEGY

An auxiliary verb in a statement can express both emphasis and surprise. Usually the auxiliary verbs are *do, does,* and *did.* Sometimes the auxiliary verbs *is, are*, *has* and *have* are also used. Often the statement begins with the word *So.* In these statements, the speaker had assumed the opposite.

PRACTICE ACTIVITY 4

Did you understand? Listen to the following sentences from your glossary. Identify the auxiliary verbs that express emphasis and surprise. Try to repeat each sentence after the speaker, using the same intonation.

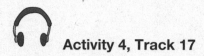

Activity 4, Track 17

<u>**EXAMPLE**</u>

T.A.
So Bill *did* apply to be a T.A.

degree
1. So you *did* graduate with a degree in music theory.

studies
2. So Jane *is* beginning her studies.

dean
3. So you *did* speak with the dean.

assignment
4. So you *do* read the assignments after all.

snack bar
5. So you *are* going to the snack bar after class.

report
6. So you *did* listen to Ken's report.

all-nighter
7. So your roommate *did* pull another all-nighter.

credit hour
8. So you *did* complete fifteen credit hours last summer.

makeup test
9. So Dr. Peterson *did* let you take a makeup test.

library card
10. So you *did* bring your library card with you.

COMPREHEND REQUESTS FOR CONFIRMATION

PRACTICAL STRATEGY

A statement that ends with the word *right* or a tag question with a rising intonation is a request for confirmation. These questions at the end mean that the speaker wants to confirm that he or she has understood correctly.

PRACTICE ACTIVITY 5

Did you understand? Listen to the following sentences from your glossary. Identify the question that signals a request for confirmation. Try to repeat each question after the speaker, using the same intonation.

Activity 5, Track 18

EXAMPLE

elective
You're going to take an elective in art appreciation, right?

    transfer
1. Dana transferred to State University, right?

    student I.D. number
2. Pat has a student I.D. number, doesn't she?

    transcript
3. You got your transcripts, didn't you?

    incomplete
4. Bill took an incomplete in sociology last semester, didn't he?

    undergrad
5. You're an undergrad, right?

    cheat
6. Gary was expelled because he cheated, right?

extra credit
7. You signed up for extra credit, right?

get caught up
8. Sue got caught up over vacation, didn't she?

fill-in-the-blank(s)
9. The test was all fill-in-the-blanks, right?

hand back
10. Dr. Mitchell hasn't handed back your exam yet, has he?

PRACTICAL STRATEGY

Sometimes the speaker asks for repetition to confirm that he or she has understood correctly. These sentences often begin with the phrase *Did you say*.

PRACTICE ACTIVITY 6

Did you understand? Listen to the following sentences from your glossary. Identify the question that signals a request for confirmation. Try to repeat each question after the speaker, using the same intonation.

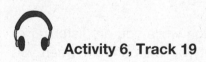 **Activity 6, Track 19**

EXAMPLE

probation
Did you say you're on probation?

fee
1. Did you say there are fees for using the recreational facilities?

admissions office
2. Did you say you couldn't find the admissions office?

flunk
3. Did you say you might have flunked the test?

fine
4. Did you say you were charged a fine for parking there?

tuition hike
5. Did you say you graduated before the tuition hike?

pop quiz
6. Did you say you passed all of the pop quizzes?

married student housing
7. Did you say there are no vacancies in married student housing?

shuttle
8. Did you say there's no shuttle on Sundays?

dorm
9. Did you say you've lived in a dorm for four years?

drop out
10. Did you say Diane dropped out after her junior year?

TAKING NOTES

Taking notes is writing down information while you are listening or reading. There are three problems that you will confront when you are taking notes.

1. **The professor determines the pace of a lecture.** This means that you have to take notes as quickly as the professor speaks.
2. **The notes must include all the main ideas and major facts.** This means that you have to know how to identify important information when you hear it or read it.
3. **The notes may be used for different reasons.** This means that you have to organize the notes to help you remember, to add to the information from another assignment, or to plan a speech or an essay.

This chapter will help you improve your note taking skills. You will learn how to

- **Separate the major and minor points**
- **Use abbreviations and symbols**

How will these strategies help you on the TOEFL? By learning to take better notes when you hear lectures, you will have the information you need to respond to the listening comprehension questions and to prepare your speaking and writing questions. You will even improve your reading comprehension. Taking excellent notes is one of the most important academic skills for success on the TOEFL and after the TOEFL when you are enrolled in a college or university program.

➤ Separate the major and minor points

In order to use two columns for notes, you must be able to classify the ideas into major and minor points. There are usually three or four major points in a short lecture or reading passage. Each of the major points is supported by examples and details. The examples and details are minor points.

PRACTICAL STRATEGY

When you hear a major point, write it on the left. When you hear a minor point, write it on the right.

PRACTICE ACTIVITY 7

Did you understand? Look at the notes under each topic. The sentences in the notes refer to either the major points or the minor points. Try to organize the notes under the topic by putting the major points in the left column and the minor points in the right column. Your answer is correct if the points are placed correctly on either the left or right. The points do not have to be in exactly the same order. The first one is completed to give you an example. The answers are printed in Chapter 7 on pages 380–381.

There are three types of managers in addition to the general manager.

The line manager is responsible for production.
For example, a production manager is a line manager.
A staff manager is in charge of support activities such as human resources.
Information systems is also overseen by a staff manager.
A functional manager is the head of a department.
A department chair at a college is a functional manager.
The manager of a sales department at a company is also a functional manager.

3 managers

line manager production	production manager
staff manager support activities	human resources information systems
functional manager head dept	dept chair college sales dept company

1. According to Mead, the self has two sides: the "I" and the "me."

   It is predictable because social conformity is expected.
   This part of the self is less predictable because it is unique.
   This part of the self is formed through socialization by others.
   The "I" represents the individuality of a person.
   For instance, a spontaneous reaction might reveal the "I."
   The "me" represents the expectations and attitudes of others.

2.   The mystery of pulsars was resolved in the 1960s.

We see pulses of light each time the beam sweeps past the Earth.
The pulsar in the Crab Nebula, for example, currently spins about thirty times per second.
We also know that pulsars are not perfectly timed because each revolution of a pulsar takes a little longer.
We know that pulsars are neutron stars, like lighthouses left by supernova explosions. It will probably spin about half as fast two thousand years from now.
Like a lighthouse, the neutron star revolves.

3.   Britain transported convicts to Australia in an effort to solve the problems of overcrowding in prisons.

There were 11 ships with 750 prisoners aboard.
Four companies of marines sailed with them as guards.
They took enough supplies for two years.
In 1787, the first fleet left for Botany Bay in New South Wales.
Shortly after arriving in 1788, the colony was moved to Sydney Cove.
In Sydney, the water supply and soil were better.
Although Sydney was the new site, for many years it was called Botany Bay.

4.   Frederick Carl Frieseke was an American impressionist.

In Normandy, he began to paint indoor settings.
In 1905, Frieseke moved to Giverney where he lived until 1920.
He studied with Whistler in the late 1800s.
Born in Michigan, he went to Paris in 1897.
In his later work, he began to use a darker palette.
From Whistler, he learned the academic style of the salons.
At Giverney, Frieseke was influenced by Monet.
Monet was experimenting with the effects of sunlight.
The style of Monet and his school is known as impressionism.
By 1920, Frieseke had left Giverney for Normandy.

5. Two types of weathering will break down rock masses into smaller particles.

Interaction between surface or ground water and chemicals causes chemical weathering.
With increased precipitation or temperature, chemicals tend to break down faster.
Mechanical weathering occurs when force and pressure grind rocks down.
A common example is the wearing away of granite facades on buildings.
The weathering of feldspar in granite can be caused by a reaction to acids in rain.
Pressure from freezing and thawing causes rocks to expand and contract.
When a rock is broken in two by physical forces, it is more vulnerable to weathering.

➤ Use abbreviations and symbols

Use abbreviations for important words and phrases that are repeated. There are two ways to do this. You can use capital letters that will remind you of the word or phrase. For example, in a lecture about Colonial America, you might use C M as an abbreviation for the phrase; in a lecture about the philosophy of John Dewey, you could use D as an abbreviation for the name. Or you can write the beginning of the word or phrase. For Colonial America, you could write Col Am; for John Dewey, J Dew. The abbreviation can be anything that will remind you of the word or phrase when you are reading your notes.

You should also use symbols and abbreviations for small words that are common in the language. The following list includes some of the most commonly used words in English. The abbreviations here are shortened forms for these frequently heard words.

+	and
w/	with
w/o	without
=	is, are, means, refers to, like, is called
Ø	different, not
#	number

X	times
→	results in, causes, produces, therefore
←	comes from, derives from
ex	example
@	about, approximately
1,2,3	first, second, third
<	less, smaller
>	more, larger
btw/	between
↑	over, up
↓	under, down

**Beyond the Book
Mini-Lesson
for the TOEFL
Note Taking**

To view the lesson, swipe
the code with the QR reader
on your smartphone or enter
the following private access
address on your computer:
*http://www.youtube.com/
watch?v=ztC_Nh6SLic&
feature=youtu.be*

PRACTICAL STRATEGY

The abbreviations in the list printed above
are part of my system for taking notes and
some of my students use it, but I encourage
you to create your own system because you will probably come up
with symbols and abbreviations that will have meaning to you, and
you will understand them later when you are reading your notes.
There is space for additional words. Be sure to choose something that
makes sense to you.

Symbol	*Word*
	and
	with
	without
	is, are, means, refers to, like, is called
	different, not
	number
	times
	results in, causes, produces, therefore
	comes from, derives from
	example
	at
	first, second, third
	less, smaller
	more, larger
	between

PRACTICE ACTIVITY 8

Did you understand? Now practice taking notes with your system. These are sentences from college lectures. Take notes as quickly as you can. First, read each of the sentences and write your notes here. When you are finished taking notes for all ten sentences, compare your notes with the example notes in Chapter 7 on page 382. Then try to write the original sentences using only your notes. Finally, compare your sentences with the original sentences printed in the answer key or on the next page. An example is shown using my system. Your answer is correct if *you* can read it and if the meaning is the same as the original sentence. The words do not have to be exactly the same. Listen to some sentences from college lectures. Take notes as quickly as you can.

Activity 8, Track 20

EXAMPLE

Friction between moving air and the ocean surface generates undulations of water called *waves.*

| Short: | Friction btw air + ocean surface → waves |
| Very short: | Fric btw air + Ø surf → waves |

Friction between air and the ocean surface causes *waves.*

1.

2.

3.

4.

5.

6.

7.

8.

9.

10.

ADVISOR'S OFFICE

This advice from Dr. Charles Swindell is framed on the wall of my office near my computer so that I can see it every day. I am happy to share it with you.

The longer I live, the more I realize the impact of attitude on life. Attitude to me is more important than facts. It is more important than the past, than education, than money, than circumstances, than failures, than successes, than what other people think or say or do. It is more important than appearance, giftedness, or skill. The remarkable thing is, we have a choice every day regarding the attitude we embrace for that day. We cannot change our past. We cannot change the fact that people may act in a certain way. We cannot change the inevitable. The only thing we can do is play on the one string we have, and that is our attitude. I am convinced that life is 10 percent what happens to me and 90 percent how I react to it. And so it is with you. We are in charge of our attitudes.

Henry Ford said it another way: "If you think you can or you think you can't, you are probably right."

PARAPHRASING

Paraphrasing means using different words to express the same meaning. When you paraphrase, you express an idea that you have heard or read, but you say or write it in your own words. Because you are including all of the information when you paraphrase, the paraphrase is usually about the same length as the original. There are three problems that you will confront when you are paraphrasing.

1. **There is a natural tendency to repeat the same words instead of paraphrasing them.** This means that you need to listen and read for meaning instead of focusing on individual words and grammatical structures.
2. **Reference materials such as a thesaurus may not be used on the TOEFL.** This means that you have to know synonyms for words and phrases.
3. **Sometimes it is not possible to think of a paraphrase.** This means that you must learn how to give credit to sources when you use them in speaking or writing.

This chapter will help you improve your paraphrasing skills. You will learn how to

- **Edit problem paraphrases**
- **Mention the source appropriately**

How will these strategies help you on the TOEFL? By learning to paraphrase well, you will achieve a higher score on all four sections of the TOEFL. There are questions that require you to recognize or produce paraphrases on the Reading, Listening, Writing, and Speaking sections. Paraphrasing is a very important academic skill for success in college or university classes as well. Using someone else's words is called *plagiarizing.* Plagiarizing is a very serious offense and can result in your being expelled from school.

➤ Edit problem paraphrases

Paraphrases begin with sentences. Here are some problems that you can learn to avoid:

- Don't change the meaning
- Don't leave out information
- Don't use too much of the original wording
- Don't copy the original

Original Sentence:

> Sometimes students plagiarize material from lectures and reading passages because they don't understand how to make the appropriate changes for an excellent paraphrase.

DON'T CHANGE THE MEANING

This is not an excellent paraphrase because the meaning has been changed from the original:

> On occasion, students use paraphrases of excellent lectures and reading passages without understanding the purpose of the changes that they have made in them.

DON'T LEAVE OUT IMPORTANT INFORMATION

This is not an excellent paraphrase because it does not include all of the important information in the original:

> On occasion, students use lecture and reading material verbatim.

DON'T USE TOO MUCH OF THE ORIGINAL WORDING

This is not an excellent paraphrase because it looks and sounds too much like the original:

> On occasion, students plagiarize material from lectures and reading passages because they don't comprehend how to make the necessary changes for an excellent paraphrase.

DON'T COPY THE ORIGINAL

This is not an excellent paraphrase because it is an exact copy of the original.

Sometimes students plagiarize material from lectures and reading passages because they don't understand how to make the appropriate changes for an excellent paraphrase.

PRACTICE ACTIVITY 9

Did you understand? Try to find the problem in each paraphrase and edit it. The first one is completed to give you an example. Example answers are printed in Chapter 7 on pages 383–385.

EXAMPLE

Original: Tides are caused by the gravitational pull of both the Sun and the Moon.

Paraphrase: Tides are produced by the gravitational pull of both the Sun and the Moon.

Problem: The paraphrase is too much like the original. Only one word was changed.

Edited
Paraphrase: The combined gravitational effects of the Sun and Moon produce tides on Earth.

Why is this better? Because synonyms have been substituted, and an alternative grammatical structure has been used, but the meaning has not changed.

1. Original: Proteins are molecules that regulate the movement of materials across cell walls.

   Paraphrase: Molecules that regulate the movement of materials across cell walls are proteins.

2. Original: The invention of the steam engine played a major role in the Industrial Revolution because it caused the factory system to extend itself to many areas of production apart from the cotton industry.

   Paraphrase: The invention of the steam engine was a primary influence in the Industrial Revolution.

3. Original: Although big companies are trying to maintain a balance between traditional advertising and some of the newer alternatives like blogging, it is often the smaller entrepreneurs who are using bloggers as an efficient way to stack their competition.

   Paraphrase: Big companies are using bloggers to defeat their smaller rivals.

4. Original: Fossils of bones have the appearance of stone, but the holes and pores are actually infused with mineral deposits from the surrounding sediments.

   Paraphrase: Fossils of bones look like stone, but there are mineral deposits from the surrounding sediments in the holes and pores.

5. Original: Pictograms found in many parts of the world about 1500 B.C.E. constitute the earliest system of writing, although written symbols have been discovered that date from as early as 3500 B.C.E.

   Paraphrase: Pictograms found in various parts of the world are the earliest evidence of a written system despite the discovery of written symbols.

6. Original: The modern atmosphere is probably the fourth atmosphere in the history of the Earth.

   Paraphrase: The modern atmosphere is probably the fourth atmosphere in the history of the Earth.

7. Original: Whereas alcohol is a depressant, coffee is a stimulant.

   Paraphrase: Alcohol is not like coffee.

8. Original: The Pacific Basin, which includes the continent of Australia and the thousands of islands grouped together as Oceania, covers one third of the surface of the Earth.

   Paraphrase: The Pacific Basin is also called Oceania because it encompasses one third of the Pacific Ocean.

9. Original: In fresco painting, the pigments may be mixed with water and applied to the plaster before it dries so that the lime in the plaster fuses with the pigments on the surface.

   Paraphrase: The lime in wet plaster bonds with the pigments on the surface when the colors are mixed.

10. Original: As Linnaeus originally conceived the biological classification chart, he segregated all living creatures solely according to their degree of physical similarity.

    Paraphrase: Linnaeus originally created the biological classification chart by categorizing all living creatures according to their degree of physical similarity.

➤ Mention the source appropriately

You already know how to introduce a source, but sometimes you need to mention the source more than one time. In that case, there is a pattern that is customarily used to mention the source appropriately.

PRACTICAL STRATEGY

When you cite the source the first time, use the first and last name. The title is optional. When you site the second time, use the last name only. If you cite a third time, use a pronoun, for example, *he* or *she*. After the third citation, you may use the pronoun again if the meaning is clear, or you may repeat the last name for clarity.

In the case of speakers or writers who are not named, the source should still be cited. You may be able to identify and cite the source as a professor, a speaker, an author, a writer, or a student, based on the context in which the information is presented. Use this general description the first time that you cite the source. If it is clear that the person is a man or woman, you can use the correct pronoun when you cite the source a second or third time. After the third citation, you may use the pronoun again if the meaning is clear, or you may repeat the general description for clarity.

PRACTICE ACTIVITY 10

Did you understand? Try to report the information in the notes. Cite the source appropriately. The first report is completed to give you an example. First read the notes, and then listen to the example answer on Track 21 and check each answer printed in Chapter 7 on pages 385–386.

EXAMPLE

Source: Edwin Hubble (man) astronomer

- demonstrated Andromeda nebula located outside our galaxy
- established the islands universe theory = galaxies exist outside our own
- study resulted in Hubble's constant = standard relationship/ galaxy's distance from Earth and speed recession

Astronomer <u>Edwin Hubble</u> demonstrated that the Andromeda nebula was located outside our galaxy. <u>Hubble</u> established the islands universe theory, which states that galaxies exist outside our own. <u>He</u> published a study that resulted in what is now called Hubble's constant, a standard relationship between a galaxy's distance from Earth and its speed of recession.

Activity 10, Track 21

1. Source: Theodore White (man)
   Book—*The Making of the President*

   - 1960 presidential debate—press conference
   - Nixon proceeded—personal debate
   - Kennedy spoke directly to TV viewers
   - estimated Kennedy gained 2 mil votes

2. Source: Paul Cezanne (man)

   - all forms in nature—based on geometric shapes
   - cone, sphere, cylinder primary
   - used outlining to emphasize shapes

3. Source: Marie Curie (woman)

    - won Nobel p physics 1903 w/husband—discovery of radium
    - won Nobel p chemistry 1911—isolation pure radium
    - 1st person 2 Nobel p

4. Source: Erik Erikson (man) psychologist

    - proposed eight stages/personal development
    - psychological crises/each stage shaped sense/self
    - lifelong process

5. Source: Margaret Mead (woman)

    - first fieldwork in Samoa 1925
    - book *Coming of Age in Samoa* best seller—translated many languages
    - still one/most well-known anthropologists
    - people/simple societies provide valuable lessons/industrialized

6. Source: Leonardo da Vinci (man)

    - quintessential Renaissance man
    - brilliant painter
    - interested in mechanics
    - work in math clear in perspective

7. Source: Peter Drucker (man) author
    - *Management Challenges for the 21st Century*
    - five transforming forces
    - trends have major implications for long-term strategies of companies

8. Source: Freidrich Mohs (man)

    - devised hardness scale/10 minerals
    - assigned 10 to diamond—hardest known
    - lesser values other min
    - scale still useful/relative hardness

9. Source: Maria Montessori (woman)

   • proposed educational model
   • not transmission knowledge
   • free to develop
   • success child working independently

10. Source: Jane Goodall (woman)

   • collaboration Louis Leaky
   • years living w/chimpanzees—Gombe Reserve
   • imitated behaviors
   • discovered chimp complex social organization
   • first document chimp making/using tools
   • also identified 20 different sounds/communication

ADVISOR'S OFFICE

Do you talk to yourself? Of course you do. Maybe not aloud, but all of us have mental conversations with ourselves. So the question is *how* do you talk to yourself?

Negative Talk	*Positive Talk*
I can't study all of this.	I am studying every day.
My English is poor.	My English is improving.
I won't get a good score.	I will do my best.
If I fail, I will be so ashamed.	If I need a higher score, I can try again.

How would you talk to good friends to encourage and support them? Be a good friend to yourself. When negative talk comes to mind, substitute positive talk. Encourage yourself to learn from mistakes.

SUMMARIZING

Summarizing is related to paraphrasing because you are using your own words to express an idea that you have heard or read. Remember that when you paraphrase, you are including all of the information, but when you summarize, you are including only the main ideas. A paraphrase is about the same length as the original, but a summary is shorter than the original. There are three problems that you will confront when you are summarizing.

1. **A summary does not include everything in the original.** This means that you should not try to write too much.
2. **Details and examples that support the main points are usually not included in a summary.** This means that you have to be able to discriminate between the main points and the details or examples.
3. **The author's point of view must be maintained.** This means that you cannot express your opinion when you report the information.

This chapter will help you improve your summarizing skills. You will learn how to

- **Use the same organization as the original**
- **Retain the original emphasis**
- **Maintain an objective point of view**

How will these strategies help you on the TOEFL? By learning to summarize, you will be able to answer the questions that are worth the most points on the Reading section. There are also questions that require you to produce summaries on the Writing and Speaking sections. Moreover, research demonstrates that students who understand how to summarize and use this skill when they prepare for tests will be able to remember information better.

➤ Use the same organization as the original

A summary should retain the same organization as the original reading or lecture. For example, if the passage identifies three different types of evergreen trees, then the organization is classification. Your summary should also be organized to classify the three different types of trees. If the passage explains the cause of deforestation in Canada, then the organization of the passage is cause and effect. Your summary should also be organized to demonstrate cause and effect. If the passage explains the life cycle of a pine tree, then the organization is chronological. Your summary should also be organized in chronological order. It is also important NOT to rearrange the order. A good summary begins with the first major point and follows with each major point in the order that it appears in the original.

PRACTICAL STRATEGY

First, determine the organization of the reading or lecture. Then list the major points in the order in which you read or heard them. This list gives you an outline for your summary.

PRACTICE ACTIVITY 11

Did you understand? Put the major points in the order that they should appear in a summary. The answers are printed in Chapter 7 on pages 386–388. Your answers are correct if they are in the same order as the original.

1. Reading

Although stage plays have been set to music since the era of the ancient Greeks when the dramas of Sophocles and Aeschylus were accompanied by lyres and flutes, the usually accepted date for the beginning of opera as we know it is 1600. As part of the celebration of the marriage of King Henry IV of France to the Italian aristocrat Maria de Medici, the Florentine composer Jacopo Peri produced his famous *Euridice*, generally considered to be the first opera. Following his example, a group of Italian musicians, poets, and noblemen called the Camerata revived the style of musical story that had been used in Greek tragedy. Taking most of the plots for their operas from Greek and Roman history and mythology, they began the process of creating an opera by writing a libretto or drama that could be used to establish the framework for the music. They called their compositions *opera in musica* or musical works. It is from this phrase that the word *opera* was borrowed and abbreviated.

For several years, the center of opera was Florence in northern Italy, but gradually, during the baroque period, it spread throughout Italy. By the late 1600s, operas were being written and performed in many places throughout Europe, especially in England, France, and Germany. However, for many years, the Italian opera was considered the ideal, and many non-Italian composers continued to use Italian librettos. The European form de-emphasized the dramatic aspect of the Italian model, however, introducing new orchestral effects and even some ballet.

Furthermore, composers acquiesced to the demands of singers, writing many operas that were little more than a succession of brilliant tricks for the voice, designed to showcase the splendid vocal talent of the singers who had requested them. It was thus that complicated arias, recitatives, and duets evolved. The aria, which is a long solo, may be compared to a song in which the characters express their thoughts and feelings. The recitative, which is also a solo of sorts, is a recitation set to music, the purpose of which is to continue the story line. The duet is a musical piece written for two voices, a musical device that may serve the function of either an aria or a recitative within the opera.

Major Points

Ⓐ Three types of musical pieces in opera
Ⓑ The first opera in Italy
Ⓒ The growth of opera throughout Europe

2. Lecture Script

Listen to part of a lecture in a biology class. Then put the major points in the same order as the lecture.

🎧 **Activity 11, Track 22**

Major Points

   Ⓐ A method of classification for protozoans—the three types motility
   Ⓑ Current research—questions, redefinitions
   Ⓒ Similarity to plants—make food from water/CO_2
   Ⓓ A definition of protozoans—single cell
   Ⓔ Considered animals—eating, breathing, reproducing

➤ Retain the original emphasis

The emphasis should be the same in both the original and the summary. For example, a passage about the three different types of leaves may include all three types, but it may dedicate half of the passage to one type—palmate leaves. In this case, your summary should retain the same emphasis by dedicating half of the summary to palmate leaves.

PRACTICAL STRATEGY

When you read, think in terms of space. How much space does the author devote to each point? When you listen, think in terms of time. How much time does the speaker devote to each point? When you do this, you are determining the emphasis for each point in the original, and you will know how much emphasis to give to these points in your summary.

PRACTICE ACTIVITY 12

Did you understand? Try to identify the emphasis for each part of the original and assign percentages. Then write a summary that retains the original emphasis. The answers and example summaries are printed in Chapter 7 on pages 388–390.

1. Reading

The Federal Reserve System, commonly called the Fed, is an independent agency of the United States government charged with overseeing the national banking system. Since 1913, the Federal Reserve System has served as the central bank for the United States. The Fed's primary function is to control monetary policy by influencing the cost and availability of money and credit through the purchase and sale of government securities. If the Federal Reserve provides too little money, interest rates tend to be high, borrowing is expensive, business activity slows down, unemployment goes up, and the danger of a recession is augmented. On the other hand, if there is too much money, interest rates decline, and borrowing can lead to excess demand, pushing up prices and fueling inflation. In addition to controlling the money supply, the Fed has several other responsibilities. In collaboration with the U.S. Department of the Treasury, the Fed puts new coins and paper currency into circulation by issuing them to banks. It also supervises the activities of member banks abroad and regulates certain aspects of international finance.

The Federal Reserve System consists of twelve district reserve banks and their branch offices along with several committees and councils. All national commercial banks are required by law to be members of the Fed, and all deposit-taking institutions like credit unions are subject to regulation by the Fed regarding the amount of deposited funds that must be held in reserve and that, by definition, therefore, are not available for loans. The most powerful body is the seven-member board of governors in Washington, appointed by the President and confirmed by the Senate. Although it is true that the Federal Reserve does not depend on Congress for budget allocations, and therefore is free from the partisan politics that influence most of the other governmental bodies, it is still responsible for frequent reports to the Congress on the conduct of monetary policies.

In many ways, the Federal Reserve is like a fourth branch of the United States government because it is composed of national policy makers. However, in practice, the Fed does not stray from the financial policies established by the executive branch of the government.

Major Points

- The function and responsibilities of the Fed
- The composition of the Fed
- A comparison of the Fed to a fourth branch of government

2. Lecture

Listen to part of a lecture in a psychology class. Then assign a percentage to each of the major points from the lecture and write a summary using the percentages to determine how much to write on each point.

Activity 12, Track 23

Major Points

- The level of sophistication for human memory
- The memory trace
- Working memory

➤ Maintain an objective point of view

An objective point of view is a neutral position. A summary is not an analysis or a commentary. A summary does not invite an opinion.

PRACTICAL STRATEGY

In your summary, you should not agree or disagree with the author's or the speaker's ideas. Don't make judgments. Don't add information. When you report, you should not include *your* opinions or comments. The conclusion should be the author's or the speaker's conclusion, not yours.

PRACTICE ACTIVITY 13

Did you understand? Try to find the opinions in the summary and delete them. Use the original reading to compare the content. The answers are printed in Chapter 7 on pages 390–391.

1. Reading

Charles Ives, who is now acclaimed as the first great American composer of the twentieth century, had to wait many years for the public recognition he deserved. Born to music as the son of a band-master, Ives played drums in his father's community band and organ at the local church. He entered Yale University at twenty to study musical composition with Horatio Parker, but after graduation he chose not to pursue a career in music. He suspected correctly that the public would not accept the music he wrote because Ives did not follow the musical fashion of his times. While his contemporaries wrote lyrical songs, Ives transfigured music and musical form. He quoted, combined, insinuated, and distorted familiar hymns, marches, and battle songs, while experimenting with the effects of polytonality, or the simultaneous use of keys with conflicting rhythms and time. Even when he could convince some musicians to show some interest in his compositions, after assessing them, conductors and performers said that they were essentially unplayable.

Ives turned his attention to business. He became a successful insurance executive, building his company into the largest agency in the country in only two decades. Although he occasionally hired musicians to play one of his works privately for him, he usually heard his music only in his imagination. After he recovered from a serious heart attack, he became reconciled to the fact that his ideas, especially the use of dissonance and special effects, were just too different for the musical mainstream to accept. Determined to share his music with the few people who might appreciate it, he published his work privately and distributed it free.

In 1939, when Ives was sixty-five, American pianist John Kirkpatrick played *Concord Sonata* in Town Hall. The reviews were laudatory. One reviewer proclaimed it "the greatest music composed by an American." By 1947, Ives was famous. His *Second Symphony* was presented to the public in a performance by the New York

Philharmonic, fifty years after it had been written. The same year, Ives received the Pulitzer Prize. He was seventy-three.

Summary

Charles Ives started his musical career as a member of his father's band and received a degree from Yale University in music, but he became a businessman instead because he was afraid that his music would not be well accepted. His music was very different from the popular songs of his era because he used small phrases from well-known music with unusual rhythms and tones. Fifty years after he wrote his *Second Symphony*, it was performed by the New York Philharmonic, and he was awarded the Pulitzer Prize.

I think that Charles Ives was wrong not to pursue his musical career from the beginning. If he had continued writing music instead of selling insurance, we would have more pieces now.

2. Lecture

Listen to part of a lecture in a geology class. Then delete the opinions from the summary.

Activity 13, Track 24

Summary

In my opinion, geysers are interesting. They happen when underground water gets hot and pressure from above causes the water to get hotter and lighter so it goes up to the surface and explodes out. Then, the water runs back into the ground and starts all over again. Geysers have to have heat, a place to store water, an opening where the water can shoot up, and cracks in the ground for the water to go back down into a pool. Geysers are in New Zealand, Iceland, and the United States. Old Faithful in Yellowstone is the most famous geyser, but the best place to see geysers is in New Zealand. I saw the Pohutu Geyser there on my vacation two years ago, and it was awesome.

ADVISOR'S OFFICE

Why are you preparing for the TOEFL? What goal is motivating you to study and improve your score? Do you want to attend a university in an English-speaking country? Do you want to try for a scholarship from a sponsor in your country or region? Is the TOEFL required for graduation from your high school? Do you plan to apply for an assistantship at a graduate school? Do you need the score for a professional license?

Goals can be experienced as mental images. You can close your eyes and imagine everything, just like a movie. See yourself achieving your goal. Watch yourself as you attend school or practice your profession in your ideal environment. See other people congratulating you. Enjoy the success.

Understand that you cannot control reality with visualization. However, it does change your attitude, it helps you to focus, provides motivation, and reduces stress. Positive visualization is an excellent way to take a short break from studying.

SYNTHESIZING

Synthesizing means to combine two or more sources in order to create something new. It is probably the most complex academic skill because it includes the other academic skills that you have studied— taking notes, paraphrasing, and summarizing. In addition, the result of a synthesis should be more than the sum of the parts. There are three problems that you will confront when you are synthesizing.

1. **The relationship between the sources may not be obvious.** This means that you may have to figure out the connection.
2. **One source appears to contain all of the necessary information.** This means that you need to be sure to balance the information so that all of the sources are used.
3. **Synthesis requires a high level of thinking.** This means that you should have a plan in order to create a synthesis.

This chapter will help you improve your synthesizing. You will learn how to

- **Identify the steps for synthesis**
- **Practice and plan**

How will these strategies help you on the TOEFL? By learning to synthesize information from readings and lectures or talks, you will develop ways of thinking that will help you prepare important integrated speaking and writing questions. The ability to synthesize is also required for success in making presentations, taking exams, and writing research papers for college or university classes.

Beyond the Book Mini-Lesson for the TOEFL Synthesizing

To view the lesson, swipe the code with the QR reader on your smartphone or enter the following private access address on your computer: *http://www.youtube.com/ watch?v=O35zSd0dL6I& feature=youtu.be*

➤ Identify the steps for synthesis

PRACTICAL STRATEGY

Three tasks on the TOEFL require synthesis: Task 3 and Task 4 in the Speaking section and Task 1 in the Writing section. Each task requires a slightly different approach, but in general, you follow the same steps for all of them:

1. Draw a chart with space for a relationship sentence at the top and 3 points underneath.

2. Read a short passage and take notes on the chart.

3. Listen to a conversation or a lecture on the same topic and take notes on the chart.

4. Write a relationship sentence.

5. Respond, using information from both the reading and the conversation or lecture.

6. Use the points on the chart to check for a complete response.

PRACTICE ACTIVITY 14

The examples below will show you specific steps for each of the integrated tasks. Take your time as you study each example. You will have an opportunity to practice the steps in Activity 15.

EXAMPLE SPEAKING TASK 3

Be careful! This task does NOT ask you for your opinion, although you will be asked about the opinions of the speakers in the conversation or talk.

1. Draw a chart with space for a relationship sentence at the top and 3 points underneath.

Relationship sentence: _____

Reading   Conversation
Point 1   Point 1

Point 2   Point 2

Point 3   Point 3

2. Read a short passage about a campus-related topic and take notes on the chart.

Reading Time: 45 seconds

Announcement from Campus Security
On Monday, all State University residence halls will begin requiring students to scan their fingerprints at the door in order to gain access to their building. As part of a continuing effort to make residence halls safer, fingerprint scanners have been installed at every building entry point. To prepare for this, students must scan their fingerprints at the campus security office in the student union. Guests are still allowed into residence halls but must now leave a valid ID in exchange for a guest pass.

Relationship sentence: _____

Reading	Conversation
Point 1	Point 1
Mon scan prints	
Access dorms	
Point 2	Point 2
Prepare scan at	
Campus Security	
S Union	
Point 3	Point 3
Guests ID-pass	

3 Listen to a conversation on the same topic and take notes on the chart.

Activity 14, Track 25

Now listen to a conversation on the same topic.

Relationship sentence: The woman approves of the security policy because it is a serious plan, it will be easy to use, and it should be a deterrent to theft and safety.

Reading	Conversation
Point 1	Point 1
Mon scan prints	Current plan not enforced
Access dorms	New plan serious
Point 2	Point 2
Prepare scan at	Easy-devices secure
Campus Security	Students too
S Union	
Point 3	Point 3
Guests ID-pass	Deterrent crime

Question

The woman expresses her opinion of the announcement. State her opinion and the reasons that she has for having that opinion.

4 Write a relationship sentence.

5 Respond, using information from both the reading and the conversation.

Example Response

The woman approves of the new security policy because it's a serious plan, it will be easy to use, and it should be a deterrent to crime. She explains that the previous system that required a pass to enter the dorm wasn't enforced. But now, without a scan, it won't be possible to go in the door. She also points out that it's really easy, like scanning to access a secure mobile device. She argues that scanning a fingerprint will be a deterrent to theft and the dorms will be safer because it'll be better than a guest pass to keep track of everyone who's in the buildings.

5 Use the points on the chart to check for a complete response.

> This is a complete response because it includes all three points that the woman makes to explain her opinion that the security policy is a good idea: It is a serious plan, easy to use, and will be a deterrent to crime.

EXAMPLE SPEAKING TASK 4

Be careful! The reading usually presents the definition of a term, a concept, a principle, or a theory, and the lecture usually provides an example, evidence, a case study, a research study, or a specific instance. In other words, this task is usually a synthesis of agreement, extension, and clarification. But sometimes, it can be a synthesis of disagreement and opposition.

1 Draw a chart with space for a relationship sentence at the top and 3 points underneath.

Relationship sentence: _____

Reading	Lecture
Point 1	Point 1
Point 2	Point 2
Point 3	Point 3

2 Read a short passage about an academic topic and take notes on the chart.

Reading Time: 45 seconds

Endangered Languages

Recent estimates of language populations indicate that half of the world's languages will likely become extinct in the 21st century. Three main criteria are used as guidelines for considering a language endangered: the number of speakers currently living, the average age of native speakers, and the percentage of the youngest generation acquiring fluency.

Given these criteria, it is obvious that language extinction occurs gradually across generations. Fewer and fewer speakers use the traditional language until only the older generation is familiar enough with the grammar to understand and express themselves in it.

Relationship sentence: _____

Reading	Lecture
Point 1	Point 1
Number speakers	
Point 2	Point 2
Average age native	
Point 3	Point 3
Percent youngest gen	

3 Listen to a lecture on the same topic and take notes on the chart.

Activity 14, Track 26

Now listen to part of a lecture in a linguistics class. The professor is talking about endangered languages.

Relationship sentence: The Christensen study in 1995 provided evidence that Ojibwa should be on the endangered language list.

Reading	Lecture
Point 1	Point 1
Number speakers	500–3 states
Point 2	Point 2
Average age native	elders 80+
Point 3	Point 3
Percent youngest gen	Almost no children

Question
The professor reports a study of the Ojibwa language. Explain why the study confirms that Ojibwa is an endangered language.

4 Write a relationship sentence.

5 Respond, using information from both the reading and the lecture.

Example Response
Ojibwa is considered an endangered language because it meets all three criteria for that classification. First, few speakers are fluent in the language. In Christensen's study in 1995, only about 500 of the tribal members in the tri-state area studied were fluent speakers. Second, the average age of native speakers is older. Among the 500 fluent speakers, most were elders 80 years of age or older. Finally, the percentage of speakers in the youngest generation is small. Among Ojibwa speakers, almost *no* children were fluent. Unfortunately, this study confirmed that Ojibwa is endangered, and despite efforts to teach the language in federally funded preschools, its future is very uncertain.

6 Use the points on the chart to check for a complete response.

The response is complete because it includes all three criteria for a language to be considered endangered and provides evidence from the Christensen study to prove that Ojibwa meets all three criteria.

EXAMPLE WRITING TASK 1: INTEGRATED ESSAY

The reading usually presents a position or argument in favor of a topic. The lecture presents information that calls into question the position or a counterargument. In other words, this task is usually a synthesis of disagreement, contrast, or opposition.

1 Draw a chart with space for a relationship sentence at the top and 3 points underneath.

Relationship sentence: _____

Reading	Lecture
Point 1	Point 1
Point 2	Point 2
Point 3	Point 3

2 Read a short passage about an academic topic and take notes on the chart.

Reading Time: 3 minutes

Homeownership is a goal for many people because they see it as a sound investment with many other positive outcomes as well.

Although it is true that the housing market can be volatile, from an individual perspective, buying a home to live in is still one of the best ways to acquire wealth. In the first place, homes appreciate. Over the long term, even initial losses reverse themselves and property values rise. Moreover, the cost for a rental tends to go up every year, whereas the cost of a 30-year mortgage is fixed. If the purchase is made when financing costs are low, then the investment is even more attractive. Traditionally, tax advantages have been offered to homeowners, providing additional financial incentives to enter the real estate market.

Another positive aspect of homeownership is the control that owners have over their living situation. Landlords can change the terms of rental agreements at the end of a short contract, forcing tenants to increase their expenditure or move. In contrast, homeowners have a sense of security and stability. By owning a home in a community, it is possible to maintain a stable environment without being compelled to make changes that may not be advantageous or well timed.

Finally, there are some unexpected social benefits for home-owners. In general, research supports positive outcomes in education, health, and crime. Specifically, the children of homeowners tend to achieve higher grades in school, both adults and children living in their own homes report better health and higher self-esteem, and crime rates are significantly lower in neighborhoods with a high percentage of resident homeowners.

Relationship sentence: _____

Reading	Lecture
Point 1 wealth creation—homes appreciate, fixed mortgage, tax incentives	Point 1
Point 2 control over living situation—rental contracts change	Point 2
Point 3 social benefits—health, education, crime	Point 3

3 Listen to a lecture on the same topic and take notes on the chart.

Activity 14, Track 27
Now listen to part of a lecture in an economics class. The professor is talking about homeownership.

Relationship sentence: The lecturer refutes the idea in the reading passage that homeownership is a goal promising positive outcomes.

Reading	Lecture
Point 1 wealth creation—homes appreciate, fixed mortgage tax incentives	Point 1 recession—high mortgage, half value
Point 2 control over living situation—rental contracts change	Point 2 foreclosure—insecurity, loss control
Point 3 social benefits—health, education, crime	Point 3 one paycheck from losing home—stress, children lower grades, less involved in school

4 Write a relationship sentence.

5 Respond, using information from both the reading and the lecture.

Question
Summarize the main points in the lecture, and then explain how they cast doubt on the ideas in the reading passage.

Example Essay
The lecturer refutes the idea in the reading passage that home-ownership is a goal promising positive outcomes. He makes a case for a reversal of this trend in the current economy, addressing the three assumptions in the passage.

First, he questions whether a home is a good way to create wealth. Although homes appreciated in the past, in today's market, homes are, in fact, depreciating to such a low that some homeowners are paying a high fixed mortgage for a home that is worth about half the value of its purchase price.

Second, the lecturer disagrees that homeownership provides control over one's living situation. During the recession, foreclosures and forced sales created a loss of control and a climate of insecurity in the market. He points out that many first-time homeowners would rather rent but cannot solve the problem of how to return to a rental without losing a significant investment in the home that they now own.

Third, studies confirm that many owners are only one paycheck away from losing their homes, a situation that creates stress for all family members, reversing the social benefits that homeownership once assured, including lower grades and less involvement in school activities on the part of the children.

Clearly, economic instability has affected the value of homeownership in serious ways.

6 Use the points on the chart to check for a complete response.

The essay is complete because it includes all three arguments proposed in the reading passage with the opposing argument for each one presented in the lecture.

➤ Practice with the plan

PRACTICAL STRATEGY

Remember that three tasks on the TOEFL require synthesis: Task 3 and Task 4 in the Speaking section and Task 1 in the Writing section. Now that you have memorized the steps, practice using them. Don't worry! The model tests in this book and on the CD-ROM will give you more practice, and soon you will be able to respond with confidence within the time limits on the iBT. For now, don't worry about timing yourself.

PRACTICE ACTIVITY 15

First, write the step after the number. Then practice the step to complete the task. Compare your answers with the example answers in Chapter 7 on pages 395–402.

Speaking Task 3

1

2

Reading Time: 45 seconds

Announcement from the Office of the President
After five months of remodeling, the Faculty Club will move into a new space on the top floor of Anderson Hall. The facilities, open to all full-time faculty, will include a restaurant open for breakfast, lunch, and dinner, a private dining area that seats twenty, and a bar that will serve beer and wine. The Club will be open next Monday. The Honors Program that formerly occupied the Anderson Hall space has moved to a smaller suite of offices and a lounge in the basement of Harkins Hall. The offices are already open and the lounge will be available for honors students to use next month.

3

Activity 15, Track 28
Now listen to a conversation on the same topic.

Question
The man expresses his opinion of the announcement. State his opinion and give the reasons that he gives for the opinion.

④

Response
⑤

⑥

After you have completed your response, listen to the example response for Speaking Task 3 in Chapter 7 on page 397.

SPEAKING TASK 4

①

②

Reading Time: 45 seconds

Courtship Display

A courtship display is a series of behaviors that an animal might use to attract a mate, and occasionally to warn rivals who may intrude. In general, the males initiate the courtship displays to arouse a female's interest and to win her selection among competing males. These behaviors may include ritualized dances or vocalizations that showcase the beauty or strength of the potential mate. In birds, these courtship displays often include postures by males to expose their plumage. Fanning and shaking the tail feathers, turning them to catch the light, and strutting around the female bird are common elements of the display.

3

Activity 15, Track 29
Now listen to a lecture in a biology class about the same topic.

Question
The professor discusses peacocks. Explain how their behavior conforms to the usual rituals for courtship displays.

4

5

Response

6

After you have completed your response, listen to the example response for Speaking Task 4 in Chapter 7 on page 399.

WRITING TASK 1

☐1☐

☐2☐

Reading Time: 3 minutes

Government censorship of the Internet benefits society in three ways. First, like other forms of mass media, including television and movies, censorship protects children. Restricting adult content and providing punitive measures for pornographic websites discourages the exposure of young children to inappropriate images and explicit language. Since children are growing up in an environment in which they can easily access the Internet, some restrictions should be in place to protect them.

Second, censorship curtails criminal activities. Censorship discovers and discourages financial frauds, theft, and harassment, or even potentially violent encounters. Because the Internet affords criminals a high degree of anonymity, unless their activities are monitored, they can sell illegal substances, threaten or bully individuals, or intrude into the lives of large numbers of people with spam advertising. Censorship reduces the instances of these disturbing contacts.

Finally, censorship assures personal privacy. Censorship laws establish standards for websites and security measures to protect identity, financial records, and personal information. Censorship restricts access to credit cards and bank accounts, as well as medical and employment records, and it reduces the incidents of identity theft.

3

Activity 15, Track 30
Now listen to a lecture about the same topic.

Question
Summarize the main points in the lecture, and then explain how they cast doubt on the ideas in the reading passage.

Question
The professor talks about censorship on the Internet. Explain how the lecture casts doubt on the information in the reading passage.

4

5

Essay

6

After you have completed your response, read the example essay for Writing Task 1 in Chapter 7 on pages 401–402.

**Beyond the Book
Mini-Lesson for the TOEFL
Synthesis**

To view the lesson, swipe the code with the QR reader on your smartphone or enter the following private access address on your computer:
https://www.youtu.be/nta5oJ9P9s4

4

MODEL TESTS

MODEL TEST 1: PRETEST

READING SECTION

The Reading section tests your ability to understand reading passages like those in college textbooks. The reading passages are presented in one complete section, which allows you to move to the next passage and return to a previous passage to change answers or answer questions that you may have left blank. The passages are about 700 words in length.

This is the short format for the Reading section. On the short format, you will read three passages. After each passage, you will answer 12–14 questions about it. You may take notes while you read, but notes are not graded. You may use your notes to answer the questions. Some passages may include a word or phrase that is underlined in blue. Click on the word or phrase to see a glossary definition or explanation.

Choose the best answer for multiple-choice questions. Follow the directions on the page or on the screen for computer-assisted questions. Most questions are worth 1 point, but the last question in each passage is worth more than 1 point.

Click on **Next** to go to the next question. Click on **Back** to return to previous questions. You may return to previous questions for all of the passages.

You can click on **Review** to see a chart of the questions you have answered and the questions you have not answered. From this screen, you can return to the question you want to answer.

Although you can spend more time on one passage and less time on another passage, you should try to pace yourself so that you are spending about 20 minutes to read each passage and answer the questions for that passage. You will have 60 minutes to complete all of the passages and answer all of the questions on the short format. A clock on the screen will show you how much time you have to complete the Reading section.

Reading 1 "Beowulf"

Historical Background

P1 → The epic poem *Beowulf*, written in Old English, is the earliest existing Germanic epic and one of four surviving Anglo-Saxon manuscripts. Although *Beowulf* was written by an anonymous Englishman in Old English, the tale takes place in that part of Scandinavia from which Germanic tribes emigrated to England. Beowulf comes from Geatland, the southeastern part of what is now Sweden. Hrothgar, king of the Danes, lives near what is now Leire, on Zealand, Denmark's largest island. The *Beowulf* epic contains three major tales about Beowulf and several minor tales that reflect a rich Germanic oral tradition of myths, legends, and folklore.

P2 → The *Beowulf* warriors have a foot in both the Bronze and Iron Ages. Their mead-halls reflect the wealthy living of the Bronze Age Northmen, and their wooden shields, wood-shafted spears, and bronze-hilted swords are those of the Bronze Age warrior. However, they carry iron-tipped spears, and their best swords have iron or iron-edged blades. Beowulf also orders an iron shield for his fight with a dragon. Iron replaced bronze because it produced a blade with a cutting edge that was stronger and sharper. The Northmen learned how to forge iron in about 500 B.C. Although they had been superior to the European Celts in bronze work, it was the Celts who taught them how to make and design iron work. Iron was accessible everywhere in Scandinavia, usually in the form of "bog-iron" found in the layers of peat in peat bogs.

P3   The *Beowulf* epic also reveals interesting aspects of the lives of the Anglo-Saxons who lived in England at the time of the anonymous *Beowulf* poet. The Germanic tribes, including the Angles, the Saxons, and the Jutes, invaded England from about A.D. 450 to

600. By the time of the Beowulf poet, Anglo-Saxon society in England was neither primitive nor uncultured. [A]

[P4] ➔ Although the *Beowulf* manuscript was written in about A.D. 1000, it was not discovered until the seventeenth century. [B] Scholars do not know whether *Beowulf* is the sole surviving epic from a flourishing Anglo-Saxon literary period that produced other great epics or whether it was unique even in its own time. [C] Many scholars think that the epic was probably written sometime between the late seventh century and the early ninth century. If they are correct, the original manuscript was probably lost during the ninth-century Viking invasions of Anglia, in which the Danes destroyed the Anglo-Saxon monasteries and their great libraries. However, other scholars think that the poet's favorable attitude toward the Danes must place the epic's composition after the Viking invasions and at the start of the eleventh century, when this *Beowulf* manuscript was written.

[P5] ➔ The identity of the *Beowulf* poet is also uncertain. [D] He apparently was a Christian who loved the pagan heroic tradition of his ancestors and blended the values of the pagan hero with the Christian values of his own country and time. Because he wrote in the Anglian dialect, he probably was either a monk in a monastery or a poet in an Anglo-Saxon court located north of the Thames River.

Appeal and Value

[P6]   *Beowulf* interests contemporary readers for many reasons. First, it is an outstanding adventure story. Grendel, Grendel's mother, and the dragon are marvelous characters, and each fight is unique, action-packed, and exciting. Second, Beowulf is a very appealing hero. He is the perfect warrior, combining extraordinary strength, skill, courage, and loyalty. Like

Hercules, he devotes his life to making the world a safer place. He chooses to risk death in order to help other people, and he faces his inevitable death with heroism and dignity. Third, the *Beowulf* poet is interested in the psychological aspects of human behavior. For example, the Danish hero's welcoming speech illustrates his jealousy of Beowulf. The behavior of Beowulf's warriors in the dragon fight reveals their cowardice. Beowulf's attitudes toward heroism reflect his maturity and experience, while King Hrothgar's attitudes toward life show the experiences of an aged nobleman.

P7   Finally, the *Beowulf* poet exhibits a mature appreciation of the transitory nature of human life and achievement. In *Beowulf*, as in the major epics of other cultures, the hero must create a meaningful life in a world that is often dangerous and uncaring. He must accept the inevitability of death. He chooses to reject despair; instead, he takes pride in himself and in his accomplishments, and he values human relationships.

1. According to paragraph 1, which of the following is true about *Beowulf*?

   Ⓐ It is the only manuscript from the Anglo-Saxon period.
   Ⓑ The original story was written in a German dialect.
   Ⓒ The author did not sign his name to the poem.
   Ⓓ It is one of several epics from the first century.

   Paragraph 1 is marked with an arrow [➔].

2. The word major in the passage is closest in meaning to

   Ⓐ basic
   Ⓑ principal
   Ⓒ distinct
   Ⓓ current

3. Why does the author mention "bog-iron" in paragraph 2?

   Ⓐ To demonstrate the availability of iron in Scandinavia
   Ⓑ To prove that iron was better than bronze for weapons
   Ⓒ To argue that the Celts provided the materials to make iron
   Ⓓ To suggest that 500 B.C. was the date that the Iron Age began

   Paragraph 2 is marked with an arrow [➜].

4. Which of the sentences below best expresses the information in the highlighted statement in the passage? The other choices change the meaning or leave out important information.

   Ⓐ Society in Anglo-Saxon England was both advanced and cultured.
   Ⓑ The society of the Anglo-Saxons was not primitive or cultured.
   Ⓒ The Anglo-Saxons had a society that was primitive, not cultured.
   Ⓓ England during the Anglo-Saxon society was advanced, not cultured.

5. The word unique in the passage is closest in meaning to

   Ⓐ old
   Ⓑ rare
   Ⓒ perfect
   Ⓓ weak

6. According to paragraph 4, why do many scholars believe that the original manuscript for *Beowulf* was lost?

   Ⓐ Because it is not like other manuscripts
   Ⓑ Because many libraries were burned
   Ⓒ Because the Danes were allies of the Anglo-Saxons
   Ⓓ Because no copies were found in monasteries

   Paragraph 4 is marked with an arrow [➜].

7. In paragraph 4, the author suggests that *Beowulf* was discovered in which century?

   Ⓐ first century
   Ⓑ ninth century
   Ⓒ eleventh century
   Ⓓ seventeenth century

   Paragraph 4 is marked with an arrow [➜].

8. Why does the author of this passage use the word "apparently" in paragraph 5?

   Ⓐ He is not certain that the author of *Beowulf* was a Christian.
   Ⓑ He is mentioning facts that are obvious to the readers.
   Ⓒ He is giving an example from a historical reference.
   Ⓓ He is introducing evidence about the author of *Beowulf*.

   Paragraph 5 is marked with an arrow [➜].

9. Why did the author compare the Beowulf character to Hercules?

   Ⓐ They are both examples of the ideal hero.
   Ⓑ Their adventures with a dragon are very similar.
   Ⓒ The speeches that they make are inspiring.
   Ⓓ They lived at about the same time.

10. The word exhibits in the passage is closest in meaning to

   Ⓐ creates
   Ⓑ demonstrates
   Ⓒ assumes
   Ⓓ terminates

11. The word reject in the passage is closest in meaning to

   Ⓐ manage
   Ⓑ evaluate
   Ⓒ refuse
   Ⓓ confront

12. Look at the four squares [■] that show where the following sentence could be inserted in the passage.

    Moreover, they disagree as to whether this *Beowulf* is a copy of an earlier manuscript.

    Where could the sentence best be added?

    Click on a square [■] to insert the sentence in the passage.

13. **Directions:** An introduction for a short summary of the passage appears below. Complete the summary by selecting the THREE answer choices that mention the most important points in the passage. Some sentences do not belong in the summary because they express ideas that are not included in the passage or are minor points from the passage. *This question is worth 2 points.*

    ***Beowulf* is the oldest Anglo-Saxon epic poem that has survived to the present day.**

    ●

    ●

    ●

Answer Choices

A The Northmen were adept in crafting tools and weapons made of bronze, but the Celts were superior in designing and working in iron.

B In the Viking invasions of England, the Danish armies destroyed monasteries, some of which contained extensive libraries.

C King Hrothgar and Beowulf become friends at the end of their lives, after having spent decades opposing each other on the battlefield.

D The poem chronicles life in Anglo-Saxon society during the Bronze and Iron Ages when Germanic tribes were invading England.

E Although *Beowulf* was written by an anonymous poet, probably a Christian, about 1000 A.D., it was not found until the seventeenth century.

F *Beowulf* is still interesting because it has engaging characters, an adventurous plot, and an appreciation for human behavior and relationships.

Reading 2 "Thermoregulation"

P1 → Mammals and birds generally maintain body temperature within a narrow range (36–38°C for most mammals and 39–42°C for most birds) that is usually considerably warmer than the environment. Because heat always flows from a warm object to cooler surroundings, birds and mammals must counteract the constant heat loss. This maintenance of warm body temperature depends on several key adaptations. The most basic mechanism is the high metabolic rate of endothermy itself. Endotherms can produce large amounts of metabolic heat that replace the flow of heat to the environment, and they can vary heat production to match changing rates of heat loss. Heat production is increased by such muscle activity as moving or shivering. In some mammals, certain hormones can cause mitochondria to increase their metabolic activity and produce heat instead of ATP. This **nonshivering thermogenesis (NST)** takes place throughout the body, but some mammals also have a tissue called **brown fat** in the neck and between the shoulders that is specialized for rapid heat production. Through shivering and NST, mammals and birds in cold environments can increase their metabolic heat production by as much as 5 to 10 times above the minimal levels that occur in warm conditions.

P2 → Another major thermoregulatory adaptation that evolved in mammals and birds is insulation (hair, feathers, and fat layers), which reduces the flow of heat and lowers the energy cost of keeping warm. Most land mammals and birds react to cold by raising their fur or feathers, thereby trapping a thicker layer of air. A Humans rely more on a layer of fat just beneath the skin as insulation; goose bumps are a vestige of hair-raising left over from our furry ancestors. B Vasodilation and vasoconstriction also regulate heat exchange and may contribute to regional temperature differences within the animal. C For example, heat loss from a human is reduced when arms and legs cool to several degrees below the temperature of the body core, where most vital organs are located. [D]

P3   → Hair loses most of its insulating power when wet. Marine mammals such as whales and seals have a very thick layer of insulation fat called blubber, just under the skin. Marine mammals swim in water colder than their body core temperature, and many species spend at least part of the year in nearly freezing polar seas. The loss of heat to water occurs 50 to 100 times more rapidly than heat loss to air, and the skin temperature of a marine mammal is close to water temperature. Even so, the blubber insulation is so effective that marine mammals maintain body core temperatures of about 36–38°C with metabolic rates about the same as those of land mammals of similar size. The flippers or tail of a whale or seal lack insulating blubber, but countercurrent heat exchangers greatly reduce heat loss in these extremities, as they do in the legs of many birds.

P4   → Through metabolic heat production, insulation, and vascular adjustments, birds and mammals are capable of astonishing feats of thermoregulation. For example, small birds called chickadees, which weigh only 20 grams, can remain active and hold body temperature nearly constant at 40°C in environmental temperatures as low as −40°C—as long as they have enough food to supply the large amount of energy necessary for heat production.

P5   Many mammals and birds live in places where thermoregulation requires cooling off as well as warming. For example, when a marine mammal moves into warm seas, as many whales do when they reproduce, excess metabolic heat is removed by vasodilation of numerous blood vessels in the outer layer of the skin. In hot climates or when vigorous exercise adds large amounts of metabolic heat to the body, many terrestrial mammals and birds may allow body temperature to rise by several degrees, which enhances heat loss by increasing the temperature gradient between the body and a warm environment.

P6 → Evaporative cooling often plays a key role in dissipating the body heat. If environmental temperature is above body temperature, animals gain heat from the environment as well as from metabolism, and evaporation is the only way to keep body temperature from rising rapidly. Panting is important in birds and many mammals. Some birds have a pouch richly supplied with blood vessels in the floor of the mouth; fluttering the pouch increases evaporation. Pigeons can use evaporative cooling to keep body temperature close to 40°C in air temperatures as high as 60°C, as long as they have sufficient water. Many terrestrial mammals have sweat glands controlled by the nervous system. Other mechanisms that promote evaporative cooling include spreading saliva on body surfaces, an adaptation of some kangaroos and rodents for combating severe heat stress. Some bats use both saliva and urine to enhance evaporative cooling.

Glossary
ATP: energy that drives certain reactions in cells
mitochondria: a membrane of ATP

14. According to paragraph 1, what is the most fundamental adaptation to maintain body temperature?

    Ⓐ The heat generated by the metabolism
    Ⓑ A shivering reflex in the muscles
    Ⓒ Migration to a warmer environment
    Ⓓ Higher caloric intake to match heat loss

    Paragraph 1 is marked with an arrow [→].

15. Based on information in paragraph 1, which of the following best explains the term "thermogenesis"?

    Ⓐ Heat loss that must be reversed
    Ⓑ The adaptation of brown fat tissue in the neck
    Ⓒ The maintenance of healthy environmental conditions
    Ⓓ Conditions that affect the metabolism

    Paragraph 1 is marked with an arrow [➜].

16. Which of the sentences below best expresses the information in the highlighted statement in the passage? The other choices change the meaning or leave out important information.

    Ⓐ An increase in heat production causes muscle activity such as moving or shivering.
    Ⓑ Muscle activity like moving and shivering will increase heat production.
    Ⓒ Moving and shivering are muscle activities that increase with heat.
    Ⓓ When heat increases, the production of muscle activity also increases.

17. The word minimal in the passage is closest in meaning to

    Ⓐ most recent
    Ⓑ most active
    Ⓒ newest
    Ⓓ smallest

18. In paragraph 2, how does the author explain the concept of vasodilation and vasoconstriction?

    Ⓐ Describing the evolution in our ancestors
    Ⓑ Giving an example of heat loss in the extremities
    Ⓒ Comparing the process in humans and animals
    Ⓓ Identifying various types of insulation

    Paragraph 2 is marked with an arrow [➜].

19. The word regulate in the passage is closest in meaning to

    Ⓐ protect
    Ⓑ create
    Ⓒ reduce
    Ⓓ control

20. According to paragraph 3, why do many marine animals require a layer of blubber?

    Ⓐ Because marine animals have lost their hair during evolution
    Ⓑ Because heat is lost in water much faster than it is in air
    Ⓒ Because dry hair does not insulate marine animals
    Ⓓ Because they are so large that they require more insulation

    Paragraph 3 is marked with an arrow [➔].

21. Why does the author mention "chickadees" in paragraph 4?

    Ⓐ To discuss an animal that regulates heat very well
    Ⓑ To demonstrate why chickadees have to eat so much
    Ⓒ To mention an exception to the rules of thermoregulation
    Ⓓ To give a reason for heat production in small animals

    Paragraph 4 is marked with an arrow [➔].

22. The word sufficient in the passage is closest in meaning to

    Ⓐ established
    Ⓑ valuable
    Ⓒ safe
    Ⓓ adequate

23. In paragraph 6, the author states that evaporative cooling is often accomplished by all of the following methods EXCEPT

    Ⓐ by spreading saliva over the area
    Ⓑ by urinating on the body
    Ⓒ by panting or fluttering a pouch
    Ⓓ by immersing themselves in water

    Paragraph 6 is marked with an arrow [➔].

24. The word enhance in the passage is closest in meaning to

    Ⓐ simplify
    Ⓑ improve
    Ⓒ replace
    Ⓓ interrupt

25. Look at the four squares [■] that show where the following sentence could be inserted in the passage.

    The insulating power of a layer of fur or feathers mainly depends on how much still air the layer traps.

    Where could the sentence best be added?

    Click on a square [■] to insert the sentence in the passage.

26. **Directions:** An introduction for a short summary of the passage appears below. Complete the summary by selecting the THREE answer choices that mention the most important points in the passage. Some sentences do not belong in the summary because they express ideas that are not included in the passage or are minor points from the passage. *This question is worth 2 points.*

    Thermoregulation is the process by which animals control body temperatures within healthy limits.

    ●

    ●

    ●

Answer Choices

A Although hair can be a very efficient insulation when it is dry and it can be raised, hair becomes ineffective when it is submerged in cold water.

B Some animals with few adaptations for thermoregulation migrate to moderate climates to avoid the extreme weather in the polar regions and the tropics.

C Mammals and birds use insulation to mitigate heat loss, including hair and feathers that can be raised to trap air as well as fat or blubber under the skin.

D Some birds have a special pouch in the mouth, which can be fluttered to increase evaporation and decrease their body temperatures by as much as 20°C.

E Endotherms generate heat by increasing muscle activity, by releasing hormones into their blood streams, or by producing heat in brown fat tissues.

F Panting, sweating, and spreading saliva or urine on their bodies are all options for the evaporative cooling of animals in hot environmental conditions.

Reading 3 "Social Readjustment Scales"

P1 → In 1967, Holmes and Rahe developed the Social Readjustment Rating Scale (SRRS) to measure life change as a form of stress. A The scale assigns numerical values to 43 major life events that are supposed to reflect the magnitude of the readjustment required by each change. In responding to the scale, respondents are asked to indicate how often they experienced any of these 43 events during a certain time period (typically, the past year). The person then adds up the numbers associated with each event checked. B

P2 → The SRRS and similar scales have been used in thousands of studies by researchers all over the world. C Overall, these studies have shown that people with higher scores on the SRRS tend to be more vulnerable to many kinds of physical illness— and many types of psychological problems as well. D More recently, however, experts have criticized this research, citing problems with the methods used and raising questions about the meaning of the findings.

P3   First, the assumption that the SRRS measures change exclusively has been shown to be inaccurate. We now have ample evidence that the desirability of events affects adaptational outcomes more than the amount of change that they require. Thus, it seems prudent to view the SRRS as a measure of diverse forms of stress, rather than as a measure of change-related stress.

P4 → Second, the SRRS fails to take into account differences among people in their subjective perception of how stressful an event is. For instance, while divorce may deserve a stress value of 73 for *most* people, a particular person's divorce might generate much less stress and merit a value of only 25.

P5   → Third, many of the events listed on the SRRS and similar scales are highly ambiguous, leading people to be inconsistent as to which events they report experiencing. For instance, what qualifies as "trouble with the boss"? Should you check that because you're sick and tired of your supervisor? What constitutes a "change in living conditions"? Does your purchase of a great new sound system qualify? As you can see, the SRRS includes many "events" that are described inadequately, producing considerable ambiguity about the meaning of one's response. Problems in recalling events over a period of a year also lead to inconsistent responding on stress scales, thus lowering their reliability.

P6   Fourth, the SRRS does not sample from the domain of stressful events very thoroughly. Do the 43 events listed on the SRRS exhaust all the major stresses that people typically experience? Studies designed to explore that question have found many significant omissions.

P7   → Fifth, the correlation between SRRS scores and health may be inflated because subjects' neuroticism affects both their responses to stress scales and their self-reports of health problems. Neurotic individuals have a tendency to recall more stress than others and to recall more symptoms of illness than others. These tendencies mean that some of the correlation between high stress and high illness may simply reflect the effects of subjects' neuroticism. The possible contaminating effects of neuroticism obscure the meaning of scores on the SRRS and similar measures of stress.

The Life Experiences Survey

P8   In the light of these problems, a number of researchers have attempted to develop improved versions of the SRRS. For example, the Life Experiences Survey (LES), assembled by Irwin Sarason and colleagues, has become a widely used measure of stress in contemporary research. The LES revises and builds on the SRRS survey in a variety of ways that correct, at least in part, most of the problems just discussed.

P9   → Specifically, the LES recognizes that stress involves more than mere change and asks respondents to indicate whether events had a positive or negative impact on them. This strategy permits the computation of positive change, negative change, and total change scores, which helps researchers gain much more insight into which facets of stress are most crucial. The LES also takes into consideration differences among people in their appraisal of stress, by dropping the normative weights and replacing them with personally assigned weightings of the impact of relevant events. Ambiguity in items is decreased by providing more elaborate descriptions of many items to clarify their meaning.

P10   The LES deals with the failure of the SRRS to sample the full domain of stressful events in several ways. First, some significant omissions from the SRRS have been added to the LES. Second, the LES allows the respondent to write in personally important events that are not included on the scale. Third, the LES has an extra section just for students. Sarason and colleagues suggest that special, tailored sections of this sort be added for specific populations whenever it is useful.

27. Based on the information in paragraph 1 and paragraph 2, what can be inferred about a person with a score of 30 on the SRRS?

    Ⓐ A person with a higher score will experience less stress than this person will.
    Ⓑ It is likely that this person has not suffered any major problems in the past year.
    Ⓒ The amount of positive change is greater than that of a person with a score of 40.
    Ⓓ This person has a greater probability to be ill than a person with a 20 score.

    Paragraph 1 and paragraph 2 are marked with arrows [➜].

28. The word outcomes in the passage is closest in meaning to

    Ⓐ opportunities
    Ⓑ conditions
    Ⓒ results
    Ⓓ issues

29. The word diverse in the passage is closest in meaning to

    Ⓐ necessary
    Ⓑ steady
    Ⓒ limited
    Ⓓ different

30. In paragraph 4, why does the author use divorce as an example?

    Ⓐ To show how most people respond to high stress situations in their lives
    Ⓑ To demonstrate the serious nature of a situation that is listed as a stressful event
    Ⓒ To illustrate the subjective importance of a situation listed on the scale
    Ⓓ To identify the numerical value for a stressful event on the SRRS

    Paragraph 4 is marked with an arrow [➜].

31. In paragraph 5, how does the author demonstrate that the response events on the SRRS are not consistent?

Ⓐ By asking questions that could be answered in more than one way

Ⓑ By giving examples of responses that are confusing

Ⓒ By comparing several ways to score the stress scales

Ⓓ By suggesting that people do not respond carefully

Paragraph 5 is marked with an arrow [➜].

32. According to paragraph 7, why is the SRRS inappropriate for people with neuroses?

Ⓐ They are ill more often, which affects their scores on the scale.

Ⓑ Their self-reporting on the scale is affected by their neuroses.

Ⓒ They tend to suffer more stress than people without neuroses.

Ⓓ Their response to stress will probably not be recorded on the scale.

Paragraph 7 is marked with an arrow [➜].

33. The word assembled in the passage is closest in meaning to

Ⓐ announced
Ⓑ influenced
Ⓒ arranged
Ⓓ distributed

34. The word relevant in the passage is closest in meaning to

Ⓐ occasional
Ⓑ modern
Ⓒ related
Ⓓ unusual

35. According to paragraph 9, why does the LES ask respondents to classify change as positive or negative?

    Ⓐ To analyze the long-term consequences of change
    Ⓑ To determine which aspects of change are personally significant
    Ⓒ To explain why some people handle stress better than others
    Ⓓ To introduce normative weighting of stress events

Paragraph 9 is marked with an arrow [➞].

36. According to the passage, which of the following is true about the SRRS as compared with the LES?

    Ⓐ The SRRS includes a space to write in personal events that have not been listed.
    Ⓑ The SRRS features a section for specific populations such as students.
    Ⓒ The SRRS assigns numbers to calculate the stress associated with events.
    Ⓓ The SRRS has hints to help people recall events that happened over a year ago.

37. Which of the following statements most accurately reflects the author's opinion of the SRRS?

    Ⓐ There are many problems associated with it.
    Ⓑ It is superior to the LES.
    Ⓒ It should be studied more carefully.
    Ⓓ The scale is most useful for students.

38. Look at the four squares [■] that show where the following sentence could be inserted in the passage.

This sum is an index of the amount of change-related stress the person has recently experienced.

Where could the sentence best be added?

Click on a square [■] to insert the sentence in the passage.

39. **Directions**: An introduction for a short summary of the passage appears below. Complete the summary by selecting the THREE answer choices that mention the most important points in the passage. Some sentences do not belong in the summary because they express ideas that are not included in the passage or are minor points from the passage. *This question is worth 2 points.*

   Several social readjustment scales have been developed to measure stress from life changing events.

   -
   -
   -

Answer Choices

A The Life Experiences Survey (LES) takes into consideration both positive and negative changes as well as the individual differences among people assigning values for stressful events.

B The Life Experiences Survey (LES) was developed to correct a number of problems in the Social Readjustment Rating Scale (SRRS).

C The Social Readjustment Rating Scale (SRRS) assigns mathematical values to major life events and collects data about the events that an individual has experienced during a specific time.

D Researchers have called into question the usefulness of instruments like the Social Readjustment Rating Scale (SRRS) and the Life Experiences Survey (LES) and have begun to develop a new scale to measure stress.

E People who have neurotic tendencies are not good candidates to take the Social Readjustment Rating Scale (SRRS) because they may provide higher values for stressful events.

F Positive events and negative events can both cause stress, according to social readjustment scales designed to measure them.

LISTENING SECTION

🎧 **Model Test 1, Listening Section, Track 31**

The Listening section tests your ability to understand spoken English that is typical of interactions and academic speech on college campuses. During the test, you will listen to conversations, lectures, and discussions, and you will answer questions about them.

This is the long format for the Listening section. On the long format, you will listen to three conversations, three lectures, and three discussions. After each listening passage, you will answer 5–6 questions about it. Only two conversations, two lectures, and two discussions will be graded. The other passages are part of an experimental section for future tests. Because you will not know which conversations, lectures, and discussions will be graded, you must try to do your best on all of them.

You will hear each passage one time. You may take notes while you listen, but notes are not graded. You may use your notes to answer the questions.

Choose the best answer for multiple-choice questions. Follow the directions on the page or on the screen for computer-assisted questions. Click on **Next** and then on **OK** to go on to the next question. You cannot return to previous questions.

The Listening section is divided into sets. Each set includes one conversation, one lecture, and one discussion. You have 10 minutes to answer all of the questions for each set. You will have 30 minutes to answer all of the questions on the long format. A clock on the screen will show you how much time you have to complete your answers for the section. The clock does NOT count the time you are listening to the conversations, lectures, and discussions.

IMPORTANT NOTE

The audio for the Listening, Speaking, and Writing sections of the 3 model tests in this book is available on MP3 CD. You will hear the audio, but you will not see visuals on the computer. The CD-ROM that supplements the larger version of this book provides computer visuals of 8 model tests that simulate the official TOEFL® iBT.

Listening 1 "Learning Center"

1. What does the woman need?

   Ⓐ A meeting with Professor Simpson
   Ⓑ An English composition class
   Ⓒ An appointment for tutoring
   Ⓓ Information about the Learning Center

2. Why does the woman say this: 🎧

   Ⓐ She is worried that she cannot afford the service.
   Ⓑ She is trying to negotiate the cost of the sessions.
   Ⓒ She is showing particular interest in the man.
   Ⓓ She is expressing surprise about the arrangement.

3. Why is the man concerned about the woman's attendance?

    Ⓐ If she is absent, her grade will be lowered.
    Ⓑ He will not get a paycheck if she is absent.
    Ⓒ She has been sick a lot during the semester.
    Ⓓ Her grades need to be improved.

4. What does the man agree to do?

    Ⓐ He will show the woman how to use the library.
    Ⓑ He will write some compositions for the woman.
    Ⓒ He will talk with the woman's English professor.
    Ⓓ He will show the woman how to improve her writing.

5. What does the man imply about the woman's teacher?

    Ⓐ The professor is very difficult to understand.
    Ⓑ He does not know where she came from.
    Ⓒ Her students seem to like her teaching style.
    Ⓓ He is familiar with her requirements.

Listening 2 "Geology Class"

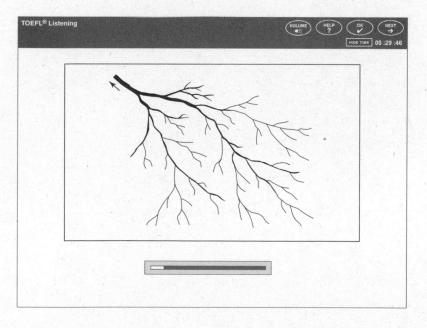

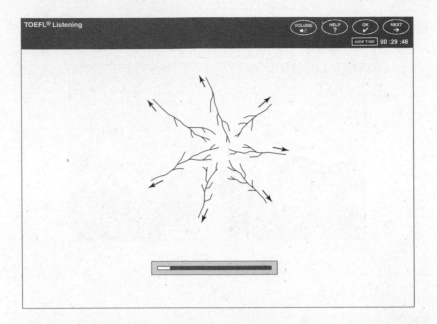

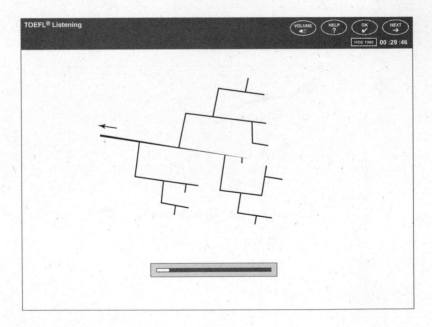

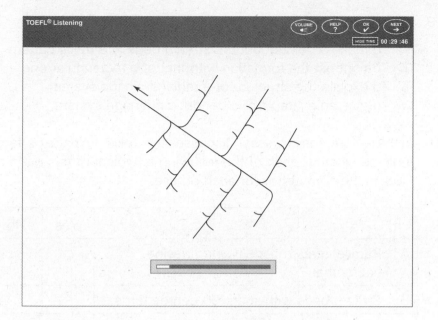

6. What is this lecture mainly about?

   Ⓐ A process for improving drainage systems
   Ⓑ A comparison of different types of drainage systems
   Ⓒ The relationship among the most common drainage systems
   Ⓓ The changes that occur in drainage systems over time

7. Why does the professor say this:

   Ⓐ To remind the students of the topic for today's session
   Ⓑ To indicate that he expects the students to read the textbook
   Ⓒ To encourage the students to participate in the discussion
   Ⓓ To demonstrate his respect for the students in his class

8. How does the professor introduce the dendritic drainage system?

   Ⓐ By demonstrating how this very old system has evolved
   Ⓑ By comparing it to both a tree and the human circulatory system
   Ⓒ By criticizing the efficiency of the branches in the system
   Ⓓ By drawing conclusions about the climate in the area

9. Why does the professor mention the spokes of a wheel?

  Ⓐ To make a point about the stream beds in a trellis pattern
  Ⓑ To contrast the formation with that of a rectangular one
  Ⓒ To explain the structure of a radial drainage system
  Ⓓ To give an example of a dendritic drainage system

10. In the lecture, the professor discusses the trellis drainage pattern. Indicate whether each of the following is typical of this pattern. Click in the correct box for each phrase.

		Yes	No
A	Parallel stream beds flowing beside each other		
B	Stream beds with sharp 90 degree turns		
C	Drainage from the top of a central peak		
D	Hard rock formations on top of soft rock formations		
E	Geological evidence of folding with outcroppings		

11. What does the professor imply when he says this:

  Ⓐ The test questions will be very difficult.
  Ⓑ The students should read their textbooks before the test.
  Ⓒ The basic patterns from the notes will be on the test.
  Ⓓ The test will influence the final grade.

Listening 3 "Psychology Class"

12. What is the discussion mainly about?

     Ⓐ The difference between suppression and repression
     Ⓑ Why Freud's theories of defense mechanisms are correct
     Ⓒ Some of the more common types of defense mechanisms
     Ⓓ How to solve a student's problem with an unfair professor

13. How does the student explain the term *repression*?

     Ⓐ He contrasts it with suppression.
     Ⓑ He identifies it as a conscious response.
     Ⓒ He gives several examples of it.
     Ⓓ He refers to a study by Freud.

14. Why does the professor say this:

     Ⓐ She is getting the class to pay attention.
     Ⓑ She is making a joke about herself.
     Ⓒ She is asking for a compliment.
     Ⓓ She is criticizing a colleague.

15. Which of the following is an example of *displacement* that was used in the discussion?

    Ⓐ Insisting that the professor dislikes you, when you really dislike him
    Ⓑ Defending the professor even when you are angry about his behavior
    Ⓒ Blaming someone in your study group instead of blaming the professor
    Ⓓ Refusing to acknowledge that a problem exists because of the low grade

16. According to the professor, what happened in the 1990s?

    Ⓐ The concept of defense mechanisms was abandoned.
    Ⓑ New terms were introduced for the same mechanisms.
    Ⓒ Modern researchers improved upon Freud's theory.
    Ⓓ Additional categories were introduced by researchers.

17. How does the professor organize the discussion?

    Ⓐ She has visual aids to explain each point.
    Ⓑ She uses a scenario that students can relate to.
    Ⓒ She provides a handout with an outline.
    Ⓓ She helps students read the textbook.

Listening 4 "Professor's Office"

18. Why does the woman go to see her professor?

    Ⓐ To get notes from a class that she has missed
    Ⓑ To clarify some of the information from a lecture
    Ⓒ To talk about her career in international business
    Ⓓ To ask some questions about a paper she is writing

19. According to the professor, which factor causes staffing patterns to vary?

    Ⓐ The yearly earnings for all of the branch offices
    Ⓑ The number of employees in a multinational company
    Ⓒ The place where a company has its home office
    Ⓓ The number of years that a company has been in business

20. Why does the professor say this: 🎧

    ⓐ To indicate that he is getting impatient
    ⓑ To encourage the woman to continue
    ⓒ To show that he does not understand
    ⓓ To correct the woman's previous comment

21. Which of the following would be an example of a third-country pattern?

    Click on 2 answer choices.

    Ⓐ A Scottish manager in an American company in Africa

    Ⓑ A German manager in a Swiss company in Germany

    Ⓒ A British manager in an American company in India

    Ⓓ A French manager in a French company in Canada

22. According to the professor, how do senior-level Japanese managers view their assignments abroad?

    ⓐ They consider them to be permanent career opportunities.
    ⓑ They use them to learn skills that they will use in Japan.
    ⓒ They understand that the assignment is only temporary.
    ⓓ They see them as a strategy for their retirement.

Listening 5 "Art Class"

23. What is the lecture mainly about?

   Ⓐ The way that drawing has influenced art
   Ⓑ The relationship between drawing and other art
   Ⓒ The distinct purposes of drawing
   Ⓓ The reason that artists prefer drawing

24. According to the professor, why do architects use sketches?

   Ⓐ Architects are not clear about the final design at the beginning.
   Ⓑ To design large buildings, architects must work in a smaller scale.
   Ⓒ Engineers use the architect's sketches to implement the details.
   Ⓓ Sketches are used as a record of the stages in development.

25. What does the professor mean when she says this: 🎧

    Ⓐ She is checking to be sure that the students understand.
    Ⓑ She is expressing uncertainty about the information.
    Ⓒ She is inviting the students to disagree with her.
    Ⓓ She is indicating that she is in a hurry to continue.

26. Why does the professor mention the drawing of Marie Antoinette?

    Ⓐ It is an example of a work copied in another medium.
    Ⓑ Drawing was typical of the way that artists were educated.
    Ⓒ The sketch was a historical account of an important event.
    Ⓓ The size of the drawing made it an exceptional work of art.

27. What is the professor's opinion of Picasso?

    Ⓐ Picasso was probably playing a joke by offering drawings for sale.
    Ⓑ At the end of his career, Picasso may have chosen drawing because it was easy.
    Ⓒ Picasso's drawings required the confidence and skill of a master artist.
    Ⓓ Cave drawings were the inspiration for many of Picasso's works.

28. According to the lecture, what are the major functions of drawing?

    Click on 3 answer choices.

    Ⓐ A technique to remember parts of a large work

    Ⓑ A method to preserve a historical record

    Ⓒ An example of earlier forms of art

    Ⓓ An educational approach to train artists

    Ⓔ A process for experimenting with media

Listening 6 *"Astronomy Class"*

29. What is the discussion mainly about?

     Ⓐ The discovery of the Alpha Centauri system
     Ⓑ The reason solar systems are confused with galaxies
     Ⓒ The vast expanse of the universe around us
     Ⓓ The model at the National Air and Space Museum

30. Why does the professor say this:

     Ⓐ The students can read the details in the textbook.
     Ⓑ The professor wants the students to concentrate on listening.
     Ⓒ The facts are probably already familiar to most of the class.
     Ⓓ This lecture is a review of material from a previous session.

31. Why wouldn't a photograph capture a true picture of the solar system walk?

     Ⓐ It would not show the distances between the bodies in space.
     Ⓑ The information on the markers would not be visible in a picture.
     Ⓒ The scale for the model was not large enough to be accurate.
     Ⓓ A photograph would make the exhibit appear much smaller.

32. How does the professor explain the term *solar system*?

     Ⓐ He identifies the key features of a solar system.
     Ⓑ He refers to the glossary in the textbook.
     Ⓒ He gives several examples of solar systems.
     Ⓓ He contrasts a solar system with a galaxy.

33. Why does the professor say this:

     Ⓐ He is trying to get the students to pay attention.
     Ⓑ He is correcting something that he said earlier in the discussion.
     Ⓒ He is beginning a summary of the important points.
     Ⓓ He is joking with the students about the lecture.

34. What can be inferred about the professor?

   Ⓐ The professor used to teach in Washington, D.C.
   Ⓑ The professor likes his students to participate in the discussion.
   Ⓒ The professor wants the students to take notes on every detail.
   Ⓓ The professor is not very interested in the subject of the discussion.

Listening 7 "Bookstore"

35. What does the man need from the bookstore?

    Ⓐ A schedule of classes for next term
    Ⓑ A form to order books
    Ⓒ Specific books for his classes
    Ⓓ Information about employment

36. What does the man need if he wants a full refund?

    Click on 2 answer choices.

    Ⓐ Identification

    Ⓑ His registration form

    Ⓒ A receipt for the purchase

    Ⓓ Proof of his deposit

37. What does the woman mean when she says this:

    Ⓐ She is not sure that the student employee will give her the form.
    Ⓑ She thinks that he will have to wait for the student employees.
    Ⓒ She does not want the man to bother her because she is busy.
    Ⓓ She is is not sure that the man understands what to do.

38. What does the woman imply about the used books she sells?

    Ⓐ They are purchased before new books.
    Ⓑ They do not have marks in them.
    Ⓒ She does not recommend buying them.
    Ⓓ She would rather sell new books.

39. What does the man need to do now?

    Ⓐ Go to the bank to get money for the deposit
    Ⓑ Sit down and fill out the form to order books
    Ⓒ Take his books back to the dormitory
    Ⓓ Locate the section numbers for his classes

Listening 8 "Environmental Science Class"

40. What is this lecture mainly about?

   Ⓐ An overview of fuel cell technology
   Ⓑ A process for producing fuel cells
   Ⓒ A comparison of fuel cell models
   Ⓓ Some problems in fuel cell distribution

41. What does the professor mean when he says this:

   Ⓐ He wants the students to take notes.
   Ⓑ He would like the students to participate.
   Ⓒ He is impressed with these options.
   Ⓓ He does not plan to talk about the alternatives.

42. Why does the professor mention the STEP program in Australia?

   Ⓐ He has personal experience in this project.
   Ⓑ He is referring to information from a previous discussion.
   Ⓒ He is comparing it to a successful program in Japan.
   Ⓓ He thinks it is a very good example of a project.

43. Why does the professor say this:

   Ⓐ To indicate that the date is not important
   Ⓑ To provide a specific date for the contract
   Ⓒ To correct a previous statement about the date
   Ⓓ To show that he is uncertain about the date

44. What are some of the problems associated with fuel cell technology?

   Click on 2 answer choices.

   Ⓐ Noise pollution

   Ⓑ Public acceptance

   Ⓒ Supplies of hydrogen

   Ⓓ Investment in infrastructures

45. What is the professor's attitude toward fuel cells?

    Ⓐ He thinks that the technology is not very efficient.

    Ⓑ He is hopeful about their development in the future.

    Ⓒ He is doubtful that fuel cells will replace fossil fuels.

    Ⓓ He is discouraged because of the delays in production.

Listening 9 "Philosophy Class"

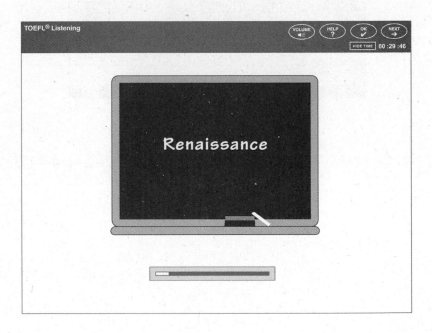

46. What is the main focus of this discussion?

    Ⓐ The Renaissance
    Ⓑ Important scholars
    Ⓒ Humanism
    Ⓓ Political reform

47. Why does the professor say this: 🎧

    Ⓐ She thinks that the spelling of the term is not important.
    Ⓑ She assumes that the students know how to spell the term.
    Ⓒ She knows that the term can be found in the textbook.
    Ⓓ She does not want to spend time explaining the term.

48. Why does the professor mention the drawing by Leonardo da Vinci?

    Ⓐ She wants the students to refer to their textbook more often.
    Ⓑ She uses it as an example of the union of art and science.
    Ⓒ She says that it is one of her personal favorites.
    Ⓓ She contrasts his work with that of other artists.

49. According to the professor, what was the effect of using Latin as a universal language of scholarship?

    Ⓐ It facilitated communication among intellectuals in many countries.
    Ⓑ It made Rome the capital of the world during the Renaissance.
    Ⓒ It caused class distinctions to be apparent throughout Europe.
    Ⓓ It created an environment in which new ideas were suppressed.

50. According to the professor, what can be inferred about a Renaissance man?

  Ⓐ He would probably be a master craftsman.
  Ⓑ He would have an aptitude for both art and science.
  Ⓒ He would be interested in classical philosophers.
  Ⓓ He would value logic at the expense of creativity.

51. All of the following characteristics are true of humanism EXCEPT

  Ⓐ Mankind is innately good.
  Ⓑ Scholars must serve society.
  Ⓒ The individual is important.
  Ⓓ Human beings are rational.

 Please turn off the audio. There is a 10-minute break between the Listening section and the Speaking section.

SPEAKING SECTION

Model Test 1, Speaking Section, Track 32

The Speaking section tests your ability to communicate in English in an academic setting. During the test, you will be presented with six speaking questions. The questions ask for a response to a single question, a conversation, a talk, or a lecture. The prompts and questions are presented only one time.

You may take notes as you listen, but notes are not graded. You may use your notes to answer the questions. Some of the questions ask for a response to a reading passage and a talk or a lecture. The reading passages and the questions are written, but the directions will be spoken.

Your speaking will be evaluated on both the fluency of the language and the accuracy of the content. You will have 15–20 seconds to prepare and 45–60 seconds to respond to each question. Typically, a good response will require all of the response time and the answer will be complete by the end of the response time.

You will have about 20 minutes to complete the Speaking section. A clock on the screen will show you how much time you have to prepare each of your answers and how much time you have to record each response.

Independent Speaking Question 1 "Marriage Partner"

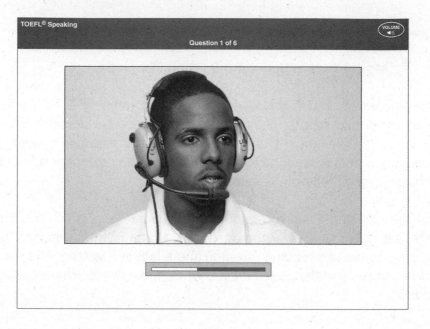

Listen for a question about a familiar topic.

Question

Describe an ideal marriage partner. What qualities do you think are most important for a husband or wife? Use specific reasons and details to explain your choices.

Preparation Time: 15 seconds
Recording Time: 45 seconds

Independent Speaking Question 2 "News"

 Listen for a question that asks your opinion about a familiar topic.

Question
Agree or disagree with the following statement:

Getting news on TV or on a computer is better than reading it in a print newspaper.

Use specific reasons and examples to support your choice.

Preparation Time: 15 seconds
Recording Time: 45 seconds

Integrated Speaking Question 3 "Meal Plan"

Read a short passage and listen to a talk on the same topic.

Reading Time: 45 seconds

Change in Meal Plans

Residence hall students are no longer required to purchase seven-day meal plans. Now two meal plan options will be offered. The traditional seven-day plan will still be available, including three meals every day at a cost of $168 per month. In addition, a five-day plan will be offered, including three meals Monday–Friday at a cost of $120 per month. Students who elect to use the five-day plan may purchase meals on the weekend at three dollars per meal. The food court in the College Union provides several fast-food alternatives. In addition to burgers and pizza, Chinese food, Mexican food, and a salad bar are also available.

Now listen to two students who are talking about the plan.

Question

The man expresses his opinion of the new meal plan. Report his opinion, and explain the reasons that he gives for having that opinion.

Preparation Time: 30 seconds
Recording Time: 60 seconds

Integrated Speaking Question 4 "Aboriginal People"

Read a short passage and listen to part of a lecture on the same topic.

Reading Time: 45 seconds

Aboriginal People

   Although the first inhabitants of Australia have been identified by physical characteristics, culture, language, and locale, none of these attributes truly establishes a person as a member of the Aboriginal People. Because the Aboriginal groups settled in various geographical areas and developed customs and lifestyles that reflected the resources available to them, there is great diversity among those groups, including more than 200 linguistic varieties. Probably the most striking comparison is that of the Aboriginal People who inhabit the desert terrain of the Australian Outback with those who live along the coast. Clearly, their societies have developed very different cultures. According to the Department of Education, the best way to establish identity as a member of the Aboriginal People is to be identified and accepted as such by the Aboriginal community.

Now listen to part of a lecture in an anthropology class. The professor is talking about Aboriginal People.

Question
Explain how the Aboriginal People are identified. Draw upon information in both the reading and the lecture.

Preparation Time: 30 seconds
Recording Time: 60 seconds

Integrated Speaking Question 5 "Scheduling Conflict"

Now listen to a conversation between a student and his friend.

Question
Describe the man's problem and the two suggestions that his friend makes about how to handle it. What do you think the man should do, and why?

Preparation Time: 20 seconds
Recording Time: 60 seconds

Integrated Speaking Question 6 "Laboratory Microscope"

Now listen to part of a talk in a biology laboratory. The teaching assistant is explaining how to use the microscope.

Question
Using the main points and examples from the talk, describe the two major systems of the laboratory microscope, and then explain how to use it.

Preparation Time: 20 seconds
Recording Time: 60 seconds

WRITING SECTION

The Writing section tests your ability to write essays in English similar to those that you would write in college courses. During the test, you will write two essays.

The Integrated Essay. First you will read an academic passage and then you will listen to a lecture on the same topic. You may take notes as you read and listen, but notes are not graded. You may use your notes to write the essay. The reading passage will disappear while you are listening to the lecture, but the passage will return to the screen for reference when you begin to write your essay. You will have 20 minutes to plan, write, and revise your response. Typically, a good essay for the integrated topic will require that you write 150–225 words.

The Independent Essay. You will read a question on the screen. It usually asks for your opinion about a familiar topic. You will have 30 minutes to plan, write, and revise your response. Typically, a good essay for the independent topic will require that you write 300–350 words.

A clock on the screen will show you how much time you have left to complete each essay.

Integrated Essay "Online Graduate Programs"

You have 20 minutes to plan, write, and revise your response to a reading passage and a lecture on the same topic. First, read the passage and take notes. Then, listen to the lecture and take notes. Finally, write your response to the writing question. Typically, a good response will require that you write 150–225 words.

Reading Passage
Time: 3 minutes

Online graduate degree programs are being offered worldwide. In many respects, the programs are like the same degree programs available in a traditional campus environment, but in several key aspects, they are very different.

First, online degree programs do not offer one-on-one time with the professors. On campus, professors hold regular office hours and expect to have conferences with their graduate students. In addition, many opportunities present themselves for informal interactions before and after class or in chance meetings on campus. Some professors invite their graduate students to their homes or otherwise make themselves available in semi-social settings. In contrast, online professors are unable to see their graduate students in person and, consequently, do not know them very well.

Second, many online graduate programs are not as challenging or as high quality as their on-campus counterparts. In fact, some courses are so easy that students are able to complete them online in one weekend. For the most part, senior faculty members refuse to teach the online courses, contributing to the difference in quality of the online and on-campus courses with the same titles. Many excellent professors view the huge numbers in the online classes as an impediment. Technology allows for more students to take the same course, and junior faculty or graders provide feedback on assignments that are graded by senior faculty teaching on campus.

Third, top schools do not offer online degree programs. Although non-credit courses or even a handful of credit courses may be available, the best schools still require that graduate students complete a more conventional program with most of their time spent in residence on campus. For students who want a graduate degree from a prestigious university, online options are not open to them.

Model Test 1, Writing Section, Track 33

Now listen to a lecture on the same topic as the passage that you have just read.

Question

Summarize the main points in the lecture and then explain how they cast doubt on the ideas in the reading passage.

Independent Essay "An Important Leader"

Question

Leaders like John F. Kennedy and Martin Luther King have made important contributions to the people of the United States. Name another world leader you think is important. Give specific reasons for your choice.

STOP

**This is the end of Model Test 1.
To check your answers, refer to "Explanatory or Example Answers and Audio Scripts for Model Tests: Model Test 1," Chapter 7, pages 403–450.
Example answers for the Speaking section can be heard on Track 34.**

5

MODEL TEST 2: PROGRESS TEST

READING SECTION

The Reading section tests your ability to understand reading passages like those in college textbooks. The reading passages are presented in one complete section, which allows you to move to the next passage and return to a previous passage to change answers or answer questions that you may have left blank. The passages are about 700 words in length.

This is the long format for the Reading section. On the long format, you will read four passages. After each passage, you will answer 12–14 questions about it. You may take notes while you read, but notes are not graded. You may use your notes to answer the questions. Some passages may include a word or phrase that is underlined in blue. Click on the word or phrase to see a glossary definition or explanation. Only three passages will be graded. The other passage is part of an experimental section for future tests. Because you will not know which passages will be graded, you must try to do your best on all of them.

Choose the best answer for multiple-choice questions. Follow the directions on the page or on the screen for computer-assisted questions. Most questions are worth 1 point, but the last question in each passage is worth more than 1 point.

Click on **Next** to go to the next question. Click on **Back** to return to previous questions. You may return to previous questions for all of the passages.

You can click on **Review** to see a chart of the questions you have answered and the questions you have not answered. From this screen, you can return to the question you want to answer.

Although you can spend more time on one passage and less time on another passage, you should try to pace yourself so that you are spending about 20 minutes to read each passage and answer the questions for that passage. You will have 80 minutes to complete all of the passages and answer all of the questions on the long format. A clock on the screen will show you how much time you have to complete the Reading section.

Reading 1 "Resources and Industrialism in Canada"

P1   → While the much-anticipated expansion of the western frontier was unfolding in accordance with the design of the National Policy, a new northern frontier was opening up to enhance the prospects of Canadian industrial development. [A] Long the preserve of the fur trade, the Canadian Shield and the western Cordilleras became a treasury of minerals, timber and hydroelectric power in the late 19th and early 20th centuries. As early as 1883, CPR [Canadian Pacific Railway] construction crews blasting through the rugged terrain of northern Ontario discovered copper and nickel deposits in the vicinity of Sudbury. [B] As refining processes, uses, and markets for the metal developed, Sudbury became the world's largest nickel producer. The building of the Temiskaming and Northern Ontario Railway led to the discovery of rich silver deposits around Cobalt north of Lake Nipissing in 1903 and touched off a mining boom that spread northward to Kirkland Lake and the Porcupine district. [C] Although the economic importance of these mining operations was enduring, they did not capture the public imagination to the same extent as the Klondike gold rush of the late 1890s. D

P2   → Fortune-seekers from all parts of the world flocked to the Klondike and Yukon River valleys to pan for gold starting in 1896. At the height of the gold rush in 1898, the previously unsettled subarctic frontier had a population of about 30,000, more than half of which was concentrated in the newly established town of Dawson. In the same year, the federal government created the Yukon Territory, administered by an appointed commissioner, in an effort to ward off the prospect of annexation to Alaska. Even if the economic significance of the Klondike strike was somewhat exaggerated and short-lived, the tales of sudden riches, heroic and tragic exploits, and the rowdiness and lawlessness of the mining frontier were immortalized through popular fiction and folklore, notably the poetic verses of Robert W. Service.

P3   → Perhaps less romantic than the mining booms, the exploitation of forest and water resources was just as vital to national development. The Douglas fir, spruce, and cedar stands of British Columbia along with the white pine forests of Ontario satisfied construction demands on the treeless prairies as well as in the growing cities and towns of central Canada and the United States. British Columbia's forests also supplied lumber to Asia. In addition, the softwood forest wealth of the Cordilleras and the Shield was a valuable source of pulpwood for the development of the pulp and paper industry, which made Canada one of the world's leading exporters of newsprint. Furthermore, the fast flowing rivers of the Shield and Cordilleras could readily be harnessed as sources of hydroelectric power, replacing coal in the booming factories of central Canada as well as in the evolving mining and pulp and paper industries. The age of electricity under public ownership and control was ushered in by the creation of the Ontario Hydro-Electric Power Commission (now Ontario Hydro) in 1906 to distribute and eventually to produce this vital source of energy.

P4 → Western settlement and the opening of the northern resource frontier stimulated industrial expansion, particularly in central Canada. As the National Policy had intended, a growing agricultural population in the West increased the demand for eastern manufactured goods, thereby giving rise to agricultural implements works, iron and steel foundries, machine shops, railway yards, textile mills, boot and shoe factories, and numerous smaller manufacturing enterprises that supplied consumer goods. By keeping out lower-priced foreign manufactured goods, the high tariff policies of the federal government received much credit for protecting existing industries and encouraging the creation of new enterprises. To climb the tariff wall, large American industrial firms opened branches in Canada, and the governments of Ontario and Quebec aggressively urged them on by offering bonuses, subsidies, and guarantees to locate new plants within their borders. Canadian industrial enterprises became increasingly attractive to foreign investors, especially from the United States and Great Britain. Much of the over $600 million of American capital that flowed into Canada from 1900 to 1913 was earmarked for mining and the pulp and paper industry, while British investors contributed near $1.8 billion, mostly in railway building, business development, and the construction of urban infrastructure. As a result, the gross value of Canadian manufactured products quadrupled from 1891 to 1916.

1. Why does the author mention "the railroads" in paragraph 1?

   Ⓐ Because miners were traveling to camps in the West
   Ⓑ Because mineral deposits were discovered when the railroads were built
   Ⓒ Because the western frontier was being settled by families
   Ⓓ Because traders used the railroads to transport their goods

   Paragraph 1 is marked with an arrow [➜].

2. In paragraph 1, how does the author identify Sudbury?

   Ⓐ An important stop on the new railroad line
   Ⓑ A large market for the metals produced in Ontario
   Ⓒ A major industrial center for the production of nickel
   Ⓓ A mining town in the Klondike region

   Paragraph 1 is marked with an arrow [➜].

3. The word enduring in the passage is closest in meaning to

   Ⓐ disruptive
   Ⓑ restored
   Ⓒ identifiable
   Ⓓ lasting

4. According to paragraph 2, why was the Yukon Territory created?

   Ⓐ To encourage people to settle the region
   Ⓑ To prevent Alaska from acquiring it
   Ⓒ To establish law and order in the area
   Ⓓ To legalize the mining claims

   Paragraph 2 is marked with an arrow [➜].

5. The word previously in the passage is closest in meaning to

   Ⓐ frequently
   Ⓑ suddenly
   Ⓒ routinely
   Ⓓ formerly

6. How did the poetry by Robert Service contribute to the development of Canada?

   Ⓐ It made the Klondike gold rush famous.
   Ⓑ It encouraged families to settle in the Klondike.
   Ⓒ It captured the beauty of the western Klondike.
   Ⓓ It prevented the Klondike's annexation to Alaska.

7. According to paragraph 3, the forest industry supported the development of Canada in all of the following ways EXCEPT

   Ⓐ by supplying wood for the construction of homes and buildings
   Ⓑ by clearing the land for expanded agricultural uses
   Ⓒ by producing the power for the hydroelectric plants
   Ⓓ by exporting wood and newsprint to foreign markets

   Paragraph 3 is marked with an arrow [➜].

8. The word Furthermore in the passage is closest in meaning to

   Ⓐ Although
   Ⓑ Because
   Ⓒ Therefore
   Ⓓ Moreover

9. The word distribute in the passage is closest in meaning to

   Ⓐ develop
   Ⓑ recognize
   Ⓒ supply
   Ⓓ continue

10. Which of the sentences below best expresses the information in the highlighted statement in the passage? The other choices change the meaning or leave out important information.

Ⓐ New businesses and industries were created by the federal government to keep the prices of manufactured goods low.

Ⓑ The lower price of manufacturing attracted many foreign businesses and new industries to the area.

Ⓒ Federal taxes on cheaper imported goods were responsible for protecting domestic industries and supporting new businesses.

Ⓓ The federal tax laws made it difficult for manufacturers to sell their goods to foreign markets.

11. According to paragraph 4, why did British and American businesses open affiliates in Canada?

Ⓐ The Canadian government offered incentives.

Ⓑ The raw materials were available in Canada.

Ⓒ The consumers in Canada were eager to buy their goods.

Ⓓ The infrastructure was attractive to investors.

Paragraph 4 is marked with an arrow [→].

12. Look at the four squares [■] that show where the following sentence could be inserted in the passage.

Railway construction through the Kootenay region of south-eastern British Columbia also led to significant discoveries of gold, silver, copper, lead, and zinc.

Where could the sentence best be added?

Click on a square [■] to insert the sentence in the passage.

13. **Directions:** An introduction for a short summary of the passage appears below. Complete the summary by selecting the THREE answer choices that mention the most important points in the passage. Some sentences do not belong in the summary because they express ideas that are not included in the passage or are minor points from the passage. *This question is worth 2 points.*

The northern frontier provided many natural resources that contributed to the industrial expansion of Canada.

-
-
-

Answer Choices

A The Yukon Territory was created in 1898 during the gold rush in the Klondike and Yukon River valleys.

B The frontier was documented in the popular press, which published tales of heroes and gold strikes.

C Significant discoveries of mineral deposits encouraged prospectors and settlers to move into the territories.

D Wheat and other agricultural crops were planted after the forests were cleared, creating the central plains.

E Powered by hydroelectricity, lumber and paper mills exploited the forests for both domestic and foreign markets.

F Incentives encouraged American and British investors to help expand manufacturing plants in Canada.

Reading 2 "Looking at Theatre History"

P1 → One of the primary ways of approaching the Greek theatre is through archeology, the systematic study of material remains such as architecture, inscriptions, sculpture, vase painting, and other forms of decorative art. A Serious on-site excavations began in Greece around 1870, but W. Dörpfeld did not begin the first extensive study of the Theatre of Dionysus until 1886. B Since that time, more than 167 other Greek theatres have been identified and many of them have been excavated. C Nevertheless, they still do not permit us to describe the precise appearance of the *skene* (illustrations printed in books are conjectural reconstructions), since many pieces are irrevocably lost because the buildings in later periods became sources of stone for other projects and what remains is usually broken and scattered. D That most of the buildings were remodeled many times has created great problems for those seeking to date the successive versions. Despite these drawbacks, archeology provides the most concrete evidence we have about the theatre structures of ancient Greece. But, if they have told us much, archeologists have not completed their work, and many sites have scarcely been touched.

P2 → Perhaps the most controversial use of archeological evidence in theatre history is vase paintings, thousands of which have survived from ancient Greece. (Most of those used by theatre scholars are reproduced in Margarete Bieber's *The History of the Greek and Roman Theatre*.) Depicting scenes from mythology and daily life, the vases are the most graphic pictorial evidence we have. But they are also easy to misinterpret. Some scholars have considered any vase that depicts a subject treated in a surviving drama or any scene showing masks, flute players, or ceremonials to be valid evidence of theatrical practice. This is a highly questionable assumption, since the Greeks made widespread use of masks, dances, and music outside the theatre and since the myths on which dramatists drew were known to everyone, including vase painters, who might well depict the same subjects as dramatists without being indebted to them. Those vases showing scenes unquestionably theatrical are few in number.

P3 → The texts to classical Greek plays were written down soon after the performance and possibly even before, though it is not always clear when or by whom. By 400 B.C.E., there was a flourishing book trade in Greece, but the texts for plays were a challenge. Hellenistic scholars dedicated years to sorting out the text and removing what they believed to be corruptions generally added by actors, but each time a text was copied there were new possibilities for errors.

P4 → The oldest surviving manuscripts of Greek plays date from around the tenth century C.E., some 1,500 years after they were first performed. Nevertheless, the scripts offer us our readiest access to the cultural and theatrical conditions out of which they came. But these scripts, like other kinds of evidence, are subject to varying interpretations. Certainly performances embodied a male perspective, for example, since the plays were written, selected, staged, and acted by men. Yet the existing plays feature numerous choruses of women and many feature strong female characters. Because these characters often seem victims of their own powerlessness and appear to be governed, especially in the comedies, by sexual desire, some critics have seen these plays as rationalizations by the male-dominated culture for keeping women segregated and cloistered. Other critics, however, have seen in these same plays an attempt by male authors to force their male audiences to examine and call into question this segregation and cloistering of Athenian women.

P5 → By far the majority of written references to Greek theatre date from several hundred years after the events they report. The writers seldom mention their sources of evidence, and thus we do not know what credence to give them. In the absence of material nearer in time to the events, however, historians have used the accounts and have been grateful to have them. Overall, historical treatment of the Greek theatre is something like assembling a jigsaw puzzle from which many pieces are missing: historians arrange what they have and imagine (with the aid of the remaining evidence and logic) what has been lost. As a result, though the broad outlines of Greek theatre history are reasonably clear, many of the details remain open to doubt.

Glossary

skene: a stage building where actors store their masks and change their costumes

14. According to paragraph 1, why is it impossible to identify the time period for theatres in Greece?

Ⓐ There are too few sites that have been excavated and very little data collected about them.

Ⓑ The archeologists from earlier periods were not careful, and many artifacts were broken.

Ⓒ It is confusing because stones from early sites were used to build later structures.

Ⓓ Because it is very difficult to date the concrete that was used in construction during early periods.

Paragraph 1 is marked with an arrow [→].

15. What can be inferred from paragraph 1 about the *skene* in theatre history?

    Ⓐ Drawings in books are the only accurate visual records.
    Ⓑ Not enough evidence is available to make a precise model.
    Ⓒ Archeologists have excavated a large number of them.
    Ⓓ It was not identified or studied until the early 1800s.

    Paragraph 1 is marked with an arrow [➜].

16. The word primary in the passage is closest in meaning to

    Ⓐ reliable
    Ⓑ important
    Ⓒ unusual
    Ⓓ accepted

17. The word precise in the passage is closest in meaning to

    Ⓐ attractive
    Ⓑ simple
    Ⓒ difficult
    Ⓓ exact

18. In paragraph 2, how does the author explain that all vases with paintings of masks or musicians may not be evidence of theatrical subjects?

    Ⓐ By arguing that the subjects could have been used by artists without reference to a drama
    Ⓑ By identifying some of the vases as reproductions that were painted years after the originals
    Ⓒ By casting doubt on the qualifications of the scholars who produced the vases as evidence
    Ⓓ By pointing out that there are very few vases that have survived from the time of early dramas

    Paragraph 2 is marked with an arrow [➜].

19. The word controversial in the passage is closest in meaning to

   Ⓐ accepted
   Ⓑ debated
   Ⓒ limited
   Ⓓ complicated

20. Which of the following statements most accurately reflects the author's opinion about vase paintings?

   Ⓐ Evidence from written documents is older than evidence from vase paintings.
   Ⓑ The sources for vase paintings are clear because of the images on them.
   Ⓒ The details in vase paintings are not obvious because of their age.
   Ⓓ There is disagreement among scholars regarding vase paintings.

21. According to paragraph 3, scripts of plays may not be accurate for which reason?

   Ⓐ The sources cited are not well known.
   Ⓑ Copies by hand may contain many errors.
   Ⓒ They are written in very old language.
   Ⓓ The printing is difficult to read.

   Paragraph 3 is marked with an arrow [➜].

22. In paragraph 4, what does the author state about female characters in Greek theatre?

   Ⓐ They had no featured parts in plays.
   Ⓑ They were mostly ignored by critics.
   Ⓒ They did not participate in the chorus.
   Ⓓ They frequently played the part of victims.

   Paragraph 4 is marked with an arrow [➜].

23. The word Overall in the passage is closest in meaning to

    Ⓐ Supposedly
    Ⓑ Generally
    Ⓒ Occasionally
    Ⓓ Finally

24. Why does the author mention a "jigsaw puzzle" in paragraph 5?

    Ⓐ To demonstrate the difficulty in drawing conclusions from partial evidence
    Ⓑ To compare the written references for plays to the paintings on vases
    Ⓒ To justify using accounts and records that historians have located
    Ⓓ To introduce the topic for the next reading passage in the textbook

    Paragraph 5 is marked with an arrow [→].

25. Look at the four squares [■] that show where the following sentence could be inserted in the passage.

    These excavations have revealed much that was previously unknown, especially about the dimensions and layout of theatres.

    Where could the sentence best be added?

    Click on a square [■] to insert the sentence in the passage.

26. **Directions:** An introduction for a short summary of the passage appears below. Complete the summary by selecting the THREE answer choices that mention the most important points in the passage. Some sentences do not belong in the summary because they express ideas that are not included in the passage or are minor points from the passage. *This question is worth 2 points.*

Greek theatre has been studied by a variety of methods.

-

-

-

Answer Choices

A Because the Greeks enjoyed dancing and music for entertainment outside of the theatre, many scenes on vases are ambiguous.

B Historical accounts assembled many years after the actual theatrical works were presented give us a broad perspective of the earlier theatre.

C Although considered less reliable, written records, including scripts, provide insights into the cultural aspects of theatre.

D Archaeological excavations have uncovered buildings and artifacts, many of which were vases with theatrical scenes painted on them.

E For the most part, men wrote the plays for Greek theatre, but choruses and even strong roles were played by women.

F Computer simulations can recreate the image of a building that is crumbling as long as the dimensions and layout are known.

Reading 3 "Geothermal Energy"

P1 → Geothermal energy is natural heat from the interior of the Earth that is converted to heat buildings and generate electricity. The idea of harnessing Earth's internal heat is not new. As early as 1904, geothermal power was used in Italy. Today, Earth's natural internal heat is being used to generate electricity in 21 countries, including Russia, Japan, New Zealand, Iceland, Mexico, Ethiopia, Guatemala, El Salvador, the Philippines, and the United States. Total worldwide production is approaching 9,000 MW (equivalent to nine large modern coal-burning or nuclear power plants)—double the amount in 1980. Some 40 million people today receive their electricity from geothermal energy at a cost competitive with that of alternative energy sources. In El Salvador, geothermal energy is supplying 30% of the total electric energy used. However, at the global level, geothermal energy supplies less than 0.15% of the total energy supply.

P2 → Geothermal energy may be considered a nonrenewable energy source when rates of extraction are greater than rates of natural replenishment. However, geothermal energy has its origin in the natural heat production within Earth, and only a small fraction of the vast total resource base is being utilized today. Although most geothermal energy production involves the tapping of high heat sources, people are also using the low-temperature geothermal energy of groundwater in some applications.

Geothermal Systems

P3 → Ⓐ The average heat flow from the interior of the Earth is very low, about 0.06 W/m². Ⓑ This amount is trivial compared with the 177 W/m² from solar heat at the surface in the United States. However, in some areas, heat flow is sufficiently high to be useful for producing energy. For the most part, areas of high heat flow are associated with plate tectonic boundaries.

Oceanic ridge systems (divergent plate boundaries) and areas where mountains are being uplifted and volcanic island arcs are forming (convergent plate boundaries) are areas where this natural heat flow is anomalously high. C

P4   On the basis of geological criteria, several types of hot geothermal systems (with temperatures greater than about 80°C, or 176°F) have been defined, and the resource base is larger than that of fossil fuels and nuclear energy combined. A common system for energy development is hydrothermal convection, characterized by the circulation of steam and/or hot water that transfers heat from depths to the surface. D

Geothermal Energy and the Environment

P5   → The environmental impact of geothermal energy may not be as extensive as that of other sources of energy. When geothermal energy is developed at a particular site, environmental problems include on-site noise, emissions of gas, and disturbance of the land at drilling sites, disposal sites, roads and pipe-lines, and power plants. Development of geothermal energy does not require large-scale transportation of raw materials or refining of chemicals, as development of fossil fuels does. Furthermore, geothermal energy does not produce the atmospheric pollutants associated with burning fossil fuels or the radioactive waste associated with nuclear energy. However, geothermal development often does produce considerable thermal pollution from hot waste-waters, which may be saline or highly corrosive.

P6   → Geothermal power is not always popular. For instance, geothermal energy has been produced for years on the island of Hawaii, where active volcanic processes provide abundant near-surface heat. There is controversy, however, over further exploration and development. Native Hawaiians and others have argued that the exploration and development of geo-thermal energy degrade the tropical forest as develop-ers construct roads, build facilities, and drill wells. In addition, religious and cultural issues in Hawaii relate to the use of geothermal energy. For example, some people are offended by using the "breath and water of Pele" (the volcano goddess) to make electricity. This issue points out the importance of being sensitive to the values and cultures of people where development is planned.

Future of Geothermal Energy

P7   At present, the United States produces only 2800 MN of geothermal energy. However, if developed, known geothermal resources in the United States could produce about 20,000 MW which is about 10% of the electricity needed for the western states. Geohydrothermal resources not yet discovered could conservatively provide four times that amount (approximately 10% of total U.S. electric capacity), about equivalent to the electricity produced from water power today.

27. In paragraph 1, how does the author introduce the concept of geothermal energy?

Ⓐ By explaining the history of this energy source worldwide
Ⓑ By arguing that this energy source has been tried unsuccessfully
Ⓒ By comparing the production with that of other energy sources
Ⓓ By describing the alternatives for generating electric power

Paragraph 1 is marked with an arrow [➜].

28. What is true about geothermal energy production worldwide?

    Ⓐ Because it is a new idea, very few countries are developing geothermal energy   sources.
    Ⓑ Only countries in the Southern Hemisphere are using geothermal energy on a large scale.
    Ⓒ Until the cost of geothermal energy becomes competitive, it will not be used globally.
    Ⓓ Geothermal energy is already being used in a number of nations, but it is not yet a major source of power.

29. The word approaching in the passage is closest in meaning to

    Ⓐ hardly
    Ⓑ mostly
    Ⓒ nearly
    Ⓓ briefly

30. The word alternative in the passage is closest in meaning to

    Ⓐ numerous
    Ⓑ optional
    Ⓒ nearby
    Ⓓ equivalent

31. In paragraph 2, why does the author state that geothermal energy is considered a nonrenewable resource?

    Ⓐ The production of geothermal energy is a natural process.
    Ⓑ Geothermal energy comes from the Earth.
    Ⓒ We are not using very much geothermal energy now.
    Ⓓ We could use more geothermal energy than is naturally replaced.

    Paragraph 2 is marked with an arrow [→].

32. Which of the sentences below best expresses the information in the highlighted statement in the passage? The other choices change the meaning or leave out important information.

   Ⓐ High heat is the source of most of the geothermal energy but low heat groundwater is also used sometimes.
   Ⓑ Even though low temperatures are possible, high heat is the best resource for energy production for groundwater.
   Ⓒ Both high heat and low heat sources are used for the production of geothermal energy from groundwater.
   Ⓓ Most high heat sources for geothermal energy are tapped from applications that involve low heat in groundwater.

33. According to paragraph 3, which statement is true about the heat flow necessary for the production of geothermal energy?

   Ⓐ It is like solar heat on the Earth's surface.
   Ⓑ It happens near tectonic plate boundaries.
   Ⓒ It must always be artificially increased.
   Ⓓ It may be impractical because of its location.

   Paragraph 3 is marked with an arrow [➔].

34. The word considerable in the passage is closest in meaning to

   Ⓐ large
   Ⓑ dangerous
   Ⓒ steady
   Ⓓ unexpected

35. In paragraph 5, why does the author mention the "atmospheric pollution" and "waste" for fossil fuel and nuclear power?

   Ⓐ To introduce the discussion of pollution caused by geothermal energy development and production
   Ⓑ To contrast pollution caused by fossil fuels and nuclear power with pollution caused by geothermal energy
   Ⓒ To argue that geothermal production does not cause pollution like other sources of energy do
   Ⓓ To discourage the use of raw materials and chemicals in the production of energy because of pollution

   Paragraph 5 is marked with an arrow [➔].

36. According to paragraph 6, the production of geothermal energy in Hawaii is controversial for all of the following reasons EXCEPT

Ⓐ The volcanoes in Hawaii could be disrupted by the rapid release of geothermal energy.

Ⓑ The rainforest might be damaged during the construction of the geothermal energy plant.

Ⓒ The native people are concerned that geothermal energy is disrespectful to their cultural traditions.

Ⓓ Some Hawaiians oppose using geothermal energy because of their religious beliefs.

Paragraph 6 is marked with an arrow [➔].

37. What is the author's opinion of geothermal energy?

Ⓐ Geothermal energy has some disadvantages, but it is probably going to be used in the future.

Ⓑ Geothermal energy is a source that should be explored further before large-scale production begins.

Ⓒ Geothermal energy offers an opportunity to supply a significant amount of power in the future.

Ⓓ Geothermal energy should replace water power in the production of electricity for the United States.

38. Look at the four squares [■] that show where the following sentence could be inserted in the passage.

One such region is located in the western United States, where recent tectonic and volcanic activity has occurred.

Where could the sentence best be added?

Click on a square [■] to insert the sentence in the passage.

39. **Directions**: An introduction for a short summary of the passage appears below. Complete the summary by selecting the THREE answer choices that mention the most important points in the passage. Some sentences do not belong in the summary because they express ideas that are not included in the passage or are minor points from the passage. *This question is worth 2 points.*

Geothermal energy is natural heat from the interior of the Earth that is converted to electricity.

-

-

-

Answer Choices

A Geothermal energy sources that convert natural heat to electricity account for 30% of the total energy supply in El Salvador at relatively competitive cost to the consumers.

B Although geothermal energy is nonrenewable when more is used than can be replaced naturally, only a small amount of the potential energy is being exploited worldwide.

C The heat from geothermal sites is thought to be the breath and water of the volcanic goddess Pele, worshiped by some native groups on the Hawaiian Islands.

D Hot geothermal systems at both divergent plate boundaries and convergent plate boundaries could provide more energy than fossil fuels and nuclear power.

E Some groups oppose the exploitation of geothermal sources because of pollution and other environmental problems or because of their cultural values.

F Thermal waste water can be very corrosive or can contain high levels of saline, which causes problems in disposal and water treatment at development sites.

Reading 4 "Migration from Asia"

P1   The Asian migration hypothesis is today supported by most of the scientific evidence. The first "hard" data linking American Indians with Asians appeared in the 1980s with the finding that Indians and northeast Asians share a common and distinctive pattern in the arrangement of the teeth. But perhaps the most compelling support for the hypothesis comes from genetic research. Studies comparing the DNA variation of populations around the world consistently demonstrate the close genetic relationship of the two populations, and recently geneticists studying a virus sequestered in the kidneys of all humans found that the strain of virus carried by Navajos and Japanese is nearly identical, while that carried by Europeans and Africans is quite different.

P2   → The migration could have begun over a land bridge connecting the continents. During the last Ice Age 70,000 to 10,000 years ago, huge glaciers locked up massive volumes of water and sea levels were as much as 300 feet lower than today. Asia and North America were joined by a huge subcontinent of ice-free, tree-less grassland, 750 miles wide. Geologists have named this area Beringia, from the Bering Straits. Summers there were warm, winters were cold, dry and almost snow-free. This was a perfect environment for large mammals—mammoth and mastodon, bison, horse, reindeer, camel, and saiga (a goatlike antelope). Small bands of Stone Age hunter-gatherers were attracted by these animal populations, which provided them not only with food but with hides for clothing and shelter, dung for fuel, and bones for tools and weapons. Accompanied by a husky-like species of dog, hunting bands gradually moved as far east as the Yukon River basin of northern Canada, where field excavations have uncovered the fossilized jawbones of several dogs and bone tools estimated to be about 27,000 years old.

P3   → Other evidence suggests that the migration from Asia began about 30,000 years ago—around the same time that Japan and Scandinavia were being settled. This evidence is based on blood type. The vast majority of modern Native Americans have type O blood and a few have type A, but almost none have type B. Because modern Asian populations include all three blood types, however, the migrations must have begun before the evolution of type B, which geneticists believe occurred about 30,000 years ago.

P4   By 25,000 years ago human communities were established in western Beringia, which is present-day Alaska. Ⓐ But access to the south was blocked by a huge glacial sheet covering much of what is today Canada. How did the hunters get over those 2,000 miles of deep ice? The argument is that the climate began to warm with the passing of the Ice Age, and about 13,000 B.C.E. glacial melting created an ice-free corridor along the eastern front range of the Rocky Mountains. Ⓑ Soon hunters of big game had reached the Great Plains.

P5   → In the past several years, however, new archaeological finds along the Pacific coast of North and South America have thrown this theory into question. Ⓒ The most spectacular find, at Monte Verde in southern Chile, produced striking evidence of tool making, house building, rock painting, and human footprints conservatively dated long before the highway had been cleared of ice. Ⓓ Many archaeologists now believe that migrants moved south in boats along a coastal route rather than overland. These people were probably gatherers and fishers rather than hunters of big game.

P6   → There were two later migrations into North America. About 5000 B.C.E. the Athapascan or Na-Dene people began to settle the forests in the northwestern

area of the continent. Eventually Athapascan speakers, the ancestors of the Navajos and Apaches,
migrated across the Great Plains to the Southwest.
The final migration began about 3000 B.C.E. after
Beringia had been submerged, when a maritime
hunting people crossed the Bering Straits in small
boats. The Inuits (also known as the Eskimos) colo-
nized the polar coasts of the Arctic, the Yupiks the
coast of southwestern Alaska, and the Aleuts the
Aleutian Islands.

P7   While scientists debate the timing and mapping of
these migrations, many Indian people hold to oral traditions that include a long journey from a distant place
of origin to a new homeland.

40. The word distinctive in the passage is closest in meaning to

   Ⓐ new
   Ⓑ simple
   Ⓒ different
   Ⓓ particular

41. According to paragraph 2, why did Stone Age tribes begin to
    migrate into Beringia?

   Ⓐ To intermarry with tribes living there
   Ⓑ To trade with tribes that made tools
   Ⓒ To hunt for animals in the area
   Ⓓ To capture domesticated dogs

   Paragraph 2 is marked with an arrow [➜].

42. The phrase Accompanied by in the passage is closest in mean-
    ing to

   Ⓐ Found with
   Ⓑ Joined by
   Ⓒ Threatened by
   Ⓓ Detoured with

43. The word estimated in the passage is closest in meaning to

    Ⓐ clarified
    Ⓑ judged
    Ⓒ changed
    Ⓓ noticed

44. Why does the author mention "blood types" in paragraph 3?

    Ⓐ Blood types offered proof that the migration had come from Scandinavia.
    Ⓑ The presence of type B in Native Americans was evidence of the migration.
    Ⓒ The blood typing was similar to data from both Japan and Scandinavia.
    Ⓓ Comparisons of blood types in Asia and North America established the date of migration.

    Paragraph 3 is marked with an arrow [➜].

45. How did groups migrate into the Great Plains?

    Ⓐ By walking on a corridor covered with ice
    Ⓑ By using the path that big game had made
    Ⓒ By detouring around a huge ice sheet
    Ⓓ By following a mountain trail

46. Why does the author mention the settlement at Monte Verde, Chile, in paragraph 5?

    Ⓐ The remains of boats suggest that people may have lived there.
    Ⓑ Artifacts suggest that humans reached this area before the ice melted on land.
    Ⓒ Bones and footprints from large animals confirm that the people were hunters.
    Ⓓ The houses and tools excavated prove that the early humans were intelligent.

    Paragraph 5 is marked with an arrow [➜].

47. The word Eventually in the passage is closest in meaning to

   Ⓐ In the end
   Ⓑ Nevertheless
   Ⓒ Without doubt
   Ⓓ In this way

48. Which of the sentences below best expresses the information in the highlighted statement in the passage? The other choices change the meaning or leave out important information.

   Ⓐ Beringia was under water when the last people crossed the straits in boats about 3000 B.C.E.
   Ⓑ Beringia sank after the last people had crossed the straits in their boats about 3000 B.C.E.
   Ⓒ About 3000 B.C.E., the final migration of people in small boats across Beringia had ended.
   Ⓓ About 3000 B.C.E., Beringia was flooded, preventing the last people from migrating in small boats.

49. According to paragraph 6, all of the following are true about the later migrations EXCEPT

   Ⓐ The Athapascans traveled into the Southwest United States.
   Ⓑ The Eskimos established homes in the Arctic polar region.
   Ⓒ The Aleuts migrated in small boats to settle coastal islands.
   Ⓓ The Yupiks established settlements on the Great Plains.

   Paragraph 6 is marked with an arrow [➜].

50. Which of the following statements most accurately reflects the author's opinion about the settlement of the North American continent?

    Ⓐ The oral traditions do not support the migration theory.

    Ⓑ The anthropological evidence for migration should be reexamined.

    Ⓒ Migration theories are probably not valid explanations for the physical evidence.

    Ⓓ Genetic markers are the best evidence of a migration from Asia.

51. Look at the four squares [■] that show where the following sentence could be inserted in the passage.

Newly excavated early human sites in Washington State, California, and Peru have been radiocarbon dated to be 11,000 to 12,000 years old.

Where could the sentence best be added?

Click on a square [■] to insert the sentence in the passage.

52. **Directions:** An introduction for a short summary of the passage appears below. Complete the summary by selecting the THREE answer choices that mention the most important points in the passage. Some sentences do not belong in the summary because they express ideas that are not included in the passage or are minor points from the passage. ***This question is worth 2 points.***

There is considerable evidence supporting a theory of multiple migrations from Asia to the Americas.

-

-

-

Answer Choices

A Ancient stories of migrations from a faraway place are common in the cultures of many Native American nations.

B The people who inhabited Monte Verde in southern Chile were a highly evolved culture as evidenced by their tools and homes.

C Genetic similarities between Native American peoples and Asians include the arrangement of teeth, viruses, and blood types.

D Hunters followed the herds of big game from Beringia south along the Rocky Mountains into what is now called the Great Plains.

E Excavations at archaeological sites provide artifacts that can be used to date the various migrations that occurred by land and sea.

F The climate began to get warmer and warmer, melting the glacial ice about 13,000 B.C.E.

LISTENING SECTION

🎧 **Model Test 2, Listening Section, Track 35**

The Listening section tests your ability to understand spoken English that is typical of interactions and academic speech on college campuses. During the test, you will listen to conversations, lectures, and discussions, and you will answer questions about them.

This is the short format for the Listening section. On the short format, you will listen to two conversations, two lectures, and two discussions. After each listening passage, you will answer 5–6 questions about it.

You will hear each passage one time. You may take notes while you listen, but notes are not graded. You may use your notes to answer the questions.

Choose the best answer for multiple-choice questions. Follow the directions on the page or on the screen for computer-assisted questions. Click on **Next** and then on **OK** to go on to the next question. You cannot return to previous questions.

The Listening section is divided into sets. Each set includes one conversation, one lecture, and one discussion. You will have 10 minutes to answer all of the questions for each set. You will have 20 minutes to answer all of the questions on the short format. A clock on the screen will show you how much time you have to complete your answers for the section. The clock does NOT count the time you are listening to the conversations, lectures, and discussions.

Listening 1 "Professor's Office"

1. Why does the man go to see his professor?

    (A) To prepare for the next midterm
    (B) To clarify a question from the midterm
    (C) To find out his grade on the midterm
    (D) To complain about his grade on the midterm

2. Why does the man say this:

    (A) He is giving something to the professor.
    (B) He is trying to justify his position.
    (C) He is apologizing because he does not understand.
    (D) He is signaling that he will explain his problem.

3. What did the man do wrong?

   Ⓐ He did not finish the test within the time limit.
   Ⓑ He did not study enough before the test.
   Ⓒ He did not answer one question completely.
   Ⓓ He did not understand a major concept.

4. According to the student, what is *divergent evolution*?

   Ⓐ A population that evolves differently does not have a common ancestor.
   Ⓑ A similar environment can affect the evolution of different species.
   Ⓒ A similar group that is separated may develop different characteristics.
   Ⓓ The climate of an area will allow scientists to predict the life forms.

5. What will Jerry probably do on the next test?

   Ⓐ He will look for questions with several parts.
   Ⓑ He will read the entire test before he begins.
   Ⓒ He will ask for more time to finish.
   Ⓓ He will write an outline for each essay.

Listening 2 "Art History Class"

6. What is the main topic of this lecture?

   Ⓐ The process of fixing a photograph
   Ⓑ The problem of exposure time
   Ⓒ The experiments by Louis Daguerre
   Ⓓ The history of early photography

7. According to the professor, what two limitations were noted in Daguerre's process for developing and fixing latent images?

   Click on 2 answer choices.

   Ⓐ The photograph disappeared after a few minutes.

   Ⓑ The images were very delicate and easily fell apart.

   Ⓒ Multiple images could not be made from the plate.

   Ⓓ The exposure time was still several hours long.

8. Why does the professor say this: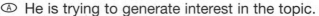

   Ⓐ He is trying to generate interest in the topic.
   Ⓑ He makes reference to a story in the textbook.
   Ⓒ He is not sure whether the information is accurate.
   Ⓓ He wants the students to use their imaginations.

9. What substance was first used to fix the images?

   Ⓐ Copper powder
   Ⓑ Table salt
   Ⓒ Mercury vapor
   Ⓓ Hot water

10. What can we assume about photographers in the 1800s?

    Ⓐ Most of them had originally been painters before they became interested in photography.

    Ⓑ Portrait photographers were in the highest demand since people wanted images of their families.

    Ⓒ There were only a few photographers who were willing to work in such a new profession.

    Ⓓ Some of them must have experienced health problems as a result of their laboratory work.

11. In what order does the professor explain photographic principles?

    Ⓐ From the least to the most important facts

    Ⓑ In a chronological sequence of events

    Ⓒ The order of the steps in the photographic process

    Ⓓ The advantages before the disadvantages

Listening 3 "Linguistics Class"

12. What is the discussion mainly about?

    Ⓐ The history of the English language
    Ⓑ Different types of grammar
    Ⓒ A linguistic perspective for Latin
    Ⓓ Standard language in schools

13. How does the professor make his point about *native intuition*?

    Ⓐ He explains how to perform an easy experiment.
    Ⓑ He tells the class about his personal experience.
    Ⓒ He provides several examples of sentences.
    Ⓓ He contrasts it with non-native intuition.

14. What are two key problems for descriptive grammar?

    Click on 2 answer choices.

    A The information is very complicated and subject to change.

    B The formal language must be enforced in all situations.

    C The language can be organized correctly in more than one way.

    D The description takes time because linguists must agree.

15. Why does the student say this:

    Ⓐ She is disagreeing with the professor.
    Ⓑ She is confirming that she has understood.
    Ⓒ She is trying to impress the other students.
    Ⓓ She is adding information to the lecture.

16. According to the professor, why were Latin rules used for English grammar?

    Ⓐ Latin was a written language with rules that did not change.
    Ⓑ The Romans had conquered England and enforced using Latin.
    Ⓒ English and Latin had many vocabulary words in common.
    Ⓓ English was taking the place of Latin among educated Europeans.

17. Why does the professor discuss the rule to avoid ending a sentence with a preposition?

    Ⓐ It is a good example of the way that descriptive grammar is used.
    Ⓑ It shows the students how to use formal grammar in their speech.
    Ⓒ It is a way to introduce a humorous story into the lecture.
    Ⓓ It demonstrates the problem in using Latin rules for English.

Listening 4 "College Campus"

18. What is the purpose of this conversation?

   Ⓐ The woman is encouraging the man to be more serious about his studies.
   Ⓑ The woman is looking for alternatives to living in dormitory housing.
   Ⓒ The man is convincing the woman to join the International Student Association.
   Ⓓ The man is trying to find out why the woman didn't go to the talent show.

19. What does the man imply about the house where he is living?

   Ⓐ He prefers the house to the dorm.
   Ⓑ He is living at the house to save money.
   Ⓒ He does not like doing chores at the house.
   Ⓓ He thinks that the house is very crowded.

20. How does the man feel about the International Student Association?

  Ⓐ He is sorry that only women can join the club.
  Ⓑ He enjoys meeting people with different backgrounds.
  Ⓒ He wishes that they would have more activities.
  Ⓓ He will probably join the organization.

21. What does the woman mean when she says this: 🎧

  Ⓐ She is trying to persuade the man.
  Ⓑ She is not sure that she understood.
  Ⓒ She is expressing doubt about the time.
  Ⓓ She is changing her mind about going.

22. What does the woman agree to do?

  Ⓐ Join the club
  Ⓑ Eat at a restaurant
  Ⓒ Go to a meeting
  Ⓓ Study with the man

Listening 5 "Zoology Class"

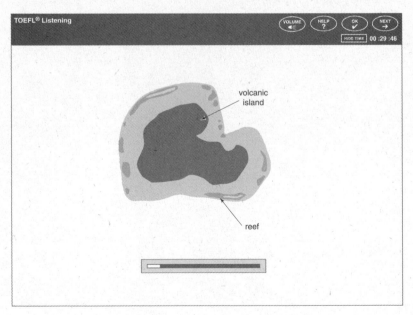

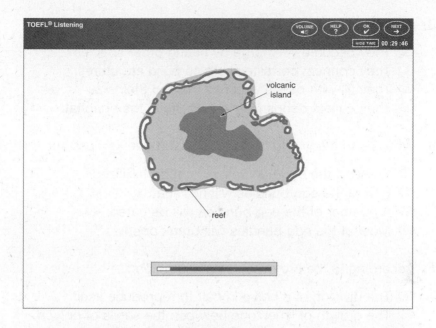

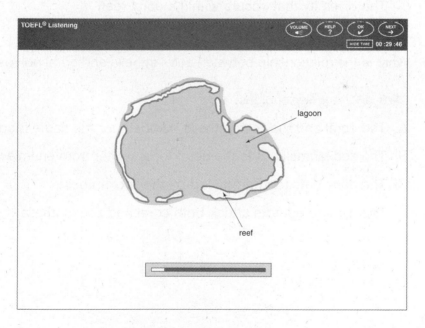

23. According to the professor, how do coral reefs grow?

    Ⓐ They become very large by eating other species.
    Ⓑ They connect corralite shells to build structures.
    Ⓒ They fill with ocean water to expand their size.
    Ⓓ They collect debris from ocean life in their habitat.

24. Why are so many egg bundles released during mass spawning?

    Ⓐ Some of the egg bundles will not be fertilized.
    Ⓑ Half of the egg bundles will not float.
    Ⓒ A number of the egg bundles will be eaten.
    Ⓓ Most of the egg bundles will break open.

25. According to the professor, what is *budding*?

    Ⓐ The division of a polyp in half to reproduce itself.
    Ⓑ The growth of limestone between the shells of polyps.
    Ⓒ The diversity that occurs within a coral reef.
    Ⓓ The increase in size of a polyp as it matures.

26. What is the relationship between zooxanthella and coral polyps?

Click on 2 answer choices.

    Ⓐ The coral and the zooxanthella compete for the same food.
    Ⓑ The zooxanthella uses the coral for a shelter from enemies.
    Ⓒ The coral eats food produced by the zooxanthella.
    Ⓓ The same predators attack both coral and zooxanthella.

27. Which of the following reefs is probably an atoll?

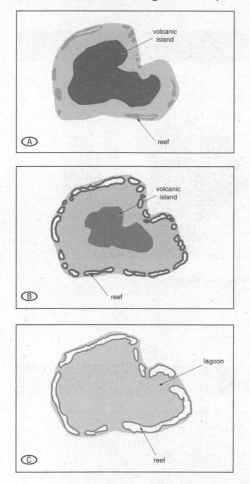

28. In the lecture, the professor explains coral reefs. Indicate whether each of the following is a true statement about coral reefs. Click in the correct box for each phrase.

	Yes	No
A In general, the organism is quite simple.		
B The structure of a reef can be very large.		
C The living coral grows on top of dead shells.		
D Mass spawning is not very effective.		

Listening 6 "Business Class"

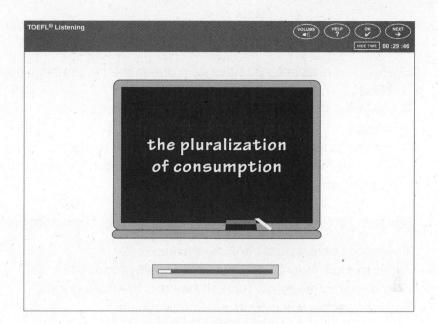

29. What is the discussion mainly about?

    Ⓐ Global marketing of food products
    Ⓑ International business in Europe
    Ⓒ Surprises in food preferences abroad
    Ⓓ Packaging food for exportation

30. How does the professor organize the discussion?

    Ⓐ He compares domestic and foreign products.
    Ⓑ He relates the textbook to his professional experience.
    Ⓒ He refers to case studies from the textbook.
    Ⓓ He presents information from most to least important.

31. Why does the student say this: 🎧

    Ⓐ She is asking the professor a question about his previous point.
    Ⓑ She is offering a possible answer to the professor's question.
    Ⓒ She is changing the subject of the class discussion.
    Ⓓ She is checking her comprehension of the professor's opinion.

32. What technique does the professor use to encourage student discussion?

    ⒶHe gives students positive reinforcement by praising their efforts.

    ⒷHe asks the students to talk among themselves in small groups.

    ⒸHe assigns a different part of the textbook to each student.

    ⒹHe calls on each student by name to contribute to the discussion.

33. What did Ted Levitt mean by "the pluralization of consumption"?

    ⒶMore people would begin to travel.

    ⒷMore multinational corporations would produce brands.

    ⒸMore consumers will have the means to afford goods.

    ⒹMore people will want the same products.

34. What does the professor say about television and movie companies?

    ⒶHe indicates that some companies hire foreign marketing experts.

    ⒷHe criticizes the way that they advertise their programs and films.

    ⒸHe notes that they are one of the most widely distributed exports.

    ⒹHe points out that they are paid to display brand-name products.

Please turn off the audio. There is a 10-minute break between the Listening section and the Speaking section.

SPEAKING SECTION

🎧 **Model Test 2, Speaking Section, Track 36**

The Speaking section tests your ability to communicate in English in an academic setting. During the test, you will be presented with six speaking questions. The questions ask for a response to a single question, a conversation, a talk, or a lecture. The prompts and questions are presented only one time.

You may take notes as you listen, but notes are not graded. You may use your notes to answer the questions. Some of the questions ask for a response to a reading passage and a talk or a lecture. The reading passages and the questions are written, but the directions will be spoken.

Your speaking will be evaluated on both the fluency of the language and the accuracy of the content. You will have 15–20 seconds to prepare and 45–60 seconds to respond to each question. Typically, a good response will require all of the response time and the answer will be complete by the end of the response time.

You will have about 20 minutes to complete the Speaking section. A clock on the screen will show you how much time you have to prepare each of your answers and how much time you have to record each response.

Independent Speaking Question 1 "Regret"

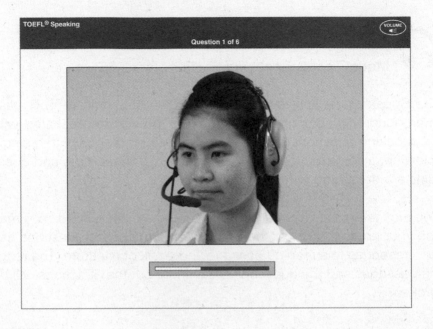

Listen for a question about a familiar topic.

Question
Explain a situation in the past when you have regretted your decision.
What would you do differently?

Preparation Time: 15 seconds
Recording Time: 45 seconds

Independent Speaking Question 2 "Course Requirements"

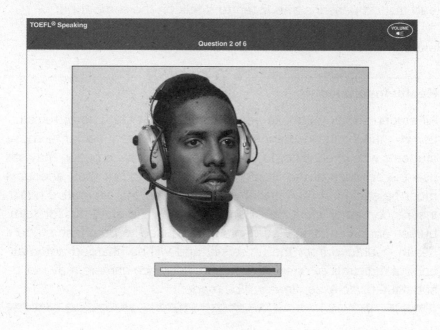

Listen for a question that asks your opinion about a familiar topic.

Question

Some students would rather write a paper than take a test. Other students would rather take a test instead of writing a paper. Which option do you prefer and why? Use specific reasons and examples to support your opinion.

Preparation Time: 15 seconds
Recording Time: 45 seconds

Integrated Speaking Question 3 "Health Insurance"

Read a short passage and listen to a talk on the same topic.

Reading Time: 45 seconds

Health Insurance

All students may purchase health insurance at the time of registration by marking the insurance box on the course request form. Those students who choose not to use the health insurance option may still use the services of the Student Health Center, but their accounts must be settled at the time of each visit, and the alternative health insurance carrier must be billed directly by the students for reimbursement. International students are required to purchase student health insurance from the university and will be charged automatically at registration. Alternative health insurance carriers may not be substituted. No exceptions will be made.

Now listen to the foreign student advisor. He is explaining the policy and expressing his opinion about it.

Question

The foreign student advisor expresses his opinion of the policy for health insurance. Report his opinion and explain the reasons that he gives for having that opinion.

Preparation Time: 30 seconds
Recording Time: 60 seconds

Integrated Speaking Question 4 "Antarctica"

Read a short passage and then listen to part of a lecture on the same topic.

Reading Time: 45 seconds

Antarctica

Antarctica and the ocean that surrounds it constitute 40 percent of the planet, but in spite of its vast area, it has remained a frontier with no permanent towns or transportation networks. Between 1895 and 1914, explorers planted their flags, claiming various sectors and the raw materials in them for their countries. Nevertheless, the remote location and the harsh environment have encouraged a spirit of cooperation among nations who maintain claims. Furthermore, because Antarctica plays a crucial role in the global environmental system, the exploitation of resources could have unpredictable consequences for the entire world. The Antarctic Treaty, signed in 1961 and expanded in 1991, ensures scientific collaboration, protects the environment, and prohibits military activities.

Now listen to part of a lecture in a geography class. The professor is talking about Antarctica.

Question
Explain why many countries have staked claims in Antarctica, and why national interests have not been pursued.

Preparation Time: 30 seconds
Recording Time: 60 seconds

Integrated Speaking Question 5 "Extra Money"

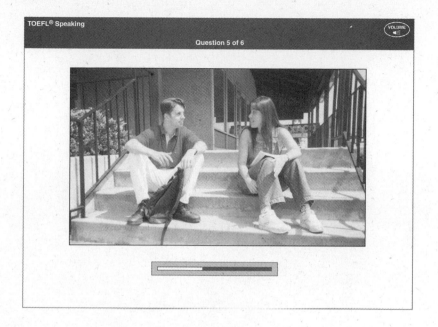

Now listen to a conversation between a student and her friend.

Question

Describe the woman's problem and the two suggestions that her friend makes about how to handle it. What do you think the woman should do, and why?

Preparation Time: 20 seconds
Recording Time: 60 seconds

Integrated Speaking Question 6 "Research References"

Now listen to part of a lecture in a sociology class. The professor is discussing the criteria for using older research references.

Question

Using the main points and examples from the lecture, describe the two criteria for using an older research reference presented by the professor.

Preparation Time: 20 seconds
Recording Time: 60 seconds

WRITING SECTION

The Writing section tests your ability to write essays in English similar to those that you would write in college courses. During the test, you will write two essays.

The Integrated Essay. First you will read an academic passage and then you will listen to a lecture on the same topic. You may take notes as you read and listen, but notes are not graded. You may use your notes to write the essay. The reading passage will disappear while you are listening to the lecture, but the passage will return to the screen for reference when you begin to write your essay. You will have 20 minutes to plan, write, and revise your response. Typically, a good essay for the integrated topic will require that you write 150–225 words.

The Independent Essay. You will read a question on the screen. It usually asks for your opinion about a familiar topic. You will have 30 minutes to plan, write, and revise your response. Typically, a good essay for the independent topic will require that you write 300–350 words.

A clock on the screen will show you how much time you have left to complete each essay.

Integrated Essay "Collapse of Easter Island"

You have 20 minutes to plan, write, and revise your response to a reading passage and a lecture on the same topic. First, read the passage and take notes. Then, listen to the lecture and take notes. Finally, write your response to the writing question. Typically, a good response will require that you write 150–225 words.

Reading Passage
Time: 3 minutes

Because of its remote location, only a few species of plants and animals thrived on Easter Island, and the water surrounding it contained very few fish. Nevertheless, beginning with extremely limited resources on an isolated island, the native people achieved a very advanced culture, as evidenced by the gigantic monolithic human figures that line the coasts, as well as by other artifacts. The complete collapse of this civilization is still a mystery, but several theories have been put forward.

One theory suggests that the natives of Easter Island cut down large palm forests to clear land for agricultural purposes, fuel for heating and cooking, construction material for pole and thatch houses, and canoes for transportation. In addition, hundreds of *ahu*, or large stone monuments, were constructed and moved to the coast on rollers made of tree trunks. Assuming that the trees could regenerate quickly enough to sustain the environment, they continued the deforestation, which, in turn, caused serious erosion.

Another theory presents a very different explanation for the decline in the population. Since there were few predators on the island, and an abundance of food, it is thought that rats may have hidden in the canoes of the earliest settlers. When the native people cut and burned trees, the rats prevented regrowth by eating the fresh shoots before they could grow into large plants. With little food and no wood to build canoes to escape, the people perished.

A third theory contends that the population was decimated by a war between short-eared and long-eared people on the island. According to oral history, a plot by the long-eared people to kill the short-eared people was discovered and the short-eared people struck first, driving the long-eared people to a ditch where they were killed and burned.

Model Test 2, Writing Section, Track 37

Now listen to a lecture on the same topic as the passage that you have just read.

Question

Summarize the main points in the lecture, and then explain how they cast doubt on the ideas in the reading passage.

Independent Essay "Family Pets"

Question

Read and think about the following statement:

Pets should be treated like family members.

Do you agree or disagree with this statement? Give reasons to support your opinion.

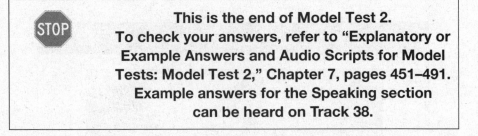

This is the end of Model Test 2.
To check your answers, refer to "Explanatory or Example Answers and Audio Scripts for Model Tests: Model Test 2," Chapter 7, pages 451–491.
Example answers for the Speaking section can be heard on Track 38.

6

MODEL TEST 3: PROGRESS TEST

READING SECTION

The Reading section tests your ability to understand reading passages like those in college textbooks. The reading passages are presented in one complete section, which allows you to move to the next passage and return to a previous passage to change answers or answer questions that you may have left blank. The passages are about 700 words in length.

This is the short format for the Reading section. On the short format, you will read three passages. After each passage, you will answer 12–14 questions about it. You may take notes while you read, but notes are not graded. You may use your notes to answer the questions. Some passages may include a word or phrase that is underlined in blue. Click on the word or phrase to see a glossary definition or explanation.

Choose the best answer for multiple-choice questions. Follow the directions on the page or on the screen for computer-assisted questions. Most questions are worth 1 point, but the last question in each passage is worth more than 1 point.

Click on **Next** to go to the next question. Click on **Back** to return to previous questions. You may return to previous questions for all of the passages.

You can click on **Review** to see a chart of the questions you have answered and the questions you have not answered. From this screen, you can return to the question you want to answer.

Although you can spend more time on one passage and less time on another passage, you should try to pace yourself so that you are spending about 20 minutes to read each passage and answer the questions for that passage. You will have 60 minutes to complete all of the passages and answer all of the questions on the short format. A clock on the screen will show you how much time you have to complete the Reading section.

Reading 1 "Symbiotic Relationships"

P1   **Symbiosis** is a close, long-lasting physical relationship between two different species. In other words, the two species are usually in physical contact and at least one of them derives some sort of benefit from this contact. There are three different categories of symbiotic relationships: parasitism, commensalism, and mutualism.

P2   **Parasitism** is a relationship in which one organism, known as the parasite, lives in or on another organism, known as the host, from which it derives nourishment. Generally, the parasite is much smaller than the host. Although the host is harmed by the interaction, it is generally not killed immediately by the parasite, and some host individuals may live a long time and be relatively little affected by their parasites. Some parasites are much more destructive than others, however. Newly established parasite-host relationships are likely to be more destructive than those that have a long evolutionary history. With a longstanding interaction between the parasite and the host, the two species generally evolve in such a way that they can accommodate one another. It is not in the parasite's best interest to kill its host. If it does, it must find another. Likewise, the host evolves defenses against the parasite, often reducing the harm done by the parasite to a level the host can·tolerate.

P3 → Parasites that live on the surface of their hosts are known as **ectoparasites**. Fleas, lice, and some molds and mildews are examples of ectoparasites. Ⓐ Many other parasites, such as tapeworms, malaria parasites, many kinds of bacteria, and some fungi, are called **endoparasites** because they live inside the bodies of their hosts. Ⓑ A tapeworm lives in the intestines of its host where it is able to resist being digested and makes use of the nutrients in the intestine. Ⓒ

P4 Even plants can be parasites. Mistletoe is a flowering plant that is parasitic on trees. It establishes itself on the surface of a tree when a bird transfers the seed to the tree. It then grows down into the water-conducting tissues of the tree and uses the water and minerals it obtains from these tissues to support its own growth. Ⓓ

P5 **Commensalism** is a relationship between organisms in which one organism benefits while the other is not affected. It is possible to visualize a parasitic relationship evolving into a commensal one. Since parasites generally evolve to do as little harm to their host as possible and the host is combating the negative effects of the parasite, they might eventually evolve to the point where the host is not harmed at all.

P6 Many examples of commensal relationships exist. Many orchids use trees as a surface upon which to grow. The tree is not harmed or helped, but the orchid needs a surface upon which to establish itself and also benefits by being close to the top of the tree, where it can get more sunlight and rain. Some mosses, ferns, and many vines also make use of the surfaces of trees in this way.

P7   In the ocean, many sharks have a smaller fish known as a remora attached to them. Remoras have a <u>sucker</u> on the top of their heads that they can use to attach to the shark. In this way, they can hitchhike a ride as the shark swims along. When the shark feeds, the remora frees itself and obtains small bits of food that the shark misses. Then, the remora reattaches. The shark does not appear to be positively or negatively affected by remoras.

P8   ➜ **Mutualism** is another kind of symbiotic relationship and is actually beneficial to both species involved. In many mutualistic relationships, the relationship is obligatory; the species cannot live without each other. In others, the species can exist separately but are more successful when they are involved in a mutualistic relationship. Some species of Acacia, a thorny tree, provide food in the form of sugar solutions in little structures on their stems. Certain species of ants feed on the solutions and live in the tree, which they will protect from other animals by attacking any animal that begins to feed on the tree. Both organisms benefit; the ants receive food and a place to live, and the tree is protected from animals that would use it as food.

P9   ➜ One soil nutrient that is usually a limiting factor for plant growth is nitrogen. Many kinds of plants, such as legumes, beans, clover, Acacia trees, and Alder trees, have bacteria that live in their roots in little <u>nodules</u>. The roots form these nodules when they are infected with certain kinds of bacteria. The bacteria do not cause disease but provide the plants with nitrogen-containing molecules that the plants can use for growth. The nitrogen-fixing bacteria benefit from the living site and nutrients that the plants provide, and the plants benefit from the nitrogen they receive.

Glossary
sucker: an adaptation for sucking nourishment or sticking to a surface
nodules: growths in the form of knots

1. The word derives in the passage is closest in meaning to

   Ⓐ requests
   Ⓑ pursues
   Ⓒ obtains
   Ⓓ rejects

2. The word categories in the passage is closest in meaning to

   Ⓐ sources
   Ⓑ ideas
   Ⓒ classifications
   Ⓓ problems

3. The word relatively in the passage is closest in meaning to

   Ⓐ comparatively
   Ⓑ routinely
   Ⓒ adversely
   Ⓓ frequently

4. Which of the sentences below best expresses the information in the highlighted statement in the passage? The other choices change the meaning or leave out important information.

 Ⓐ A parasite is less likely to destroy the host when it attaches itself at first.

 Ⓑ Parasites that have lived on a host for a long time have probably done a lot of damage.

 Ⓒ The most destructive phase for a host is when the parasite first invades it.

 Ⓓ The relationship between a parasite and a host will evolve over time.

5. The word tolerate in the passage is closest in meaning to

 Ⓐ permit
 Ⓑ oppose
 Ⓒ profit
 Ⓓ avoid

6. According to paragraph 3, how do ectoparasites survive?

 Ⓐ They live in mold and mildew on their hosts.
 Ⓑ They digest food in the intestines of their hosts.
 Ⓒ They live on the nutrients in their bacterial hosts.
 Ⓓ They inhabit the outside parts of their hosts.

Paragraph 3 is marked with an arrow [➔].

7. Which of the following is mentioned as an example of a commensal relationship?

 Ⓐ Orchids
 Ⓑ Mistletoe
 Ⓒ Ants
 Ⓓ Fungus

8. The word actually in the passage is closest in meaning to

 Ⓐ frequently
 Ⓑ initially
 Ⓒ really
 Ⓓ usually

9. In paragraph 8, why does the author use the example of the *Acacia* tree?

   Ⓐ To demonstrate how ants survive by living in trees
   Ⓑ To explain how two species can benefit from contact
   Ⓒ To show the relationship between plants and animals
   Ⓓ To present a problem that occurs often in nature

   Paragraph 8 is marked with an arrow [➜].

10. According to paragraph 9, how does bacteria affect beans and clover?

    Ⓐ It causes many of the plants to die.
    Ⓑ It limits the growth of young plants.
    Ⓒ It supplies nitrogen to the crops.
    Ⓓ It infects the roots with harmful nodules.

    Paragraph 9 is marked with an arrow [➜].

11. Look at the four squares [■] that show where the following sentence could be inserted in the passage.

    They live on the feathers of birds or the fur of animals.

    Where could the sentence best be added?

    Click on a square [■] to insert the sentence in the passage.

12. In which of the following chapters would this passage most probably appear?

    Ⓐ Environment and Organisms
    Ⓑ Pollution and Policies
    Ⓒ Human Influences on Ecosystems
    Ⓓ Energy Resources

13. **Directions:** An introduction for a short summary of the passage appears below. Complete the summary by selecting the THREE answer choices that mention the most important points in the passage. Some sentences do not belong in the summary because they express ideas that are not included in the passage or are minor points from the passage. *This question is worth 2 points.*

Symbiosis is a close, continuing physical relationship between two species.

-

-

-

Answer Choices

A Parasitic species will feed on the host species, causing varying degrees of damage to the host as a result of the relationship.

B Orchids benefit from being near the top of a tree where they can be exposed to more sunlight and rain.

C Nodules in the roots of plants supply nitrogen from bacteria, thereby enriching the soil.

D In commensalism, one species will benefit from the relationship, but the other species is not affected by it.

E Certain species form mutualistic relationships in which both species benefit from the physical contact.

F Evolutionary changes in species may allow them to live in close physical contact with little damage to each other.

Reading 2 "Civilization"

P1   Between 4000 and 3000 B.C., significant technological developments began to transform the Neolithic
towns. The invention of writing enabled records to
be kept, and the use of metals marked a new level of
human control over the environment and its resources.
Already before 4000 B.C., craftspeople had discovered
that metal-bearing rocks could be heated to liquefy
metals, which could then be cast in molds to produce
tools and weapons that were more useful than stone
instruments. Although copper was the first metal to be
utilized in producing tools, after 4000 B.C. craftspeople
in western Asia discovered that a combination of copper and tin produced bronze, a much harder and more
durable metal than copper. Its widespread use has led
historians to call the period the Bronze Age; thereafter,
from around 3000 to 1200 B.C., bronze was increasingly
replaced by iron.

P2   → At first, Neolithic settlements were hardly more
than villages. But as their inhabitants mastered the art
of farming, more complex human societies emerged.
As wealth increased, these societies began to develop
armies and to build walled cities. By the beginning of
the Bronze Age, the concentration of larger numbers
of people in the river valleys of Southwest Asia and
Egypt was leading to a whole new pattern for human
life.

P3   → As we have seen, early human beings formed
small groups that developed a simple culture that
enabled them to survive. As human societies grew
and developed greater complexity, a new form of
human existence—called civilization—came into
being. A civilization is a complex culture in which large
numbers of human beings share a number of com-

mon elements. Historians have identified a number of basic characteristics of civilization, most of which are evident in the Southwest Asian and Egyptian civilizations. These include (1) an urban focus: cities became the centers of political, economic, social, cultural, and religious development; (2) a distinct religious structure: the gods were deemed crucial to the community's success, and professional priestly classes, as stewards of the gods' property, regulated relations with the gods; (3) new political and military structures: an organized government bureaucracy arose to meet the administrative demands of the growing population while armies were organized to gain land and power and for defense; (4) a new social structure based on economic power: while kings and an upper class of priests, political leaders, and warriors dominated, there also existed large groups of free people (farmers, artisans, craftspeople) and at the very bottom, socially, a class of slaves; (5) the development of writing: kings, priests, merchants, and artisans used writing to keep records; and (6) new forms of significant artistic and intellectual activity: monumental architectural structures, usually religious, occupied a prominent place in urban environments.

P4   → Why early civilizations developed remains difficult to explain. A Since civilizations developed independently in India, China, Mesopotamia, and Egypt, can general causes be identified that would explain why all of these civilizations emerged? B A number of possible explanations of the beginning of civilization have been suggested. A theory of challenge and response maintains that challenges forced human beings to make efforts that resulted in the rise of civilization. Some scholars have adhered to a material explanation. C Material forces, such as the growth of food surpluses, made possible the specialization of labor and development of large communities with bureaucratic organization. D But the area of the Fertile

Crescent, in which civilization emerged in Southwest Asia, was not naturally conducive to agriculture. Abundant food could be produced only with a massive human effort to carefully manage the water, an effort that created the need for organization and bureaucratic control and led to civilized cities. Some historians have argued that nonmaterial forces, primarily religious, provided the sense of unity and purpose that made such organized activities possible. Finally, some scholars doubt that we are capable of ever discovering the actual causes of early civilization.

14. Which of the following is the best definition of a "civilization"?

    Ⓐ Neolithic towns and cities
    Ⓑ Types of complex cultures
    Ⓒ An agricultural community
    Ⓓ Large population centers

15. The word utilized in the passage is closest in meaning to

    Ⓐ located
    Ⓑ used
    Ⓒ described
    Ⓓ improved

16. According to paragraph 2, what happens as societies become more prosperous?

    Ⓐ More goods are produced.
    Ⓑ Walled cities are built.
    Ⓒ Laws are instituted.
    Ⓓ The size of families increased.

    Paragraph 2 is marked with an arrow [➜].

17. The word hardly in the passage is closest in meaning to

    Ⓐ frequently
    Ⓑ likely
    Ⓒ barely
    Ⓓ obviously

18. Why does the author mention "Neolithic settlements" in paragraph 2?

  Ⓐ To give an example of a civilization
  Ⓑ To explain the invention of writing systems
  Ⓒ To argue that they should be classified as villages
  Ⓓ To contrast them with the civilizations that evolved

  Paragraph 2 is marked with an arrow [➜].

19. According to paragraph 3, how was the class system structured?

  Ⓐ An upper class and a lower class
  Ⓑ Slaves, free people, and a ruling class
  Ⓒ A king, an army, and slaves
  Ⓓ Intellectuals and uneducated farmers and workers

  Paragraph 3 is marked with an arrow [➜].

20. Which of the sentences below best expresses the information in the highlighted statement in the passage? The other choices change the meaning or leave out important information.

  Ⓐ Southwest Asian and Egyptian civilizations exhibit the majority of the characteristics identified by historians.
  Ⓑ The characteristics that historians have identified are not found in the Egyptian and Southwest Asian cultures.
  Ⓒ Civilizations in Southwest Asia and Egypt were identified by historians who were studying the characteristics of early cultures.
  Ⓓ The identification of most historical civilizations includes either Egypt or Southwest Asia on the list.

21. The word crucial in the passage is closest in meaning to

  Ⓐ fundamental
  Ⓑ arbitrary
  Ⓒ disruptive
  Ⓓ suitable

22. The word prominent in the passage is closest in meaning to

    Ⓐ weak
    Ⓑ important
    Ⓒ small
    Ⓓ new

23. According to paragraph 4, how can the independent development of civilization in different geographic regions be explained?

    Ⓐ Scholars agree that food surpluses encouraged populations to be concentrated in certain areas.
    Ⓑ There are several theories that explain the rise of civilization in the ancient world.
    Ⓒ The model of civilization was probably carried from one region to another along trade routes.
    Ⓓ Historians attribute the emergence of early cities at about the same time as a coincidence.

Paragraph 4 is marked with an arrow [→].

24. All of the following are cited as reasons why civilizations developed EXCEPT

    Ⓐ Religious practices unified the population.
    Ⓑ The management of water required organization.
    Ⓒ A major climate change made living in groups necessary.
    Ⓓ Extra food resulted in the expansion of population centers.

25. Look at the four squares [■] that show where the following sentence could be inserted in the passage.

Some historians believe they can be established.

Where could the sentence best be added?

Click on a square [■] to insert the sentence in the passage.

26. **Directions:** An introduction for a short summary of the passage appears below. Complete the summary by selecting the THREE answer choices that mention the most important points in the passage. Some sentences do not belong in the summary because they express ideas that are not included in the passage or they are minor points from the passage. *This question is worth 2 points.*

Certain qualities appear to define a civilization.

-

-

-

Answer Choices

A Free citizens who work in professions for pay

B Bureaucracies for the government and armies

C Libraries to house art and written records

D A strategic location near rivers or the sea

E Organized religion, writing, and art

F A densely populated group with a class structure

Reading 3 "Life in Our Solar System"

P1   Although we can imagine life based on something other than carbon chemistry, we know of no examples to tell us how such life might arise and survive. We must limit our discussion to life as we know it and the conditions it requires. The most important requirement is the presence of liquid water, not only as part of the chemical reactions of life, but also as a medium to transport nutrients and wastes within the organism.

P2   The water requirement automatically eliminates many worlds in our solar system. The moon is airless, and although some data suggest ice frozen in the soil at its poles, it has never had liquid water on its surface. In the vacuum of the lunar surface, liquid water would boil away rapidly. Mercury too is airless and cannot have had liquid water on its surface for long periods of time. Venus has some traces of water vapor in its atmosphere, but it is much too hot for liquid water to survive. If there were any lakes or oceans of water on its surface when it was young, they must have evaporated quickly. Even if life began there, no traces would be left now.

P3   The inner solar system seems too hot, and the outer solar system seems too cold. The Jovian planets have deep atmospheres, and at a certain level, they have moderate temperatures where water might condense into liquid droplets. But it seems unlikely that life could begin there. The Jovian planets have no surfaces where oceans could nurture the beginning of life, and currents in the atmosphere seem destined to circulate gas and water droplets from regions of moderate temperature to other levels that are much too hot or too cold for life to survive.

P4   A few of the satellites of the Jovian planets might have suitable conditions for life. Jupiter's moon Europa seems to have a liquid-water ocean below its icy crust, and minerals dissolved in that water would provide a rich broth of possibilities for chemical evolution. A Nevertheless, Europa is not a promising site to search for life because conditions may not have remained stable for the billions of years needed for life to evolve beyond the microscopic stage. B If Jupiter's moons interact gravitationally and modify their orbits, Europa may have been frozen solid at some points in history. C

P5 → Saturn's moon Titan has an atmosphere of nitrogen, argon, and methane and may have oceans of liquid methane and ethane on its surface. D The chemistry of life that might crawl or swim on such a world is unknown, but life there may be unlikely because of the temperature. The surface of Titan is a deadly –179°C (–290°F). Chemical reactions occur slowly or not at all at such low temperatures, so the chemical evolution needed to begin life may never have occurred on Titan.

P6 → Mars is the most likely place for life in our solar system. The evidence, however, is not encouraging. Meteorite ALH84001 was found on the Antarctic ice in 1984. It was probably part of debris ejected into space by a large impact on Mars. ALH84001 is important because a team of scientists studied it and announced in 1996 that it contained chemical and physical traces of ancient life on Mars.

P7   Scientists were excited too, but being professionally skeptical, they began testing the results immediately. In many cases, the results did not confirm the conclusion that life once existed on Mars. Some chemical contamination from water on Earth has occurred, and some chemicals in the meteorite may have originated without the presence of life. The physical features that look like fossil bacteria may be mineral formations in the rock.

P8   Spacecraft now visiting Mars may help us understand the past history of water there and paint a more detailed picture of present conditions. Nevertheless, conclusive evidence may have to wait until a geologist in a space suit can wander the dry streambeds of Mars cracking open rocks and searching for fossils.

P9   We are left to conclude that, so far as we know, our solar system is bare of life except for Earth. Consequently, our search for life in the universe takes us to other planetary systems.

27. The word automatically in the passage is closest in meaning to

   Ⓐ partially
   Ⓑ actually
   Ⓒ occasionally
   Ⓓ naturally

28. The word data in the passage is closest in meaning to

   Ⓐ improvements
   Ⓑ agreements
   Ⓒ facts
   Ⓓ methods

29. Which of the following statements about the water on Venus is true?

   Ⓐ The water evaporated because of the high temperatures.
   Ⓑ The water became frozen in the polar regions.
   Ⓒ Only a little water is left in small lakes on the surface.
   Ⓓ Rain does not fall because there is no atmosphere.

30. The word stable in the passage is closest in meaning to

   Ⓐ visible
   Ⓑ active
   Ⓒ constant
   Ⓓ strong

31. What can be inferred from the passage about the Jovian planets?

    Ⓐ Some of the Jovian planets may have conditions that could support life.
    Ⓑ Jupiter is classified as one of the Jovian planets.
    Ⓒ Europa is the largest of the moons that revolve around Jupiter.
    Ⓓ The orbits of the Jovian planets have changed over time.

32. According to paragraph 5, why would life on Titan be improbable?

    Ⓐ It does not have an ocean.
    Ⓑ It is not a planet.
    Ⓒ It is too cold.
    Ⓓ It has a low atmosphere.

    Paragraph 5 is marked with an arrow [➜].

33. Which of the sentences below best expresses the information in the highlighted statement in the passage? The other choices change the meaning or leave out important information.

    Ⓐ Life on Mars was found as a result of research in many cases.
    Ⓑ The evidence did not demonstrate that there was life on Mars in the past.
    Ⓒ Many cases of life were concluded in the history of Mars.
    Ⓓ The conclusion was that only one instance of life on Mars was verified.

34. The word originated in the passage is closest in meaning to

    Ⓐ turned
    Ⓑ changed
    Ⓒ begun
    Ⓓ disappeared

35. Why does the author mention the meteorite "ALH84001" in paragraph 6?

    Ⓐ Because it was found in Antarctica about fifty years ago
    Ⓑ Because it was evidence of a recent impact on Mars
    Ⓒ Because scientists thought that it contained evidence of life on Mars
    Ⓓ Because the meteorite probably came from Mars a long time ago

    Paragraph 6 is marked with an arrow [→].

36. How will scientists confirm the existence of life on Mars?

    Ⓐ By sending unmanned spacecraft to Mars
    Ⓑ By looking at fossils on Mars
    Ⓒ By viewing pictures taken of Mars
    Ⓓ By studying the present conditions on Mars

37. Which of the following statements most accurately reflects the author's opinion about life in our solar system?

    Ⓐ Life is probably limited to planets in the inner solar system.
    Ⓑ There is a large body of evidence supporting life on Mars.
    Ⓒ There is little probability of life on other planets.
    Ⓓ We should explore our solar system for conditions that support life.

38. Look at the four squares [■] that show where the following sentence could be inserted in the passage.

    Such periods of freezing would probably prevent life from developing.

    Where could the sentence best be added?

    Click on a square [■] to insert the sentence in the passage.

39. **Directions:** An introduction for a short summary of the passage appears below. Complete the summary by selecting the
THREE answer choices that mention the most important points
in the passage. Some sentences do not belong in the summary
because they express ideas that are not included in the passage
or are minor points from the passage. ***This question is worth
2 points.***

**Current evidence does not support the theory of life in our
solar system.**

- ●

- ●

- ●

Answer Choices

Ⓐ The meteorite that was discovered in the Antarctic in the
1980s was thought to contain
evidence of early life on Mars,
but it was later disputed.

Ⓑ The planet that has the greatest probability for life in the
past or now is Mars, but more
investigation is required to
draw conclusions.

Ⓒ Europa has an ocean under
the ice on the surface of the
moon, which may contain
the chemical combinations
required for life to evolve.

Ⓓ Although some of the moons
that revolve around Saturn
and Jupiter have conditions
that might support life, the
evidence contradicts this
possibility.

Ⓔ Other planetary systems must
have life that is similar to that
which has evolved on Earth
because of the principles of
carbon chemistry.

Ⓕ It is too hot for life on the
planets near the Sun in the
inner solar system and too
cold on the planets most
removed from the Sun in the
outer solar system.

LISTENING SECTION

🎧 **Model Test 3, Listening Section, Track 39**

The Listening section tests your ability to understand spoken English that is typical of interactions and academic speech on college campuses. During the test, you will listen to conversations, lectures, and discussions, and you will answer questions about them.

This is the long format for the Listening section. On the long format, you will listen to three conversations, three lectures, and three discussions. After each listening passage, you will answer 5–6 questions about it. Only two conversations, two lectures, and two discussions will be graded. The other passages are part of an experimental section for future tests. Because you will not know which conversations, lectures, and discussions will be graded, you must try to do your best on all of them.

You will hear each passage one time. You may take notes while you listen, but notes are not graded. You may use your notes to answer the questions.

Choose the best answer for multiple-choice questions. Follow the directions on the page or on the screen for computer-assisted questions. Click on **Next** and then on **OK** to go on to the next question. You cannot return to previous questions.

The Listening section is divided into sets. Each set includes one conversation, one lecture, and one discussion. You have 10 minutes to answer all of the questions for each set. You will have 30 minutes to answer all of the questions on the long format. A clock on the screen will show you how much time you have to complete your answers for the section. The clock does NOT count the time you are listening to the conversations, lectures, and discussions.

Listening 1 "Students on Campus"

1. What are the students mainly discussing?

   Ⓐ Group sessions in the Office of Career Development
   Ⓑ The advantages of career counseling for the man
   Ⓒ The woman's internship in the Office of Career Development
   Ⓓ How to find employment in the field of career counseling

2. What is the man's problem?

   Ⓐ He does not have time to see an advisor.
   Ⓑ He does not have an internship yet.
   Ⓒ He does not know which career to choose.
   Ⓓ He does not have a job offer after graduation.

3. Why does the woman tell the man about her experience?

   Ⓐ To demonstrate the benefits of going to the Office of Career Development
   Ⓑ To encourage the man to talk with an advisor about an internship
   Ⓒ To suggest that he change his major from math to library science
   Ⓓ To give the man her opinion about his career decision

4. What is the woman's attitude toward her internship?

    Ⓐ She would rather go to graduate school.
    Ⓑ She is looking forward to interning.
    Ⓒ She thinks that it is a very positive experience.
    Ⓓ She will be happy when she completes it.

5. What will the man probably do?

    Ⓐ He will make an appointment with his academic advisor.
    Ⓑ He will go to the Office of Career Development.
    Ⓒ He will apply for a job at the library.
    Ⓓ He will ask the woman to help him with his tests.

Listening 2 "Sociology Class"

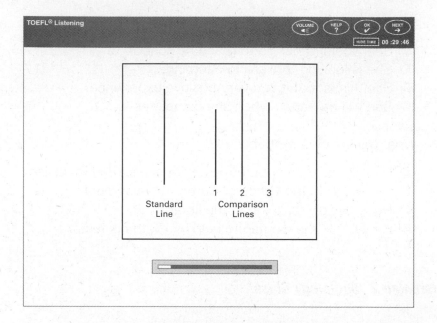

6. What is the main topic of the lecture?

   Ⓐ The problems inherent in group decisions
   Ⓑ Ways that individuals become popular in groups
   Ⓒ The influence of groups on individual behavior
   Ⓓ The differences in social influence across cultures

7. According to the professor, what two results were reported in the Asch and Abrams studies?

   Click on 2 answer choices.

   Ⓐ A larger group exerts significantly more pressure than a smaller group.

   Ⓑ Subjects conformed to group opinion in more than one-third of the trials.

   Ⓒ When the subject knows the group socially, there is greater pressure to conform.

   Ⓓ A majority opinion has as much influence as a unanimous opinion.

8. Why does the professor say this:

   Ⓐ She regretted the result of the experiment.
   Ⓑ She knew that the students would not like the information.
   Ⓒ She needed to correct what she had said in a previous statement.
   Ⓓ She neglected to mention important facts.

9. What generally happens after a group makes a decision?

   Ⓐ Some group members regret their decision.
   Ⓑ At least one group member presents a new idea.
   Ⓒ As a whole, the group is even more united in its judgment.
   Ⓓ The popular group members compete for leadership.

10. Based on information in the lecture, indicate whether the statements describe the Asch study.

For each sentence, click in the Yes or No column.

		Yes	No
A	Only one subject is being tested.		
B	The cards can be interpreted several ways.		
C	Some of the group collaborate with the experimenter.		

11. What is the professor's attitude about the studies on social influence?

Ⓐ She seems surprised by the results.
Ⓑ She appears to be very interested in them.
Ⓒ She needs more information about them.
Ⓓ She doubts that there is practical application.

Listening 3 "Art History Class"

12. What is the discussion mainly about?

    Ⓐ Catherine de Medici's entertainments
    Ⓑ The figures for court dancing
    Ⓒ The development of the ballet
    Ⓓ The relationship between dance and meals

13. Why does the professor say this: 🎧

    Ⓐ To end his explanation and begin the lecture
    Ⓑ To apologize to the students about their tests
    Ⓒ To comment about the students' grades
    Ⓓ To regain the attention of the class

14. According to the professor, what does the term *balletti* mean?

    Ⓐ A dramatic story
    Ⓑ A parade of horses
    Ⓒ A dance done in figures
    Ⓓ An outdoor entertainment

15. How did the early choreographers accommodate the abilities of amateur performers?

    Ⓐ The steps were quite simple.
    Ⓑ The same performance was repeated.
    Ⓒ Practice sessions were lengthy.
    Ⓓ The dance was seen from a distance.

16. Why does the professor mention that he checked several references about the length of *Queen Louise's Ballet*?

    Ⓐ He was very interested in the ballet.
    Ⓑ He did not know much about it.
    Ⓒ He wasn't sure that it was accurate.
    Ⓓ He wanted to impress the class.

17. What can be inferred about the professor?

    Ⓐ He is not very polite to his class.
    Ⓑ He encourages the students to participate.
    Ⓒ He is not very interested in the topic.
    Ⓓ He is probably a good dancer.

Listening 4 "Admissions Office"

18. Why does the student go to the admissions office?

    Ⓐ He is applying for financial aid.
    Ⓑ He is requesting an official transcript.
    Ⓒ He is transferring to another college.
    Ⓓ He is trying to enroll in classes.

19. What is missing from the student's file?

    Ⓐ A financial aid application
    Ⓑ A transcript from County Community College
    Ⓒ Grades from Regional College
    Ⓓ An official copy of the application

20. Why does the woman say this:

    Ⓐ She is asking the man to finish explaining the situation.
    Ⓑ She is confirming that she understands the problem.
    Ⓒ She is expressing impatience with the man's explanation.
    Ⓓ She is trying to comprehend a difficult question.

21. What does the woman suggest that the man do?

    Ⓐ Make a copy of his transcripts for his personal file
    Ⓑ Complete all of the admissions forms as soon as possible
    Ⓒ Change his provisional status to regular status before registering
    Ⓓ Continue to request an official transcript from County Community College

22. What will the student most probably do now?

    Ⓐ Return later in the day to see the woman in the admissions office
    Ⓑ Go to the office for transfer students to be assigned an advisor
    Ⓒ Enter information in the computer to complete the application process
    Ⓓ See the woman's superior to get a provisional admission to State University

Listening 5 "Geology Class"

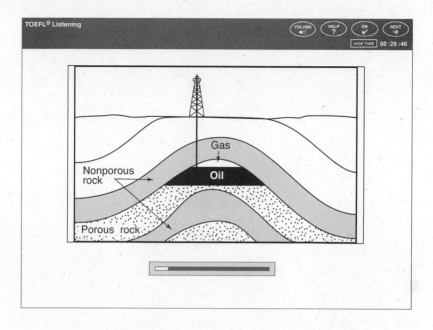

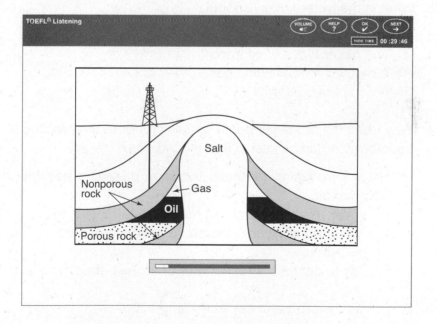

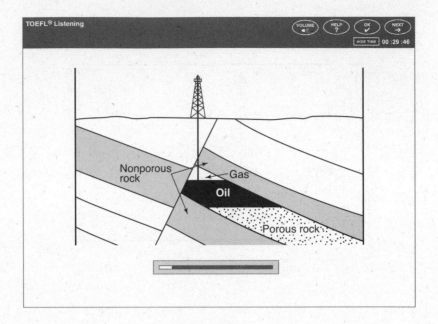

23. What is the lecture mainly about?

    Ⓐ The process of photosynthesis
    Ⓑ The major types of oil traps
    Ⓒ A method for collecting gas
    Ⓓ A comparison of gas and oil

24. Why does the professor begin by talking about the process that transforms organic material into oil and gas?

    Ⓐ He is introducing the main topic by providing background information.
    Ⓑ He is not very organized and he digresses a lot in the lecture.
    Ⓒ He wants the class to understand why hydrocarbons remain on the surface.
    Ⓓ He has to define a large number of terms before proceeding.

25. Why does the professor say this:

    Ⓐ He wants the class to participate more.
    Ⓑ He thinks that the reason is not logical.
    Ⓒ He wants all of the students to reply.
    Ⓓ He plans to answer the question.

26. Select the diagram of the anticline trap that was described in the lecture.

Click on the correct diagram.

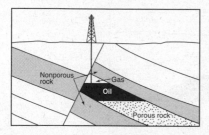

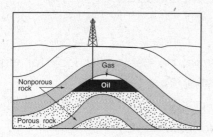

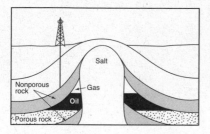

27. Identify the nonporous rock in the diagram.

    Click on the correct letter.

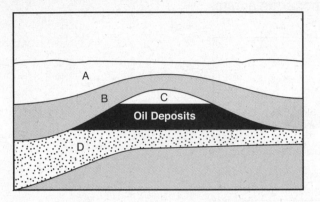

28. According to the professor, what do geologists look for when they are trying to locate a salt dome?

    Ⓐ A bulge in an otherwise flat area
    Ⓑ Underground rocks shaped like an arch
    Ⓒ Salt on the surface of a large area
    Ⓓ A deep crack in the Earth

Listening 6 "Anthropology Class"

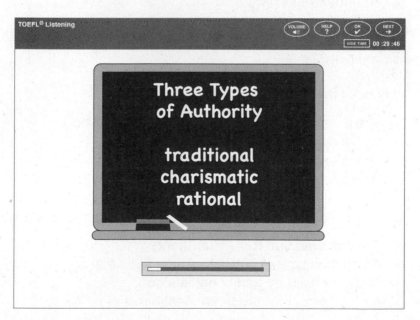

29. What is the main purpose of this discussion?

    Ⓐ To discuss three types of authority
    Ⓑ To distinguish between power and authority
    Ⓒ To examine alternatives to Weber's model
    Ⓓ To argue in favor of a legal rational system

30. Why do the students mention Kennedy and Reagan?

    Ⓐ They were founders of political movements.
    Ⓑ They were examples of charismatic leaders.
    Ⓒ They were attorneys who led by the law.
    Ⓓ They had contrasting types of authority.

31. According to the professor, what two factors are associated with charismatic authority?

    Click on 2 answer choices.

    Ⓐ Sacred customs

    Ⓑ An attractive leader

    Ⓒ A social cause

    Ⓓ Legal elections

32. Why does the professor say this: 🎧

    Ⓐ She is asking the students to answer a question.
    Ⓑ She is introducing the topic of the lecture.
    Ⓒ She is expressing an opinion about the subject.
    Ⓓ She is reminding students of a previous point.

33. In an evolutionary model, how is rational legal authority viewed?

    Ⓐ The most modern form of authority
    Ⓑ A common type of authority in the industrial age
    Ⓒ Authority used by traditional leaders
    Ⓓ A replacement for the three ideal types of authority

34. What does the professor imply about the three types of authority?

Ⓐ There is only one legitimate type of authority in modern societies.

Ⓑ Sociologists do not agree about the development of the types of authority.

Ⓒ Societies tend to select and retain one type of authority indefinitely.

Ⓓ Weber's model explains why the social structure rejects power over time.

Listening 7 "Library"

35. What does the man need from the librarian?

    Ⓐ A DVD player
    Ⓑ Material for a class
    Ⓒ Research by Dr. Parsons
    Ⓓ His student ID

36. What is the man's problem?

    Ⓐ He has to study for an important exam.
    Ⓑ He needs to prepare for a class discussion.
    Ⓒ He owes a fine at the library.
    Ⓓ He does not own a DVD player.

37. What does the man feel when he says this:

    Ⓐ Amused
    Ⓑ Worried
    Ⓒ Confused
    Ⓓ Interested

38. What is the policy for materials on reserve?

    Ⓐ The materials cannot leave the library without exception.
    Ⓑ There is a ten-dollar fine for each hour the materials are late.
    Ⓒ Students must show the professor's signature to use the materials.
    Ⓓ Materials may be checked out overnight two hours before closing.

39. What does the librarian imply when she tells the man to return at nine o'clock?

    Ⓐ She will see the man after work.
    Ⓑ The library probably closes at eleven.
    Ⓒ She is too busy to help the man now.
    Ⓓ Her supervisor will be there at that time.

Listening 8 *"Literature Class"*

40. What does this lecturer mainly discuss?

Ⓐ Transcendentalism
Ⓑ Puritanism
Ⓒ Ralph Waldo Emerson
Ⓓ Nature

41. Why does the professor say this: 🎧

Ⓐ She is joking with the students.
Ⓑ She is drawing a conclusion.
Ⓒ She is correcting the students' behavior.
Ⓓ She is reasoning aloud.

42. According to the professor, what was true about the Puritans?

Ⓐ They stressed the essential importance of the individual.
Ⓑ They supported the ideals of the Transcendental Club.
Ⓒ They believed that society should be respected above persons.
Ⓓ They thought that people should live in communes like Brook Farm.

43. Why did the church oppose the Transcendental movement?

 Ⓐ The authority of the church would be challenged by a code of personal ethics.
 Ⓑ The leaders of the Transcendentalists were not as well educated as the clergy.
 Ⓒ Church members were competing with Transcendentalists for teaching positions.
 Ⓓ Professors at Harvard College convinced the church to support their position.

44. Why did the professor mention *Walden*?

 Ⓐ It is probably well-known to many of the students in the class.
 Ⓑ It is considered an excellent example of Transcendental literature.
 Ⓒ It is required reading for the course that she is teaching.
 Ⓓ It is her personal favorite of nineteenth-century essays.

45. According to the professor, what was the most lasting contribution of Transcendentalism?

 Ⓐ Educational reorganization
 Ⓑ Religious reformation
 Ⓒ Experimental communities
 Ⓓ Political changes

Listening 9 "General Science Class"

46. What is this discussion mainly about?

   Ⓐ A model of the universe
   Ⓑ Interpretations of facts
   Ⓒ A definition of a hypothesis
   Ⓓ The scientific method

47. Why did the professor give the example of the ancient Egyptians?

   Ⓐ To explain the rotation of the Earth and the Sun
   Ⓑ To prove that facts may be interpreted differently
   Ⓒ To present a fact that can be verified by the students
   Ⓓ To discard a model that was widely accepted

48. Why did the professor say this: 🎧

   Ⓐ He is asking whether students need repetition.
   Ⓑ He is beginning a review of the process.
   Ⓒ He is complaining because students don't understand.
   Ⓓ He is making a suggestion before he proceeds.

49. According to the professor, what did Kepler do to verify his theory of planetary motion?

   Ⓐ He made predictions based on the model.
   Ⓑ He asked other scientists to make predictions.
   Ⓒ He used prior observations to test the model.
   Ⓓ He relied on insight to verify the theory.

50. What can be concluded from information in this discussion?

   Ⓐ A model does not always reflect observations.
   Ⓑ A model is not subject to change like a theory is.
   Ⓒ A model is considered true without doubt.
   Ⓓ A model does not require further experimentation.

51. What technique does the professor use to explain the practical application of the scientific method?

    Ⓐ A summary
    Ⓑ An example
    Ⓒ A prediction
    Ⓓ A formula

 Please turn off the audio. There is a 10-minute break between the Listening section and the Speaking section.

SPEAKING SECTION

🎧 **Model Test 3, Speaking Section, Track 40**

The Speaking section tests your ability to communicate in English in an academic setting. During the test, you will be presented with six speaking questions. The questions ask for a response to a single question, a conversation, a talk, or a lecture. The prompts and questions are presented only one time.

You may take notes as you listen, but notes are not graded. You may use your notes to answer the questions. Some of the questions ask for a response to a reading passage and a talk or a lecture. The reading passages and the questions are written, but the directions will be spoken.

Your speaking will be evaluated on both the fluency of the language and the accuracy of the content. You will have 15–20 seconds to prepare and 45–60 seconds to respond to each question. Typically, a good response will require all of the response time and the answer will be complete by the end of the response time.

You will have about 20 minutes to complete the Speaking section. A clock on the screen will show you how much time you have to prepare each of your answers and how much time you have to record each response.

Independent Speaking Question 1 "Advice"

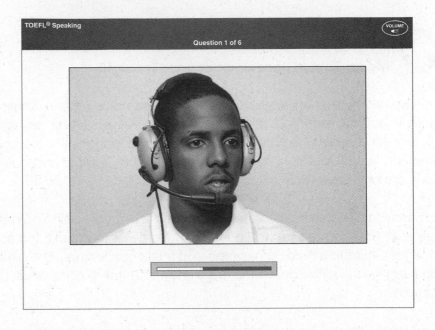

🎧 Listen for a question about a familiar topic.

Question
The older generation often gives advice to younger family members.
Describe a valuable piece of advice that an older person gave you.
Why did it help you?

Preparation Time: 15 seconds
Recording Time: 45 seconds

Independent Speaking Question 2 "Climate"

Listen for a question that asks your opinion about a familiar topic.

Question

Some people enjoy living in a location that has a warm climate all year. Other people like to live in a place where the seasons change. Which type of climate do you prefer and why? Use specific reasons and examples to support your opinion.

Preparation Time: 15 seconds
Recording Time: 45 seconds

Integrated Speaking Question 3 "Withdrawal from Classes"

Read a short passage and listen to a talk on the same topic.

Reading Time: 45 seconds

Withdrawal from Classes

In order to qualify for a refund of 100 percent at any time during the semester, you must first establish eligibility. Serious illness or injury must be verified by a written statement signed by a doctor or a psychologist. The death of a family member must be verified by a death certificate. Military duty must be verified by a copy of the orders. Students who wish to withdraw without submitting official documentation may do so before the end of the drop-add period without penalty. After the end of the second week of classes, students may petition for a 90 percent reimbursement. After the end of the fourth week, students are eligible for a 50 percent refund.

Now listen to the students discuss the policy with each other.

Question

The student expresses her opinion of the policy for reimbursement. Report her opinion and explain the reasons that she gives for having that opinion.

Preparation Time: 30 seconds
Recording Time: 60 seconds

Integrated Speaking Question 4 "Ballads"

Read a short passage and then listen to part of a lecture on the same topic.

Reading Time: 45 seconds

Ballads

A *ballad* is a poem that tells a story and is sung to music. Usually the story is of unknown origin, and a number of versions may be found for one song, a characteristic that stems from the oral tradition. As the song is passed on from one singer to another, a word is added or changed, or a slight alteration is made in the tune. In short, ballads represent a living tradition that evolves as the song is performed and passed to the next musician. A collection of ballads has been preserved in written form in the volume *English and Scottish Popular Ballads* by Francis James Child, and many ballads are still referred to by their "Child number."

Now listen to part of a lecture in a music appreciation class. The professor is talking about the ballad of "Barbara Allen."

Question
Define a ballad, and then explain why "Barbara Allen" can be classified as a ballad.

Preparation Time: 30 seconds
Recording Time: 60 seconds

Integrated Speaking Question 5 "The Assignment"

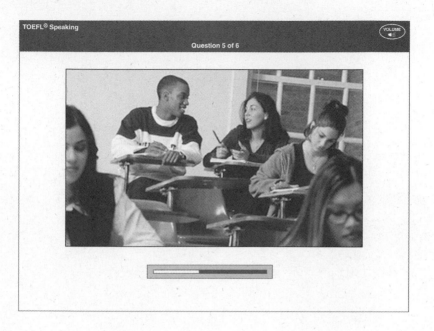

Now listen to a conversation between a student and her friend.

Question

Describe the woman's problem and the two suggestions that her friend makes about how to handle it. What do you think the woman should do, and why?

Preparation Time: 20 seconds
Recording Time: 60 seconds

Integrated Speaking Question 6 "Ultrasound"

Now listen to part of a lecture in a general science class. The professor is discussing the way that ultrasound works.

Question

Using the main points and examples from the lecture, describe the kind of information that ultrasound can provide, and then explain the way that ultrasound is used in medical diagnosis.

Preparation Time: 20 seconds
Recording Time: 60 seconds

WRITING SECTION

The Writing section tests your ability to write essays in English similar to those that you would write in college courses. During the test, you will write two essays.

The Integrated Essay. First you will read an academic passage and then you will listen to a lecture on the same topic. You may take notes as you read and listen, but notes are not graded. You may use your notes to write the essay. The reading passage will disappear while you are listening to the lecture, but the passage will return to the screen for reference when you begin to write your essay. You will have 20 minutes to plan, write, and revise your response. Typically, a good essay for the integrated topic will require that you write 150–225 words.

The Independent Essay. You will read a question on the screen. It usually asks for your opinion about a familiar topic. You will have 30 minutes to plan, write, and revise your response. Typically, a good essay for the independent topic will require that you write 300–350 words.

A clock on the screen will show you how much time you have left to complete each essay.

Integrated Essay "Emperor Penguins"

You have 20 minutes to plan, write, and revise your response to a reading passage and a lecture on the same topic. First, read the passage and take notes. Then, listen to the lecture and take notes. Finally, write your response to the writing question. Typically, a good response will require that you write 150–225 words.

Reading Passage
Time: 3 minutes

Emperor penguins are not only the largest species of penguin in the world but also one of the most unique. They are very social, living in colonies that can include hundreds of thousands of individuals. Nevertheless, emperor penguins are monogamous. Having selected a mate, emperor penguins remain faithful to each other for life, using vocal calls to find one another when they return to their breeding site on the compacted ice of the Antarctic continent. It is believed that different frequencies alert mates to the sound of their partner's call.

Another interesting aspect of emperor penguins is that they return to the same site, called a rookery, to nest each year. Although their path to the rookery is different every year due to the shifting sea ice, in general, the penguins continue to use the rookery where they were hatched. Their loyalty to a particular breeding ground results in increasingly larger penguin colonies, some with more than a million birds. Males tend to arrive first to reestablish and defend their preferred nesting sites and females return a day or so later.

Emperor penguins are not considered endangered and are not currently protected under international law. In fact, in areas where reliable population counts have been conducted, the evidence suggests that populations are stable. However, due to harsh environmental conditions, some colonies have not been monitored on a consistent basis. Estimates of population sizes are at about 240,000 breeding pairs. Taking into consideration the non-breeding birds as well, the total translates into about 600,000 adult birds. Emperor chicks that reach adulthood can survive for 20 years.

Model Test 3, Writing Section, Track 41

Now listen to a lecture on the same topic as the passage that you have just read.

Question

Summarize the main points in the lecture, and then explain how they cast doubt on the ideas in the reading passage.

Independent Essay "The College Years"

Question

Read and think about the following statement:

The college years are the best time in a person's life.

Do you agree or disagree with this statement?
Give reasons to support your opinion.

**This is the end of Model Test 3.
To check your answers, refer to "Explanatory or Example Answers and Audio Scripts for Model Tests: Model Test 3," Chapter 7, pages 492–540. Example answers for the Speaking section can be heard on Track 42.**

7

ANSWERS AND AUDIO SCRIPTS FOR ACTIVITIES, QUIZZES, AND MODEL TESTS

ANSWERS AND AUDIO SCRIPTS FOR QUIZZES IN CHAPTER 2

Reading

➤ Progress Chart for the Reading Quiz

The following chart will help you evaluate your progress and determine what you need to read again. First, use the Correct Answer column to grade the quiz. Next, check the Problem Types to locate which ones you answered incorrectly. Review the Referral Pages that correspond to the Reading Problem for each question that you missed. Finally, review the Academic Skills in Chapter 3.

Quiz Question	Problem Types	Correct Answer	Academic Skill	Question Type Referral Pages
1	True-False	B	Paraphrasing	Question 1, page 42
2	Paraphrase	A	Paraphrasing	Question 7, page 44
3	Vocabulary	D	Paraphrasing	Question 2, page 42
4	Purpose	B	Paraphrasing	Question 6, page 44
5	Inference	A		Question 4, page 43
6	Cause	B	Paraphrasing	Question 9, page 45
7	Reference	B		Question 5, page 44
8	Terms	A	Paraphrasing	Question 3, page 43
9	Detail	D	Paraphrasing	Question 8, page 45
10	Exception	D	Taking Notes	Question 12, page 47
11	Opinion	C		Question 10, page 46
12	Insert	B		Question 11, page 46
13	Classification: Hereditarian Environmentalist	D E I B F G H	Summarizing	Question 13, page 47
14	Summary	D B F	Summarizing	Question 14, page 48

Listening

➤ Script for the Listening Quiz

This is a quiz for the Listening section of the TOEFL iBT. This section tests your ability to understand campus conversations and academic lectures. During the quiz, you will listen to one conversation and one lecture. You will hear each conversation or lecture one time and respond to questions about them. You may take notes while you listen. You may use your notes to answer the questions. Once you begin, do not pause the audio. [To check your answers, refer to the question number in the margin beside the shaded area in the script to which that question refers.]

CONVERSATION

🎧 **Questions 1–4, Conversation, Track 4**
Listen to a conversation on campus between a professor and a student.

	Student:	Hi Professor Taylor.
	Professor:	Hi Jack.
Q1	Student:	I was hoping that I could talk with you for a few minutes. It's about the test.
	Professor:	Oh, okay.
	Student:	Well, I've never taken an open-book test, and I just don't know what to expect. Does that mean I can use my book during the test . . . as a reference?
	Professor:	Exactly. And you can use your notes and the handouts, too.
	Student:	Really?
Q2	Professor:	Yes, but Jack, since you've never taken an open-book test, I should warn you. It isn't as easy as it seems.
	Student:	Because?
	Professor:	Because you don't have enough time to look up every answer and still finish the test.
	Student:	Oh.

Professor:	That's the mistake that most students make. You see, the purpose of an open-book test is to allow you to look up a detail or make a citation. But the students who are looking up every answer spend too much time on the first few questions, and then they have to leave some of the questions at the end blank.
Student:	So it's important to pace yourself.
Professor:	It is. The test is one hour long and there are twenty questions so you have to be working on question ten in half an hour.
Student:	Right. That's clear enough. So, how do I prepare for an open-book test?
Professor:	Well, the first thing to do is to organize your notes into subject categories, so you can refer easily to topics that might appear in the test questions. And then study your book, just like you would for any other test. Well, some people mark passages in the book with flags to make it easier to locate certain facts, but other than that, just prepare for a test like you usually do.
Student:	Right . . . Uh, Professor Taylor, could I ask you . . . um . . . why are you making this test open-book? I mean, we have to study for it like always, so . . . I hope you don't mind that I asked. I'm . . . I'm just curious.
Professor:	I don't mind at all. Jack, I think an open-book test provides an opportunity for real learning. Too many of my students used to memorize small facts for a test and then forget all about the broad concepts. I want you to study the concepts so you will leave my class with a general perspective that you won't forget.
Student:	Wow. I can relate to that.
Professor:	Most people can. But, the way I see it, this is a psychology class, not a memory class.
Student:	Well, thanks for taking the time to explain everything, Dr. Taylor.
Professor:	You're welcome, Jack. See you next week then.
Student:	Okay. Have a nice weekend.
Professor:	You, too.

Audio	1. Why does the man go to see his professor?
Answer	**C** To get advice about studying for the test
Audio	2. Listen again to part of the conversation. Then answer the following question.

Q3 · Q4

Replay	Yes, but Jack, since you've never taken an open-book test, I should warn you. It isn't as easy as it seems. Because? Because you don't have enough time to look up every answer and still finish the test.
Audio	Why does the student say this:
Replay	Because?
Answer	**B** To encourage the professor to explain. When it is asked in a neutral tone, this one-word question invites further explanation.
Audio	3. How should Jack prepare for the test?
Answer	**C** He should organize his notes by topic.
Audio	4. Why does the professor give open-book tests?
Answer	**D** Because she thinks it provides a better learning experience.

LECTURE

🎧 **Questions 5–14, Lecture, Track 4 continued**

Listen to part of a lecture in an economics class. The professor is talking about supply-side economics.

Q5 The fundamental concept in supply-side economics is that tax cuts will spur economic growth because these tax cuts will allow entrepreneurs to invest their tax savings, thereby creating more jobs and profits, which ultimately allow the entrepreneur and the additional employees to pay more taxes, **Q13** even though the rates are lower. Let's go through that again, step by step. First, taxes are lowered. Then business owners use their tax savings to hire more workers. This increases profits so the business owner pays more taxes at a lower rate, and in addition, the newly hired workers all pay taxes as well. So there's more income flowing into the government through taxes.

Q6 Historically in the United States, several presidents have championed tax cuts to get the economy moving. Although this top-down economic theory is more popular among Republicans who have traditionally been aligned **Q7** with business interests, in 1960, John Fitzgerald Kennedy, a Democratic president, also used tax cuts to improve economic conditions. He probably wouldn't qualify as a true supply-sider, but he *did* understand and capitalize on the basic concept. But it's perhaps Ronald Reagan who is most closely associated with supply-side economics. So much so that his policies in the

1980s were referred to as Reaganomics. During his term of office, Reagan cut taxes, but actually, the huge increases in spending, especially for the military budget, caused supply-siders to debate with their conservative cousins.

You see, *conservative* and *supply-side* are not the same thing. Traditional conservative economists insist that tax cuts should be accompanied by fiscal responsibility, that is, spending cuts by government. But supply-side economists aren't concerned with spending. They rely on tax cuts to do the job. Period. Back to the supply-side policies under Reagan, well, the supply-siders believed that the economic growth resulting from tax cuts would be so great and the total increase in taxes so high that the United States economy would grow beyond its deficit spending. When this didn't happen, some economists distanced themselves from the label *supply-side* while advocating tax cuts with greater attention to spending.

Even Milton Friedman, Nobel laureate and an influential member of the Chicago School of Economics—even Friedman is now pointing out that the problem is how to hold down government spending, which accounts for about half of the national income. But he still looks to tax cuts as a solution.

So, a more recent problem for supply-siders, in addition to the fiscal responsibility issue, is that corporate business tends to move their investment and jobs overseas, which critics say eventually will lead to high unemployment in the United States. But Friedman insists that by moving jobs abroad, incomes and dollars are created that sooner or later will be used to purchase goods that are made in the United States and produce jobs in the United States. It's supply-side economics with a global perspective. [Q8]

In fact, conservatives and supply-siders alike argue that progress in the American economy has been made from technological changes and increased productivity—producing different goods or more goods with fewer workers. Dr. Barry Asmus cites the example of the millions of tons of copper wire that had to be produced for us to communicate by telephone across country. Now, a few satellites will do the job. Clearly, the people who were employed in the copper wire industry suffered unemployment when the change in technology occurred. Or, another example, in the case [Q11] of manufacturing, thirty years ago, a General Electric plant required 3000 workers to produce one dishwasher every minute. Now, the same plant [Q12] needs 300 people to produce one dishwasher every six seconds. So, you might focus on the fact that many workers will be without jobs making dishwashers, but what do you suppose supply-siders would say? Think this through. They would counter with the argument that the dishwasher will be cheaper as a result of the increased productivity, so more people can buy dishwashers and still have some money left. Again Asmus reasons that if the [Q9] consumers spend money on more goods, they create jobs because workers are needed to produce the goods they buy. If they invest their money, they also create more jobs by supporting the economy.

So some people do lose jobs because of technology, productivity, and the shift of manufacturing overseas, and only 70 percent find better-paying jobs when they transition to another job. Yes, that's true, and it's a personally painful transition for those involved. But the argument by supply-siders and many conservatives as well is that this is temporary unemployment and the important word here is *temporary*. So the temporary unemployment occurs in the process of shifting people not just from one job to another but from one segment of the economy to another. To use an analogy, it would be like the shift from farming to manufacturing that's occurred worldwide as better methods allowed fewer farmers to produce food and resulted in the movement of farmers from the country to the cities where they became employed in manufacturing. And now there's a shift from manufacturing to technology, which, if supply-siders and conservative economists are to be believed, will result in an even higher standard of living in the United States and globally. But, of course, the success of the United States within the global economy will largely depend on a favorable balance of trade—how much we can produce in this country in the new segments of the economy and how much we can sell abroad.

| **Audio** | 5. What is the lecture mainly about? |
| **Answer** | **C** Supply-side economics |

| **Audio** | 6. How does the professor organize the lecture? |
| **Answer** | **B** By taking an historical perspective |

| **Audio** | 7. According to the lecturer, what did Kennedy and Reagan have in common? |
| **Answer** | **B** They cut taxes to spur the economy during their administrations. |

| **Audio** | 8. What would Milton Friedman most likely say about moving a manufacturing plant from the United States to a site abroad? |
| **Answer** | **C** He would view it as a natural process in the shift to technology. |

Audio	9. According to Barry Asmus, what are two key ways that consumers contribute to the creation of new jobs?
Answer	**A** By investing their tax savings
	D By spending more money

Q10

Audio   10. How does the professor explain the shift from manufacturing to technology?

Answer   **C** He compares it with the change from agriculture to manufacturing.

Audio   11. Why does the professor mention the General Electric plant?

Answer   **A** Because the plant is a good example of increased productivity

Audio   12. Listen again to part of the lecture. Then answer the following question.

Replay   Now, the same plant needs 300 people to produce one dishwasher every six seconds. So, you might focus on the fact that many workers will be without jobs making dishwashers, but what do you suppose supply-siders would say? Think this through.

Audio   Why does the professor say this:

Replay   Think this through.

Answer   **C** He wants the students to follow his logical answer.

Audio   13. In the lecture, the professor explains supply-side economics. Indicate whether each of the following strategies supports the theory.

Answer

	Yes	No
A Reduce tax rates	✔	
B Cut government spending		✔
C Increase productivity	✔	
D Tolerate temporary unemployment	✔	
E Discourage consumer spending		✔

Audio   14. Put the following events in the correct order.

Answer   **B** The government works to affect a reduction in taxes.

A Businesses hire more employees with the tax savings.

D Profits increase because of the growth in businesses.

C The businesses and their employees pay more taxes.

➤ Progress Chart for the Listening Quiz

The chart below will help you evaluate your progress and determine what you need to read again. First use the Correct Answer column to grade the quiz. Next, check the Problem Types to locate which ones you answered incorrectly and review the Referral Pages that correspond to the Listening Problem for each question that you missed. Finally, review the Academic Skills in Chapter 3.

Quiz Question	Problem Types	Correct Answer	Academic Skill	Question Type Referral Pages
1	Purpose	C	Taking Notes Summarizing	Question 1, page 67
2	Pragmatics	B		Question 4, page 69
3	Inference	C		Question 3, page 68
4	Detail	D	Taking Notes Paraphrasing	Question 2, page 68
5	Main Idea	C	Summarizing	Question 5, page 72
6	Organization	B	Taking Notes	Question 6, page 72
7	Detail	B	Taking Notes Paraphrasing	Question 2, page 68
8	Inference	C		Question 3, page 68
9	Details	A D	Taking Notes Paraphrasing	Question 7, page 72
10	Technique	C		Question 8, page 73
11	Inference	A		Question 3, page 68
12	Pragmatics	C		Question 4, page 69

Quiz Question	Problem Types	Correct Answer	Academic Skill	Question Type Referral Pages
13	Yes-No	A C D Yes B E No	Taking Notes Paraphrasing	Question 9, page 73
14	Connections	B A D C	Summarizing	Question 10, page 74

Speaking

➤ Script for the Speaking Quiz

This is a quiz for the Speaking section of the TOEFL® iBT. This section tests your ability to communicate in English in an academic context. During the quiz, you will respond to six speaking questions. You may take notes as you listen. You may use your notes to answer the questions. The reading passages and the questions are written [printed in the book], but the directions will be spoken. Once you begin, do not pause the audio.

Speaking Quiz, Track 11

Narrator 2: Number 1. Listen for a question about a familiar topic. After you hear the question, you have 15 seconds to prepare and 45 seconds to record your answer.

Narrator 1: If you were asked to choose one movie that has influenced your thinking, which one would you choose? Why? What was especially impressive about the movie? Use specific reasons and details to explain your choice.

Narrator 2: Please prepare your answer after the beep.

Beep

[Preparation Time: 15 seconds]

Narrator 2: Please begin speaking after the beep.

Beep

[Recording Time: 45 seconds]

Beep

Narrator 2: Number 2. Listen for a question that asks your opinion about a familiar topic. After you hear the question, you have 15 seconds to prepare and 45 seconds to record your answer.

Narrator 1: Some people think that teachers should be evaluated by the performance of their students on standardized tests at the end of the term. Other people maintain that teachers should be judged by their own performance in the classroom, and not by the scores that their students achieve on tests. Which approach do you think is better and why? Use specific reasons and examples to support your opinion.

Narrator 2: Please prepare your answer after the beep.

Beep

[Preparation Time: 15 seconds]

Narrator 2: Please begin speaking after the beep.

Beep

[Recording Time: 45 seconds]

Beep

Narrator 2: Number 3. Read a short passage and listen to a talk on the same topic. Then listen for a question about them. After you hear the question, you have 30 seconds to prepare and 60 seconds to record your answer.

Narrator 1: A meeting is planned to explain the residence requirements for instate tuition. Read the policy in the college catalogue [printed on page 110]. You have 45 seconds to complete it. Please begin reading now.

[Reading Time: 45 seconds]

Narrator 1: Now listen to a student who is speaking at the meeting. He is expressing his opinion about the policy.

Student:
Well, I agree with most of the policy, but what I don't understand is why I have to use my parents' address as my permanent address. This is my third year in a dorm on campus, and I've gone to school every summer, so I've lived in this state for three consecutive years. I don't pay state taxes because I don't earn enough as a full-time student to, uh, to pay taxes, but I don't receive support from my parents either. I have a small grant and a student loan that I'm responsible for, and . . . and I plan to live and work in this state after I graduate, so, um, I think students like me should be eligible for a waiver.

Narrator 1: The student expresses his opinion of the policy for instate tuition. Report his opinion and explain the reasons that he gives for having that opinion.

Narrator 2: Please prepare your answer after the beep.

Beep

[Preparation Time: 30 seconds]

Narrator 2: Please begin speaking after the beep.

Beep

[Recording Time: 60 seconds]

Beep

Narrator 2: Number 4. Read a short passage and listen to a lecture on the same topic. Then listen for a question about them. After you hear the question, you have 30 seconds to prepare and 60 seconds to record your answer.

Narrator 1: Now read the passage about communication with primates [printed on page 111]. You have 45 seconds to complete it. Please begin reading now.

[Reading Time: 45 seconds]

Narrator 1: Now listen to part of a lecture in a zoology class. The professor is talking about a primate experiment.

Professor:
Probably one of the most publicized linguistic research studies with primates is the Kanzi experiment. Dr. Sue Savage-Rumbaugh had been trying to train a bonobo chimpanzee to communicate, using a keyboard adapted with symbols. What is interesting about the experiment is that the chimpanzee's adopted son Kanzi, also a bonobo chimpanzee, well, Kanzi had been observing and had acquired a rather impressive vocabulary. Savage-Rumbaugh and her colleagues kept adding symbols to Kanzi's keyboard and then started a file of laminated flash cards. In addition to the more than 350 symbols that Kanzi learned to use, he also understood the meaning of about 3000 spoken English words and could respond appropriately to spoken commands. In addition, Kanzi picked up some American sign language by watching videos of Koko, a gorilla who used sign language to communicate with his keeper, Penny Patterson. But what about speaking? What about actually vocalizing? Well, yes and no. Kanzi made attempts to vocalize in order to communicate by using speech to identify the symbols that he had learned, but because of the very different vocal tract, the sounds were very high-pitched and distorted. So, for now, communicating with primates appears to be limited to symbolic language. Nevertheless, Kanzi has more than proven that communication is possible.

Narrator 1: Explain how the example of the Kanzi experiment demonstrates progress in research on primate communication.

Narrator 2: Please prepare your answer after the beep.

Beep

[Preparation Time: 30 seconds]

Narrator 2: Please begin speaking after the beep.

Beep

[Recording Time: 60 seconds]

Beep

Narrator 2: Number 5. Listen to a short conversation. Then listen for a question about it. After you hear the question, you have 20 seconds to prepare and 60 seconds to record your answer.

Narrator 1: Now listen to a conversation between a student and her friend.

Friend:	Did you decide to take Johnson's class?
Student:	Yeah. I'm going to work it out somehow. Yesterday I walked from the chemistry lab to Hamilton Hall—that's where Johnson's class is.
Friend:	And?
Student:	And it took me twenty minutes.
Friend:	Uh-oh. You only have fifteen minutes between classes, so that means you'll be five minutes late. Listen, why don't you buy a bike? I'm sure you could cut at least five minutes off your time if you took the bike trail.
Student:	I thought about that. But then I'd have to get a license, and I'd have to find somewhere to store it at night. I thought it might be a hassle.
Friend:	Oh, it's not so bad. I have a bike. The license is only ten dollars, and I just park my bike on the deck outside my apartment when the weather's good. And the weather should be okay for most of spring semester.
Student:	That's true.
Friend:	Well, your other option is to talk with Dr. Johnson. Maybe he'll give you permission to be five minutes late to his class because of the distance from your lab. Actually, I've had several classes with him, and he seems very approachable. Anyway, it's an alternative to the bike, if you don't want to do that.

Narrator 1: Describe the woman's problem, and the two suggestions that her friend makes about how to handle it. What do you think the woman should do, and why?

Narrator 2: Please prepare your answer after the beep.

Beep

[Preparation Time: 20 seconds]

Narrator 2: Please begin speaking after the beep.

Beep

[Recording Time: 60 seconds]

Beep

Narrator 2: Number 6. Listen to part of a lecture. Then listen for a question about it. After you hear the question, you have 20 seconds to prepare, and 60 seconds to record your answer.

Narrator 1: Now listen to part of a lecture in an astronomy class. The professor is discussing the habitable zone.

Professor:
Of course, stars are too hot to support life, but the light from a star warms orbiting planets or moons, supplying the energy needed for life to develop. Besides energy, a liquid, let's say, a chemical solvent of some kind, is also necessary. On Earth, the solvent in which life developed was water, but others such as ammonia, hydrogen fluoride, or methane might also be appropriate. So, in order for the solvent to remain in liquid form, the planet or moon must lie within a certain range of distances from the star. Why is this so? Well, think about it. If the planet is too close to the star, the solvent will change into a gas, boiling and evaporating. If it is too far from the star, the solvent will freeze, transforming into a solid. For our Sun and life as we know it, the habitable zone appears to lie between the orbits of Venus and Mars. Within this range, water remains liquid. And until recently, this area was indeed the accepted scientific definition of the habitable zone for our solar system. But now scientists have postulated that the habitable zone may be larger than originally supposed. They speculate that the strong gravitational pull caused by larger planets may produce enough energy to heat the cores of orbiting moons. So that means that these moons may support life. There may be habitable zones far beyond Venus!

Narrator 1: Using the main points and examples from the lecture, describe the habitable zone, and then explain how the definition has been expanded by modern scientists.

Narrator 2: Please prepare your answer after the beep.

Beep

[Preparation Time: 20 seconds]

Narrator 2: Please begin speaking after the beep.

Beep

[Recording Time: 60 seconds]

Beep

Progress Chart for the Speaking Quiz

The chart below will help you evaluate your progress and determine what you need to practice again. First, compare your answers on the quiz with the Example Answers. Use the Checklists in the Review to evaluate specific features of your speech. Next, check the Problem Types to locate which ones were most difficult for you. Review the Referral Pages that correspond to the Speaking Problem for each question that you missed. Finally, review the Academic Skills in Chapter 3.

Quiz Question	Problem Types	Correct Answer	Academic Skill	Question Type Referral Pages
1	Experiences	1	Summarizing Taking Notes	Question 1, pages 86–88
2	Preferences	2	Summarizing Taking Notes	Question 2, pages 88–89
3	Reports	3	Synthesizing Taking Notes	Question 3, pages 89–92
4	Examples	4	Synthesizing Taking Notes	Question 4, pages 92–95
5	Problems	5	Summarizing Taking Notes	Question 5, pages 95–97
6	Summaries	6	Summarizing Taking Notes	Question 6, pages 97–100

🎧 **Example Answers, Track 12**

QUESTION 1: EXAMPLE ANSWER

The movie that has influenced my thinking the most is *Fantasia* because it's my first memory of classical music and ballet. One reason the movie was so impressive is, um, I was at a very impressionable age when I saw it—five years old. Besides that, it was made using the latest technology. In the 1950s, it was amazing to see detailed animation and . . . and hear high quality sound. But what really influenced me was the music and the dance scenes. I especially remember Mickey Mouse dancing with the brooms and I'm sure I took ballet lessons because of it. The coordination of the storm scene with the music from *The Hall of the Mountain King* still impresses me when I see it today and, thanks to Walt Disney, classical music is still my favorite music.

QUESTION 2: EXAMPLE ANSWER

I think it's good to evaluate teachers by their student's performace on standardized tests because when teachers and students are judged by the same criteria, they'll work efficiently toward the same goals. Now some teachers argue that tests aren't important but still, students need good scores for admission to universities so the tests are important to them. If teachers were evaluated on the same basis, then they would pay more attention to the criteria on tests to design their lessons so both students and teachers would benefit. Another reason to use this evaluation is to compare teachers from different schools on a standardized scale. And this system would be more fair, too, because the possibility of a teacher getting a high evaluation because of friendship with the supervisor is also eliminated.

QUESTION 3: EXAMPLE ANSWER

The student said that he mostly agreed with the policy for instate tuition but he disagreed with a couple of requirements. For one thing, you can't use a campus address as a permanent address, but he's a dorm student, and he explained that he's lived in the dorm for three years because he's gone to school every summer without returning to his parents' home to live so the dorm really is his permanent address right now. He doesn't think he should have to use his parent's out-of-state address. Besides that, he hasn't been subsidized by his parents. In the policy, the most recent taxes must be filed in the state of residence but, uh, he didn't make enough money to pay taxes. He didn't mention in which state he had his voter's registration or car registration and driver's licenses, but he said that he plans to continue living and working in the state after graduation, and he thought that he should be eligible for a waiver of the out-of-state fees.

QUESTION 4: EXAMPLE ANSWER

The studies by Savage-Rumbaugh and colleagues with Kanzi, a bonobo chimpanzee, demonstrate progress in research on primate communication. Although the experiments confirm that auditory speech communication can't happen because of the different vocal tracts between species, they also prove that primates can communicate using sign language and symbols. In fact, Kanzi learned more than 350 symbols on a keyboard and on flash cards, understood 3000 spoken English words, and . . . and he was able to respond to spoken commands. So . . . the research substantiates the information in the reading passage that um, vocal organs and not intelligence . . . they inhibit communication between primates and humans.

QUESTION 5: EXAMPLE ANSWER

The problem is that the woman has only fifteen minutes between classes but it takes twenty minutes to walk from the chemistry lab to Hamilton Hall where Professor Johnson's class is held. So she would like to take the class with Johnson but she would be late. Um, her friend suggests that she buy a bike but her concern is that she would need a license and would have to store the bike somewhere at night. The other recommendation is . . . is to ask Dr. Johnson for permission to enter the class five minutes late. So . . . I think the woman should talk with the professor first. Her friend says he's approachable and he might give her permission to be late for class. The first five minutes in a class is usually just business anyway—taking attendance and handing back papers—so she wouldn't miss much. And, if he refuses, then she can always resort to the other alternative. She can buy a bike and a license, and she can find a place to store it.

QUESTION 6: EXAMPLE ANSWER

The habitable zone is an area in which life can develop. There are several requirements, including an energy source and a chemical solvent that retains its liquid form. Okay, that means that the moon or the planet where life may develop has to be close enough to the energy source—probably a star—close enough that the solvent will remain a liquid. Outside the habitable zone, it would freeze or boil, depending on whether it was far way or too close to the star. In the case of Earth, the Sun supplied the energy and water was the chemical solvent. So, for life to evolve in ways similar to our own, the habitable zone would have to fall between Venus and Mars. But, modern scientists are questioning whether the forces of gravity on larger planets might not generate enough energy to heat up the cores of the moons that orbit them. Now, if that's the case, then there could be habitable zones at a great distance from Venus, which was the previously determined limit for a habitable zone in our solar system.

Writing

➤ Script for the Writing Quiz

This is a quiz for the Writing section of the TOEFL (iBT). This section tests your ability to write essays in English. During the quiz, you will respond to two writing questions. You may take notes as you read and listen to academic information. You may use your notes to write the essays. Once you begin, you have 20 minutes to write the first essay and 30 minutes to write the second essay.

🎧 Question 1, Track 14

Now listen to a lecture on the same topic as the passage you have just read.

Professor:
Although there's a great deal of excitement about the Stonehenge Riverside Project, I'm less enthusiastic about it than many of my colleagues. Here's why. The theory that the monument was constructed as a burial site rests on three assumptions. First, the researchers report that they've found human remains, suggesting that ritual cremations and burials were performed at the site. But this discovery isn't new. We've known about the remains since the first excavations at the site more than 200 years ago. Because people were buried in Stonehenge, it doesn't necessarily follow that the site was constructed for that purpose. Previous research studies have noted the evidence of burials but haven't come to the same conclusion.

Second, let's consider the bluestones that stand in front of the larger sarsen stones. Clearly, since these stones aren't native to the area and had to be carried long distances from quarry sites as far as 250 miles away, well, that's convincing evidence that they served an important purpose, but what that purpose is, well that remains unclear. Yes, they've been associated with burials. Still, some studies believe that the stones were important for their acoustical properties, and when bluestones along the Carn Menyn ridge were tested, a high proportion of them would actually ring when struck, so any number of rituals, including but not limited to burials, could have been enhanced by ancient music. Other studies maintain that the bluestones held a magical purpose and were thought to aid in the healing of people recovering from illness or injury. So, instead of a burial site, Stonehenge could have been a healing site. The discovery of small pieces of bluestones chipped from the originals and scattered throughout the site might indicate that prehistoric people who made the pilgrimage to Stonehenge carried small pieces of the magical stones with them. And the burials there may have been secondary to their attempt to find a cure. In other words, some died in the effort to be healed.

Finally, we have to consider the artifacts, specifically the stone mace, which was certainly an object that belonged to a person of high rank. But here's the problem: the mace is one object, and not enough artifacts have been located in addition to this one exciting find for us to draw conclusions. Furthermore, Stonehenge has been subjected to so many excavations and so much theft that it would be difficult to determine who was buried within the stone circles.

➤ Progress Chart for the Writing Quiz

The chart below will help you to evaluate your progress and determine what you need to practice again. First, compare your answers on the quiz with the Example Essays. Use the Checklists in the Review to evaluate specific features of your writing. Next, check the Problem Types to locate which was most difficult for you. Read the Referral Pages that correspond to the Writing Problem for the question that you found most difficult. Finally, review the Academic Skills in Chapter 3.

Quiz Question	Problem Types	Checklists	Academic Skill	Question Type Referral Pages
1	Integrated	Synthesis of Opposing Ideas	Paraphrasing Summarizing Synthesizing	Question 1, pages 116–121
2	Independent	Opinion		Question 2, pages 121–123

QUESTION 1: EXAMPLE ESSAY

The lecturer refutes the three arguments presented in the reading passage, calling into question the new hypothesis to explain the purpose of Stonehenge. According to the hypothesis, the site was constructed as a burial ground for elite members of society in approximately 3000 B.C.E. The researchers in the Riverside Project cited the discovery of human remains, the presence of bluestones, and several important artifacts as evidence for their claim. However, the lecturer presents a counterargument for each assertion.

First, he maintains that the discovery of human remains is not unique to this project. Excavations as early as 200 years ago provided evidence of burials in Stonehenge. Although the remains prove that ritual burials were performed at Stonehenge, it does not necessarily follow that the monument was built for the purpose of burials. Previous researchers evaluating the same evidence have not come to the same conclusion.

Moreover, the bluestones could have been brought to the area for purposes other than burial rites. Since they have acoustical properties, ancient music could have been played on the stones. Some studies suggest that the stones may have had a magical purpose or could have been used for healing, in which case the burials could have been performed when healing was not successful.

In spite of the discovery of two significant artifacts that probably belonged to highly important people, the lecturer points out that the number of objects is insufficient to draw conclusions and, furthermore, that the current excavation may have been corrupted by previous digs and theft.

QUESTION 2: EXAMPLE ESSAY

Although it can be argued that voice mail and email are more efficient, and in many ways, more convenient, I still prefer to communicate in person, or if that is not possible, by telephone. In my experience, face-to-face interactions are best for a number of reasons. In the first place, when you hear the speaker's tone of voice, you are better able to judge the attitude and emotions that can be easily hidden in a written reply. In addition, the exchange is more immediate. Even instant messaging isn't as fast as a verbal interaction in person or by phone. Email seems efficient; however, sometimes multiple messages over several days are required to clarify the information that a short phone call would have taken care of in one communication. We have all tried to return a voice mail only to hear a recording on the original caller's voice mail. Clearly, no real communication is possible in a situation that allows only one person to talk. Moreover, the body language and the expression on the speaker's face often communicate more than the words themselves. Research indicates that more than 80 percent of a message is nonverbal. The way that a speaker stands or sits can indicate interest or disagreement. The eye contact and the movement of the eyebrows and the mouth can actually communicate the opposite of the words that the speaker is saying. Finally, no technology has succeeded in duplicating a firm handshake to close a deal, a hug to encourage a friend, or a kiss goodbye. Until email and voice mail can provide the subtle communication, the immediate interaction, and the emotional satisfaction of a face-to-face conversation, complete with facial expressions and gestures, I will prefer to talk instead of to type.

ANSWERS AND AUDIO SCRIPTS FOR PRACTICE ACTIVITIES IN CHAPTER 3

Practice Activity 7

1. According to Mead, the self has two sides: the "I" and the "me."

The "I" represents the individuality of a person.	For instance, a spontaneous reaction might reveal the "I." This part of the self is less predictable because it is unique.
The "me" represents the expectations and attitudes of others.	This part of the self is formed through socialization by others. It is predictable because social conformity is expected.

2. The mystery of pulsars was resolved in the 1960s.

We know that pulsars are neutron stars, like lighthouses left by supernova explosions.	Like a lighthouse, the neutron star revolves. We see pulses of light each time the beam sweeps past the Earth.
We also know that pulsars are not perfectly timed because each revolution of a pulsar takes a little longer.	The pulsar in the Crab Nebula, for example, currently spins about thirty times per second. It will probably spin about half as fast two thousand years from now.

3. Britain transported convicts to Australia in an effort to solve the problems of overcrowding in prisons.

In 1787, the first fleet left for Botany Bay in New South Wales.	There were 11 ships with 750 prisoners aboard. Four companies of marines sailed with them as guards. They took enough supplies for two years.

| Shortly after arriving in 1788, the colony was moved to Sydney Cove. | In Sydney, the water supply and soil were better.
Although Sydney was the new site, for many years it was called Botany Bay. |

4. Frederick Carl Frieseke was an American impressionist.

Born in Michigan, he went to Paris in 1897.	He studied with Whistler in the late 1800s. From Whistler, he learned the academic style of the salons.
In 1905, Frieseke moved to Giverney where he lived until 1920.	At Giverney, Frieseke was influenced by Monet. Monet was experimenting with the effects of sunlight. The style of Monet and his school is known as impressionism.
By 1920, Frieseke had left Giverney for Normandy.	In Normandy, he began to paint indoor settings. In his later work, he began to use a darker palette.

5. Two types of weathering will break down rock masses into smaller particles.

| Interaction between surface or ground water and chemicals causes chemical weathering. | With increased precipitation or temperature, chemicals tend to break down faster.
The weathering of feldspar in granite can be caused by a reaction to acids in rain.
A common example is the wearing away of granite facades on buildings. |
| Mechanical weathering occurs when force and pressure grind rocks down. | Pressure from freezing and thawing causes rocks to expand and contract.
When a rock is broken in two by physical forces, it is more vulnerable to weathering. |

PRACTICE ACTIVITY 8

🎧 **Activity 8, Track 20**

Listen to some sentences from college lectures. Take notes as quickly as you can.

1. The Nineteenth Amendment to the U.S. Constitution gave women the right to vote, beginning with the elections of 1920.
   19 → women vote/1920

2. In a suspension bridge, there are two towers with one or more flexible cables firmly attached at each end.
   suspension = 2 towers w/flex cables @ ends

3. A perennial is any plant that continues to grow for more than two years, as for example, trees and shrubs.
   perennial = plant 2+ yrs ex. trees, shrubs

4. Famous for innovations in punctuation, typography, and language, Edward Estlin Cummings, known to us as e.e. cummings, published his collected poems in 1954.
   ee. cummings → innovations punct, typo, lang 1954 poems

5. Absolute zero, the temperature at which all substances have zero thermal energy, and thus the lowest possible temperatures, is unattainable in practice.
   absolute zero = temp. all subs 0 therm en → lowest temps

6. Because Columbus, Ohio, is considered a typical metropolitan area, it is often used for market research to test new products.
   Columbus, O = typical metro → market res new prod

7. The cacao bean was cultivated by the Aztecs not only to drink but also as currency in their society.
   cocao bean ← Aztecs = curr

8. The blue whale is the largest known animal, reaching a length of more than one hundred feet, which is five times its size at birth.
   blue whale = largest an 100′ = 5× birth size

9. Ontario is the heartland of Canada, both geographically, and, I would say, historically as well.
   Ontario = heartland Can geo + hist

10. Nuclear particles called hadrons, which include the proton and neutron, are made from quarks—very odd particles that have a slight electrical charge but that cannot exist alone in nature.
    nuclear particles = hadrons = proton + neutron ← quarks = part slight elec charge Ø nature

PRACTICE ACTIVITY 9

1. Problem: The paraphrase is too much like the original. Only the subject and complement have been reversed in this alternative grammatical structure.

Edited
Paraphrase: Molecules that function as regulators in the transmission of substances across cell walls are known as proteins.

Why is this better? Because synonyms have been substituted for all the nontechnical vocabulary and the subject and complement are reversed in an alternative grammatical structure.

2. Problem: The paraphrase is not complete. Information about the factory system and the cotton industry are not included.

Edited
Paraphrase: The factory system spread across a large number of enterprises in addition to cotton manufacturing as a result of the introduction of steam engines.

Why is this better? Because the relationship between cause and effect has been retained using different vocabulary and grammar, and both the factory system and the cotton industry are included.

3. Problem: The paraphrase is not correct. The meaning has been changed.

Edited
Paraphrase: Small enterprises are frequently using bloggers to compete effectively with large businesses that are still employing more conventional marketing strategies as well as some of the more recent options.

Why is this better? Because the meaning of the original sentence has been retained.

4. Problem: The paraphrase is too much like the original. Too many words and phrases are the same, and the grammatical structure is too similar.

   Edited
   Paraphrase: Although fossilized bones may look like stone, minerals from sedimentary material fill the spaces.

   Why is this better? Because synonyms have been substituted for all the nontechnical vocabulary, and the subject and complement are reversed in an alternative grammatical structure.

5. Problem: The paraphrase is incomplete. The dates are important here.

   Edited
   Paraphrase: About 3500 B.C., two thousand years before written symbols were introduced in 1500 B.C., the first pictographic writing system appeared simultaneously in various regions of the known world.

   Why is this better? Because the chronology is not clear without a time frame. The date solves this problem.

6. Problem: This is not a paraphrase. It is copied directly from the original.

   Edited
   Paraphrase: In all likelihood, the Earth's current atmosphere was preceded by three earlier atmospheres.

   Why is this better? Because copying directly from a source is the worst kind of plagiarism. Even when you are in a hurry, be sure that you are not copying.

7. Problem: This is not a paraphrase. It is too general.
   Edited
   Paraphrase: Alcohol depresses the central nervous system, but coffee increases neural transmission.

   Why is this better? Because details are necessary for a paraphrase to be specific. A general statement does not include enough information.

8. Problem: This paraphrase changes the meaning of the original statement.

Edited
Paraphrase: Australia and the islands of Oceania comprise the Pacific Basin, an area that encompasses about 33 percent of the Earth's surface.

Why is this better? Because this paraphrase retains the original meaning. The area is one third of the surface of the Earth, not one third of the Pacific Ocean.

9. Problem: The paraphrase is incomplete. It does not identify the process as fresco painting.

Edited
Paraphrase: The lime in wet plaster bonds with the colors on the surface when the paints are mixed for frescos.

Why is this better? Because the process described in the paraphrase is identified as fresco painting.

10. Problem: The paraphrase is too much like the original. Too many words and phrases are repeated.

Edited
Paraphrase: The Linnaean chart used to classify all biological species was initially created to categorize each specimen in conformity with its resemblance to other organisms.

Why is this better? Because the edited paraphrase retains the meaning of the original, but the words and phrases are different, and the grammatical structure is changed.

PRACTICE ACTIVITY 10

Activity 10, Track 21

1. In his book, *The Making of the President,* Theodore White noted that the 1960 presidential debate was more like a press conference. According to White, Nixon proceeded as though he were engaged in a personal debate. In contrast, Kennedy spoke directly to the TV viewers. He estimated that Kennedy gained two million votes as a result.
2. Paul Cezanne believed that all forms in nature were based on geometric shapes. Cezanne identified the cone, sphere, and cylinder as the primary forms. He used outlining to emphasize these shapes.

3. Along with her husband, Marie Curie won the Nobel prize for physics in 1903 for the discovery of radium. Curie then received the Nobel prize for chemistry in 1911 for the isolation of pure radium. She was the first person to be awarded two Nobel prizes.
4. Psychologist Erik Erikson proposed eight stages of personal development. Erikson claimed that psychological crises at each stage shaped the sense of self. He believed that development was a lifelong process.
5. Margaret Mead did her first fieldwork in Samoa in 1925. Mead's book, *Coming of Age in Samoa*, was a best seller that was translated into many languages. She is still one of the most well-known anthropologists in the world. Mead believed that people in simple societies could provide valuable lessons for the industrialized world.
6. Leonardo da Vinci was the quintessential Renaissance man. A brilliant painter, da Vinci was perhaps best remembered for his art. But he was also interested in mechanics, and his understanding of mathematics is clear in his use of perspective.
7. Author Peter Drucker wrote *Management Challenges for the 21st Century*. In this book, Drucker proposed five transforming forces. He predicted that these trends will have major implications for the long-term strategies of companies.
8. Freidrich Mohs devised a scale of hardness for ten minerals. By assigning 10 to diamond, the hardest known mineral, Mohs was able to attribute relative values to all the other minerals. His scale is still useful in the study of minerals today.
9. Maria Montessori proposed an educational model that has become known as the Montessori method. Montessori insisted that education should not be merely the transmission of knowledge but the freedom to develop as a person. She felt her greatest success was achieved when a child began working independently.
10. In collaboration with Louis Leaky, Jane Goodall spent years living with chimpanzees on the Gombe Reserve. Goodall imitated their behaviors and discovered that chimpanzees lived within a complex social organization. She was the first to document chimpanzees making and using tools, and she also identified twenty different sounds that were part of a communication system.

PRACTICE ACTIVITY 11

1. Reading

1. **B** The first opera in Italy
2. **C** The growth of opera throughout Europe
3. **A** Three types of musical pieces in opera

2. Lecture

🎧 **Activity 11, Track 22**

Listen to part of a lecture in a biology class.

The protozoans, minute aquatic creatures, each of which consists of a single cell of protoplasm, constitute a classification of the most primitive forms of animal life. The very name protozoan indicates the scientific understanding of the animals. *Proto* means "first" or "primitive" and *zoa* refers to the animal.

They are fantastically diverse, but three major groups may be identified on the basis of their motility. The Mastigophora have one or more long tails that they use to propel themselves forward. The Ciliata, which use the same basic means for locomotion as the Mastigophora, have a larger number of short tails. The Sarcodina, which include amoebae, float or row themselves about on their crusted bodies.

In addition to their form of movement, several other features discriminate among the three groups of protozoans. For example, at least two nuclei per cell have been identified in the Ciliata, usually a large nucleus that regulates growth but decomposes during reproduction, and a smaller one that contains the genetic code necessary to generate the large nucleus.

So all of this seems very straightforward to this point, but now we are going to complicate the picture. Chlorophyll, which is the green substance in plants, is also found in the bodies of some protozoans, enabling them to make at least some of their own food from water and carbon dioxide. Sounds like photosynthesis, doesn't it? But protozoans are animals, right? And plants are the life forms that use photosynthesis. Okay. Well protozoans are not considered plants because, unlike pigmented plants to which some protozoans are otherwise almost identical, they don't live on simple organic compounds. Their cells demonstrate all of the major characteristics of the cells of higher animals, such as eating, breathing, and reproducing.

Now many species of protozoans collect into colonies, physically connected to one another and responding uniformly to outside stimuli. Current research into this phenomenon along with investigations carried out with advanced microscopes may necessitate a redefinition of what constitutes protozoans, even calling into question the basic premise that they have only one cell. Nevertheless, with the current data available, almost 40,000 species of protozoans have been identified. No doubt, as technology improves methods of observation, better models of classification of these simple single cells will be proposed.

1. **D** A definition of protozoans—single cell
2. **A** A method of classification for protozoans—the three types motility

3. **C** Similarity to plants—make food from water + CO_2
4. **E** Considered animals—eating, breathing, reproducing
5. **B** Current research—questions, redefinitions

PRACTICE ACTIVITY 12

1. Reading

50% The function and responsibilities of the Fed
40% The composition of the Fed
10% A comparison of the Fed to a fourth branch of government

Although the summary below is actually closer to 50%, 30%, 20%, it still maintains a reasonably accurate emphasis.

Summary

The function of the Federal Reserve System is to regulate money and credit by buying and selling government securities, thereby influencing periods of recession and inflation. Moreover, the Fed cooperates with the Department of the Treasury to issue new coins and paper notes to banks and participates in international financial policies through member banks overseas.

The Fed includes twelve district reserve banks and branches, all national commercial banks and credit unions, as well as several committees and councils, including the powerful board of governors appointed by the president.

Because of its powerful membership, the Fed has been compared to a fourth branch of government, but the president's policies are usually implemented.

2. Lecture

Activity 12, Track 23
Listen to part of a lecture in a psychology class.

Okay then, let's talk about human memory, which was formerly believed to be rather inefficient as compared with, for example, computers. But we are finding that we probably have a much more sophisticated mechanism than we had originally assumed. Researchers approaching the problem from a variety of points of view have all concluded that there is a great deal more stored in our minds than has been generally supposed. Here's what I mean—Dr. Wilder

Penfield, a Canadian neurosurgeon, proved that by stimulating their brains electrically, he could elicit the total recall of complex events in his subjects' lives. Even dreams and other minor events supposedly forgotten for many years suddenly emerged in detail.

The *memory trace* is the term for whatever forms the internal representation of the specific information about an event stored in the memory. So, the trace is probably made by structural changes in the brain, but the problem is that the memory trace isn't really subject to direct observation because it's . . . it's . . . more a theoretical construct that we use to speculate about how information presented at a particular time can cause performance at a later time. So most theories include the strength of the memory trace as a variable in the degree of learning, retention, and retrieval possible for a memory. One theory is that the fantastic capacity for storage in the brain is the result of an almost unlimited combination of interconnections between brain cells, stimulated by patterns of activity. And repeated references to the same information supports recall. Or, to say that another way, improved performance is the result of strengthening the chemical bonds in the memory.

Now here's the interesting part. Psychologists generally divide memory into at least two types—short-term memory and long-term memory, which combine to form what we call *working memory*. Short-term memory contains what we are actively focusing on at any particular time but items aren't retained longer than twenty or thirty seconds without verbal rehearsal. We use short-term memory when we look up a telephone number and repeat it to ourselves until we can place the call. In contrast, long-term memory can store facts, concepts, and experiences after we stop thinking about them. All conscious processing of information, as in problem solving, for example, involves both short-term and long-term memory. As we repeat, rehearse, and recycle information, the memory trace is strengthened, allowing that information to move from short-term memory to long-term memory.

25%	The level of sophistication for human memory
40%	The memory trace
35%	Working memory

Although the summary below is actually closer to 25%, 35%, 40%, it still maintains a reasonably accurate emphasis.

Summary

Human memory is more highly developed than previously thought. Penfield's experiments prove that detailed memories can be recalled when the brain is stimulated electrically. Using the memory trace, a theoretical model, we can conjecture how facts are retrieved and used at a later time. Current thinking assumes that chemical bonds can be improved by repeated exposure to the same information. The concept of working memory includes both short-term memory, which includes recall for twenty or thirty seconds, and long-term memory, which stores facts and experiences more permanently. Information is transferred from short-term to long-term memory when the memory trace is reinforced.

PRACTICE ACTIVITY 13

1. Reading

Summary

Charles Ives started his musical career as a member of his father's band and received a degree from Yale University in music, but he became a businessman instead because he was afraid that his music would not be well accepted. His music was very different from the popular songs of his era because he used small phrases from well-known music with unusual rhythms and tones. Fifty years after he wrote his *Second Symphony*, it was performed by the New York Philharmonic, and he was awarded the Pulitzer Prize. I think that Charles Ives was wrong not to pursue his musical career from the beginning. If he had continued writing music instead of selling insurance, we would have more pieces now.

2. Lecture

Activity 13, Track 24
Listen to part of a lecture in a geology class.

A geyser is the result of underground water under the combined conditions of high temperatures and increased pressure beneath the surface of the Earth. Now, temperature rises about maybe 1 degree Fahrenheit for every 60 feet under the Earth's surface, and we know that pressure also increases with depth, water that seeps down in cracks and fissures, so when the water, . . . when the water reaches very hot rocks in the Earth's interior, it becomes heated to the temperature of, let's say, 290 degrees.

Okay, then, water under pressure can remain liquid at temperatures above the normal boiling point, but in a geyser, the weight of the water nearer the surface exerts so much pressure on the deeper water that the water at the bottom of the geyser reaches much higher temperatures than the water at the top. And as the deep water becomes hotter, and consequently lighter, it suddenly rises to the surface and shoots out of the ground in the form of steam and hot water. In turn, the explosion agitates all of the water in the geyser reservoir, and what do you think happens then? More explosions. So immediately afterward, the water goes back into the underground reservoir, it starts to heat up again, and the whole process repeats itself.

So, in order to function, then, a geyser must have a source of heat, a reservoir where water can be stored until the temperature rises to an unstable point, an opening through which the hot water and steam can escape, and underground channels for resupplying water after an eruption.

Now, favorable conditions for geysers exist in regions of geologically recent volcanic activity, especially in areas of more than average precipitation. For the most part, geysers are located in three regions of the world— New Zealand, Iceland, and the Yellowstone park area of the United States. I'd say that the most famous geyser in the world is Old Faithful in Yellowstone. It erupts every hour, rising to a height of 125 to 170 feet and expelling more than ten thousand gallons of hot water during each eruption. Old Faithful earned its name, because unlike most geysers, it has never failed to erupt on schedule even once in eighty years of observation.

Summary

In my opinion, geysers are interesting. They happen when underground water gets hot and pressure from above causes the water to get hotter and lighter so it goes up to the surface and explodes out. Then, the water runs back into the ground and starts all over again. Geysers have to have heat, a place to store water, an opening where the water can shoot up, and cracks in the ground for the water to go back down into a pool. Geysers are in New Zealand, Iceland, and the United States. Old Faithful in Yellowstone is the most famous geyser, but the best place to see geysers is in New Zealand. I saw the Pohutu Geyser there on my vacation two years ago, and it was awesome.

Practice Activity 14

1. Draw a chart with a relationship sentence at the top and three points underneath

2. Read a short passage and take notes on the chart

3. Listen to a conversation or a lecture on the same topic and take notes on the chart

4 Respond, using information from both the reading and
the conversation or lecture

5 Use the chart to check for a complete response

EXAMPLE SPEAKING TASK 3

🎧 **Activity 14, Track 25**
Now listen to a conversation on the same topic.

Woman: I know you think it's a hassle, but I'm really happy about the new security measures. You wouldn't believe the people who parade through our dorm in the middle of the night.

Man: And the scans will help that?

Woman: Maybe. At least we'll know who's there. And people who just walk in from who-knows-where will have to get guest passes.

Man: Don't they have to do that now?

Woman: Well, yes, but it isn't really enforced. And this looks like a serious plan.

Man: I'll give you that.

Woman: And for students—well, how long does it take to scan a fingerprint at the door?

Man: True.

Woman: It won't be any different from opening up your phone or tablet with your fingerprint.

Man: I hadn't thought about that. I guess it's just the time to go get your fingerprint scanned at the security office.

Woman: Look, back to the issue of phones and tablets. You want to keep those secure. Why wouldn't you want to keep students secure?

Man: That's a point.

Woman: It stands to reason that someone who wants to steal something or even hurt someone, well, maybe they'll think about it if they have to scan their prints or leave their ID at the desk. I know I'm going to feel better about living in the dorm.

Man: Okay. I'm convinced. It isn't such a big deal to go to the security office. I can just stop by there when I'm in the student union the next time. But . . . I hope there isn't a line a mile long.

Question
The woman expresses her opinion of the announcement. State her opinion and the reasons that she has for having that opinion.

Example Response

The woman approves of the new security policy because it's a serious plan, it will be easy to use, and it should be a deterrent to crime. She explains that the previous system that required a pass to enter the dorm wasn't enforced, but now, without a scan, it won't be possible to go in the door. She also points out that it's really easy, like scanning to access a secure mobile device. She argues that scanning a fingerprint will be a deterrent to theft and the dorms will be safer because it'll be better than a guest pass to keep track of everyone who's in the buildings.

EXAMPLE SPEAKING TASK 4

Activity 14, Track 26

Now listen to part of a lecture in a linguistics class. The professor is talking about endangered languages.

Today I want to give you an example of a language that, unfortunately, meets all the criteria to be considered an endangered language. Like many other Native American languages, Ojibwa, also known as Chippewa, is struggling to survive. A North American indigenous language of the Algonquian language family, Ojibwa has traditionally been spoken in Canada and along the Northern border of the United States. It was very important during the fur-trading era in the Great Lakes region—to such an extent, in fact, that French traders often used Ojibwa to speak with other tribes. But although the total ethnic population still includes more than 200 thousand people, and that number comes from self-identification—the people who claim Ojibwa tribal membership—well, of those 200 thousand, only about 30 thousand still speak Ojibwa on any level of proficiency. And the number of children in the youngest generation who are fluent in Ojibwa is almost non-existent.

In a study in 1995 of Ojibwa language usage in a three-state area consisting of Michigan, Wisconsin, and Minnesota, Rosemary Christensen was able to locate only 500 fluent Ojibwa speakers. Of those speakers, most were elders, over the age of 80, and none were under the age of 45. She found no children who were fluent in Ojibwa.

Partly in response to this study, and with funding from the Department of Health and Human Services, four preschools were opened in Minneapolis in 2006. In cooperation with the 100 remaining Ojibwa speakers in the area, immersion classrooms in Ojibwa began teaching young children in their ancestral language. Will it be too little too late? Only time will tell. As for now, Ojibwa remains on the endangered list, a language with an uncertain future.

Question

The professor reports a study of the Ojibwa language. Explain why the study confirms that Ojibwa is an endangered language.

Example Response

Ojibwa is considered an endangered language because it meets all three criteria for that classification. First, few speakers are fluent in the language. In Christensen's study in 1995, only about 500 of the tribal members in the tri-state area studied were fluent speakers. Second, the average age of native speakers is older. Among the 500 fluent speakers, most were elders 80 years of age or older. Finally, the percentage of speakers in the youngest generation is small. Among Ojibwa speakers, almost *no* children were fluent. Unfortunately, this study confirmed that Ojibwa is endangered, and despite efforts to teach the language in federally funded preschools, its future is very uncertain.

EXAMPLE WRITING TASK 1: INTEGRATED ESSAY

🎧 **Activity 14, Track 27**
Now listen to part of a lecture in an economics class. The professor is talking about home ownership.

The reading passage lists three reasons to own a home, but recent changes in the economy persuade us to reassess the assumptions.

First, we have to question whether owning a home is a sound investment in today's economy. Although it was once considered a strategy in the creation of wealth, it is now being reexamined. During recessions like the one recently experienced, the value of homes has dramatically fallen. So much so that many homeowners were paying a high mortgage for a home that was worth only half of its value at the time of the purchase. Whether owning a home that has depreciated in value so rapidly will be a sound investment long term—well, the verdict will have to wait for a decade to give us that kind of data. But short term, for many homeowners, the plan to create wealth is a disappointment.

The sharp increase in foreclosures and forced sales has also decreased the sense of security that homeowners once experienced. Struggling to pay a mortgage and a looming possibility that the property will be foreclosed leads to a loss of control and a sense of insecurity—the exact opposite of the anticipated stability that homeowners used to enjoy. A significant number of first-time owners report that they would prefer to rent but don't know how to reverse their situation without losing their initial investment.

As for the social benefits, the pressures associated with owning and maintaining a home are taking a toll on the psychological and physical health of homeowners. Many homeowners report that they're only one paycheck away from being unable to pay the costs of owning a home. The stress affects *all* of the family members, even the children, who seem to respond to the pressures by bringing home lower grades and by being less involved in school activities than was previously reported. So, as you see, times have changed.

Question

Summarize the main points in the lecture and then explain how they cast doubt on the ideas in the lecture.

Practice Activity 15

SPEAKING TASK 3

1. Draw a chart with a relationship sentence at the top and three points underneath.

Relationship sentence: The man is not happy about the relocation of the honors program to Harkins Hall because the other location in Andersen Hall was larger and had a better view.

Point 1	Harkins to Anderson	Point 1	inferior space—smaller, no view, dark
Point 2	Faculty Club	Point 2	uses lounge more
Point 3	Honors smaller suite	Point 3	honors program not important

2. Read a short passage about a campus-related topic and take notes on the chart.

3. Listen to a conversation on the same topic and take notes on the chart.

Activity 15, Track 28
Now listen to a conversation on the same topic.

Man: You're an honors student, aren't you?

Woman: Yes.

Man: So I guess you've been over to Harkins Hall.

Woman: Umhum. It's pretty grim. But they aren't done yet, so maybe it will be okay.

Man: Always the optimist. How can a basement be better than the top floor of Anderson Hall? That was really a nice place to hang out. The view was phenomenal.

Woman: It still is. It's just not our view anymore. That's why the faculty wanted it.

Man: Right.

Woman: But you spend more time there than I do so it doesn't matter so much to me. I just go over there when I need my advisor's signature for something. I haven't used the lounge that much.

Man: Well, since I live off campus, I'm there between classes and I even eat my lunch there sometimes. There's always a chess game going, and I'm friends with a lot of the regulars.

Woman: Then it's a big change for you.

Man: It *is*. And it bugs me that the new space is so inferior to what we had. I think they should have tried harder to find something better than a basement. It just communicates that the Honors Program isn't important.

Woman: Oh, I don't know about that. I feel lucky to be in smaller classes and to be able to take graduate courses while I'm still an undergrad, don't you?

Man: Sure. Of course I do. But the lounge is supposed to be our place to meet up with other honors students, and, besides, how do you think the advisors feel? Their offices are cramped and dark compared with the program offices that they had in Anderson.

Woman: Of course, they can always use the Faculty Club when they want to.

Man: Unlike us. Listen, are you always so upbeat? It seems like you just take everything in stride.

Woman: Pretty much. Especially when it's something I can't change anyway.

Question

The man expresses his opinion of the announcement. State this opinion and the reasons that he gives for having that opinion.

4 Respond, using information from both the reading and the conversation.

Example Response

The man isn't happy about the relocation of the Honors Program to Harkins Hall because the other location in Anderson Hall was larger and had a better view. He uses the lounge to hang out with friends and eat lunch because he lives off campus, and the new space isn't as nice. It's dark, small, and it doesn't have a view because it's in a basement. He feels that moving the Honors Program to an inferior space indicates that the program isn't very important to the college.

5 Use the chart to check for a complete response.

All three points in the chart are included in the response.

SPEAKING TASK 4

1 Draw a chart with a relationship sentence at the top and three points underneath.

Relationship sentence: Peacocks are a good example of animals that use courtship displays to compete with other males and attract a mate.

Point 1	ritualized dances	Point 1	strut and dance around female
Point 2	postures tail-feathers	Point 2	large fan w/ many eyespots
Point 3	vocalization	Point 3	mating calls— vibrations train 20 hertz

2 Read a short passage about an academic topic and take notes on the chart.

3 Listen to a lecture on the same topic and take notes on the chart.

🎧 **Activity 15, Track 29**
Now listen to a lecture in a biology class about the same topic.

Peacocks are large, colorful birds, known for their beautiful blue-green tail feathers, which they spread out in a distinctive fan. When extended, the fantail represents more than 60 percent of the peacock's total body weight. Arched into a magnificent train, it surrounds the bird's back and spreads out onto the ground on either side. Female birds choose their mates according to the size, color, and quality of the feathered trains. In addition to the blue-green feathers, colorful eye markings of red and gold and many other colors enhance the beauty of individual birds and form very different patterns from one bird to another.

Although the term *peacock* is commonly used to refer to both males and females, technically only the male is a peacock. The *peahens* watch the display in order to make a selection. In general, the more eyespots and the more evenly spaced their pattern, the more attractive a male peacock appears to the female. A large fan is also appealing; however, tails that are too big are considered too burdensome for mating. And as though the beautiful feathers and the graceful movements of the males were not enough, as they strut and perform an elaborate dance in front of their potential mates, well, these beautiful birds also communicate in very low-pitched mating calls that are produced by the vibrations of the feather train at a level of 20 hertz, far too low to be heard by the human ear, but just right for a peahen to notice.

Question
The professor discusses peacocks. Explain how their behavior conforms to the usual rituals for courtship displays.

4 Respond, using information from both the reading and the lecture.

Example Response

Peacocks are a good example of animals that use courtship displays to compete with other males and attract a mate. Like other birds, peacocks engage in ritualized dances, strutting gracefully around the female. In addition, they display their magnificent fan of blue-green tail feathers, posturing to show the eyespots and beautiful colors to advantage. They also use vocalizations, in this case, mating calls that are generated by vibrations when they shake their feathers.

5 Use the chart to check for a complete response.

All three points in the chart are included in the response.

WRITING TASK 1

1 Draw a chart with a relationship sentence at the top and three points underneath.

Relationship sentence: The lecturer refutes the idea that government censorship of the Internet should be instituted to protect children, curtail crime, and assure personal privacy.

Point 1 Protects children	Point 1	Parents, guardians monitor
Point 2 Curtails crime	Point 2	Personal responsibility better—passwords, firewalls, anti-virus, no attach, good judgment
Point 3 Assures personal privacy	Point 3	Laws not enforced—take care ourselves—separate email, don't disclose personal info social media

2 Read a short passage about an academic topic and take notes on the chart.

Reading Time: 3 minutes

> Government censorship of the Internet benefits society in three ways. First, like other forms of mass media, including television and movies, censorship protects children. Restricting adult content and providing punitive measures for pornographic websites discourages the exposure of young children to inappropriate images and explicit language. Since children are growing up in an environment in which they can easily access the Internet, some restrictions should be in place to protect them.
>
> Second, censorship curtails criminal activities. Censorship discovers and discourages financial frauds, theft, and harassment, or even potentially violent encounters. Because the Internet affords criminals a high degree of anonymity, unless their activities are monitored, they can sell illegal substances, threaten or bully individuals, or intrude into the lives of large numbers of people with spam advertising. Censorship reduces the instances of these disturbing contacts.
>
> Finally, censorship assures personal privacy. Censorship laws establish standards for websites and security measures to protect identity, financial records, and personal information. Censorship restricts access to credit cards and bank accounts, as well as medical and employment records, and it reduces the incidents of identity theft.

3 Listen to a lecture on the same topic and take notes on the chart.

🎧 **Activity 15, Track 30**
Now listen to a lecture about the same topic.

Although it may be true that government censorship has the potential to benefit society, realistically, it's just not possible to enforce. That aside, let's look at each of the advantages that are mentioned in the reading passage. Hardly anyone would disagree that children should be protected from pornography and other inappropriate websites. The issue is, *who* should protect them—the government or their parents? Software that installs parental controls is readily available and relatively cheap. My position is that responsible adults should monitor their children's Internet access. Even if censorship *does* restrict some viewing, it's still up to the parents or guardians to take care of their children.

Now, as for criminal activities, no one wants to deal with this, especially since the Internet intrudes into our workspaces and our homes. And censorship helps somewhat. But again, personal responsibility is a better deterrent. Everyone needs to choose and use strong passwords, install firewalls and antivirus software, avoid opening attachments from unidentified sources, and use good judgment when interacting with unfamiliar people or businesses—but, of course, that's true for face-to-face encounters and purchases as well. And we don't want the government to censor those, that's for sure.

So last, of course, we want to guard our identities and our personal and financial information. And censorship laws may establish standards. But, as I said in the beginning, the laws are very difficult, even impossible to enforce. So in the long run, it comes down to taking care of ourselves. How can we do that? Well, first we should establish a separate email account for Internet transactions—one that we can close down easily if we need to. In other words, we have a disposable identity in cyberspace. Second, never give out personal information like a social security number, credit card or bank account numbers unless *you* initiate the interaction. And this is important— don't divulge too much personal information on social media. If we want to protect ourselves even more, we have the option to subscribe to an identity theft plan.

The bottom line is this: To keep our children safe and to avoid being victims of crime or identity theft, we have to take personal responsibility. Censorship on the Internet isn't necessary, and it doesn't work.

Question
Summarize the main points in the lecture and then explain how they cast doubt on the ideas in the reading passage.

4 Respond, using information from both the reading and the lecture.

Example Essay
The lecturer refutes the idea that government censorship of the Internet should be instituted to protect children, curtail crime, and assure personal privacy. He contends that censorship cannot be enforced, and that, in any case, personal responsibility is better than censorship.

According to the lecturer, parents and guardians, not the government, should monitor their children's Internet use to protect them from inappropriate sites and images.

Moreover, users should assume individual responsibility to avoid becoming victims of crime. We can do this by using strong passwords and by installing firewalls and antivirus software, as well as by using good judgment about opening attachments and interacting with unfamiliar people and businesses online.

Furthermore, he claims that we should take care of our own identities by using email accounts that can be closed if they are breached by intrusive sources. Finally, he recommends that we not disclose too much personal information on social media.

In short, the lecturer is an advocate for personal responsibility instead of for government censorship.

5 *Use the chart to check for a complete response.*

All three points in the chart are included in the response.

EXPLANATORY OR EXAMPLE ANSWERS AND AUDIO SCRIPTS FOR MODEL TESTS

Model Test 1: PRETEST

➤ Reading

READING 1 "BEOWULF"

1. **C** ". . . *Beowulf* was written by an anonymous [author unknown] Englishman in Old English." Choice A is not correct because it is one of four surviving manuscripts. Choice B is not correct because it was written in old English about Germanic characters. Choice D is not correct because scholars do not know if it is the sole surviving epic from about A.D. 1000.

2. **B** In this passage, *principal* is a synonym for "major." Context comes from the contrast with "minor" in the same sentence.

3. **A** "Iron was accessible everywhere in Scandinavia, usually in the form of 'bog iron' found in the layers of peat in peat bogs." Choice B is not correct because the author had already stated that the best swords had iron or iron-edged blades. Choice C is not correct because the Celts taught the Northmen how to use the materials, but they did not provide the bog iron. Choice D is not correct because the bog iron does not relate to the date, although 500 B.C. is mentioned as the time when the Northmen learned how to forge iron.

4. **A** *Society in Anglo-Saxon England* paraphrases "Anglo-Saxon society." . . . *both advanced* paraphrases "neither primitive," and *cultured* paraphrases "nor uncultured." Two negatives [*nor* and *–un*] produce an affirmative meaning.

5. **B** In this passage, *rare* is a synonym for "unique." Context comes from the reference to the "sole surviving epic" in the beginning of the same sentence.

6. **B** ". . . the original manuscript was probably lost during the ninth century . . ., in which the Danes destroyed the Anglo-Saxon monasteries and their great libraries." Choice A is true but it is not the reason that scholars believe the original manuscript was lost. Choice C is not correct because the Danes were invaders, not poets. Choice

D is not correct because the location of the discovery is not mentioned, although the author may have been a monk.

7. **D** "Although the *Beowulf* manuscript was written in about A.D. 1000, it was not discovered until the seventeenth century." Choice A is not correct because the first century was the date the manuscript was written, not discovered. Choice B is not correct because the ninth century was the date when the original manuscript may have been lost. Choice C is not correct because some scholars think that the manuscript was written in the eleventh century.

8. **A** Because the word "apparently" means "appearing to be so," the author is expressing doubt about the information that follows, ". . . [the *Beowulf* poet] was a Christian." Choice B is not correct because the word "obviously" would be used. Choice C is not correct because the phrases "for example" or "for instance" would signal an example. Choice D is not correct because evidence would not be presented as "appearing to be so."

9. **A** ". . . Beowulf is a very appealing hero . . . Like Hercules." Choice B is not correct because a fight with a dragon is mentioned in reference to Beowulf but not to Hercules. Choice C is not correct because the Danish hero's welcome is the only reference to a speech, and it was jealous, not inspiring. Choice D is not correct because the time period for the life of Hercules is not mentioned.

10. **B** In this passage, *demonstrates* is a synonym for "exhibits."

11. **C** In this passage, *refuse* is a synonym for "reject." Context comes from the contrast with "accept" in the previous sentence.

12. **C** Addition is a transitional device that connects the insert sentence with the previous sentence. *Moreover* signals that additional, related information will follow. ". . . they [scholars] disagree" refers to "Scholars do not know" in the previous sentence.

13. **E, D, F** summarize the passage. Choice A is true, but it is a minor point that establishes the time period for the poem and refers to major point D. Choice B is true, but it is a detail that refers to major point E and explains why there may be only one manuscript. Choice C is not clear from the information in the passage.

READING 2 "THERMOREGULATION"

14. **A** "The most basic mechanism [for maintenance of warm body temperature] is the high metabolic rate." Choices B, C, and D are all ways to maintain body temperature, but they are not the most fundamental adaptation.

15. **D** "In some mammals, certain hormones can cause mitochondria to increase their metabolic activity and produce heat instead of ATP. This **nonshivering thermogenesis (NST)**. . . ." Choice A is not correct because thermogenesis is the activity that generates heat, not the heat loss. Choice B is not correct because brown fat is one example of a more generalized process. Choice C is not correct because thermogenesis is a response to the environment to maintain the health of the animal, not a process that maintains the environment.

16. **B** A passive grammatical structure in the passage is paraphrased by an active grammatical structure in the answer choice.

17. **D** In this passage, *smallest* is a synonym for "minimal."

18. **B** "For example, heat loss from a human is reduced when arms and legs cool." Choice A is not correct because goose bumps, not heat loss in the extremities, is a vestige of our evolution. Choice C is not correct because no direct comparisons of these processes are made in the paragraph. Choice D is not correct because the types of insulation are mentioned before the concept of vasodilatation and vasoconstriction are introduced.

19. **D** In this passage, *control* is a synonym for "regulate." Context comes from the reference to "temperature differences" at the end of the same sentence.

20. **B** "The loss of heat to water occurs 50 to 100 times more rapidly than heat loss to air." Choice A is not correct because hair loses insulating power when wet, but the evolution of marine animals is not mentioned. Choice C is not correct because dry hair insulates better than wet hair. Choice D is not correct because there are land animals that are of similar size.

21. **A** ". . . capable of astonishing feats of thermoregulation. For example, small birds called chickadees . . . hold body temperature nearly constant." Choice B is not correct because the food supply supports thermoregulation, which is the main point of the example. Choice C is not correct because chickadees are capable of astonishing feats of thermoregulation. Choice D is not correct because the reason for heat production in animals is explained before the example of the chickadee.

22. **D** In this passage, *adequate* is a synonym for "sufficient."

23. **D** Choice A is mentioned in paragraph 6, sentence 7. Choice B is mentioned in paragraph 6, sentence 8. Choice C is mentioned in paragraph 6, sentences 3 and 4.

24. **B** In this passage, *improve* is a synonym for "enhance." Context comes from the reference to "promote" in the previous sentence.

25. **A** Reference is a transitional device that connects the insert sentence with the previous sentence. ". . . a layer of fur or feathers" and "how much still air the layer [of fur or feathers] traps" in the insert sentence refers to ". . . fur or feathers" and "a thicker layer of air" in the previous sentence.

26. **E, C, F** summarize the passage. Choice A is a minor point that supports major point C. Choice B is true but it is not mentioned in the passage. Choice D is a minor point that supports major point F.

READING 3 "SOCIAL READJUSTMENT SCALES"

27. **D** "Overall, these studies have shown that people with higher scores on the SRRS tend to be more vulnerable to many kinds of physical illness." Choice A is not correct because a person with a higher score will experience more, not less, stress. Choice B is not correct because the numerical values for major problems are not identified, and a score of 30 does not have meaning unless it is compared with a higher or lower score. Choice C is not correct because the effects of positive or negative change are not mentioned in the first two paragraphs.

28. **C** In this passage, *results* is a synonym for "outcomes."

29. **D** In this passage, *different* is a synonym for "diverse."

30. **C** ". . . divorce may deserve a stress value of 73 for *most* people, a particular person's divorce might generate much less stress and merit a value of only 25." Choice A is not correct because a particular person is compared with most people. Choice B is not correct because the serious nature of divorce is not mentioned. Choice D is not correct because the numerical value of 73 for most people is questioned.

31. **A** ". . . what qualifies as 'trouble with the boss'? Should you check that because you're sick and tired of your supervisor? What constitutes a 'change in living conditions'? Does your purchase of a great new sound system qualify?" Choice B is not correct because the author does not offer examples of responses to the questions posed. Choice C is not correct because options for scores are not provided in paragraph 5. Choice D is not correct because the author suggests that people do not respond consistently but whether they respond carefully is not mentioned.

32. **B** ". . . subjects' neuroticism affects both their responses to stress scales and their self-reports of health problems." Choice A is not correct because they recall more symptoms, but they are not ill more often. Choice C is not correct because they recall more stress, but they do not necessarily suffer more actual stress. Choice D is not correct because the effects of neuroticism obscures the meaning of the scores that are recorded.

33. **C** In this passage, *arranged* is a synonym for "assembled."

34. **C** In this passage, *related* is a synonym for "relevant."

35. **B** ". . . dropping the normative weights and replacing them with personally assigned weightings." Choice A is not correct because long-term consequences are not included in positive, negative, and total change scores. Choice C is not correct because the differences in people reflect their appraisal of stress, not how they handle stress. Choice D is not correct because normative weighting is replaced by personally assigned weightings.

36. **C** In paragraph 1, the authors state that the SRRS ". . . assigns numerical values." Choices A and B are not correct because they are mentioned in paragraph 10 in reference to the LES, not the SRRS. Choice D is not correct because recalling events from one year ago is a problem on the SRRS.

37. **A** "The LES deals with the failure of the SRRS to sample the full domain of stressful events." Choice B is not correct because the author explains several ways that the LES deals with the failure of the SRRS. Choice C is not correct because it has been used in thousands of studies by researchers all over the world. Choice D is not correct because the LES, not the SRRS, has a special section for students.

38. **B** Reference is a transitional device that connects the insert sentence with the previous sentence. "This sum" in the insert sentence refers to the phrase "adds up the numbers" in the previous sentence.

39. **A, B, C** summarize the passage. Choice D is true but it is not mentioned in the passage. Choice E is a minor point that supports major point B. Choice F is a minor point that supports major point A.

➤ Listening

🎧 **Model Test 1, Listening Section, Track 31**

LISTENING 1 "LEARNING CENTER"

Audio Conversation

Narrator:	Listen to a conversation on campus between two students.
Man:	Hi. Are you Paula?
Woman:	Jim?
Man:	Hi. Nice to meet you.
Woman:	Glad to meet you.
Man:	So, you need some tutoring in English?
Woman:	Yeah. I'm taking English composition, and I'm not doing very well on my essays.
Man:	Right. Um, well, first let's see if we can figure out a time to meet . . . that we're both free.
Woman:	Okay.
Man:	How about Mondays? Maybe in the morning? I don't have any classes until eleven on Mondays.
Woman:	That would work, but I was hoping we could, you know, meet more than once a week.
Man:	Oh. Well, Tuesdays are out. I've got classes and I work at the library part time on Tuesdays and Thursdays. But I could get together on Wednesdays.
Woman:	In the morning?
Man:	Probably nine-thirty would be best. That way we'd have an hour to work before I'd have to get ready for my eleven o'clock.
Woman:	So that would be two hours a week then?
Man:	I could do that.
Woman:	Oh, but, would that be extra? You know, would I need to pay you for the extra session?
Man:	No. Just so you meet me here at the Learning Center, and we both sign in, then I'll get paid. Tutoring is free, to you, I mean. The school pays me. But we both have to show up. If you don't show up and sign in for a session, then I don't get paid. So . . .
Woman:	Oh, don't worry about that. I really need the help. I won't miss any sessions unless I'm sick or something.
Man:	Okay then. So you want me to help you with your essays?

Q1

Q2

Q3

Woman:	Right. I could bring you some that have, you know, comments on them. I'm getting C's and . . .
Man:	Well, that's not too bad. Once I see some of your writing, we should be able to pull that up to a B.
Woman:	You think so?
Q4 Man:	Sure. But I need to explain something. Some of my students in the past . . . they expected me to write their essays for them. But that's not what a tutor is supposed to do. My job is to help you be a better writer.
Woman:	Oh, I understand that. But you'll read my essays, right?
Man:	Oh yeah. No problem. We'll read them together, and I'll make suggestions.
Woman:	Great. I think part of the problem is I just don't understand the teacher's comments. Maybe you can help me figure them out.
Man:	Sure. Who's the teacher?
Woman:	Simpson.
Q5 Man:	No problem. I've tutored a couple of her students, so I know more or less where she's coming from. Okay, then. I guess we'll meet here on Monday.
Woman:	I'll be here. Nine-thirty you said.
Man:	Just sign in when you get here.

Audio	1.	What does the woman need?
Answer	**C**	An appointment for tutoring
Audio	2.	Listen again to part of the conversation and then answer the following question.
Replay		"Oh, but, would that be extra? You know, would I need to pay you for the extra session?"
Audio		Why does the woman say this:
Replay		"Oh, but would that be extra?"
Answer	**A**	Her tone indicates that she is worried.
Audio	3.	Why is the man concerned about the woman's attendance?
Answer	**B**	He will not get a paycheck if she is absent.
Audio	4.	What does the man agree to do?
Answer	**D**	He will show the woman how to improve her writing.
Audio	5.	What does the man imply about the woman's teacher?
Answer	**D**	". . . know . . . where she's coming from" means "to understand her."

LISTENING 2 "GEOLOGY CLASS"

Audio Lecture
Narrator: Listen to part of a lecture in a geology class.

Professor:
Okay, today we're going to discuss the four major types of drainage pat- Q6
terns. I trust you've already read the chapter so you'll recall that a drainage Q7
pattern is the arrangement of channels that carry water in an area. And
these patterns can be very distinctive since they're determined by the climate, the topography, and the composition of the rock that underlies the
formations. So, consequently, we can see that a drainage pattern is really
a good visual summary of the characteristics of a particular region, both
geologically and climatically. In other words, when we look at drainage patterns, we can draw conclusions about the structural formation and relief of
the land as well as the climate.

Now all drainage systems are composed of an interconnected network
of streams, and, when we view them together, they form distinctive patterns. Although there are at least seven identifiable kinds of drainage patterns, for our purposes, we're going to limit our study to the four major
types. Probably the most familiar pattern is the dendritic drainage pattern.

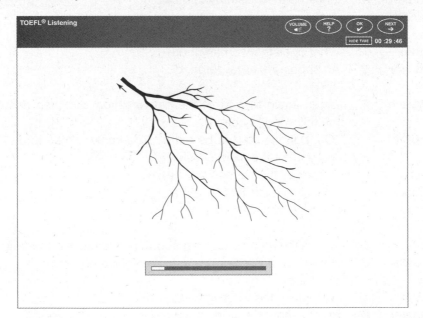

TOEFL® Listening
VOLUME   HELP   OK   NEXT
?
HIDE TIME   00 :29 :46

Q8 This is a stream that looks like the branches of a tree. Here's an example of a dendritic pattern. As you can see, it's similar to many systems in nature. In addition to the structure of a tree, it also resembles the human circulation system. This is a very efficient drainage system because the overall length of any one branch is fairly short, and there are many branches, so that allows the water to flow quickly and efficiently from the source or sources.

Okay, let's look at the next example.

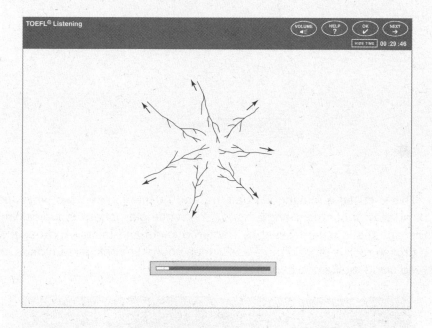

This drainage pattern is referred to as a radial pattern. Notice how the
Q9 streams flow from a central point. This is usually a high mountain, or a volcano. It kind of looks like the spokes that radiate out from the hub of a wheel. When we see a radial pattern, we know that the area has experienced uplift and that the direction of the drainage is down the slopes of a relatively isolated central point.

Going back to the dendritic for a moment. The pattern is determined by the direction of the slope of the land, but it, uh, . . . the streams flow in more or less the same direction and so it's unlike the radial that had multiple directions of flow from the highest point.

Now this pattern is very different from either the dendritic or the radial.

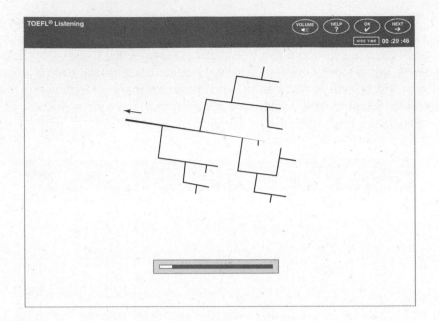

This is called a rectangular pattern, and I think you can see why. Just look at all of those right-angle turns. The rectangle pattern is typical of a landscape that's been formed by fractured joints and faults. And because this broken rock is eroded more easily than unbroken rock, stream beds are carved along the jointed bedrock.

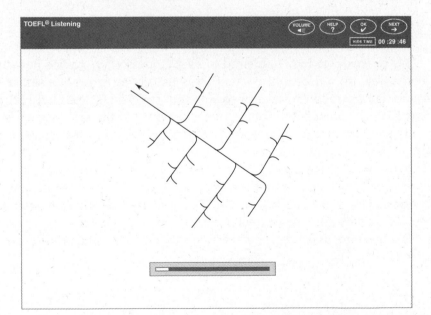

Finally we have the trellis pattern. And here in this example, you can see quite clearly how the tributaries of an almost parallel structure drain into valleys and form the appearance of a garden trellis. This pattern forms in areas where there are alternating bands of variable resistance, and by that I mean

Q10 that the bands of rock that are very strong and resistant to erosion alternate with bands of rock that are weak and easily eroded. This often happens when a horizontal plain folds and outcroppings appear.

So, as I said, as a whole, these patterns are dictated by the structure and relief of the land. The kinds of rocks on which the streams are developed, the structural pattern of the folds, uh, faults, and . . . uplift will usually determine a drainage system. However, I should also mention that drainage patterns can occasionally appear to be, well, out of sync with the landscape. And this can happen when a stream flows over older structures that have been uncovered by erosion or when a stream keeps its original drainage system when rocks are uplifted. So when that happens, the pat-

Q11 tern appears to be contrary to the expected course of the stream. But I'm interested in your understanding the basic drainage systems. So I don't plan to trick you with test questions about exceptional patterns, but I expect you to know that exceptions to the patterns can occur when geological events influence them.

Audio	6.	What is this lecture mainly about?
Answer	**B**	A comparison of different types of drainage systems
Audio	7.	Listen again to part of the lecture and then answer the following question.
Replay		"Okay, today we're going to discuss the four major types of drainage patterns. I trust you've already read the chapter so you'll recall that a drainage pattern is the arrangement of channels that carry water in an area."
Audio		Why does the professor say this:
Replay		"I trust you've already read the chapter so you'll recall that a drainage pattern is the arrangement of channels that carry water in an area."
Answer	**B**	"I trust you" means "I expect you to."
Audio	8.	How does the professor introduce the dendritic drainage system?
Answer	**B**	By comparing it to both a tree and the human circulatory system

Audio   9.   Why does the professor mention the spokes of a wheel?
Answer **C**   To explain the structure of a radial drainage system

Audio   10.   In the lecture, the professor discusses the trellis drainage pattern. Indicate whether each of the following is typical of this pattern. Click in the correct box for each phrase.

Answer   **A, D, E:** YES   **B** refers to the rectangular pattern, and **C** refers to the dendritic.

Audio   11.   What does the professor imply when he says this:
Replay   "So I don't plan to trick you with test questions about exceptional patterns."

Answer   **C**   The basic patterns from the notes will be on the test. Professors who "trick" students ask questions that have not been discussed in class.

LISTENING 3 "PSYCHOLOGY CLASS"

Audio Discussion
Narrator: Listen to part of a discussion in a psychology class. The professor is discussing defense mechanisms.

Professor:
Okay, we know from our earlier study of Freud that defense mechanisms Q12
protect us from bringing painful thoughts or feelings to the surface of
our consciousness. We do this because our minds simply can't tolerate
these thoughts. So, defense mechanisms help us to express these painful thoughts or feelings in another way, while we repress the real problem.
The function of defense mechanisms is to keep from being overwhelmed.
Of course, the avoidance of problems can result in additional emotional
issues. And there's a huge distinction between repression and suppression.
Anybody want to explain the difference?

Student 1:
I'll try it. I think repression is an unconscious response to serious events Q13
or images but suppression is more conscious and deals with something
unpleasant but not usually, well, terrible experiences.

Professor:
I couldn't have said it better. Now remember that the thoughts or feelings that we're trying to *repress* may include, just to mention a few, anger, depression, competition, fear, envy, hate, and so on. For instance, let's

suppose that you're very angry with your professor. Not me, of course. I'm referring to another professor. So, you're very angry because he's treated you unfairly in some way that . . . that could cause you to lose your scholarship. Maybe he failed you on an examination that didn't really cover the material that he'd gone over in class, and an F grade in the course is going to be unacceptable to your sponsors. So, this would be very painful, as I'm sure you'd agree. And I'd say it would qualify as a serious event.

So let's take a look at several different types of defense mechanisms that you might employ to repress the feelings of disappointment, rage perhaps, and . . . and even violence that you'd feel toward the professor. Most of them are named so the mechanism is fairly obvious and one of the most common mechanisms is *denial*, which is . . .

Student 2:   If I want to deny something, I'll just say I'm not angry with the professor.

Professor:
Exactly. You may even extend the denial to include the sponsors, and you could tell your friends that they'd never revoke your scholarship. And this mechanism would allow you to deny the problem, even in the face of direct evidence to the contrary. Let's say, a letter from the sponsor indicating that you won't receive a scholarship for the next term. . . . Okay on that one? Okay. How about *rationalization*?

Student 2:   Well, in rationalization, you come up with some reasons *why* the professor might have given an unfair test.

Professor: And how would you do that?

Student 2:   Well, you might defend him. You could say that he gave the test to encourage students to learn information on their own. Is that what you mean?

Professor:
Sure. Because you'd be rationalizing . . . providing a reason that justifies an otherwise mentally intolerable situation. Okay, another example of rationalizing is to excuse the sponsor for refusing to hear your side of the situation. You might say that sponsors are too busy to investigate why students are having problems in their classes. And you might do that while you deny your true feelings that sponsors really should be more open to hearing you out.

Student 3:   So when you deny something, I mean when you use denial, you're refusing to acknowledge a situation, but . . . when you use rationalization, you're excusing the behavior?

Professor:
Excellent summary. So, now let me give you another option. If you use a *reaction formation* as a defense mechanism, you'll proclaim the *opposite* of your feelings. In this case, what would you say about the professor?

Student 4:   I'd say that I like the professor when, in fact, I hate him for depriving me of my opportunity.

Professor:
And you might insist that you have no hard feelings and even go so far as to tell your friends that he's an excellent teacher. You see, a reaction formation turns the expression of your feelings into the opposite reaction, that is, on the surface.
    And that brings us to *projection*, which is a defense mechanism that tricks your mind into believing that someone else is guilty of the negative thought or feeling that *you* have.

Student 1:   Can you give us an example of that one?

Professor:
Okay. Feelings of hate for the professor might be expressed by telling class-mates about *another* student who hates the professor, or, uh, . . . or even suggesting that the professor has strong feelings of hate for *you* but you really like the professor yourself. So you would project, um, . . . attribute your feelings . . . to someone else. Get it?

Student 1:   So if I hate someone, I'd believe that another person hates him or that he hates me.

Professor: But you wouldn't admit that *you* hate him yourself.

Student 1:   Okay. That's projection.

Professor:
Now *displacement* serves as a defense mechanism when a less threatening person or object is substituted for the person or object that's really the cause of your anxiety. So, instead of confronting the professor about the unfair test, well, you might direct your anger toward the friend who studied for the test [Q15]

with you, and you could blame him for wasting your time on the material that was in the book and notes.

Of course, there are several other defense mechanisms like *fantasy*, which includes daydreaming or watching television maybe to escape the problems at school. Or *regression,* which includes immature behaviors that are no longer appropriate, like maybe expressing temper in the same way that a preschooler might respond to having a toy snatched away. And your textbook contains a few more that we haven't touched on in class.

Just one more thing, it's good to understand that the notion of unconscious thoughts and the mechanisms that allow us to manage them, that this is a concept that goes in and out of fashion. Many psychologists rejected defense mechanisms altogether during the 70s and 80s, and then in the **Q16** 90s, cognitive psychologists showed a renewed interest in research in this area. But I must warn you, that although they found similar responses, they tended to give them different names. For instance, *denial* might appear in a more recent study as *positive illusion*, or *scapegoating* might be referred to instead of *displacement*. But when you get right down to it, the same categories of behavior for defense mechanisms still exist in the research even if they're labeled differently. And, uh, in my view, if you compare Freud's traditional defense mechanisms with those that are being presented by more modern researchers, you'll find that Freud is easier to understand and gives us a broader perspective. And, if you understand Freud's categories, well, you'll certainly be able to get a handle on the newer terms. What is exciting about the modern studies is the focus on coping skills and what's being referred to as healthy defenses. So next time, we'll take a look at some of these processes.

Audio	12.	What is the discussion mainly about?
Answer	**C**	Some of the more common types of defense mechanisms
Audio	13.	How does the student explain the term *repression*?
Answer	**A**	He contrasts it with suppression.
Audio	14.	Listen again to part of the discussion and then answer the following question.
Replay		"For instance, let's suppose that you're very angry with your professor. Not me, of course. I'm referring to another professor. So, you're very angry because he's treated you unfairly in some way that . . . that could cause you to lose your scholarship."
Audio		Why does the professor say this:
Replay		"Not me, of course. I'm referring to another professor."
Answer	**B**	The professor's tone is not serious. She is joking.

Audio 15. Which of the following is an example of *displacement* that was used in the discussion?

Answer C Blaming someone in your study group instead of blaming the professor

Audio 16. According to the professor, what happened in the 1990s?

Answer B New terms were introduced for the same mechanisms.

Audio 17. How does the professor organize the discussion?

Answer B She uses a scenario that students can relate to. She talks about the way that a student might respond to a professor by using defense mechanisms.

LISTENING 4 "PROFESSOR'S OFFICE"

Audio Conversation

Narrator: Listen to a conversation on campus between a student and a professor.

Student: Thanks for seeing me, Professor Williams.

Professor: Glad to, Alice. What do you have on your mind?

Student: Well, I got a little mixed up when I started to go over my notes from the last class, so I had a few questions. [Q18]

Professor: Shoot.

Student: Okay. I understand the three basic sources of personnel for multinational companies. That's fairly self-explanatory.

Professor: Host country, home country, and third country.

Student: Right. But then you started talking about staffing patterns that . . . let me see . . . okay . . . you said, "staffing patterns may vary depending on the length of time that the multinational company has been operating," and you gave some examples, but I got confused and now I can't read my notes. [Q19]

Professor: Okay. Well, one pattern is to rely on home country managers to staff the key positions when the company opens, but gradually moving more host country nationals into upper management as the company grows.

Student: So, for example, if a French company opened a factory in Canada, then French management would gradually replace themselves with Canadian managers. Is that what you mean?

Professor: Right. I think I used that very example in class. So do you want to try to explain the second pattern to me?

Student:	Sure. I think it's the one where home country nationals are put in charge of the company if it's located in a developed country, but in a developing country, then home country nationals manage the company sort of indefinitely.
Q20 Professor:	Right again. And an example of that would be . . .
Student:	. . . maybe using German management for a Swiss company in Germany, but, uh, they might send Swiss management to provide leadership for a Swiss company in . . . in . . .
Professor:	How about Zimbabwe?
Student:	This is one of the confusing parts. Zimbabwe has a very old and highly developed culture, so...
Professor:	. . . but it's still defined as a developing country because of the economic base—which is being developed now.
Q21 Student:	Oh, okay. I guess that makes sense. Then the example of the American company with British management . . . when the company is in India . . . that would be a third-country pattern?
Professor:	Yes. In fact, this pattern is fairly prevalent among multinational companies in the United States. Many Scottish or English managers have been hired for top management positions at United States subsidiaries in the former British colonies—India, Jamaica, the West Indies, some parts of Africa . . .
Student:	Okay. So I've got all the examples right now.
Professor:	Anything else?
Student:	Just one thing. There were some typical patterns for certain countries.
Professor:	Like the last example.
Student:	No. This came later in the lecture. Something about Japan and Europe?
Q22 Professor:	Oh. Right. I probably said that both Japanese multinational companies and European companies tend to assign senior-level home country managers to overseas locations for their entire careers, whereas multinational companies in the United States view overseas assignments as temporary, so they may actually find themselves reporting to a senior-level manager from the host country who has more experience.
Student:	So, for example, a Japanese company in the United States would most probably have senior-level Japanese managers with mid-level managers maybe from the United States. But in Japan, the senior-level Japanese managers at an

	American company would probably have mid-level American managers reporting to them.
Professor:	Well, generalities are always a little tricky, but for the most part, that would be a typical scenario. Because living as a permanent expatriate is a career move in Japan, but a temporary strategy in the United States.
Student:	Okay. That's interesting.
Professor:	And important for you to know as a business major with an interest in international business. You're still on that track, aren't you?
Student:	I sure am. But, you know, I wasn't thinking in terms of living abroad for my entire career. That really is a huge commitment, and something to ask about going in. Anyway, like you say, most American companies view overseas assignments as temporary. That's more what I have in mind, for myself, I mean.

Audio	18.	Why does the woman go to see her professor?
Answer	**B**	To clarify some of the information from a lecture
Audio	19.	According to the professor, which factor causes staffing patterns to vary?
Answer	**D**	The number of years that a company has been in business
Audio	20.	Listen again to part of the conversation and then answer the following question.
Replay		"I think it's the one where home country nationals are put in charge of the company if it's located in a developed country, but in a developing country, then home country nationals manage the company sort of indefinitely."
		"Right again. And an example of that would be . . . "
Audio		Why does the professor say this:
Replay		"And an example of that would be . . . "
Answer	**B**	Sometimes professors begin a statement and pause to allow the student to continue.
Audio	21.	Which of the following would be an example of a third-country pattern?
Answer	**A**	A Scottish manager in an American company in Africa
	C	A British manager in an American company in India

Audio   22.   According to the professor, how do senior-level Japanese managers view their assignments abroad?

Answer   **A**   They consider them to be permanent career opportunities.

LISTENING 5 "ART CLASS"

Audio Lecture

Narrator: Listen to part of a lecture in an art class. The professor is discussing drawing.

Professor:

Drawing is a very basic art form. It's appealing because it can be used to make a very quick record of the ideas that an artist may be envisioning, so, a drawing can serve as a visual aid for the artist to remember a certain moment of inspiration and maybe use it for a more detailed work later on. Okay, usually such sketches allow the artist to visualize the proportions and the shapes without much attention to details so these images can be used by painters, architects, sculptors—any artist really. And large renderings, sketches of parts of the whole . . . these can be helpful in the creative process when a huge image might be more difficult to conceive of in its entirety. Or, a sketch of just one face in a crowd can allow the artist to focus on creating just that part of the image. So, in many artists' studios, countless drawings are strewn about as the final painting or sculpture takes form. And this gives us insight into the creative process, as well as the opportunity to see changes from the images at the beginning in the images of the finished work. It's rare, in fact, for an artist to use permanent materials to begin a piece of art. And some painters, for example, even sketch onto the surface of the canvas before applying the pigments. Now, architects are especially prone

Q24   to sketches because, of course, their buildings are so large that an image in smaller scale is necessary to the imagination and implementation of such

Q25   projects. So these studies become the basis for future works. And again, this is very interesting as a record of the creative process. Okay so far?

Q23   Okay, drawing has several other functions besides as a temporary reference. For centuries, artists have used drawing as a traditional method of education. By copying the great works, especially of the Old Masters, aspiring artists could learn a lot about proportion, how to capture light and shadow and . . . and so forth. In fact, some artists who later achieve recognition, still continue to use this practice to hone their skills or simply to pay homage to another artist, as is often the case when a work of art originally created in another medium like a sculpture . . . when it's recreated in the form of a drawing. Many examples of drawings of Michelangelo's sculptures were re-created by well-known artists. One that comes to mind is the *Study of Michelangelo's Bound Slave* by Edgar Degas. The original by Michelangelo was a marble sculpture that was, oh, about seven feet in height, but the small drawing was made in a sketchpad. In any case, the study is also considered a masterpiece, on a small scale, of course.

So . . . what additional purposes might be served by the medium of drawing? [Q23] Well, let's remember that photography is a relatively new art form, so prior to the use of photographs to record historical events, a quick drawing by an artist was about the only way to preserve a real-time visual account of an important moment. Although a more permanent visual impression might be rendered later, it would be based on memory and not on the artist's actual observation. Probably the most often cited example of a sketch [Q26] that preserved an historical record would be the small drawing of Marie Antoinette as she was taken to the guillotine in a cart through the streets of Paris. Jacques-Louis David sketched this famous drawing on a piece of paper about the size of the palm of his hand. And the artist, the artist as reporter, is still important even in modern times, when photography isn't possible, for example, when judges won't permit cameras in the courtroom.

Okay, to review, we've talked about three functions for drawing—as a [Q28] visual aid for the artist to complete a future work, as a method of education for aspiring artists or even practiced artists, and a way to report an event. But the sketchbook has . . . other possibilities. Sometimes a drawing is the final execution of the art. Picasso produced hundreds of drawings in, well, every conceivable medium, but especially in pencil and crayon. I find it very interesting that Picasso did so much of this kind of work . . . drawing, I mean, in his last years. Some critics have argued that he was just laughing at the art world, which was willing to pay outrageous sums for anything with his name on it, and clearly, a drawing can be executed in a short period of time. But others, other critics, they feel as I do that Picasso was drawing because it was so basic, and because it was so spontaneous, and so much [Q27] fun. And also, think about how difficult it really is to produce a quick drawing with a few lines and no opportunity to . . . to recreate the original, either by painting it out or remodeling the clay or changing the building materials or any of the other methods for revision of a finished artistic work that artists have at their disposal. So, what I'm saying is that drawing when it's elevated to a finished piece, it must be done with confidence and it must show a high degree of creativity and mastery of the art form. In a way, it harkens back to the beginnings of art itself, when some unknown artist must have stuck a finger in the earth to draw an image or . . . maybe he picked up a stone and made a drawing on the wall of a cave.

Okay, so, as a first assignment, I want you to make a couple of sketches yourself. I'm not going to grade them. This isn't a studio art class. I just want you to use a few basic strokes to capture an image. You can do the first one in pencil, crayon, ink, chalk, or even charcoal . . . whatever you like. Then, I want you to sketch the same image in a different medium. So, if you do a face in pencil, I want you to do the same face but in chalk or crayon. Bring them to class next week and we'll continue our discussion of drawing, but we'll talk more about the materials artists use to produce drawings, and we'll refer to your sketches as examples.

Audio   23.   What is the lecture mainly about?
Answer   C   The distinct purposes of drawing

Audio   24.   According to the professor, why do architects use sketches?
Answer   B   To design large buildings, architects must work in a smaller scale.

Audio   25.   Listen again to part of the lecture and then answer the following question.
Replay   "So these studies become the basis for future works. And again, this is very interesting as a record of the creative process. Okay so far?"
Audio   What does the professor mean when she says this:
Replay   "Okay so far?"
Answer   A   Professors sometimes pause for a comprehension check by asking if everything is okay. This gives students an opportunity to answer questions.

Audio   26.   Why does the professor mention the drawing of Marie Antoinette?
Answer   C   The sketch was an historical account of an important event.

Audio   27.   What is the professor's opinion of Picasso?
Answer   C   Picasso's drawings required the confidence and skill of a master artist.

Audio   28.   According to the lecture, what are the major functions of drawing?
Answer   A   A technique to remember parts of a large work
    B   A method to preserve an historical record
    D   An educational approach to train artists

LISTENING 6 "ASTRONOMY CLASS"

Audio Discussion

Narrator: Listen to part of a discussion in an astronomy class. The professor is talking about the solar system.

Professor:

Okay, let's get started. Um, as you know, today I promised to take you on a walk through the solar system, so let's start here with the central object of our solar system—the Sun. As you can see, the Sun is about five inches in diameter and that's about the size of a large grapefruit, which is exactly what I've used to represent it here in our model. So, I'm going to take two steps and that will bring me to the planet closest to the Sun. That would be Mercury. Two more steps to Venus. And one step from Venus to Earth. Let's continue walking three steps from Earth to Mars. And that's as far as I can go here in the classroom, but we can visualize the rest of the journey. Don't | Q30 bother writing this down. Just stay with me on this. So, to go from Mars to Jupiter, we'd have to walk a little over half the length of a football field, so that would put us about at the library here on campus, and then to get from Jupiter to Saturn, we'd have to walk another 75 yards, so by then we'd be at Harmon Hall. From Saturn to Uranus, we'd have to walk again as far as we'd gone in our journey from the Sun to Saturn, and so we'd probably be at the Student Union. From Uranus to Neptune we'd have to walk the same distance again, which would take us all the way to the graduate dormitory towers. From Neptune to Pluto, another 125 yards. So, we'd end up about one third of a mile from this classroom at the entrance to the campus.

Okay. That's interesting, but now I want you to think about the orbits of the planets in those locations. Clearly, the first four planets could orbit fairly comfortably in this room, but to include the others, we'd have to occupy an area of more than six-tenths of a mile, which is all the way from College Avenue to Campus Drive. Remember that for this scale, the Sun is five inches, and most of the planets are smaller than the lead on a sharpened pencil. Okay, with that in mind, I want you to think about space. Sure, there are some moons around a few planets, and a scattering of asteroids and comets, but really, there isn't a lot out there in such a vast area. It's, well, it's pretty empty. And that's what I really want to demonstrate with this exercise.

Now, it would really be even more impressive if you could actually make that walk, and actually you can, if you visit Washington, D.C., where a scale model is set up on the National Mall, starting at the National Air and Space | Q34 Museum and ending up at the Arts and Industries Museum. I did that a couple of years ago, and it was, well amazing. Even though I knew the distances intellectually, there is nothing like the experience. Has anybody else done that walk?

Student 1:
I have. And you're right. It's an eye-opener. It took me about twenty minutes to go from the Sun to Pluto because I stopped to read the information at each planet, but when I made the return trip, it was about ten minutes.

Q34 | Professor: Did you take pictures?

Student 1:   I didn't. But, you know, I don't think it would have captured it anyway.

Professor:
Q31 | I think you're right. What impressed me about doing it was to see what was not there. I mean, how much space was between the bodies in the solar system. And a photograph wouldn't have shown that.

So back to our model. Here's another thought for you. The scale for our model is 1 to 10 billion. Now, let's suppose that we want to go to the nearest star system, the neighbor to our solar system. That would be the Alpha Centauri system, which is a little less than four and a half light years away. Okay. Let's walk it on our model. Here we are on the East Coast of the United States. So if we want to make it all the way to Alpha Centauri, we have to hike all the way to the West Coast, roughly a distance of 2,700 miles. And that's just the closest one. To make a model of the Milky Way Galaxy would require a completely different scale because . . . because the surface of the Earth wouldn't be large enough to accommodate a model at the scale of 1 to 10 billion.

Now, let's stop here for a minute because I just want to be sure that Q32 | we're all together on the terms *solar system* and *galaxy*. Remember that our solar system is a single star, the Sun, with various bodies orbiting around it—nine planets and their moons, and asteroids, comets, meteors. But the galaxy has a lot of star systems—probably 100 billion of them. Okay? This is important because you can be off by almost 100 billion if you get confused by these terms. Not a good idea.

Okay, then, even if we could figure out a different scale that would let us make a model of the Milky Way Galaxy, even then, it would be challenging to make 100 billion stars, which is what you'd have to do to complete the model. How many would that be exactly? Well, just try to count all the grains of sand on all the beaches on Earth. That would be about 100 billion. But of course, you couldn't even count them in your lifetime, could you? If you'd started counting in 1000 B.C.E. you'd be finishing just about now, with the counting, I mean. But of course, that assumes that you wouldn't sleep or take any breaks.

So, what am I hoping for from this lecture? What do you think I want you to remember? Q33

Student 2:   Well, for one thing, the enormous distances . . .   Q29

Student 3:   . . . and the vast emptiness in space.

Professor:
That's good. I hope that you'll also begin to appreciate the fact that the Earth isn't the center of the universe. Our planet, although it's very beautiful and unique, it's still just one planet, orbiting around just one star in just one galaxy.

Audio   29.   What is the discussion mainly about?
Answer **C**   The vast expanse of the universe around us.

Audio   30.   Why does the professor say this:
Replay   "Don't bother writing this down. Just stay with me on this."
Answer **B**   Sometimes a professor will tell students to stop taking notes, which usually means that the information is not a main point or, in this case, the professor wants the students to concentrate on listening.

Audio   31.   Why wouldn't a photograph capture a true picture of the solar system walk?
Answer **A**   It would not show the distances between the bodies in space.

Audio   32.   How does the professor explain the term *solar system*?
Answer **D**   He contrasts a solar system with a galaxy.

Audio   33.   Listen again to part of the discussion and then answer the following question.
Replay   "So, what am I hoping for from this lecture? What do you think I want you to remember?"
"Well, for one thing, the enormous distances . . . "
". . . and the vast emptiness in space."
"That's good. I hope that you'll also begin to appreciate the fact that the Earth isn't the center of the universe."
Audio   Why does the professor say this:

Replay	"So, what am I hoping for from this lecture? What do you think I want you to remember?"
Answer C	When professors ask their students to think about what they might want them to remember, this usually signals the beginning of a summary of the important points.

Audio	34.	What can be inferred about the professor?
Answer	**B**	The professor likes his students to participate in the discussion. He asks questions.

LISTENING 7 "BOOKSTORE"

Audio Conversation

Narrator:	Listen to part of a conversation in the bookstore.
Student:	Excuse me. I'm looking for someone who can help me with the textbook reservation program.
Manager:	Oh, well, I can do that. What do you need?
Student:	Okay. Um, my friend told me that I could get used books if I order, I mean, preorder them now.
Manager:	That's right. Do you want to do that?
Student:	I think so, but I'm not sure how it works.
Manager:	Actually, it's fairly straightforward. We have a short form for you to fill out. Do you know what you're going to take next semester?
Student:	Yeah, I do.
Manager:	And you have the course names and the schedule numbers for all your classes?
Student:	Unhuh.
Manager:	Okay, then, just put that information down on the form and, uh, make a checkmark in the box if you want recommended books as well as required books. And you said you were interested in used books, right?
Student:	Right.
Manager:	So mark the box for used books, sign the form and bring it back to me.
Student:	Do I have to pay now? Or, do you want a deposit?
Manager:	No, you can pay when you pick up the books.
Student:	And when can I do that?
Manager:	The week before classes begin.
Student:	That's good, but, um, what if I change my schedule? I mean, I don't plan to but . . .

Q35 appears beside the Student line "I think so, but I'm not sure how it works."

Manager:	. . . it happens. Don't worry. If you change classes, you can just bring the books back any time two weeks from the first day of class to get a full refund. Of course, you'll need the original cash register receipt and a photo ID and, if it's a new book, you can't have any marks in it. But you said you wanted used books, so it won't matter. Q36
Student:	Yeah, that's the main reason why I want to do this—because I'll have a better chance to get used books.
Manager:	If there are used books available and you marked the form, that's what we'll pull for you.
Student:	Okay, thanks a lot. I'll just fill this out and bring it back to you later today. I don't have all the numbers with me, the section numbers for the classes.
Manager:	Fine. We need those numbers because when different professors are teaching the same class, they don't always order the same books.
Student:	Right. So, will you be here this afternoon?
Manager:	I probably will, but if I'm not, just give the form to the person in this office. Don't give it to one of the student employees, though. They're usually very good about getting the forms back to the office, but sometimes it gets really busy and . . . you know how it is. Q37
Student:	Sure. Well, I'll bring it back to the office myself.
Manager:	That's probably a good idea. And, oh, uh, one more thing. I should tell you that the used books tend to go first, so, if you want to be sure that you get used books . . . Q38
Student:	You know what? I'm going to go right back to the dorm to get those numbers now, while you're still here. Q39
Manager:	Okay. That's good.

Audio 35. What does the man need from the bookstore?
Answer **B** A form to order books

Audio 36. What does the man need if he wants a full refund?
Answer **A** Identification
C A receipt for the purchase

Audio 37. Listen again to part of the conversation and then answer the following question.
Replay "Don't give it to one of the student employees, though. They're usually very good about getting the forms back to the office, but sometimes it gets really busy and . . . you know how it is."

Audio	What does the woman mean when she says this:
Replay	". . . sometimes it gets really busy and . . . you know how it is."
Answer A	She is not sure that the student employee will give her the form. The phrase "you know how it is" implies that the man will be able to make a logical conclusion. If the student employees are very busy, they might forget to take the forms to the office.

Audio 38.	What does the woman imply about the used books she sells?
Answer A	They are purchased before new books.

Audio 39.	What does the man need to do now?
Answer D	Locate the section numbers for his classes. They are in his room at the dorm.

LISTENING 8 "ENVIRONMENTAL SCIENCE CLASS"

Audio Lecture

Narrator: Listen to part of a lecture in an environmental science class.

Professor:

Q40 Hydrogen is the most recent and, I'd say, one of the most promising, in a
Q41 long list of alternatives to petroleum. Some of the possibilities include batteries, methanol, natural gas, and, well, you name it. But hydrogen fuel cells have a couple of advantages over some of the other options. First of all, they're really quiet, and they don't pollute the atmosphere. Besides that, hydrogen is the most abundant element in the universe, and it can be produced from a number of sources, including ammonia, or . . . or even water. So, it's renewable, and there's an almost unlimited supply.

Okay. Now fuel cells represent a radical departure from the conventional internal combustion engine and even a fairly fundamental change from electric battery power. Like batteries, fuel cells run on electric motors; however, batteries use electricity from an external source and store it for use in the battery while the fuel cells create their own electricity through a chemical process that uses hydrogen and oxygen from the air. Are you with me? Look, by producing energy in a chemical reaction rather than through combustion, a fuel cell can convert, say 40–60 percent of the energy from the hydrogen into electricity. And when this ratio is compared with that of a combustion engine that runs at about half the efficiency of a fuel cell, well, it's obvious that fuel cell technology has the potential to revolutionize the energy industry.

So, fuel cells have the potential to generate power for almost any kind of machinery or equipment that fossil fuels run, but, the most important, let's say goal, the goal of fuel cell technology is the introduction of fuel cell powered vehicles. Internationally, the competition is fierce to commercialize fuel cell cars. I guess all of the leading automobile manufacturers worldwide have concept cars that use fuel cells, and some of them can reach speeds of as high as 90 miles per hour. Even more impressive is the per tank storage capacity. Can you believe this? Some of those cars can run for 220 miles between refills. But many of those cars were designed decades ago, so . . . what's the holdup?

Well, the problem in introducing fuel cell technology is really twofold. In the first place, industries will have to invest millions, maybe even billions of dollars to refine the technology—and here's the real cost—the infrastructure to support the fueling of the cars. And by infrastructure, I mean basic facilities and services like hydrogen stations to refuel cars and mechanics who know how to repair them. I think you get the picture. And then, consumers will have to accept and use the new products powered by fuel cells. So, we're going to need educational programs to inform the public about the safety and convenience of fuel cells, if we're going to achieve a successful transition to fuel cell products. But, unfortunately, major funding efforts get interrupted. Here's what I mean. When oil prices are high, then there seems to be more funding and greater interest in basic research and development, and more public awareness of fuel cells, and then the price of oil goes down a little and the funding dries up and people just go back to using their fossil fueled products. And this has been going on for more than thirty years. [Q44]

Some government sponsored initiatives have created incentives for fuel cell powered vehicles but probably one of the most successful programs, at least in my opinion, is the STEP program, which is an acronym for the Sustainable Transportation Energy Program. STEP is a demonstration project sponsored by the government of Western Australia. Now, in this project, gasoline-driven buses have been replaced with fuel cell buses on regular transportation routes. I think that British Petroleum is the supplier of the hydrogen fuel, which is produced at an oil refinery in Kwinana, south of Perth. So we need to watch this carefully. Another collaborative research effort is being undertaken by the European Union and the United States. Scientists and engineers are trying to develop a fuel cell that's effectively engineered and attractive to the commercial market. Now, under an agreement signed in about 2000, if memory serves, it was 2003, but anyway, the joint projects include the writing of codes and standards, the design of fueling infrastructures, the refinement of fuel cell models, and the demonstration of fuel cell vehicles. In Europe, the private sector will combine efforts with government agencies in the public sector to create a long-term plan [Q42] [Q43] for the introduction of fuel cells throughout the E.U. And the World Bank is providing funding to promote the development and manufacture of fuel cell buses for public transportation in China, Egypt, Mexico, and India, and we're starting to see some really interesting projects in these areas. So, uh, clearly, fuel cell technology is an international effort.

Okay, at the present time, Japan leads the way in addressing the issues of modifying the infrastructure. Several fueling stations that dispense hydrogen by the cubic meter are already in place, with plans for more. But even when a nationwide system is completed, decisions about how and where to produce the hydrogen and how to transport it will still have to be figured out. Most countries share the view that fleets of vehicles have significant advantages for the introduction of fuel cell powered transportation because, well obviously they can be fueled at a limited number of central locations. And, uh, and other benefits of a fleet are the opportunity to provide training for a maintenance crew and for the drivers. As for consumer education, no one country seems to have made the advances there that . . . that would serve as a model for the rest of us. But perhaps, when the demonstration projects have concluded and a few model cars are available to the public, well, more attention will be directed to public information programs.

Q45

Audio	40.	What is this lecture mainly about?
Answer	**A**	An overview of fuel cell technology. The professor discusses the process for producing energy, the efficiency of the cells, the problems, and some model programs.
Audio	41.	Listen again to part of the lecture and then answer the following question.
Replay		"Hydrogen is the most recent and, I'd say, one of the most promising, in a long list of alternatives to petroleum. Some of the possibilities include batteries, methanol, natural gas, and, well, you name it."
Audio		What does the professor mean when he says this:
Replay		"Some of the possibilities include batteries, methanol, natural gas, and, well, you name it."
Answer	**D**	He does not plan to talk about the alternatives. The comment "you name it" implies that there are a large number of alternatives and that he is not interested in them.
Audio	42.	Why does the professor mention the STEP program in Australia?
Answer	**D**	He thinks it is a very good example of a project.

Audio	43.	Listen again to part of the lecture and then answer the following question.
Replay		"Now, under an agreement signed in about 2000, if memory serves, it was 2003, but anyway, the joint projects include the writing of codes and standards, the design of fueling infrastructures, the refinement of fuel cell models, and the demonstration of fuel cell vehicles."
Audio		Why does the professor say this:
Replay		" . . . if memory serves, it was 2003 . . . "
Answer	**D**	To show that he is uncertain about the date

Audio	44.	What are some of the problems associated with fuel cell technology?
Answer	**B**	Public acceptance
	D	Investment in infrastructures

Audio	45.	What is the professor's attitude toward fuel cells?
Answer	**B**	He is hopeful about their development in the future. He would like more attention to be directed to public information programs, which would solve one of the major problems for fuel cell technology.

LISTENING 9 "PHILOSOPHY CLASS"

Audio Discussion

Narrator: Listen to part of a discussion in a philosophy class.

Professor:

Humanism is a philosophical position that places the dignity of the individual at the center of its movement. A primary principle of humanism—I don't need to spell that for you, do I? Okay, a primary principle of humanism is that human beings are rational and have an innate predisposition for good. Although humanism is associated with the beginning of the Reformation, the humanist philosophy was not new when it became popular in Italy during the Middle Ages. In fact, according to the ancient Greek philosopher, Protagoras, mankind was "the measure of all things." And this idea was echoed by Sophocles when he said, "Many are the wonders of the world, and none so wonderful as mankind." This is classical humanism. Man as the ideal at the center of all creation. Even the ancient Greek gods were viewed as resembling man both physically and psychologically. And, in a sense, isn't this personification of the deity just another way to exalt human beings? But that aside, it was precisely the rediscovery and translation of

Q46

Q47

classical manuscripts that coincided with the invention of printing presses around the mid-15th century, which provided a catalyst for the humanistic movement throughout Europe. As the clergy and upper classes participated in the rediscovery and dissemination of classical literature, humanism became popular among theologians and scholars, and soon set the stage for the Renaissance. This one, I'll spell. Does anybody remember the meaning of the word *renaissance*?

Student 1:   Rebirth, renewal.

Professor:
Right you are. *Renaissance* literally means "rebirth," and it refers to the return to ancient Greek and Roman art and literature, which, like all things in the humanistic tradition, they were measured by human standards. Art returned to the classical principles of harmony and balance. In the field of architecture, we see both religious and secular buildings styled after ancient Roman designs, with mathematical proportions and . . . a human scale, a scale that contrasted with the Medieval Gothic buildings of the previous era. Public works such as bridges and aqueducts from the Roman occupation were repaired, restored, or rebuilt. In the sculptures of the period, nude figures were modeled in life-sized images, with true proportions, and it was also at this point that realism became the standard for painting, with a preference for naturalistic settings and the placement of figures in . . . realistic proportion to those settings. It was also evident that the portraits tended to be more personal and authentic. And artists even produced self-portraits at this time. Remember, the figures in the paintings of the previous era tended to be of another world, but Renaissance painters placed recognizable human beings in this world. In music, uh, there was an effort to create harmonies that were pleasing to the human ear and melodies that were compatible with the human voice. In addition, music lessons became more widespread as a source of education and enjoyment. Dancing increased in popularity with a concurrent trend toward music that had rhythm and invited movement as a pleasurable activity.

Student 2:   Wasn't that why Latin became so important?

Professor:
Yes. Both Greek and Latin became important as tools for scholarship, and classical Latin became the basis for an international language of the intellectuals throughout Europe. To be true to humanism, and all it represented, it was necessary to be knowledgeable about and faithful to the ancient philosophies as expressed in their writing, and how best to express them

than in the original languages? By the way, Latin as a universal language Q49 for clerics and the aristocracy, this encouraged the exchange of ideas on a wider scale than ever before, and legitimized in a sense the presumption that mankind was at the center of all things. It also made it possible for individual scholars to make a name for themselves and establish their place in the history of mankind.

Well, it was at this time that a close association, almost a partnership Q48 was forged between art and science. In their efforts to be precise, sculptors and painters studied the human form. In effect, they became anatomists. You may recall the drawing in your textbook, the one by Leonardo da Vinci which demonstrates the geometrical proportions of the human body. And, of course, Alberti, in his many books on architecture, sculpture, and painting . . . he emphasized the study of mathematics as the underlying principle of all the arts. Whereas artists had considered themselves craftsmen in the Middle Ages, the great Renaissance artists viewed themselves as intellectuals, philosophers, if you will, of humanism. They were designing a world for human beings to live in and enjoy. One that was in proportion and in harmony with mankind. So, perhaps you can see why the so-called Renaissance man emerged.

Student 1:	Okay. But exactly what is the definition of a Renaissance man? I know it means a very talented person, but . . .

Professor:
Good question. Sometimes we use these terms without really defining them. Q50 So I would say that a Renaissance man would be talented, as you said, but would also have to demonstrate broad interests . . . in both the arts and the sciences. The quality that was most admired in the Renaissance was the extraordinary, maybe even . . . universality of talents in diverse fields of endeavor. After all, this quality proved that mankind was capable of reason and creation, that humanism was justified in placing man in the center of the world, as the measure of all things in it. With the humanistic philosophy as a justification, scholars would interpret the ancient classics and some of them would argue to a reasonable conclusion a very new and more secular society built on individual, human effort. It was not difficult for the Renaissance man to make the leap of logic from classical humanism to political humanism, which encouraged freedom of thought, and indeed even democracy, within both the church and the state. But that is a topic for another day.

Audio	46.	What is the main focus of this discussion?
Answer	C	The other topics are mentioned in the discussion as they relate to the main focus: Humanism.

Audio	47.	Listen again to part of the discussion and then answer the following question.
Replay		"A primary principle of humanism—I don't need to spell that for you, do I? Okay, a primary principle of humanism is that human beings are rational and have an innate predisposition for good."
Audio		Why does the professor say this:
Replay		"I don't need to spell that for you, do I?"
Answer	**B**	Her tone indicates that she assumes that the students know how to spell the term. Later, she spells a more difficult term.

Audio	48.	Why does the professor mention the drawing by Leonardo da Vinci?
Answer	**B**	She uses it as an example of the union of art and science.

Audio	49.	According to the professor, what was the effect of using Latin as a universal language of scholarship?
Answer	**A**	It facilitated communication among intellectuals in many countries.

Audio	50.	According to the professor, what can be inferred about a Renaissance man?
Answer	**B**	He would have an aptitude for both art and science.

Audio	51.	All of the following characteristics are true of humanism EXCEPT
Answer	**B**	Scholars must serve society.

➤ Speaking

🎧 **Model Test 1, Speaking Section, Track 32**

INDEPENDENT SPEAKING QUESTION 1 "MARRIAGE PARTNER"

Narrator 2: Number 1. Listen for a question about a familiar topic. After you hear the question, you have 15 seconds to prepare and 45 seconds to record your answer.

Narrator 1: Describe an ideal marriage partner. What qualities do you think are most important for a husband or wife? Use specific reasons and details to explain your choices.

Narrator 2: Please prepare your answer after the beep.

Beep

[Preparation Time: 15 seconds]

Narrator 2: Please begin speaking after the beep.

Beep

[Recording Time: 45 seconds]

Beep

INDEPENDENT SPEAKING QUESTION 2 "NEWS"

Narrator 2: Number 2. Listen for a question that asks your opinion about a familiar topic. After you hear the question, you have 15 seconds to prepare and 45 seconds to record your answer.

Narrator 1: Agree or disagree with the following statement:

Getting news on TV or on a computer is better than reading it in a print newspaper.

Use specific reasons and examples to support your choice.

Narrator 2: Please prepare your answer after the beep.

Beep

[Preparation Time: 15 seconds]

Narrator 2: Please begin speaking after the beep.

Beep

[Recording Time: 45 seconds]

Beep

INTEGRATED SPEAKING QUESTION 3 "MEAL PLAN"

Narrator 2: Number 3. Read a short passage and listen to a talk on the same topic. Then listen for a question about them. After you hear the question, you have 30 seconds to prepare and 60 seconds to record your answer.

Narrator 1: A new meal plan is being offered by the college. Read the plan in the college newspaper [printed on page 236]. You have 45 seconds to complete it. Please begin reading now.

[Reading Time: 45 seconds]

Narrator 1: Now listen to two students who are talking about the plan.

Man:	I don't like to cook, but I don't like to eat in the cafeteria every day either.
Woman:	True. The food does get kind of . . . same old same old.
Man:	My point exactly. And besides, I go home about every other weekend, so paying for my meals when I'm not there doesn't make a lot of sense.
Woman:	Right. So you'll probably sign up for the five-day plan next semester.
Man:	I already did. If I want to eat in the cafeteria some weekend, I can just buy a meal, but I'd probably go out somewhere with my friends if I'm here over the weekend.
Woman:	Well, I don't go home on the weekends as much as you do, but I still eat out a lot on the weekends.
Man:	So the five-day plan might work out better for you, too. I'm really glad to have the option.

Narrator 1: The man expresses his opinion of the new meal plan. Report his opinion, and explain the reasons that he gives for having that opinion.

Narrator 2: Please prepare your answer after the beep.

Beep

[Preparation Time: 30 seconds]

Narrator 2: Please begin speaking after the beep.

Beep

[Recording Time: 60 seconds]

Beep

INTEGRATED SPEAKING QUESTION 4 "ABORIGINAL PEOPLE"

Narrator 2: Number 4. Read a short passage and listen to a lecture on the same topic. Then listen for a question about them. After you hear the question, you have 30 seconds to prepare and 60 seconds to record your answer.

Narrator 1: Now read the passage about Aboriginal People [printed on page 237]. You have 45 seconds to complete it. Please begin reading now.

[Reading Time: 45 seconds]

Narrator 1: Now listen to part of a lecture in an anthropology class. The professor is talking about Aboriginal People.

Professor:
According to your textbook, the Aboriginal People are very diverse, and, I would agree with that; however, there are certain beliefs that unite the groups, and in fact, allow them to identify themselves and others as members of the diverse Aboriginal societies. For one thing, unlike the anthropologists who believe that tribes arrived in eastern Australia from Tasmania about 40,000 years ago, the Aboriginal People believe that they have always been in Australia, and that they have sprung from the land. Evidence for this resides in the oral history that has been recorded in stories and passed down for at least fifty generations. This history is referred to as the "Dreaming." The stories teach moral and spiritual values and provide each member of the group with an identity that reflects the landscape where the person's mother first becomes aware of the unborn baby, or to put it in terms of the "Dreaming," where the spirit enters the mother's body. So, I am saying that the way that the Aboriginal People identify themselves and each other, even across groups, is by their membership in the oral history that they share.

Narrator 1: Explain how the Aboriginal People are identified. Draw upon information in both the reading and the lecture.

Narrator 2: Please prepare your answer after the beep.

Beep

[Preparation Time: 30 seconds]

Narrator 2: Please begin speaking after the beep.

Beep

[Recording Time: 60 seconds]

Beep

Integrated Speaking Question 5 "Scheduling Conflict"

Narrator 2: Number 5. Listen to a short conversation. Then listen for a question about it. After you hear the question, you have 20 seconds to prepare and 60 seconds to record your answer.

Narrator 1: Now listen to a conversation between a student and his friend.

Friend:	So what time should we pick you up on Friday? Can you be ready by noon or do you need another hour or so?
Student:	I really wanted to spend the weekend with my family, and the ride with you would have made it even more fun, but . . .
Friend:	You mean you aren't going?
Student:	I can't. I'm not doing too well in my economics class, and I have a lecture Friday afternoon. I don't think I should miss it.
Friend:	Well, why don't you borrow the notes from someone? Isn't your roommate in that class?
Student:	Yeah, he is. But I've already asked to borrow his notes once this semester. He didn't seem to mind though.
Friend:	Well, there you are. Unless you want to go to class on Thursday. I'm fairly sure that Dr. Collins teaches the same class Thursday night.
Student:	Really? She probably wouldn't mind if I sat in on the Thursday class, but I wonder if she'll give the same lecture. You know, maybe they're one week behind or one week ahead of us.
Friend:	I suppose that's possible, but it would be easy enough to find out. You could just tell her that you'd like to attend the Thursday session this week because you need to go out of town. Then you can ride home with us. If there's a problem, you can still borrow your roommate's notes on Sunday when we get back.

Narrator 1: Describe the man's problem and the two suggestions that his friend makes about how to handle it. What do you think the man should do, and why?

Narrator 2: Please prepare your answer after the beep.

Beep

[Preparation Time: 20 seconds]

Narrator 2: Please begin speaking after the beep.

Beep

[Recording Time: 60 seconds]

Beep

INTEGRATED SPEAKING QUESTION 6 "LABORATORY MICROSCOPE"

Narrator 2: Number 6. Listen to part of a talk. Then listen for a question about it. After you hear the question, you have 20 seconds to prepare and 60 seconds to record your answer.

Narrator 1: Now listen to part of a talk in a biology laboratory. The teaching assistant is explaining how to use the microscope.

Teaching Assistant:
All right, now that you all have microscopes at your tables, I want to explain how they work and how to use them. First of all, you should know that they are compound microscopes so they can magnify objects up to 1,000 times their size. These microscopes have two systems—an illuminating system and an imaging system. You'll see that the illuminating system has a light source built in, and you can control it by adjusting the lever on the side. Why is this important? Well, the specimen must be pretty thin, or let's say, transparent enough to let light pass through it. So the light source controls the amount of light that passes through the specimen. Okay. The other system provides magnification. Use this lever to switch powers. So, when you switch to a higher power, you see a larger image, and when you switch to a lower power, you see a smaller image. But, I should remind you that the field of view is smaller at a higher power. In other words, at a higher magnification, you see a larger image of a smaller area. Okay. So what about the focus? Well, these microscopes are parfocal, and that means you usually

don't have to refocus when you switch to a higher or lower power of magnification. But there are two adjustment knobs—the larger one for coarse adjustment and the smaller one for fine adjustment, just in case.

Narrator 1: Using the main points and examples from the talk, describe the two major systems of the laboratory microscope, and then explain how to use it.

Narrator 2: Please prepare your answer after the beep.

Beep

[Preparation Time: 20 seconds]

Narrator 2: Please begin speaking after the beep.

Beep

[Recording Time: 60 seconds]

Beep

➤ Writing

🎧 **Model Test 1, Writing Section, Track 33**

Integrated Essay "Online Graduate Programs"
First, read the passage [printed on pages 242–243] and take notes.

Narrator: Now listen to a lecture on the same topic as the passage that you have just read.

Professor:
Today we're going to question some of the claims made in the reading about online graduate degree programs. First of all, the one-on-one time with professors that a student has, as in a traditional course, is really up to the student. Those who want to talk with their professors, do so. The main difference is the way that professors communicate in online courses. Whereas student interaction with faculty in traditional on-campus programs is often face to face, faculty interaction online is more likely to be by email and chat, or occasionally by telephone conference.

Second, the claim that the difficulty level and the quality of the courses are inferior in online degree programs just doesn't hold up under scrutiny. In order to be accredited, the online program must meet the same standards as those of the on-campus program at the same institution. And this is also interesting—of the 20 programs in my study, students reported that they *thought* the online courses would be easier, but, in fact, they were more difficult because they required more self-discipline and personal time management than the courses that were offered on campus on a regular schedule. In many cases, online students complained that they had to learn how to manage the technology in an online course in addition to learning the content of the course.

Last then. Although I'll concede that some online degree programs aren't accredited and not worth the time, it's simply not true that top schools don't offer online degree programs. Just as an example, every Ivy League school except Princeton provides online degrees and even Princeton offers a large number of courses online. A few of the Ivy League programs require a one-term residency requirement on campus, but many allow students to complete the entire degree online. And most of the other top schools also provide online degree options.

Question

Summarize the main points in the lecture and then explain how they cast doubt on the ideas in the reading passage.

➤ Example Answers and Checklists for Speaking and Writing

🎧 **Model Test 1, Example Answers, Track 34**

EXAMPLE ANSWER FOR INDEPENDENT SPEAKING QUESTION 1 "MARRIAGE PARTNER"

In my view, three characteristics are essential for a marriage partner. Compatibility is very important because spending the rest of your life with someone is a huge commitment, and without compatibility in values and interests, and goals, it could be a struggle rather than a partnership. Um, I also think that a good marriage partner should fit into your family. Without acceptance and affection for you as a couple, you could risk the relationships you have with family members. And attraction is another factor. Since fidelity is part of the marriage contract, the expression of love will be limited to your partner, so it should be a person you're attracted to.

Checklist 1

✔ The talk answers the topic question.
✔ The point of view or position is clear.
✔ The talk is direct and well organized.
✔ The sentences are logically connected.
✔ Details and examples support the main idea.
✔ The speaker expresses complete thoughts.
✔ The meaning is easy to comprehend.
✔ A wide range of vocabulary is used.
✔ There are only minor errors in grammar.
✔ The talk is within a range of 125–150 words.

EXAMPLE ANSWER FOR INDEPENDENT SPEAKING QUESTION 2 "NEWS"

Although newspapers contain some information that's limited to local interests and I like to turn to those pages, for the most part, I agree that getting news on TV and on my computer is better than reading it in a print newspaper. The problem with printed news is it takes so long to produce it that the stories could have changed or more important news could have happened minutes after the newspaper is delivered. So, I scan the local stories in the paper when I get home from work, then I watch the international news on TV at night for the most current information, and the following morning, I click on one of the websites that offer the most recent updates of the lead stories. That way, I'm taking advantage of the best aspects of all the news media, and I stay current locally and internationally.

Checklist 2

✔ The talk answers the topic question.
✔ The point of view or position is clear.
✔ The talk is direct and well organized.
✔ The sentences are logically connected.
✔ Details and examples support the main idea.
✔ The speaker expresses complete thoughts.
✔ The meaning is easy to comprehend.
✔ A wide range of vocabulary is used.
✔ There are only minor errors in grammar.
✔ The talk is within a range of 125–150 words.

EXAMPLE ANSWER FOR INTEGRATED SPEAKING QUESTION 3 "MEAL PLAN"

The man is glad that an alternative to the seven-day meal plan is now available for students who live in the dorms. He'll purchase the five-day meal plan, which provides three meals on weekdays and the option to buy meals on the weekends for $3 each. The new five-day meal plan is better for him because he likes to go home every other weekend, and when he's on campus, he likes to go out with his friends. So he wasn't taking advantage of the cafeteria on the weekends even though he was paying for it. The Student Union has fast-food as well as booths in the food court for Chinese or Mexican food or even a salad bar. Besides, if he wants to eat in the cafeteria on a weekend, he can buy a meal. He should save about $48 a month by using the new plan, and he can use that money to eat out.

Checklist 3

✔ The talk summarizes the situation and opinion.
✔ The point of view or position is clear.
✔ The talk is direct and well organized.
✔ The sentences are logically connected.
✔ Details and examples support the opinion.
✔ The speaker expresses complete thoughts.
✔ The meaning is easy to comprehend.
✔ A wide range of vocabulary is used.
✔ Errors in grammar are minor.
✔ The talk is within a range of 125–150 words.

EXAMPLE ANSWER FOR INTEGRATED SPEAKING QUESTION 4 "ABORIGINAL PEOPLE"

The Aboriginal People are culturally and linguistically diverse, in part because the geography dictated both limitations and opportunities for their communities. So the establishment of identity as a member of the Aboriginal People because of appearance, language, culture, or geographical location isn't considered accurate. The Department of Education suggests that the best means of identification is to be recognized and accepted by other members of the Aboriginal society. Um, according to the lecturer, even diverse groups have certain unifying beliefs that are passed down as oral tradition, called the "Dreaming." The stories associated with this tradition are used to teach ethical principles and spiritual lessons. It would probably be through knowledge of this shared oral history that Aborigines would identify each other.

Checklist 4

✔ The talk relates an example to a concept.
✔ Inaccuracies in the content are minor.
✔ The talk is direct and well organized.
✔ The sentences are logically connected.
✔ Details and examples support the opinion.
✔ The speaker expresses complete thoughts.
✔ The meaning is easy to comprehend.
✔ A wide range of vocabulary is used.
✔ The speaker paraphrases in his/her own words.
✔ The speaker credits the lecturer with wording.
✔ Errors in grammar are minor.
✔ The talk is within a range of 125–150 words.

EXAMPLE ANSWER FOR INTEGRATED SPEAKING QUESTION 5 "SCHEDULING CONFLICT"

The man would like to visit his family over the weekend, but his friends are leaving before his economics class on Friday. He doesn't want to miss the class because he needs to bring his grade up. His friend suggests that he borrow the notes from the class. His roommate didn't have a problem lending him notes from that class earlier in the semester, but he's reluctant to do that. The other possibility that his friend mentions is for him to attend another section of the same class on Thursday night, but he isn't sure that the professor will give him the same lecture. To find out, he would have to ask the professor. In my opinion, the man should stay for his economics class and take notes. It's hard to read someone else's notes, and besides, if he's in the class, he can ask questions. If he wants to visit his family, he should try to find a ride on Saturday or on Friday after the class.

Checklist 5

✔ The talk summarizes the problem and recommendations.
✔ The speaker's point of view or position is clear.
✔ The talk is direct and well organized.
✔ The sentences are logically connected.
✔ Details and examples support the opinion.
✔ The speaker expresses complete thoughts.
✔ The meaning is easy to comprehend.
✔ A wide range of vocabulary is used.
✔ Errors in grammar are minor.
✔ The talk is within a range of 125–150 words.

EXAMPLE ANSWER FOR INTEGRATED SPEAKING QUESTION 6 "LABORATORY MICROSCOPE"

The two major systems of the laboratory microscope are the illuminating system and the imaging system. The illuminating system has a light source that can be controlled to let more or less light pass through the specimen you're viewing when you move a lever on the side of the microscope. The imaging system is actually a magnification feature, which can be calibrated by using the other lever to change powers. When you look through a higher power, the image appears to be larger, and conversely, when you look through a lower power, it appears to be smaller. What that really means is when you use a higher magnification, the image actually shows you a smaller part of the specimen because it's enlarged. Now when you switch powers, the lenses will focus automatically, but the big knob will allow you to make a rough adjustment, and the small knob will let you make a more detailed adjustment, if you want.

Checklist 6

✔ The talk summarizes a short lecture.
✔ Inaccuracies in the content are minor.
✔ The talk is direct and well organized.
✔ The sentences are logically connected.
✔ Details and examples support the main idea.
✔ The speaker expresses complete thoughts.
✔ The meaning is easy to comprehend.
✔ A wide range of vocabulary is used.
✔ The speaker paraphrases in his/her own words.
✔ The speaker credits the lecturer with wording.
✔ Errors in grammar are minor.
✔ The talk is within a range of 125–150 words.

EXAMPLE RESPONSE FOR INTEGRATED ESSAY "ONLINE GRADUDATE PROGRAMS"

Many writers begin with a chart like those you practiced in Chapter 3. Only the essay will be scored.

Chart

Online Graduate Degree Programs
question claims

Relationship w prof

o no 1-1 c office hrs c inform inter	o + c same amount o diff way—email, chat o phone conf

Quality courses

Complete in wkend o jr faculty, graders o large	o + c ame accred o thought easy—not o content + tech

No top schools

c best schools c conventional w/ residence	o most top o all ivy except Princeton o some l term res—most all

Example Essay "Online Graduate Programs"

The lecture questions the claims in the reading that the relationship with professors, the quality of courses, and the access to top schools are inferior in online graduate degree programs.

According to the lecturer, the relationship with online and on-campus professors is the same in terms of the amount of interaction. The way that the interaction occurs is different because online professors use email, chat, and telephone conference calls to communicate with their students.

The reading passage asserts that the professors who teach online are not as qualified and the courses themselves do not compare with the more challenging on-campus courses; however, the lecturer makes a strong case against this claim. The lecturer explains that both online and on-campus graduate courses must demonstrate the same standards for accreditation.

Furthermore, students who take online courses in the mistaken belief that they will be easier often report that they were more difficult because of the added technology that had to be learned in order to navigate the course and complete the requirements.

The lecturer also refutes the idea that the best schools do not offer online graduate degree programs. Using the example of Ivy League schools, known for their prestige, the lecturer indicates that all Ivy League schools with the exception of Princeton offer online graduate degrees. Although some top schools may require one term residence, they offer the degree program online.

Checklist for Integrated Essay

✔ The essay answers the topic question.
✔ Inaccuracies in the content are minor.
✔ The essay is direct and well organized.
✔ The sentences are logically connected.
✔ Details and examples support the main idea.
✔ The writer expresses complete thoughts.
✔ The meaning is easy to comprehend.
✔ A wide range of vocabulary is used.
✔ The writer paraphrases in his/her own words.
✔ The writer credits the author with wording.
✔ Errors in grammar and idioms are minor.
✔ The essay is within a range of 150–225 words.

EXAMPLE RESPONSE FOR INDEPENDENT ESSAY "AN IMPORTANT LEADER"

Some writers begin with an outline and others begin with a map of their ideas. Only the essay will be scored.

Outline

William Lyon Mackenzie King
• Offices
    Parliament
    Head Liberal Party
    Prime minister
• Longevity
    21 years P.M.
    50 years public service
• Accomplishments
    Unity French + English provinces
    Represented all Canadians

Map

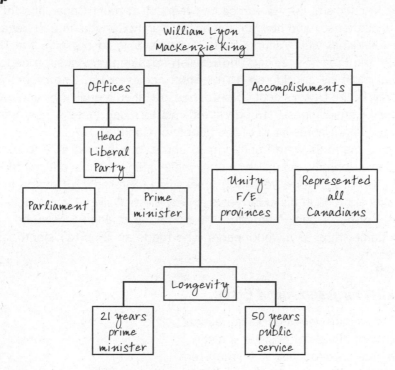

Example Essay

William Lyon Mackenzie King was a member of the Canadian parliament and head of the Liberal Party in the first half of the twentieth century. He held the office of prime minister for a total of twenty-one years, which is a longer period of time than that of any public servant in the history of Canada. Because his terms of office as prime minister were not consecutive, he held other positions of public service in many appointed and elected offices as well over a period of fifty years. Although it could be argued that he was an important world leader on the basis of longevity alone, I admire him because of his qualities of leadership. He was active in government during two world wars and the Great Depression and played a key role in guiding Canada during those very difficult years. He understood the importance of a unified nation and worked to bring various partisan groups together for the higher good of the country. Under his tenure in office, Canada became a participant in world affairs.

His three terms of office as prime minister were marked by compromise and often criticism, but he earned the respect of most Canadians for his political astuteness and his determination to unify Canada. In part because of his friendship with Wilfrid Laurier, he was able to preserve the unity between the French-speaking and English-speaking provinces, a negotiation that must be considered his greatest achievement. One biographer, John Moir of the University of Toronto, has identified a quality in King called "essential Canadianness." I understand this to mean that he was able to understand and represent all of the people of Canada.

King's methods were frustrating to some, but he was able to extend Canadian autonomy and maintain unity while acting within a difficult federal system. He did so for a very long time, even representing Canada in the international arena in his elder years. In my view, William Lyon Mackenzie King is worthy of being named in the company of John F. Kennedy and Martin Luther King as a world leader who made an important contribution to humanity.

Checklist for Independent Essay

✔ The essay answers the topic question.
✔ The point of view or position is clear.
✔ The essay is direct and well organized.
✔ The sentences are logically connected.
✔ Details and examples support the main idea.
✔ The writer expresses complete thoughts.
✔ The meaning is easy to comprehend.
✔ A wide range of vocabulary is used.
✔ Various types of sentences are included.
✔ Errors in grammar and idioms are minor.
✔ The essay is within a range of 300–350 words.

MODEL TEST 2: PROGRESS TEST

➤ Reading

READING 1 "RESOURCES AND INDUSTRIALISM IN CANADA"

1. **B** "The building of the Temiskaming and Northern Ontario Railway led to the discovery of rich silver deposits." Choices A, C, and D are true, but they do not relate to the main point in paragraph 1, the resources in the western frontier.

2. **C** ". . . Sudbury became the world's largest nickel producer." Choice A is not correct because it is not mentioned directly in the paragraph. Choice B is not correct because Sudbury was a supplier, not a market for metals. Choice D is not correct because Sudbury is in Ontario, not in the Klondike.

3. **D** In this passage, *lasting* is a synonym for "enduring."

4. **B** ". . . the federal government created the Yukon Territory . . . in an effort to ward off the prospect of annexation to Alaska." Choice A is not correct because fortune-seekers were flocking there already. Choice C is not correct because the tales of lawlessness were told in popular fiction, but no effort to establish law and order was mentioned. Choice D is not correct because the legality of the mining claims was not mentioned.

5. **D** In this passage, *formerly* is a synonym for "previously." Context comes from the reference to "unsettled" for an area that was increasing in population.

6. **A** ". . . the tales [of the Klondike strike] . . . were immortalized through . . . the poetic verses of Robert W. Service." Choices B and C may have been true, but they were not mentioned in connection with the poetry of Robert Service. Choice D is not correct because the creation of the Yukon Territory, not the poetry, prevented the Klondike's annexation to Alaska.

7. **B** Choice A is mentioned in paragraph 3, sentence 2. Choice C is mentioned in paragraph 3, sentence 5. Choice D is mentioned in paragraph 3, sentence 4.

8. **D** In this passage, *Moreover* is a synonym for "Furthermore." Context comes from the addition of another way that the forest and water resources were exploited.

9. **C** In this passage, *supply* is a synonym for "distribute."

10. **C** *Federal taxes* paraphrases "the high tariff policies" and *cheaper imported goods* paraphrases "lower-priced foreign manufactured

goods." . . . *protecting domestic industries* paraphrases "protecting existing industries" and *supporting new businesses* paraphrases "encouraging the creation of new enterprises."

11. **A**   ". . . the governments of Ontario and Quebec . . . [offered] bonuses, subsidies, and guarantees to locate new plants within their borders." Choice B is true, but it is not the reason why British and American businesses opened affiliates. Choice C is not correct because the consumers in western Canada were eager to buy goods from eastern and central Canada, not from abroad. Choice D is not correct because British investors contributed to the construction of urban infrastructure.

12. **C**   Vocabulary reference is a transitional device that connects the insert sentence with the previous sentence. The connection is "Railway construction" and "discoveries of gold, silver, copper, lead, and zinc" to "The building of the . . . Railway" and "rich silver deposits."

13. **C, E, F** summarize the passage. Choices A and B are minor points that support major point C. Choice D is a minor point that supports major point E.

READING 2 "LOOKING AT THEATRE HISTORY"

14. **C**   ". . . the buildings in later periods became sources of stone for other projects and what remains is usually broken and scattered." Choice A is not correct because other theatres have been identified and many of them have been excavated. Choice B is not correct because the archeologists were not the ones who broke the stones. Choice D is not correct because concrete was not mentioned as construction material during early periods. The word "concrete" in the passage means "true" or "verifiable" in reference to "evidence."

15. **B**   ". . . many pieces are irrevocably lost." Choice A is not correct because drawings are conjectural. Choice C is not correct because the number of skenes that archeologists have excavated is not specified. Choice D is not correct because excavations did not begin until the late 1800s, not the early 1800s.

16. **B**   In this passage, *important* is a synonym for "primary." Context comes from the phrase, "most concrete evidence."

17. **D**   In this passage, *exact* is a synonym for "precise." Context comes from the contrast with the word "conjectural" in the same sentence.

18. **A**   ". . . the myths on which dramatists drew were known to everyone, including vase painters, who might well depict the same subjects as dramatists." Choice B is not correct because reproductions were

not mentioned. Choice C is not correct because the qualifications of scholars were not discussed. Choice D is not correct because thousands of vases have survived.

19. **B** In this passage, *debated* is a synonym for "controversial." Context comes from the phrases "easy to misinterpret" and "questionable assumption" in later sentences.

20. **D** Because the author refers to the archeological evidence in vase paintings as "controversial," it must be concluded that there is disagreement among scholars. Choice A is not correct because the oldest surviving manuscripts date from 1500 years after they were first performed. Choice B is not correct because they are easy to misinterpret. Choice C is not correct because the author does not mention the condition of the vases.

21. **B** ". . . each time a text was copied, there were new possibilities for errors." Choice A is not correct because the problem of sources was identified for archeological findings, not written evidence. Choices C and D are not mentioned as problems for written evidence.

22. **D** ". . . these characters [women] often seem victims of their own powerlessness." Choice A is not correct because many plays featured strong female characters. Choice B is not correct because some critics have seen these plays [with women as victims] as rationalizations by the male-dominated culture and other critics have seen them as an attempt to examine this aspect of the culture. Choice C is not correct because plays featured numerous choruses of women.

23. **B** In this passage, *Generally* is a synonym for "Overall."

24. **A** ". . . historical treatment of Greek theatre is something like assembling a jigsaw puzzle of which many pieces are missing." The reference to "missing pieces" is an analogy to the partial evidence for Greek theatre. Choice B is not correct because no comparison is made between written references and the paintings in paragraph 4. Choice C is not correct because the author does not use words and phrases that suggest justification. Choice D is not correct because the last sentence is a summary of the reading passage, not an opening sentence for a new topic.

25. **C** Vocabulary reference and contrast are two transitional devices that connect the previous and following sentences to the insert sentence. The connection is "theatres . . . have been excavated" in the previous sentence and "These excavations" in the insert sentence as well as the contrast with "Nevertheless, they" [the theatres or excavations of theatres] in the following sentence.

26. **B, D, C** summarize the passage. Choice A is a minor point that supports major point D. Choice E is a minor point that supports major point C. Choice F is reasonable, but it is not mentioned in the passage.

Reading 3 "Geothermal Energy"

27. **A** The author mentions geothermal power in 1904 in Italy, and then lists a number of countries worldwide that are using geothermal energy. Choice B is not correct because only successful production is mentioned. Choices C and D are discussed later in the passage.

28. **D** ". . . at the global level, geothermal energy supplies less than 0.15% of the total energy supply." Choice A is not correct because geothermal energy was used as early as 1904. Choice B is not correct because Russia, Iceland, Mexico, and the United States are in the Northern Hemisphere. Choice C is not correct because several advantages of using geothermal power are noted, but the comparative cost was not mentioned.

29. **C** In this passage *nearly* is a synonym for "approaching." Context comes from the number after the word.

30. **B** In this passage, *optional* is a synonym for "alternative." Context comes from the contrast of "geothermal energy" and "other" energy sources.

31. **D** ". . . considered a nonrenewable energy source when rates of extraction are greater than rates of natural replenishment." Choices A, B, and C are true, but they do not explain the term "nonrenewable."

32. **A** *High heat is the source of most of the geothermal energy* paraphrases ". . . most geothermal energy production involves the tapping of high heat sources," and *low heat groundwater is also used sometimes* paraphrases "people are also using the low-temperature geothermal energy of groundwater in some applications."

33. **B** ". . . areas of high heat flow are associated with plate tectonic boundaries." Choice A is not correct because geothermal heat flow is very low compared with solar heat. Choice C is not correct because, in some areas, heat flow is sufficiently high. Choice D is not correct because geothermal energy is very practical along plate boundaries.

34. **A** In this passage, *large* is a synonym for "considerable" in reference to "thermal pollution." Context comes from the contrast with the phrase "atmospheric pollutants" in the previous sentence.

35. **B** ". . . geothermal energy does not produce the atmospheric pollutants associated with burning fossil fuels." Choice A is not correct

because the pollution caused by geothermal energy was introduced before the discussion on atmospheric pollution. Choice C is not correct because environmental problems caused by geothermal energy are mentioned. Choice D is not correct because the author points out the problem of pollution, but does not suggest that the use of raw materials and chemicals be discontinued.

36. **A**   Choice B is mentioned in paragraph 6, sentence 4. Choices C and D are mentioned in paragraph 6, sentences 5 and 6.

37. **C**   ". . . known geothermal resources . . . could produce . . . 10% of the electricity . . . for the western states. . . . Geohydrothermal resources not yet discovered could . . . provide . . . [the] equivalent [of] the electricity produced from water power today." Choice A is not correct because the author points out the disadvantages but argues in favor of using geothermal energy. Choice B is not correct because the author does not mention exploration as a prerequisite to further production. Choice D is not correct because the author cites the potential for geothermal energy to equal the production of water power, not to replace water power.

38. **C**   Vocabulary reference is a transitional device that connects the insert sentence with the previous sentence. "One such region" is a phrase in the insert sentence that refers to "Oceanic ridge systems" in the previous sentence.

39. **B, D, E** summarize the passage. Choice A is true, but it is a minor point that provides an example for major point B. Choice C is true, but it refers to one example of cultural values developed in major point E. Choice F is true, but it is a detail that provides support for the environmental problems mentioned in major point E.

READING 4 "MIGRATION FROM ASIA"

40. **D**   In this passage, *particular* is a synonym for "distinctive."

41. **C**   ". . . Stone Age hunter-gatherers were attracted by these animal populations [large animals]." Choice A is not mentioned. Choice B is not correct because the tools were made from the animals, not traded with other tribes. Choice D is not correct because the dogs accompanied them.

42. **B**   In this passage, the phrase *Joined by* is a synonym for "Accompanied by." Context comes from the word part, "company."

43. **B**   In this passage, *judged* is a synonym for "estimated." Context comes from the phrase "about 27,000 years old" in the same sentence.

44. **D**   ". . . the migrations must have begun before the evolution of type B." Choice A is not correct because the time frame was the same

as the settlement of Scandinavia, but the origin of the migration was not Scandinavian. Choice B is not correct because almost no Native Americans have type B. Choice C is not correct because the blood typing was done with Native Americans and Asians, not Scandinavians.

45. **D** ". . . glacial melting created an ice-free corridor along the eastern front range of the Rocky Mountains. Soon hunters . . . had reached the Great Plains." Choices A and C are not correct because the corridor was ice-free. Choice B is not correct because the hunters were looking for big game, but the game did not leave a migration path.

46. **B** "The most spectacular find, at Monte Verde in southern Chile, produced striking evidence of tool making, house building . . . before the highway had been cleared of ice." Choice A is not correct because archeologists believe that migration in boats may have occurred, but no boats were found. Choice C is not correct because the footprints found there were human, not those of large animals. Choice D is not correct because no conclusions were made about the intelligence of the early humans.

47. **A** In this passage, *In the end* is a synonym for "Eventually." Context comes from the phrase "The final migration" in the following sentence.

48. **A** *Beringia was under water* paraphrases "Beringia had been submerged" and *the last people* paraphrases "The final migration."

49. **D** Choice A is mentioned in paragraph 6, sentence 3. Choices B and C are mentioned in paragraph 6, sentence 5. Choice D is not true because the Yuptiks settled the coast of Alaska, not the Great Plains.

50. **D** ". . . the most compelling support [for migration] . . . comes from genetic research." Choice A is not correct because oral traditions include a long journey from a distant place to a new homeland. Choice B is not correct because the author presents the evidence without commenting on the authenticity. Choice C is not correct because the author states that the Asian migration hypothesis is supported by most of the scientific evidence.

51. **C** Chronological order and place reference are transitional devices that connect the insert sentence with the previous sentence. The date, 13,000 B.C.E. in the previous paragraph is a date that precedes 11,000 to 12,000 years old in the insert sentence. In addition, Washington State, California, and Peru in the insert sentence refer to the Pacific coast of North and South America in the previous sentence.

52. **E, D, C** summarize the passage. Choice A is a concluding point that is not developed with examples and details. Choice B is a minor point that supports major point E. Choice F is a minor point that supports major point D.

➤ Listening

Model Test 2, Listening Section, Track 35

LISTENING 1 "PROFESSOR'S OFFICE"

Audio Conversation

Narrator:	Listen to part of a conversation between a student and a professor.

Student:	Professor James. Do you have a minute?
Professor:	Sure. Come on in. What can I do for you?
Student:	Well, I did pretty well on the midterm . . .
Professor:	You sure did. One of the best grades, as I recall.
Q1 Student:	But I missed a question, and I'd appreciate it if you could help me understand what I did wrong. I have the test right here, and I just can't figure it out.
Professor:	Okay. Fire away.
Student:	It's question 7 . . . the one on biotic provinces and biomes.
Professor:	Oh, that one. Um, quite a few people missed it. I was thinking that we should go over it again in class. But anyway, let's look at your answer.
Q2 Student:	Thanks. Here's the thing. I said that a biotic province was a region with similar life, but with boundaries that prevent plants and animals from spreading to other regions. So an animal, for example, a mammal . . . it may have a genetic ancestor in common with another mammal. But a biome is a similar environment, an ecosystem really, like a desert or a tropical rainforest. So, in the case of a biome, well, the similar climate causes the plants and animals to evolve . . . to adapt to the climate, and that's why they look alike.
Q3 Professor:	That's good, very good . . . as far as you went. But there's a second part to the question. Look, right here. "Include an explanation of convergent and divergent evolution." So . . . I was looking for a more complete answer. Next time, be

	sure to include both parts of a question . . . when there are two parts like this one. . . . Do you know how to explain convergent and divergent evolution?
Student:	I think so. Isn't it . . . like when a group of plants or animals . . . when they're separated by mountains or a large body of water . . . then subpopulations evolve from a common ancestor and they have similar characteristics but their development diverges because of the separation, so that's why we call it divergent evolution.

Q4

Professor:	Right. Even when the habitat is similar, if they're separated, then they diverge. How about convergent evolution then?
Student:	Well, that would be a situation where a similar environment . . . a habitat . . . it may cause plants and animals to evolve in order to adapt to the conditions. So a species that isn't really related can evolve with similar characteristics because . . . it can look like a species in another geographic region because of adaptation . . . and that would be convergent evolution?
Professor:	Right again. So temperature and rainfall, proximity to water, latitude and longitude all combine to determine the climate, and if we know the climate of an area, then we can actually predict what kind of life will inhabit it.
Student:	Okay. And I really did know that. I just didn't put it down. To tell the truth, I didn't see the second part. Not until you pointed it out to me.
Professor:	That's what I thought. Well, Jerry, it's a good idea to double-check all the questions on a test . . . not just my test . . . any test . . . to make sure you've answered each part of the question completely. Otherwise, you won't get full credit.
Student:	I see that. Well, live and learn.
Professor:	Jerry, you're one of my best students.
Student:	Thanks. I really like biology. In fact, I'm thinking of majoring in it.
Professor:	Good. That means you'll be in some of my upper-level classes.
Student:	And I'll be watching out for those two-part questions on your exams.
Professor:	And all the rest of your exams. I'll be honest with you. My questions usually have two parts so the students will have an insight into the grading system . . . and a lot of professors do that. In an essay question, it's difficult to know what to include and how much to write. Just read the question carefully, and be sure to include all the parts. There may be

three or four in some essay questions. This is the way that the professor helps you organize your answer. I'm giving my students a hint about what I'm looking for by including several parts to the question. But if you miss one of the parts, then it lowers your score.

Student: That makes sense. I think I was just trying to finish within the time limit, and I didn't read as carefully as I should have. **On the final, I'll spend more time reading the questions before I start to answer them.**

Professor: Good plan.

Audio 1. Why does the man go to see his professor?
Answer **B** To clarify a question from the midterm

Audio 2. Listen again to part of the conversation and then answer the following question.
Replay "Thanks. Here's the thing. I said that a biotic province was a region with similar life, but with boundaries that prevent plants and animals from spreading to other regions."
Audio Why does the man say this:
Replay "Thanks. Here's the thing."
Answer **D** He is signaling that he will explain his problem.

Audio 3. What did the man do wrong?
Answer **C** He did not answer one question completely. He did not see the second part.

Audio 4. According to the student, what is *divergent evolution*?
Answer **C** A similar group that is separated may develop different characteristics.

Audio 5. What will Jerry probably do on the next test?
Answer **A** To avoid the same problem that he had on the midterm, he will look for questions with several parts.

LISTENING 2 "ART HISTORY CLASS"

Audio Lecture
Narrator: Listen to part of a lecture in an art history class.

Professor:
We know that the Chinese had been aware of basic photographic principles as early as the fifth century B.C.E., and Leonardo da Vinci had experimented

with a dark room in the 1500s, but it was a number of discoveries in chemistry during the eighteenth century that, uh, uh, accelerated the development of modern photography. The discovery that silver salts were light sensitive led to . . . experimentation with images of light on a surface that had been coated with silver. Often glass was used in the early images. But the problem was that these images were ephemeral—fading after only a short time. Some of the chemists who worked with them called them fairy pictures, and considered them . . . that they were only momentary creations . . . that they would disappear.

Okay. How to fix the image permanently was one of the most important challenges . . . of the early photographer chemists. In France, in about 1820, Nicephore Niepce discovered a method for fixing the image after a long exposure time, oh, probably eight hours. So, although his work was considered interesting, it was . . . largely dismissed as impractical. Nevertheless, one of his associates, Louis Daguerre, managed to find a way to reduce . . . the exposure time to less than twenty minutes. So the story goes, in 1835, Daguerre was experimenting with some exposed plates, and he put a couple of them into his chemical cupboard, so a few days later, he opened the cupboard, and to his surprise, the latent images on the plates had developed. At first, he couldn't figure out why, but eventually, he concluded that this must have occurred as a result of mercury vapor . . . from a broken thermometer that was also in the . . . enclosed in the cupboard. Supposedly, from this fortunate accident, he was able to invent a process for developing latent images on . . . on exposed plates.

Q8

The process itself was somewhat complicated. First, he exposed copper plates to iodine which released fumes of light-sensitive silver iodide. These copper plates were used to capture the image, and by the way, they had to be used almost immediately after their exposure to the iodine. So, the image on the plate was then exposed to light for ten to twenty minutes. The plate was developed over mercury heated to about 75 degrees centigrade, which caused the mercury to amalgamate with the silver. Now here's the ingenious part—he then fixed the image in a warm solution of common salt, but later he began using sodium sulphite. Anyway, after he rinsed the plate in hot distilled water, a white image was left permanently on the plate. And the quality was really quite amazing.

Q9

But, um . . . the process had its limitations. First, the images couldn't be reproduced, so each one was a unique piece, and that greatly increased the cost of photography. Second, the image was reversed, so the subjects would actually see themselves as though they were looking in a mirror, although in the case of portraits, the fact that people were accustomed to seeing themselves in a mirror made this less . . . this problem less urgent than some of the others. Nevertheless, some photographers did point their

Q7

cameras at a mirrored reflection of the image that they wanted to capture so that the reflection would be reversed, and a true image could be pro-

Q10 duced. Okay. Third, the chemicals and the fumes that they released were highly toxic, so photography was a very dangerous occupation. Fourth, the

Q7 surface of the image was extremely fragile and . . . had to be protected, often under glass, so they didn't disintegrate from handling. The beautiful cases that were made to hold the early images became popular not only for aesthetic purposes but, uh, but also for very practical reasons. And finally, although the exposure time had been radically reduced, it was still . . . inconveniently long . . . at twenty minutes, especially for portraits, since people would have to sit still in the sun for that length of time. Elaborate headrests were constructed to keep the subjects from moving so that the image wouldn't be ruined, and many people simply didn't want to endure the discomfort.

Q11   But, by the mid 1800s, improvements in chemistry and optics had resolved most of these issues. Bromide as well as iodine sensitized the plates, and some photographers were even using chlorine in an effort to decrease exposure time. The portrait lens was also improved by reducing the size of the opening, and limiting the amount of light that could enter, so the exposure time was about twenty seconds instead of twenty minutes. And negative film had been introduced in France, sorry, in England, and negatives permitted the production of multiple copies from a single image. So, photography was on its way to becoming a popular profession and pastime.

Audio	6.	What is the main topic of this lecture?
Answer	**D**	The other choices are all mentioned in order to develop the main topic: the history of early photography.

Audio	7.	According to the professor, what two limitations were noted in Daguerre's process for developing and fixing latent images?
Answer	**B**	The images were very delicate and easily fell apart.
	C	Multiple images could not be made from the plate.

Audio	8.	Listen again to part of the lecture and then answer the following question.
Replay		" At first, he couldn't figure out why, but eventually, he concluded that this must have occurred as a result of mercury vapor . . . from a broken thermometer that was also in the . . . enclosed in the cupboard. Supposedly, from this fortunate accident, he was able to invent a process for developing latent images on . . . on exposed plates."

Audio		Why does the professor say this:
Replay		"Supposedly, from this fortunate accident, he was able to invent a process for developing latent images on . . . on exposed plates."
Answer	**C**	The word "supposedly" implies that the speaker is not sure whether the information is accurate.
Audio	9.	What substance was first used to fix the images?
Answer	**B**	Table salt
Audio	10.	What can we assume about photographers in the 1800s?
Answer	**D**	Some of them must have experienced health problems as a result of their laboratory work because the chemicals and the fumes that they released were highly toxic.
Audio	11.	In what order does the professor explain photographic principles?
Answer	**B**	In a chronological sequence of events, beginning with the fifth century B.C.E. and ending with the mid-1800s

Listening 3 "Linguistics Class"

Audio Discussion

Narrator:	Listen to part of a discussion in a linguistics class.
Professor:	What comes to mind when I say the word *grammar*?
Student 1:	That's easy. English class and lots of rules.
Student 2:	Memorizing parts of speech . . . like nouns and verbs.
Student 3:	Diagramming sentences.

Professor:
Well, yes, that's fairly typical. But today we're going to look at grammar [Q12] from the point of view of the linguist, and to do that, we really have to consider three distinct grammars for every language.

The first grammar is referred to as a *mental grammar*. And that's what a speaker of a language knows, often implicitly, about the grammar of that language. This has also been called *linguistic competence* and from that term *competence grammar* has become popular. I like to think of it, of mental or competence grammar, I mean . . . I like to think of it as an incredibly complex system that allows a speaker to produce language that other speakers can understand. It includes the sounds, the vocabulary, the order of words in sentences and . . . even the appropriateness of a topic or a word in a particular social situation. And what's so amazing is that most of us carry this knowledge around in our heads and use it without much reflection.

Q13 One way to clarify mental or competence grammar is to ask a friend a question about a sentence. Your friend probably won't know why it's correct, but that friend will know if it's correct. So one of the features of mental or competence grammar is this incredible sense of correctness and the ability to hear something that "sounds odd" in a language. Haven't you had the experience of hearing a sentence, and it stood out to you? It just wasn't quite right? For native speakers we can call this ability native intuition, but even language learners who've achieved a high level of competence in a second language will be able to give similar intuitive responses even if they can't explain the rules. So that's mental grammar or competence grammar.

Okay then, that brings us to the second type of grammar, and this is what linguists are most concerned about. This is *descriptive grammar*, which is a description of what the speakers know intuitively about a language. Linguists try to discover the underlying rules of mental or competence grammar and describe them objectively. So descriptive grammar is a *model* of competence grammar, and as such, it has to be based on the best effort of a linguist, and consequently, subject to criticism and even disagreement from *other* linguists. Because no matter how skilled a linguist is, describing **Q14** grammar is an enormous task. In the first place, the knowledge is incredibly vast and complex; in the second place, the language itself is changing even while it's being described; and finally, the same data can be organized in different but equally correct ways in order to arrive at generalizations. And the ultimate goal of a descriptive grammar is to formulate generalizations about a language that accurately reflect the mental rules that speakers have in their heads.

But, getting back to what most people think of as grammar—the grammar that we may have learned in school. That's very different from either competence grammar or descriptive grammar because the rules aren't meant to describe language at all. They're meant to prescribe and judge language as good or bad. And this kind of grammar is called, not surprisingly, *prescriptive grammar* because of its judgmental perspective. Again, to contrast prescriptive grammar with descriptive grammar, just think of descriptive generalizations as accepting the language that a speaker uses in an effort to describe it and recognizing that there may be several dialects that are used by various groups of speakers and that any one speaker will probably choose to use different language depending on the formality, for example, of the situation. On the other hand, prescriptive rules are rigid and subject to enforcement. Prescriptivists want to make all speakers conform to one standard in all situations, and that tends to be a very formal level of language all the time.

Now which of these types of grammar do you think you were learning in school when you had to memorize parts of speech and rules and diagram sentences?

Student 2:   Sounds like prescriptive grammar to me.

Professor:
Precisely. But how did prescriptive rules get to be accepted, at least in the schools? And probably even more important, why are so many of these rules disregarded even by well-educated speakers in normal situations?

Student 1:   Did you say *disregarded*?   Q15

Professor:
I did. Some of you may recall that during the seventeenth and eighteenth centuries in Europe, Latin was considered the perfect language and was used by the educated classes. The argument for the perfection of Latin was   Q16 reinforced by the fact that Latin had become a written language and, con- sequently . . . Latin had stopped changing in the normal ways that spoken languages do, so the rules were also fixed, and for many writers of English during that period, the rules of Latin were held as a standard for all lan- guages, including English. But the problem was that English had a different origin and very different constructions. For example, how many times have   Q17 you heard the prescriptive rule, "never end a sentence with a preposition?" This is a Latin rule, but it doesn't apply to English, so it sounds very formal and even strange when this Latin rule is enforced. Now, how many of you would say, "What are we waiting for?" I think most of us would prefer it to "For what are we waiting?" But as you see, this breaks the rule—the Latin rule, that is.

Student 2:
So we're really learning Latin rules in English classes. No wonder I was confused. But wouldn't you think that . . . well, that things would change? I mean, Latin hasn't been recognized as a world language for a long time.

Professor:
You're right. But the reason that prescriptive rules survive is the school system. Teachers promote the prescriptive grammar as the standard for the school, and consequently for the educated class. And "good" language is

a requisite for social mobility, even when it's very dissimilar to the mental grammar or the descriptive grammar of a language.

Audio   12.   What is the discussion mainly about?
Answer   **B**   Different types of grammar

Audio   13.   How does the professor make his point about *native intuition*?
Answer   **A**   He explains how to perform an easy experiment. By asking a friend about a sentence, the students will understand the concept.

Audio   14.   What are two key problems for descriptive grammar?
Answer   **A**   The information is very complicated and subject to change.
             C   The language can be organized correctly in more than one way.

Audio   15.   Listen again to part of the discussion and then answer the following question.
Replay   "But how did prescriptive rules get to be accepted, at least in the schools?
                    And probably even more important, why are so many of these rules disregarded even by well-educated speakers in normal situations?"
                    "Did you say *disregarded*?"
Audio   Why does the student say this:
Replay   "Did you say *disregarded*?"
Answer   **B**   She is confirming that she has understood. Her tone is confused, not challenging.

Audio   16.   According to the professor, why were Latin rules used for English grammar?
Answer   **A**   Latin was a written language with rules that did not change.

Audio   17.   Why does the professor discuss the rule to avoid ending a sentence with a preposition?
Answer   **D**   It demonstrates the problem in using Latin rules for English.

LISTENING 4 "COLLEGE CAMPUS"

Audio Conversation

Narrator:	Listen to part of a conversation on campus between two students.
Man:	I didn't see you at the International Talent Show.
Woman:	No time for that kind of thing.
Man:	You mean you don't belong to the ISA?
Woman:	The ISA?
Man:	International Student Association.
Woman:	Oh, no. I don't belong to any clubs.
Man:	But this isn't like a regular club.
Woman:	How so?
Man:	Well, we have a house. You know, the brick house on fraternity row and . . .
Woman:	You live there, right?
Man:	Yeah. I moved in last year. It's really inexpensive because we take care of the house ourselves and we cook our own meals.
Woman:	That sounds like it would take a lot of time.
Man:	Not really. There's a list of chores posted every week, and you can choose something you like to do, so I usually put my name down for yard work. I like being outside so it's fun for me.
Woman:	But you have to cook too, right?
Man:	Okay, it's like this: twenty of us live there so every night two of the guys cook and two of the guys clean up, so you only have to cook about once a week and clean up once.
Woman:	What about breakfast and lunch?
Man:	Oh, well, you're on your own for that, but the dinners are just fantastic. It's like eating in a different ethnic restaurant every night. You know, because the guys are from different countries.
Woman:	That sounds good.
Man:	And it costs about half what it did to live in the dorm. But really, I'm doing it because it's a great experience living with people from so many different countries. My best friend in the house is from Korea. My roommate's from Brazil. And I've got friends from . . . well, just about everywhere.
Woman:	But you don't have to live in the house to belong to the club.

Q19

Q20

Man:	No, no. There are about a hundred members in the International Student Association. Only guys live in the house, but there are a lot of women in the association.
Woman:	I wish I had time to do it. It really sounds interesting.
Man:	You've got to relax sometimes. Anyway, we meet at the house the first Friday of the month from seven to ten. We have a buffet dinner and after that, we have a short meeting. That's when we plan our activities, like the talent show and picnics and dances. Then a lot of the people stay for music and a party, but some people leave after the meeting.
Woman:	So it's only a couple hours a month?
Man:	Right. Listen, why don't you come over next Friday for the meeting, as my guest, I mean. You have to eat anyway. And if you have a good time, you can think about joining.
Woman:	Next Friday? Well, I don't know . . . I usually study on Friday night, but . . . I could take a break . . . Sure I'll come over . . . but I might have to leave early.
Man:	Great.

Q21 (left margin)
Q18 (left margin)
Q22 (left margin)

Audio   18.   What is the purpose of this conversation?
Answer   **C**   The man is convincing the woman to join the International Student Association. He invites the woman to attend a meeting as his guest.

Audio   19.   What does the man imply about the house where he is living?
Answer   **A**   He is saving money by living at the house, but he prefers the house to the dorm because it is a great experience.

Audio   20.   How does the man feel about the International Student Association?
Answer   **B**   He enjoys meeting people with different backgrounds.

Audio   21.   Listen again to part of the conversation and then answer the following question.
Replay   "Then a lot of the people stay for music and a party, but some people leave after the meeting."
"So it's only a couple hours a month?"
Audio   What does the woman mean when she says this:
Replay   "So it's only a couple hours a month?"
Answer   **D**   Her tone indicates indecision. She is changing her mind about going.

Audio   22.   What does the woman agree to do?
Answer   C   Go to a meeting

LISTENING 5 "ZOOLOGY CLASS"

Audio Lecture
Narrator: Listen to part of a lecture in a zoology class. The professor is discussing coral reefs.

Professor:
Every ecosystem on Earth is unique, but the coral reef is perhaps the most unusual of all because it's the only ecosystem made *by* and made *of*—animals. All coral reefs are constructed by coral polyps, which are generally small, about the size of this pencil eraser. But, the structures themselves are, well, enormous. Astronauts have been able to identify the Great Barrier Reef in Australia from space. Can you believe that? And the diversity of species in large coral reefs is second only to the rainforest habitats. In fact, we estimate that for every species we've identified on a coral reef, there are probably a hundred times that number that remain to be classified and studied. | Q28

But how do these little polyps build such impressive reefs? Well, hard coral secrete a shell of calcium carbonate around their bodies. The polyp *isn't* hard, you see, but the shell *is*. And these shells are the material that forms a coral reef. So a coral reef is just a colony—millions and millions of coral animals whose shells are connected. And reproduction is really the basis for the construction of a large reef. You see, as each polyp matures, it converts the calcium and other minerals in ocean water to a hard limestone exoskeleton called a corallite. And this is fascinating. Although the polyps themselves don't appreciably increase in size, they continue to build new shells periodically, um, connecting them with . . . with partitions. | Q23

Now coral can reproduce sexually through an activity called mass spawning. During one night in the spring when the moon is full, coral polyps release egg bundles that contain both eggs and sperm. Most polyps have both male and female reproductive cells. The egg bundles are round, about half the size of marbles, I would say. They're brightly colored in orange or red or pink, and they float up to the surface to form a thick layer of, uh . . . well think of them as rather fragrant beads. So with the water so saturated with them, predators will only be able to devour a small number compared with the huge number that will survive and break open. The sperm cells swim away to fertilize the eggs from another bundle. So . . . once fertilized, the little egg begins to mature from a coral larva to a planulae, which can swim for a few hours, days, or even a few weeks. Ultimately it locates a hard surface on which to attach itself and from which it will *not* move for the rest | Q24 of its life, except for the movement involved in the process of building a new, neighboring shell as . . . as it continues to mature.

But actually sexual reproduction isn't the way that coral reefs are really constructed. When a polyp matures on the site it's selected, the habitat is identified as being conducive to reef building. So the mature polyp doesn't just grow bigger, it actually replicates itself in a process called budding. After the genetic material is duplicated, then the polyp divides itself in half, and each half becomes a completely mature polyp. This budding process repeats itself, eventually producing thousands of asexually budded coral polyps connected by a tissue that grows over the limestone shells between the polyps. So, as you can imagine, budding will produce a large number of individual polyps, but they'll all have exactly the same genetic code as the first polyp. And this creates the beginning of a coral reef, but without the diversity that eventually populates the habitat. Wherever a coral reef is constructed, abundant sea life congregates. In fact, it's been estimated that about 25 percent of all ocean species can be found within the coral reefs.

Now most coral polyps eat plankton—single-celled microscopic organisms that float or swim very slowly in the ocean water in their habitat. But a coral reef has such a high concentration of polyps, they can't rely solely on plankton to survive. So coral polyps have developed a symbiotic relationship with a single-celled algae called zooxanthella. Remember that to qualify as symbiotic, a relationship must be mutually beneficial. So the zooxanthella produces food for the coral through the by-products of photosynthesis, and the coral provides a safe home for the zooxanthella, because it's hidden from predators that inhabit the coral reef.

Every species of coral grows at a different rate, some as much as six inches a year. But faster growing colonies are more prone to breaking apart either from their own weight or from the continuous force of the ocean waves. Some species tend to grow more slowly, but they may live as long as a thousand years. Even so, only the top portion of any reef is actually alive and growing and the lower structure is comprised of the skeletal remains . . . that's limestone corallite from coral that has died.

And what I find incredibly interesting about coral reefs is that each is a unique structure. But, of course, scientists need to classify, and so there's a classification system for coral reefs. A *fringing reef* grows around islands and the shorelines of continents and extends out from the shore. In order to flourish, fringing reefs must have clean water, lots of sunshine, and a moderately high concentration of salt. Some good examples of fringing reefs can be found around the Hawaiian Islands. Oh, yes, these are the most common and also the most recently formed class of coral reefs. Here's a drawing of a fringing reef.

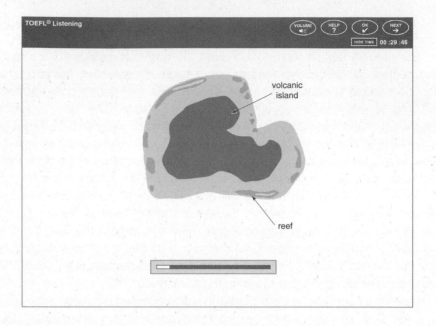

I think this is actually one of the Hawaiian reefs.

Now, *barrier reefs*—they're found further from shore, and they're usually separated from the shoreline by a shallow body of water, maybe a lagoon. As in the case of the Great Barrier Reef off the shore of Australia, the body of water can be miles wide, so the reef is miles away from the shoreline. And there may actually be a collection of coral reefs fused together. This is a drawing of a reef in the Great Barrier chain.

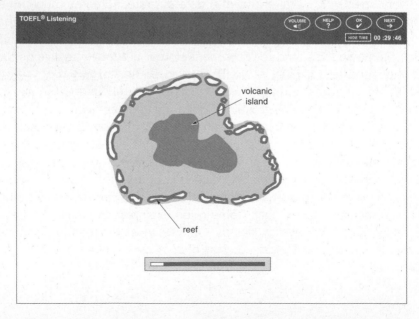

As I recall there are about twenty-five, or maybe even more individual coral reefs connected to form the Great Barrier Reef. As a general rule, barrier reefs are larger and older than fringing reefs.

Q27 But the oldest class of coral reef is the atoll, which is a ring-shaped reef with a lagoon in the middle and deep water surrounding the ring. These are scattered throughout the South Pacific, kind of like oasis settlements in the desert. And they abound with a diversity of sea life. This is one of the South Pacific atolls.

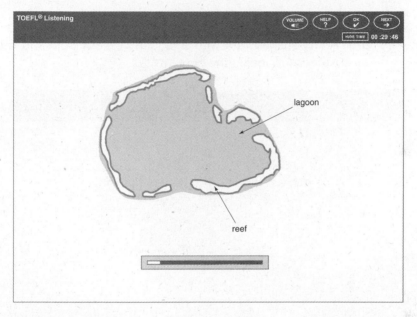

Q28 So, as we reflect on everything we've said about coral, we know that it's a relatively simple organism with a body ending in a mouth and tentacles. It reproduces both sexually and asexually by budding, and it survives by forming a symbiotic relationship with zooxanthella. But none of this is very extraordinary. What *is* unique about coral in the animal kingdom is its ability to construct a variety of reefs, creating habitats that are absolutely unlike any others on Earth.

Audio   23.   According to the professor, how do coral reefs grow?
Answer   **B**   They connect corallite shells to build structures.

Audio   24.   Why are so many egg bundles released during mass spawning?
Answer   **C**   A number of the egg bundles will be eaten [by predators].

Audio   25. According to the professor, what is *budding*?

Answer   A The division of a polyp in half to reproduce itself.

Audio   26. What is the relationship between zooxanthella and coral polyps?

Answer   B The zooxanthella uses the coral for a shelter from enemies.
            C The coral eats food produced by the zooxanthella.
            The relationship is symbiotic.

Audio   27. Which of the following reefs is probably an atoll?

Answer   C A ring-shaped reef with a lagoon in the middle and deep water surrounding the ring.

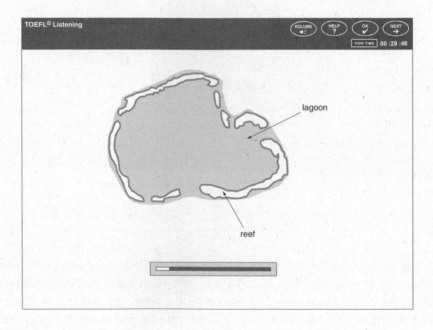

Audio   28. In the lecture, the professor explains coral reefs. Indicate whether each of the following is a true statement about coral reefs. Click in the correct box for each phrase.

		Yes	No
A	In general, the organism is quite simple.	✔	
B	The structure of a reef can be very large.	✔	
C	The living coral grows on top of dead shells.	✔	
D	Mass spawning is not very effective.		✔

LISTENING 6 "BUSINESS CLASS"

Audio Discussion

Narrator: Listen to part of a discussion in a business class.

Professor:

Q29 Industry analysts report that multinational food companies are trying to use the same types of strategies that automobile and electronics manufacturers have found to be successful in the global marketplace. The problem is that general rules for products that tend to be traditional for national or even regional tastes . . . these products are very difficult to identify and sales aren't easy to project. But, the companies that tend to do best are those that are the most responsive to local tastes. And they spend development dollars on taste testing in the local markets before they formulate the final

Q30 product. Can anyone recall any examples from the case studies in the text? Sandy?

Student 1:

McDonald's Big Mac has more mustard in the special sauce in Paris than it does in New York.

Professor: Because?

Student 1:

Because taste tests verified that people in the United States liked sweeter condiments than people did in France. In fact, I think the . . . the sugar content for export foods in general usually has to be modified when American products are taste tested overseas.

Professor:

Right you are. Probably the company that's adapted most to local tastes is Nestle. Can you believe that they produce more than 200 slightly different blends of Nescafe for export to different countries? Amazing but true. But sometimes taste is less a problem of ingredients and more a matter of the way a food product looks or feels. One case study that comes to mind is the one about the soft cookies that just don't sell as well in England as crisp cookies. So, you can see that taste extends way beyond just flavor. It's really a combination of flavor preferences and local expectations.

Look, here's another example of accommodation that had more to do with the expectation for a process than the flavor of the product. In this case study, it was cake. Remember when Betty Crocker cake mixes were introduced in England, they weren't accepted because the English homemaker felt more comfortable with convenience foods that required more than water to prepare them. Go figure. But that was the problem uncovered by extensive market research. So when the mix was reformulated without an egg, and the preparation included adding an egg with the water before mixing it, well, Betty Crocker cake mixes became very popular in England.

Any other examples come to mind? They don't have to be from the case `Q31` studies in the book.

Student 2:   How about serving sizes?

Professor: Go on.

Student 2:
Well soft drinks for one. Just compare the serving sizes in the United States and many foreign markets where soft drinks are sold. The cans in foreign markets are much smaller because consumers expect it. But, uh, in the United States, well, super sizing is probably a consideration when a foreign company is trying to crack the American market.

Professor:
That's a great example. So the taste can be acceptable, but the packag- `Q32` ing has to compare favorably with the competing brands and the public's expectations.

Student 3:
Yeah, but that makes products more expensive, doesn't it? I mean you can't standardize the product or the packaging so that would make it more . . . more costly to produce, wouldn't it?

Professor:
Right you are, Chris. In fact, you've really gone to the heart of the issue. A compromise has to occur between the requirement that products be adapted to please the taste and the expectations of local consumers and the pressure to standardize products for maximum cost effectiveness. Now, let's complicate that even further. Even the experts don't agree on the importance of how far to go in adapting products for local markets. A few years ago, Ted Levitt—he's the editor of the *Harvard Business Review*— Levitt predicted what he called a "pluralization of consumption." What he `Q33` means is that at least in some areas, tastes are likely to converge, which makes sense when you think about the increased opportunities for travel and sampling of foods, as well as the continued global marketing efforts by multinational corporations. So logically, it's smarter to simply identify the

areas in which tastes are most likely to be the same, and concentrate efforts on those food products.

But there's also the issue of global marketing. How about the potential to create taste? I mean, selling the image that surrounds using a product. If consumers want to associate themselves with that image, won't they develop a taste for the product that does that for them? For example, there's some evidence that the popularity of products seen in movies and television spills into the foreign marketplace. This subtle brand association with the movie or the celebrities in it translates into high dollar deals for certain brands to be visibly displayed in widely distributed films.

Student 3:
Oh, right. I was reading about that. It was in a couple of the case studies. The bottle, a can, or . . . or a package appears as part of the character's persona, and if it's a character that audiences choose to identify with, then the taste for the product may follow, or at least that's what the marketing experts are betting on.

Professor:
And that includes foreign audiences. Anyone drink Starbucks coffee? Well, Starbucks began as a regional coffee in Seattle, Washington, and made the global leap in 2000, opening shops in China, a huge market surely, but also a traditionally *tea-drinking* society. So what's the attraction? Starbucks is marketing to the cosmopolitan consumer, the young trendy set looking for a modern image as well as a different taste.

Still, there have been some real surprises in the multinational dinner party. No one has really figured out why the Italians, Germans, and British love Kraft's Philadelphia cream cheese, and the Greeks simply don't buy it. And why did Perrier, a mineral water from France . . . why did Perrier take America by storm while other imported mineral waters . . . didn't? In short, success in the food export industry is probably a combination of the real taste . . . the flavor of the product, with some adaptation for the local markets, the satisfaction of certain expectations for the preparation and packaging, and the taste for the product created by images in the global marketing plan. Add to this mix the potential for a short shelf life or even perishable products and, well, you have a very challenging problem for the multinational food industry.

Audio	29.	What is the discussion mainly about?
Answer	**A**	The other choices relate to the main topic: the global marketing of food products.

Audio 30. How does the professor organize the discussion?

Answer C He refers to case studies from the textbook.

Audio 31. Listen again to part of the discussion and then answer the following question.

Replay "Any other examples come to mind? They don't have to be from the case studies in the book."
"How about serving sizes?"

Audio Why does the student say this:

Replay "How about serving sizes?"

Answer B She is offering a possible answer to the professor's question. "How about" is a polite way to offer a possibility.

Audio 32. What technique does the professor use to encourage student discussion?

Answer A He gives students positive reinforcement by praising their efforts.

Audio 33. What did Ted Levitt mean by "the pluralization of consumption"?

Answer D More people will want the same products.

Audio 34. What does the professor say about television and movie companies?

Answer D He points out that they are paid to display brand-name products.

➤ Speaking

Model Test 2, Speaking Section, Track 36

INDEPENDENT SPEAKING QUESTION 1 "REGRET"

Narrator 2: Number 1. Listen for a question about a familiar topic. After you hear the question, you have 15 seconds to prepare and 45 seconds to record your answer.

Narrator 1: Explain a situation in the past when you have regretted your decision. What would you do differently?

Narrator 2: Please prepare your answer after the beep.

Beep

[Preparation Time: 15 seconds]

Narrator 2: Please begin speaking after the beep.

Beep

[Recording Time: 45 seconds]

Beep

INDEPENDENT SPEAKING QUESTION 2 "COURSE REQUIREMENTS"

Narrator 2: Number 2. Listen for a question that asks your opinion about a familiar topic. After you hear the question, you have 15 seconds to prepare and 45 seconds to record your answer.

Narrator 1: Some students would rather write a paper than take a test. Other students would rather take a test instead of writing a paper. Which option do you prefer and why? Use specific reasons and examples to support your opinion.

Narrator 2: Please prepare your answer after the beep.

Beep

[Preparation Time: 15 seconds]

Narrator 2: Please begin speaking after the beep.

Beep

[Recording Time: 45 seconds]

Beep

INTEGRATED SPEAKING QUESTION 3 "HEALTH INSURANCE"

Narrator 2: Number 3. Read a short passage and listen to a talk on the same topic. Then listen for a question about them. After you hear the question, you have 30 seconds to prepare and 60 seconds to record your answer.

Narrator 1: A student is discussing the university's health insurance policy with the foreign student advisor. Read the policy in the college schedule [printed on page 294]. You have 45 seconds to complete it. Please begin reading now.

[Reading Time: 45 seconds]

Narrator 1: Now listen to the foreign student advisor. He is explaining the policy and expressing his opinion about it.

Advisor:
I think it's very important for you to know that this policy wasn't instituted in order to increase fees for international students. In fact, the university doesn't make a profit from the sale of health insurance. The problem is that health care costs in this country are so high that it could be financially disastrous for the family of an international student who needed more than just a simple visit to the doctor's office. A trip to the emergency room at the hospital could cost thousands of dollars without health insurance! Most families abroad just don't realize how costly it is. As for foreign health insurance providers—well, it was just too difficult to validate their coverage for medical services, and the local doctors and hospitals simply stopped accepting them. So . . . to be sure that our students are protected, we're offering low-cost health insurance through the school.

Narrator 1: The foreign student advisor expresses his opinion of the policy for health insurance. Report his opinion and explain the reasons that he gives for having that opinion.

Narrator 2: Please prepare your answer after the beep.

Beep

[Preparation Time: 30 seconds]

Narrator 2: Please begin speaking after the beep.

Beep

[Recording Time: 60 seconds]

Beep

INTEGRATED SPEAKING QUESTION 4 "ANTARCTICA"

Narrator 2: Number 4. Read a short passage and then listen to part of a lecture on the same topic. Then listen for a question about them. After you hear the question, you have 30 seconds to prepare and 60 seconds to record your answer.

Narrator 1: Now read the passage about Antarctica [printed on page 295]. You have 45 seconds to complete it. Please begin reading now.

[Reading Time: 45 seconds]

Narrator 1: Now listen to part of a lecture in a geography class. The professor is talking about Antarctica.

Professor:
With the increasing pressure to replace raw materials that are being consumed in other parts of the world, Antarctica and the waters offshore could become a stage for international conflict in the future. During the eighteenth and nineteenth centuries, hunters decimated huge populations of whales and seals, and the race to reach the South Pole resulted in national claims by explorers from a variety of countries, which finally resulted in the partitioning of pie-shaped sectors radiating away from the center at the pole. So today several claims overlap, and only one sector remains unclaimed. Virtually all of these claims are covered by an ice sheet about two miles thick, but the question is, what's beneath the ice? Scientific experiments indicate that proteins, fuels, and minerals exist in abundance, and that means that in spite of the difficulties and challenges involved in the exploitation of these natural resources, the countries with claims haven't demonstrated an intention to relinquish their stake in the area. While resources are available in more convenient sites, the remote areas in Antarctica appear to be relatively safe from exploitation. In addition, as the reading passage suggests, global self-interest may engender international cooperation in this crucial environmental system.

Narrator 1: Explain why many countries have staked claims in Antarctica, and why national interests have not been pursued.

Narrator 2: Please prepare your answer after the beep.

Beep

[Preparation Time: 30 seconds]

Narrator 2: Please begin speaking after the beep.

Beep

[Recording Time: 60 seconds]

Beep

INTEGRATED SPEAKING QUESTION 5 "EXTRA MONEY"

Narrator 2: Number 5. Listen to a short conversation. Then listen for a question about it. After you hear the question, you have 20 seconds to prepare and 60 seconds to record your answer.

Narrator 1: Now listen to a conversation between a student and her friend.

Student:	I need to earn some extra money. My budget's just out of control.
Friend:	I hear you. I had the same problem last semester.
Student:	So what did you do?
Friend:	I got a job at the cafeteria. I don't really like the work, but the good thing is that you get free meals.
Student:	Really? Are they hiring?
Friend:	I don't know, but I could ask. The pay isn't great though. See, the meals are the thing.
Student:	Oh. Still, that would cut down on the grocery bill.
Friend:	Yeah . . . Or, you know what? You could rent that extra room in your apartment. I'll bet you could get $250 a month, at least.
Student:	I've been thinking about that. It would help with the rent and the utilities, and I wouldn't have to work so I could use my time for my classes, but, I keep thinking, what if my roommate doesn't pay on time, or what if there's a lot of noise.
Friend:	Well, you'd have to have a deposit and a contract . . . something in writing so you could keep the deposit if there were problems, and you could break the contract if it didn't work out.

Narrator 1: Describe the woman's problem, and the two suggestions that her friend makes about how to handle it. What do you think the woman should do, and why?

Narrator 2: Please prepare your answer after the beep.

Beep

[Preparation Time: 20 seconds]

Narrator 2: Please begin speaking after the beep.

Beep

[Recording Time: 60 seconds]

Beep

INTEGRATED SPEAKING QUESTION 6 "RESEARCH REFERENCES"

Narrator 2: Number 6. Listen to part of a lecture. Then listen for a question about it. After you hear the question, you have 20 seconds to prepare, and 60 seconds to record your answer.

Narrator 1: Now listen to part of a lecture in a sociology class. The professor is discussing the criteria for using older research references.

Professor:
Well, first of all you have to understand that there's no hard and fast rule for deciding when a research reference is too old. But that doesn't help you much. So, I'll try to give you a couple of guidelines, and then you'll just have to use good judgment. Okay, let's just say for our purposes, that the research is thirty years old. Then the next thing to think about is whether any changes have occurred in society to call the data into question. For example, in a study that looks at diet, we know logically that many changes have occurred in eating patterns over the past thirty years, so this study would probably be out of date. But a study of, uh, say language development may be okay because the way that babies learn their native language hasn't changed much in the same period of time. So, what I'm saying is . . . the date is less important than the potential for change. Okay, then the second criteria to consider is whether the citation is a *finding* or an *opinion*. If you have a study that indicates, uh, for example, that college students are drinking more, that's a *finding*, but if you have a statement by the researcher

that drinking is the most serious problem on campus, then you have an *opinion*. And opinions are accurate over the years as long as they're attributed to the person and the date is cited. But the finding for an older study may be too old. In that case, it's probably better to use a more recent study.

Narrator 1: Using the main points and examples from the lecture, describe the two criteria for using an older research reference presented by the professor.

Narrator 2: Please prepare your answer after the beep.

Beep

[Preparation Time: 20 seconds]

Narrator 2: Please begin speaking after the beep.

Beep

[Recording Time: 60 seconds]

Beep

➤ Writing

 Model Test 2, Writing Section, Track 37

INTEGRATED ESSAY "COLLAPSE OF EASTER ISLAND"

First, read the passage [printed on pages 300–301] and take notes.

Narrator: Now listen to a lecture on the same topic as the passage that you have just read.

Professor:
Well, all of the theories explaining the collapse of the civilization on Easter Island have some serious flaws. Let's start with deforestation. A credible study by Hunt and Lipo provides evidence that even though the Easter Islanders cleared most of the forests, they replaced them with grasslands, which would have prevented the erosion that supposedly made the ground

impossible to cultivate. So the absence of trees, although serious in terms of shelter, cooking, and transportation, wouldn't necessarily have precluded an agricultural base that could have supported the population.

As for the theory that rats ate the new tree shoots, preventing the regrowth of the forests, it's probably true that rats contributed to a disruption of the island's ecosystem, but it's also likely that the native people used rats as a food source while they tried to establish a long-term plan. Rat bones have been found along with chicken bones in the garbage dumps on the island, suggesting that the islanders were eating rats as well as chicken.

Okay then, what about the fighting between the long-eared and short-eared people? Historical records confirm that when the Spanish Viceroy of Peru sent an expedition to the island in 1770, the explorers estimated a native population of about 3000 people, but four years later when Sir James Cook arrived, the population had been decimated. Some records indicate that more than two-thirds of the population had perished. But island tradition dates the war between the long-eared and the short-eared people at about 1680—that's about one hundred years earlier. And it doesn't add up, does it?

So, you see, we still have a mystery because none of the three theories really provides a scenario that explains why the civilization on Easter Island collapsed.

Question

Summarize the main points in the lecture and then explain how they cast doubt on the ideas in the reading passage.

➤ Example Answers and Checklists for Speaking and Writing

Model Test 2, Example Answers, Track 38

Example Answer for Independent Speaking Question 1 "Regret"

I regret that I moved out of my apartment with my roommate without trying harder to make things better. In the first place, I should have talked with her about the problems and listened to what she had to say. Maybe if I'd understood *her* side, it would have made a difference. In the second place, I should have tried to include my roommate in some of my plans with my other friends. Maybe she felt left out. And when I think about it, I probably should have been a better roommate myself, to set a good example, I mean.

If I'd been the kind of roommate I wanted to have, I could have shown her by example. Just leaving wasn't a good idea and I regret it.

Checklist 1

✔ The talk answers the topic question.
✔ The point of view or position is clear.
✔ The talk is direct and well organized.
✔ The sentences are logically connected.
✔ Details and examples support the main idea.
✔ The speaker expresses complete thoughts.
✔ The meaning is easy to comprehend.
✔ A wide range of vocabulary is used.
✔ There are only minor errors in grammar.
✔ The talk is within a range of 125–150 words.

EXAMPLE ANSWER FOR INDEPENDENT SPEAKING QUESTION 2 "COURSE REQUIREMENTS"

I prefer to write a paper instead of taking a test because I know exactly what the topic is when I'm researching a paper, but there are a large number of possibilities for questions on a test and that makes it much more difficult to prepare for. Besides, in my experience, some teachers aren't very straight-forward about their tests, and even though I've studied and understand the subject, well, sometimes the questions that you would expect to see aren't on the test and some obscure information is tested instead. But probably the most important reason for my preference is that I get very nervous when I'm taking a test, and that can affect my performance. Writing a paper doesn't cause me the same level of anxiety.

Checklist 2

✔ The talk answers the topic question.
✔ The point of view or position is clear.
✔ The talk is direct and well organized.
✔ The sentences are logically connected.
✔ Details and examples support the main idea.
✔ The speaker expresses complete thoughts.
✔ The meaning is easy to comprehend.
✔ A wide range of vocabulary is used.
✔ There are only minor errors in grammar.
✔ The talk is within a range of 125–150 words.

EXAMPLE ANSWER FOR INTEGRATED SPEAKING QUESTION 3 "HEALTH INSURANCE"

The foreign student advisor agrees with the policy that requires international students to purchase health insurance from the university at registration. He assures students that the university isn't trying to increase fees for international students by doing this. He explains that health care is very expensive. For example, a visit to the emergency room can be a financial burden to a family who doesn't have medical insurance. He says that most families of international students don't expect the costs to be so excessive. And the reason that the university doesn't allow students to substitute other health care providers is because the local medical community has had problems with validation for health insurance plans from abroad and now refuses to accept them. So, um, in order to protect the students, the school doesn't make any exceptions to the policy.

Checklist 3

✔ The talk summarizes the situation and opinion.
✔ The point of view or position is clear.
✔ The talk is direct and well organized.
✔ The sentences are logically connected.
✔ Details and examples support the opinion.
✔ The speaker expresses complete thoughts.
✔ The meaning is easy to comprehend.
✔ A wide range of vocabulary is used.
✔ Errors in grammar are minor.
✔ The talk is within a range of 125–150 words.

EXAMPLE ANSWER FOR INTEGRATED SPEAKING QUESTION 4 "ANTARCTICA"

Many countries have staked claims in Antarctica because the natural resources in other areas are being depleted and, uh, research indicates that minerals, fuels, and even some sources of protein are probably under the ice in large quantities. So, the implication is that as raw materials are exploited in areas that are relatively easy to reach, nations will think about taking advantage of their claims. For the time being, the location and climate have discouraged exploitation, and so have the treaties that protect the environment and encourage scientists to collaborate. It's also worth mentioning that Antarctica is vitally important to the balance that's maintained in the environment worldwide. So, in addition to all the difficulties that would have to be overcome to take advantage of the resources in their claims, individual nations also recognize the danger to the global environment and, at least for now, they're not pursuing their national interests.

Checklist 4

✔ The talk relates an example to a concept.
✔ Inaccuracies in the content are minor.
✔ The talk is direct and well organized.
✔ The sentences are logically connected.
✔ Details and examples support the opinion.
✔ The speaker expresses complete thoughts.
✔ The meaning is easy to comprehend.
✔ A wide range of vocabulary is used.
✔ The speaker paraphrases in his/her own words.
✔ The speaker credits the lecturer with wording.
✔ Errors in grammar are minor.
✔ The talk is within a range of 125–150 words.

EXAMPLE ANSWER FOR INTEGRATED SPEAKING QUESTION 5 "EXTRA MONEY"

The woman needs additional income to meet her expenses so her friend suggests that she get a job at the cafeteria. Even though the salary isn't very high, the free meals are helpful. He isn't sure whether there's a job available but he agrees to find out. He also recommends that she rent the second bedroom in her apartment for a minimum of $250 a month, which would subsidize the rent and utilities. The problem she points out is that room-mates can be disruptive, and sometimes they aren't financially responsible. But, she would have more time to study if she didn't have to work and her friend reminds her that she could require an agreement in writing, along with a deposit. Okay, in my opinion, she should try to get a job either in the cafeteria or someplace else on campus because if she lives alone, she can maintain a quiet environment for study, and she won't have to worry about a contract that could be difficult to enforce.

Checklist 5

✔ The talk summarizes the problem and recommendations.
✔ The speaker's point of view or position is clear.
✔ The talk is direct and well organized.
✔ The sentences are logically connected.
✔ Details and examples support the opinion.
✔ The speaker expresses complete thoughts.
✔ The meaning is easy to comprehend.
✔ A wide range of vocabulary is used.
✔ Errors in grammar are minor.
✔ The talk is within a range of 125–150 words.

EXAMPLE ANSWER FOR INTEGRATED SPEAKING QUESTION 6 "RESEARCH REFERENCES"

According to the lecturer, there are two major criteria for using an older research reference. First, she mentions, and I'm quoting here, the "potential for change." For example, research on diet may be too old after thirty years because many changes have occurred in dietary practices during that time, but research on language development may be okay because fewer changes have taken place in language acquisition in the same number of years. The other criteria requires that you first identify the research as a conclusion or an opinion. Because, uh, in general, a conclusion may be outdated when a newer study is published, but an opinion credited to a person with the date of the opinion in the citation, um, that's correct over time. In other words, there's no exact number of years to decide whether a reference is acceptable so the date isn't as significant as the criteria. So, an older study can be used if changes in the research haven't taken place or if the results are worded as opinions with the dates cited.

Checklist 6

✔ The talk summarizes a short lecture.
✔ Inaccuracies in the content are minor.
✔ The talk is direct and well organized.
✔ The sentences are logically connected.
✔ Details and examples support the main idea.
✔ The speaker expresses complete thoughts.
✔ The meaning is easy to comprehend.
✔ A wide range of vocabulary is used.
✔ The speaker paraphrases in his/her own words.
✔ The speaker credits the lecturer with wording.
✔ Errors in grammar are minor.
✔ The talk is within a range of 125–150 words.

EXAMPLE RESPONSE FOR INTEGRATED ESSAY "COLLAPSE OF EASTER ISLAND"

Many writers begin with a chart like those you practiced in Chapter 3. Only the essay will be scored.

Chart

Collapse of Easter Island
flaws in theories

Deforestation	
Cleared palms—ag, cooking, houses, canoes Moved ahu → erosion	Replaced w/grass → prevent e Ag base could support pop Hunt, Lipo

Rats	
Rats in canoes Ate young trees → prevented regrowth	Rats = food source Rat bones in garbage

War	
Short v Long ear L burned in ditch	Historical records 1680 100 yrs earlier

Example Essay "Collapse of Easter Island"

The reading lists three theories to explain the collapse of the civilization on Easter Island, but the lecture points out flaws in all three theories presented in the reading. The lecturer concedes that palm trees were cleared for agricultural purposes, cooking, the construction of homes and canoes, as well as the transportation of *ahu*. Nevertheless, the lecturer explains that the islanders replaced the palm trees with grass, which would have prevented erosion and would have allowed for an agricultural base that could have supported the population.

Although rats may have eaten many of the young trees, preventing their regrowth, the lecturer maintains that the rats could have been used as a food source for the islanders. In fact, rat bones found in garbage dumps provide evidence that the islanders were eating rats. In other words, they replaced plants with protein in their diet.

It is documented that a war occurred between the short-eared and long-eared people on the island, killing many of the islanders on both sides; however, the lecturer presents historical records substantiating that the war was fought in about 1770, which would have been 100 years after the islanders' traditional stories of the war. The difference in the dates brings the entire theory into question.

Therefore, none of the three theories accounts for the collapse of the advanced culture that once thrived on Easter Island. What happened is still a mystery.

Checklist for Integrated Essay

✔ The essay answers the topic question.
✔ Inaccuracies in the content are minor.
✔ The essay is direct and well organized.
✔ The sentences are logically connected.
✔ Details and examples support the main idea.
✔ The writer expresses complete thoughts.
✔ The meaning is easy to comprehend.
✔ A wide range of vocabulary is used.
✔ The writer paraphrases in his/her own words.
✔ The writer credits the author with wording.
✔ Errors in grammar and idioms are minor.
✔ The essay is within a range of 150–225 words.

EXAMPLE RESPONSE FOR INDEPENDENT ESSAY "FAMILY PETS"

Some writers begin with an outline and others begin with a map of their ideas. Only the essay will be scored.

Outline

Agree that pets should be treated like family members
• Children—learn how to care for brother, sister
• Couple—substitute for babies
• Disabled, elderly—help, caring like family members
• Every stage in life

Map

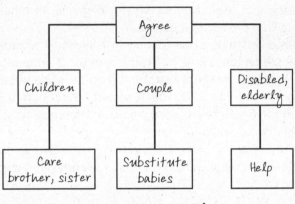

Every stage in life

Example Essay

Although the argument has been made that money spent on pets could better be directed to programs that provide assistance for needy people, I agree that pets should be treated like family members because they live in our homes and interact with us like family members do. Often parents allow children to have pets in order to teach them to be responsible. By feeding, walking, and grooming a dog, children learn to be dependable and kind. Parents expect their children to take care of the pets as if they were members of the family in order to learn these valuable lessons. For many children, a dog or a kitten is also a best friend and a wonderful way to learn how to treat a new brother or sister when the family expands.

Besides the friendship that children enjoy with animals, pets can sub-stitute for the absence of other family members. Sometimes a couple who is unable to have children will adopt pets and treat them like babies. They shower the love on their cats that they might have provided a child, and receive affection and companionship in return. Many people who are living alone enjoy the companionship of a pet instead of loved ones who are at a distance or have passed away. The pet becomes a family member for these people and deserves the same kind of treatment that a family member would receive.

Many articles have appeared in the popular press citing the benefits of pets to the disabled and the elderly. In addition to the usual services that pets may provide, such as bringing objects to their owners or helping a vision-impaired owner to walk in unfamiliar surroundings, there is evidence that pets actually extend the life expectancy of their owners. In a real sense, these pets are caring for their owners like family members would, and for this reason, they should be treated like family.

At every stage in life we interact with our pets in the same ways that we interact with family. Children, young married couples, and elderly people have reason to treat their pets like family members.

Checklist for Independent Essay

✔ The essay answers the topic question.
✔ The point of view or position is clear.
✔ The essay is direct and well organized.
✔ The sentences are logically connected.
✔ Details and examples support the main idea.
✔ The writer expresses complete thoughts.
✔ The meaning is easy to comprehend.
✔ A wide range of vocabulary is used.
✔ Various types of sentences are included.
✔ Errors in grammar and idioms are minor.
✔ The essay is within a range of 300–350 words.

MODEL TEST 3: PROGRESS TEST

➤ Reading

READING 1 "SYMBIOTIC RELATIONSHIPS"

1. **C** In this passage, *obtains* is a synonym for "derives." Context comes from the close association with the word "benefit."

2. **C** In this passage, *classifications* is a synonym for "categories." Context comes from the phrase "three different" in the same sentence.

3. **A** In this passage, *comparatively* is a synonym for "relatively." Context comes from the phrase "not killed immediately" in the same sentence.

4. **C** . . . *when the parasite first invades* paraphrases "Newly established" and *the most destructive phase* paraphrases "more destructive."

5. **A** In this passage, *permit* is a synonym for "tolerate." Context comes from the phrase "reducing the harm" in the same sentence.

6. **D** "Parasites that live on the surface of their hosts are known as **ectoparasites**." . . . *surface* means "outside." Choice A is not correct because "mold and mildew" are ectoparasites, not ways that ectoparasites survive. Choices B and C refer to endoparasites, not to ectoparasites.

7. **A** "Many examples of commensal relationships exist. Orchids use trees as a surface upon which to grow." Choices B and D are mentioned as examples of parasites. Choice C is not correct because ants are mentioned with the Acacia as an example of mutualism, not a commensal relationship.

8. **C** In this passage, *really* is a synonym for "actually."

9. **B** The author uses the example of the Acacia to explain how two species can benefit from contact. "Some species of Acacia, a thorny tree, provide food in the form of sugar . . . Certain species of ants . . . receive food and a place to live, and the [Acacia] tree is protected from animals. . . " Both organisms benefit.

10. **C** "The bacteria do not cause disease but provide the plants with nitrogen-containing molecules." Choice A is not correct because the bacteria do not cause disease. Choice B is not correct because the bacteria is used for growth. Choice D is not correct because the nodules supply nitrogen, which is beneficial.

11. **A** Pronoun reference is a transitional device that connects the insert sentence with the previous sentence. "Fleas, lice and some molds

and mildews are examples of ectoparasites. They [fleas, lice and some molds] live on the feathers of birds or the fur of animals." Choices B, C, and D are not correct because the pronoun does not refer to endoparasites, which live inside the host and are explained later in the passage.

12. **A** Because the text explains the types of relationships between species, it must be concluded that the passage would be found in a chapter about the environment and organisms. Choices B, C, and D are not correct because they are not as closely associated with the main idea.

13. **A, D, E** summarize the passage. Choice B is true, but it is an example of a commensal relationship described in major point D. Choice C refers to a mutualistic relationship developed in major point E. Choice F is mentioned as a minor point in the discussion of parasitic relationships described in major point A.

READING 2 "CIVILIZATION"

14. **B** ". . . Neolithic settlements were hardly more than villages. But as their inhabitants mastered the art of farming, more complex human societies [civilizations] emerged." Choice A is not correct because the Neolithic settlements preceded civilizations. Choice C is not correct because agriculture is mentioned as a cause of the rise in complex cultures, not as a definition of civilization. Choice D is not correct because the population centers increased in size as civilizations grew, but other basic characteristics had to be present as well.

15. **B** In this passage, *used* is a synonym for "utilized."

16. **B** "As wealth increased, such societies began to develop armies and to build walled cities." Choices A, C, and D may be logical, but they are not mentioned and may not be concluded from information in the passage.

17. **C** In this passage, *hardly* is a synonym for "barely."

18. **D** Because the author states that from Neolithic towns "more complex human societies emerged," it may be concluded that they are mentioned to contrast them with the civilizations that evolved. Choice A is not correct because a Neolithic town does not qualify as a civilization. Choice B is not correct because writing systems were not part of Neolithic settlements. Choice C is not correct because Neolithic settlements were referred to as villages, and no argument was made for the classification.

19. **B** "... a new social structure ... [included] kings and an upper class ... free people ... and a class of slaves." Choice A is not correct because it does not include free people. Choice C is not correct because it does not include free people. Choice D is not mentioned and may not be concluded from information in the passage. The new structure described is based on economics, not on education.

20. **A** ... *the majority* paraphrases "most of which."

21. **A** In this passage, *fundamental* is a synonym for "crucial."

22. **B** In this passage, *important* is a synonym for "prominent." Context comes from the word "monumental" in the same sentence.

23. **B** "A number of possible explanations of the beginning of civilization have been suggested." Choice A is not correct because scholars do not agree on one explanation. Choice C is not correct because trade routes are not mentioned in paragraph 4. Choice D is not correct because coincidence is not mentioned as one of the possible explanations.

24. **C** Choice A is mentioned in paragraph 4, sentence 9. Choice B is mentioned in paragraph 4, sentence 8. Choice D is mentioned in paragraph 4, sentence 6.

25. **B** A rhetorical question is a question that is asked and answered by the same speaker. Response is a transitional device that connects the insert sentence with the previous rhetorical question. Choices A, C, and D are not correct because the pronoun "they" in the insert sentence does not refer to plural nouns in the previous sentence.

26. **B, E, F** summarize the passage. Choice A is true, but it is a minor point that is mentioned as an example of the characteristics of a class structure. Choice C may be one of the architectural structures built, but it is not specified. Choice D is true of Mesopotamia and Egypt, but is not developed as a major point.

READING 3 "LIFE IN OUR SOLAR SYSTEM"

27. **D** In this passage, *naturally* is a synonym for "automatically." Context comes from the prefix *auto*, which means "self" and the root *matic*, which is found in many words that refer to "machines."

28. **C** In this passage, *facts* is a synonym for "data."

29. **A** "Venus has some traces of water vapor in its atmosphere, but it is much too hot for liquid water to survive." Choice B is not correct because the water transformed to vapor, not ice. Ice refers to our moon, not to Venus. Choice C is not correct because the lakes or oceans evaporated quickly. Choice D is not correct because the airless atmosphere refers to Mercury, not to Venus.

30. **C** In this passage, *constant* is a synonym for "stable." Context comes from the contrast with "evolve" later in the sentence.

31. **B** Because Jupiter's moon is used as an example of satellites of Jovian planets, it must be concluded that Jupiter is a Jovian planet. Choice A is not correct because the satellites, not the planets, have conditions that support life. Choice C is not correct because the size of Europa is not mentioned. Choice D is not correct because the author draws no conclusion about the change of orbits. If orbits were modified, then a conclusion could be drawn about whether Europa was frozen.

32. **C** ". . . life there may be unlikely because of the temperature. The surface of Titan is a deadly $-179°C$." Choice A is not correct because there are oceans of liquid methane and ethane. Choice B is true, but it is not the reason why life would be improbable. Choice D is not correct because it is the temperature, not the atmosphere, that is low.

33. **B** . . . *the evidence did not demonstrate* paraphrases "the results did not confirm."

34. **C** In this passage, *begun* is a synonym for "originated." Context comes from the root *origin*, which means "beginning."

35. **C** "ALH84001 is important because a team of scientists studied it and announced in 1996 that it contained chemical and physical traces of ancient life on Mars." Choice A is not correct because the meteorite was found closer to twenty years ago. Choice B is not correct because the impact on Mars was not recent. Choice D is true, but it is not the reason why the author mentions the meteorite.

36. **B** ". . . conclusive evidence [of life] may have to wait until a geologist in a space suit can . . . open rocks . . . searching for fossils." Choice A is not correct because a geologist will travel in the spacecraft. Choice C is not correct because pictures are not mentioned as a way to confirm the existence of life on Mars. Choice D is not correct because the present conditions could be studied in a variety of ways, but conclusive evidence depends on a manned flight that will allow a geologist to study the physical evidence.

37. **C** "We are left to conclude that, so far as we know, our solar system is bare of life except for Earth." Choice A is not correct because the author states that our solar system is bare of life. Choice B is not correct because the evidence is not encouraging. Choice D is not correct because the search takes us to other planetary systems.

38. **C** Reference is a transitional device that connects the insert sentence with the previous sentence. *Such periods* refers to "some points in

history." Choices A, B, and D are not correct because *such periods* does not refer to phrases in the sentences that precede the insert options.

39. **F, D, B** summarize the passage. Choice A is a minor point that supports the major point in Choice B. Choice C is a minor point that supports the major point in Choice D. Choice E is not true because the author entertains the possibility of life based on something other than carbon chemistry.

➤ Listening

Model Test 3, Listening Section, Track 39

LISTENING 1 "STUDENTS ON CAMPUS"

Audio Conversation

Narrator:	Listen to part of a conversation on campus between two students.
Man:	I wish I were as sure about my future as you seem to be. I . . . I really don't know what I want to do after I graduate. [Q2]
Woman:	Well, have you talked with a counselor over at the Office of Career Development?
Man:	No. . . . I talked to my academic advisor, though.
Woman:	That's good, but it's really better to see someone who specializes in helping people make career decisions. You see, an academic advisor is there to help you work out your academic program. You know, figure out what your major is going to be and which courses to take and all that. But a career counselor has a lot of experience and resources to help you decide what you want to do in the work world. [Q1]
Man:	Did you see a career counselor?
Woman:	I sure did. Last semester. I was . . . well, I didn't even know what I would be good at, for a career, I mean. So I made an appointment at the Office of Career Development, and I talked with a counselor.
Man:	Do you remember who it was?
Woman:	Sure. It was Ruth Jackson.
Man:	Oh, but since I'm interested in careers for math majors, probably I should see someone else.

Woman:	Not really. Any of the counselors can help you. Look, first I took some aptitude tests and something called a . . . uh . . . I think it was called a *career inventory*. Anyway, I took several tests, and then the counselor gave me some ideas about different careers. I even went to some group sessions with some other students for a few weeks. Mrs. Jackson was the group leader, so, um, that's how I met her, and then I just sort of naturally started making my appointments with her when I needed some advice.
Man:	It sounds like it took a lot of time. I'm so busy already.
Woman:	Well, it did take time. Probably three hours for the tests, and I think I went to maybe four group sessions, and then I saw Ruth a couple of times. I guess about nine or ten hours probably. But it was worth it.

Q3

| Man: | So, is that why you decided to go into library science? Because of the tests and everything? |
| Woman: | In part. But, mostly it was because of the internship. You see, I also got my internship through the Office of Career Development. And when I was working as an intern in the public library, it all sort of came together for me. I really liked what I was doing, and I realized that I didn't want the internship to end. |

Q4

Man:	And you get paid for working there in the library too, don't you?
Woman:	I get paid, and I get credit toward my degree. But even better, I have a job offer from the library where I'm doing my internship.
Man:	Wow! Are you going to take it?
Woman:	I think so. I have to let them know next week. If I do take the job, I'll have to go to graduate school to get a degree in library science, but I can do that part-time while I'm working, and I had thought about graduate school anyway. So, I'm leaning toward taking the job.

Q5

| Man: | That's great, Anne. I'm glad for you. So, uh, I guess I'd better make an appointment with Ruth Jackson. Maybe she can find me an internship. |
| Woman: | Maybe. |

Audio   1.   What are the students mainly discussing?
Answer **B**   Choices A and C are mentioned in reference to the main topic: the advantages of career counseling for the man.

Audio   2.   What is the man's problem?
Answer **C**   He does not know which career to choose.

Audio   3.   Why does the woman tell the man about her experience?
Answer **A**   Because the woman's experience was positive, she probably told the man about it in order to demonstrate the benefits.

Audio   4.   What is the woman's attitude toward her internship?
Answer **C**   She thinks that it is a very positive experience.

Audio   5.   What will the man probably do?
Answer **B**   He will go to the Office of Career Development [to see Ruth Jackson].

LISTENING 2 "SOCIOLOGY CLASS"

Audio Lecture
Narrator: Listen to part of a lecture in a sociology class.

Professor:
Social influence involves the changes in behavior influenced by the actions Q6 of other people. Social influence can come about for a variety of reasons, on a continuum from mere suggestion to, in the more severe form, well, to torture. How does social influence work? Well, first we must become aware of a difference between ourselves and the values or behaviors of other people. There are a great many studies of social influence that demonstrate how the presence of others can cause us to change our attitudes or actions. Studies show that people eat more when dining with others than, and I'm talking about dining out here, so they eat more in the company of others than they do when they're alone. They also run faster when others are running with them. There's even some interesting research on social influence among animals with similar results to those of human studies.

Probably one of the most interesting aspects of social influence is the pressure for conformity. Conformity is a process by which an individual's opinion or behavior moves toward the norms of the group. In a classic study by Solomon Asch, seven people were shown cards with three lines drawn on them. Here's an example:

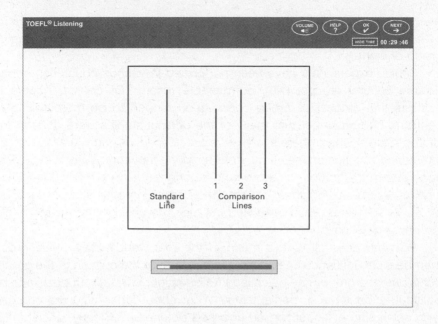

So, they were shown the lines, and then they were asked to select the line among the three that matched the standard line. Here's the standard. **Q10** So there's no question as to the comparison. This has to be easy, right? Wrong. You see, Asch enlisted the cooperation of six of the seven participants in the experiment. On the first card, the six respond correctly—they identify the lines of the same length—so the seventh person, who is the only real subject in the experiment, well, the seventh person answers correctly, in agreement with the others. But on the next card, four of the cooperating participants choose an incorrect answer, but they're in agreement, so the problem for the subject is whether to conform to the opinion of the peer group, even though the answer is in conflict with the answer that the subject knows to be correct.

So what do you think happened? Well, subjects who were tested alone made errors in answers fewer than 1 percent of the time. This was the control group. But of those tested in groups of seven, let's see, uh, 75 percent yielded at least once to conform to a group answer that was clearly incorrect, **Q7** and on average, subjects conformed to the group in about 37 percent of the critical trials. This means that they were bringing their behavior into agreement with group norms in spite of what they were seeing.

Q8 Later Asch manipulated the size of the control group . . . I'm sorry, the experimental group . . . to see whether group size would affect pressure, and it did, but probably less than you might expect. Um . . . groups of four demonstrated about the same results as groups of eight. Interestingly enough, a unanimous agreement by the group was more important than the number. In other words, a unanimous opinion by three exerted more pressure to conform than a majority of seven with a dissenting opinion in a group of eight.

Similar experiments have been performed in various countries, among diverse cultural groups, with, comparable results. Of course, people in cultures that emphasize group cooperation tended to be more willing to conform, but remember that many of the original studies were done in the United States where there's a high value placed on individualism. In an interesting variation on the study, Abrams found that conformity is especially strong when the group is selected from among those people that the subject clearly identifies with, either because they have characteristics in common or . . . or they know each other and interact in a peer group outside of the experimental situation.

Q7

So what does all of this mean in the real world? Well, since group members can influence one another to conform to the opinion of the group, decisions of a group may be called into question. What about decisions by political committees or parliaments? What about juries who are charged with convicting or acquitting an accused defendant? Clearly, social influence will play a part in these critical group decisions.

Also interesting is the fact that after a decision is made by a group, there's a tendency to solidify, and by that I mean that the group becomes even more convinced of the validity of the group opinion. This may happen because individual group members who strongly support the group tend to be more popular with the group members.

Q9

Q11

Audio	6.	What is the main topic of the lecture?
Answer	**C**	The influence of groups on individual behavior

Audio	7.	According to the professor, what two results were reported in the Asch and Abrams studies?
Answer	**B**	Subjects conformed to group opinion in more than one-third of the trials.
	C	When the subject knows the group socially, there is greater pressure to conform.

Audio	8.	Listen again to part of the lecture and then answer the following question.
Replay		"Later Asch manipulated the size of the control group . . . I'm sorry, the experimental group . . . to see whether group size would affect pressure, and it did, but probably less than you might expect."
Audio		Why does the professor say this:

Replay   "I'm sorry, the experimental group . . ."
Answer   C   She needed to correct what she had said in a previous statement. Professors occasionally misspeak, apologize briefly, and provide the correct information.

Audio   9.   What generally happens after a group makes a decision?
Answer   C   As a whole, the group is even more united in its judgment.

Audio   10.   Based on information in the lecture, indicate whether the statements describe the Asch study. For each sentence, click in the YES or NO column.

Answer

		Yes	No
A	Only one subject is being tested.	✔	
B	The cards can be interpreted several ways.		✔
C	Some of the group collaborate with the experimenter.	✔	

Audio   11.   What is the professor's attitude about the studies on social influence?
Answer   B   She appears to be very interested in them. Her tone indicates interest and she cites some of the facts as "interesting."

LISTENING 3 "ART HISTORY CLASS"

Audio Discussion
Narrator: Listen to part of a discussion in an art history class.

Professor:
Sorry about the tests. I don't have them finished. They just took longer to grade than I thought they would. So . . . I'll have them for you next time. | Q12 |
Okay then. Let's begin our discussion of the ballet. If you read the chapter | Q13 |
in your text, you already know that in 1489, a performance that was something like a dinner theater was organized to celebrate the marriage of the Duke of Milan, and . . . a dance representing Jason and the Argonauts was performed just before the roasted lamb was served. By the way, it's interesting that the dance was called an *entree* and that name has been retained for courses in meals. Anyway, about the same time, outdoor entertainment,

you know . . . parades and equestrian events . . . they were becoming more popular, and we have evidence that they were referred to as "horse ballets."

Student 1:
So this . . . the horse ballet . . . was it the first time the term "ballet" was used?

Professor:
Right. The actual term in Italian was balletti, which meant "a dance done in figures." And it was characterized by the arrangement of the performers in various patterns. Actually, the balletti were staged versions of the social dances that were popular at court, and the steps . . . the basic movements . . . they were walking, swaying, and turning . . . so they combined in a variety of sequences, each of which was named so that they could be referred to in the directions for individual dances. In fact, specific instructions for the placement of the dancer's feet probably provided the first, . . . the first record of the five positions of classical ballet. Question?

Q14

Student 2:
Sorry. I'm trying to get clear on the dancers. Um . . . could you explain what the book means about court dancing and, uh . . . I'm not saying this very well.

Professor:
I think I know where you're going. You see, the directions that were written down were intended as a reference for social dancing, but they were important in the history of ballet because the theatrical dances or entertainments that preceded ballet were . . . not performed by professional dancers. Members of the court danced for the entertainment of society, and in general, the performances were in the central halls of castles and palaces with the audience seated in galleries above so that the floor figures could be seen when the people looked down. But back to your question . . . because of the limitations of the performers and the arrangement of the staging, well, the best way to impress the audience was to keep the steps simple enough for the amateur dancers but the geometrical patterns had to be, uh, . . . intricate and . . . and fresh . . . so the spectators would go away pleased because they'd seen something new.

Q15

Student 2:
Oh, I get it now. That makes sense, too, because everyone would be looking down at the dancers.

Professor:
Exactly. Now to continue that thought for a moment . . . by the middle of the sixteenth century, variety shows were being presented on a grand scale in Northern Italy. They included both indoor and outdoor entertainment, and most people called them *spectaculi*. And, uh . . . France had begun to make a significant contribution to the dance form that evolved into modern ballet.

But, to be precise, it was Catherine de Medici who used dance as part of her court entertainments and is credited with the use of the term *ballet*. In 1573 . . . I think it was 1573 . . . anyway, she organized a huge celebration to welcome the ambassadors from Poland who had arrived to offer their country's throne to her son Henri. So she called it the *Polish Ballet*, and the production was staged on a landing at the top of a grand staircase. Sixteen ladies . . . and these would not have been dancers . . . just members of court . . . so they represented the sixteen provinces of France, and they performed a choreographed dance with a variety of floor figures. Afterward, the audience joined in court dances, similar to the ballroom dancing that evolved later. . . . So that's a long answer to your original question.

Q17 Student 1:   Now I have a question.

Professor: Okay.

Student 1:
You said that the *Polish Ballet* was the first ballet, but I thought the book said the first ballet was *Queen Louise's Ballet*.

Professor:
Good question. Well, I said the *Polish Ballet* was the first use of the term *ballet* for a dance performance, but *Queen Louise's Ballet* is generally considered the first modern ballet. As you'll remember, from the book, the ballet was performed before ten thousand guests, and it was five hours long. Q16 When I was doing the research for this lecture, I saw several references to the time, so . . . so I know that this is accurate, but I kept thinking, no one would watch a ballet for five hours. But it must be correct. I can only assume that other activities were going on simultaneously, like a banquet and conversation. Don't you think?

Anyway, what makes *Queen Louise's Ballet* so unique, besides the length, and why it's the first *modern* ballet, is that it was connected by a story line or, in technical terms, it's called *dramatic cohesion*. Each scene was related to the tales of Circe, a Greek enchantress, who used her powers to battle with man and the gods. The triumph of good, portrayed by Jupiter, over evil, portrayed by Circe, was told in a . . . let's call it a unified production.

Audio	12.	What is the discussion mainly about?
Answer	C	All of the other choices are mentioned in relationship to the main topic: the development of the ballet.

Audio	13.	Listen again to part of the discussion and then answer the following question.
Replay		"So . . . I'll have them for you next time. Okay then. Let's begin our discussion of the ballet. . . . "
Audio		Why does the professor say this:
Replay		"Okay then."
Answer	A	To end his explanation and begin the discussion. Professors often use the word "Okay" as a transition from classroom management activities before the class to the beginning of their lectures.

Audio	14.	According to the professor, what does the term *balletti* mean?
Answer	C	A dance done in figures

Audio	15.	How did the early choreographers accommodate the abilities of amateur performers?
Answer	A	The steps were quite simple.

Audio	16.	Why does the professor mention that he checked several references about the length of *Queen Louise's Ballet*?
Answer	C	He wasn't sure that it was accurate.

Audio	17.	What can be inferred about the professor?
Answer	B	He encourages the students to participate.

LISTENING 4 "ADMISSIONS OFFICE"

Audio Conversation

Narrator:	Listen to part of a conversation between a student and an admissions assistant.
Student:	Excuse me, but the secretary referred me to your office.
Assistant:	Yes?
Student:	I'm a new student . . . well, actually, I'm not enrolled yet, but I'm trying to get all my admissions applications turned in today.
Assistant:	What's your name?
Student:	Robert Franklin.

Q18

Assistant:		Middle initial?
Student:		T.
Assistant:		Oh, I see. Wait a minute and we'll find out what you have to do. . . . Well, according to the records here, you have your admissions form, a financial aid application, three letters of recommendation, transcripts from Regional College . . . so that's everything you need except a transcript from County Community College.
Student:		That's what I thought. You see, I took a couple of courses there during the summer because it's close to my parent's house. Anyway, almost all of my first two years is from Regional College, and, uh, that's where I'm transferring from. In fact, the credit for the community college courses appears on the transcript from Regional College as transfer credit, but, uh, it doesn't show my final grades in the courses.
Assistant:		Oh, and you haven't been able to register for your courses here at State University because the computer shows that you are missing some of your application materials. Is that it?
Student:		Exactly. What I was wondering is whether you have, like a policy for this kind of situation so I could go ahead and register for this first semester while we wait for the transcript to get here. It should be here now. I requested it the same time that I requested a transcript from Regional College, but they're just slow at County Community.
Assistant:		That happens sometimes. . . . Do you have a copy of your transcript from County Community College?
Student:		Yes, I do. It's right here. Of course, it isn't an official copy. It's stamped "unofficial copy."
Assistant:		But I can use this one until the official copy gets here. Here's the best way to handle this. We can give you a provisional admission. That means that you're admitted contingent upon the receipt of your official transcript. That will allow you to register for your courses this semester. When County Community College sends us your official transcript, then I can change your status from provisional admission to regular admission.
Student:		Oh, that's great!
Assistant:		Is this the only copy you have of your transcript?
Student:		No. I have another one.
Assistant:		Good. Then I'll just keep this in your file.

Q19

Q20

Student:	Okay.
Assistant:	Now the only problem is you can't register for next semes- [Q21] ter without regular admission status, and you need the official transcript for me to do that, so you still need to keep after them to get everything sent to us as soon as possible.
Student:	Right. Well, I'll do that. But at least I have some time to get it done. . . . Um . . . what do I need to do now . . . to get registered, I mean.
Assistant:	Just wait here while I enter everything into the computer, [Q22] and then you can take a copy of your provisional admission along with you to the office for transfer students. They'll assign you an advisor and help you get registered later today.

Audio 18. Why does the student go to the admissions office?
Answer **D** He is trying to enroll in classes.

Audio 19. What is missing from the student's file?
Answer **B** A transcript from County Community College

Audio 20. Listen again to part of the conversation and then answer the following question.
Replay "Oh, and you haven't been able to register for your courses here at State University because the computer shows that you are missing some of your application materials. Is that it?"
Audio Why does the woman say this:
Replay "Is that it?"
Answer **B** The admissions assistant paraphrases the problem and then asks for confirmation that she has understood it. "Is that it?" means "Is that correct?"

Audio 21. What does the woman suggest that the man do?
Answer **D** Continue to request an official transcript from County Community College

Audio 22. What will the student most probably do now?
Answer **B** Go to the office for transfer students to be assigned an advisor

LISTENING 5 "GEOLOGY CLASS"

Audio Lecture
Narrator: Listen to part of a lecture in a geology class.

Professor:
The original source of energy is what? The Sun. Then plants use the Sun's energy during photosynthesis to convert water and carbon dioxide into sugar and oxygen, and they store the energy in the chemicals that the plant produces. When animals eat plants, the energy is transferred to their bodies. So then, the plants and animals die and decay, and they sink to the bottom of the sea or . . . or disintegrate into the soil and then they're covered by more and more sediment as rivers deposit mud and sand into the sea or the seas advance and retreat. Of course, it's a very gradual process . . . one that takes place over, well, millions of years. But finally, the organic material begins to transform into the hydrocarbons, and the hydrocarbons eventually become oil and gas deposits. So how does this happen? Well, at first, the oil and gas are mixed with sand and sediment but . . . as the layers on top increase, then so does the pressure. And under pressure, mixtures of oil and sand and water . . . they seep down through the layers of porous rock . . . that's usually sandstone or limestone . . . so they sink down until they reach a layer of nonporous rock, and that's where they pool because they can't pass through the nonporous rock.

Okay. Sometimes there are breaks in the layers of rocks and the breaks allow oil and gas to bubble up and . . . and eventually they reach the surface of the Earth again. So, when this happens, the gas and some oil evaporate into the air . . . but they leave a sticky black tar that appears in pools or pits on the surface. But most crude oil is found in underground formations, which

Q23 we call traps. So today, I want to talk about the major types of oil traps. In all the different types of traps, the oil collects in porous rocks, along with gas and water. And, over time, the oil moves up toward the surface of the Earth through cracks and holes in the porous rock until it reaches a nonporous rock deposit . . . and the nonporous rock, remember, it won't allow the oil to continue moving. So the oil becomes trapped under the nonporous rock deposit.

Now think for a moment. While oil was forming and moving, the Earth was also undergoing changes. In fact, there were enormous movements of the crust as the center began to cool. When *folding* happened, well, it was like the Earth fell back onto itself. And when *faulting* happened, it was . . . well, one layer was forced by rocks above down through the layers below. So, you can see that the . . .the repositioning of porous and nonporous rock . . . this repositioning would have affected the movement of oil. When the Earth shifted, cracks would have been opened, and nonporous layers would have been . . . dropped . . . dropped over channels that had previously been used as . . . as pathways for the transfer of oil and gas to the surface.

Okay, as geologists, we're interested in locating the traps. Now why **Q24** would that be so? Because that's where we'll find the oil and gas reserves. And that's what I really want to talk about today. So, there are several differ- **Q25** ent types of traps, but today we're going to talk about the three most common ones—the anticline trap, the salt dome trap, and the fault trap.

Look at this diagram. Here's an example of an anticline. As you can see, **Q26** the oil is trapped under a formation of rock that resembles an arch. That's because the arch was bent from a previously flat formation by uplifting. In this anticline, the petroleum is trapped under a formation of nonporous rock with a gas deposit directly over it. This is fairly typical of an anticline. Because gas isn't as dense as oil, it rises above it. The dome over the top can be rock as in this example, or it could be a layer of clay. The important thing is that the **Q27** cap of nonporous material won't let the oil or gas pass upwards or sideways around it.

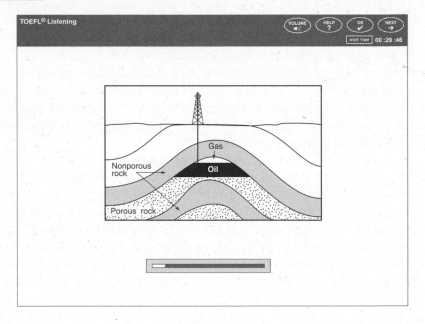

Now let's look at a diagram of a salt dome. This salt dome shows how a **Q28** cylinder-shaped salt deposit has pushed up through a layer of sedimentary rocks, causing them to arch and fracture. The oil deposits have collected along the sides of the salt dome. Salt is a unique substance. With enough heat and pressure on it, the salt will slowly flow, kind of like a glacier, but unlike glaciers, salt that's buried below the surface of the Earth can move upward until it reaches the Earth's surface, where it's then dissolved by groundwater or rain. Well, to get all the way to the Earth's surface, salt has to lift and break through many layers of rock. And that's what ultimately creates the salt dome.

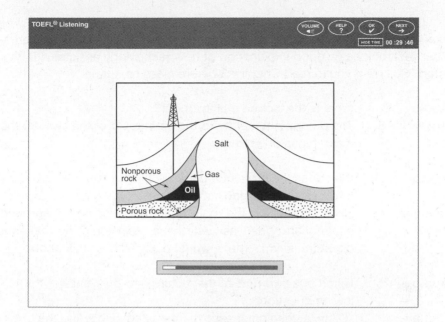

Finally, I want to show you a fault trap. Fault traps are formed by the movement of rock along a fault line. This diagram represents a fracture in the Earth that's shifted a nonporous rock formation on top of a porous formation. In this case, the reservoir rock, which is porous, has moved opposite a layer of nonporous rock. The nonporous rock prevents the oil from escaping. Remember, as in all traps, the oil is collected in the porous rock and trapped underground by the nonporous rock.

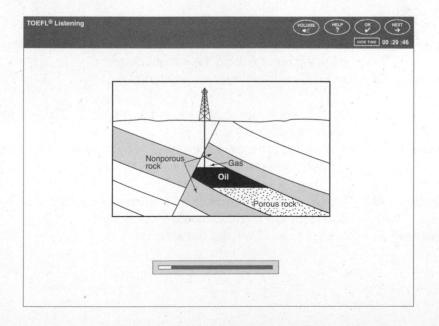

Geologists study the terrain for indications of possible oil traps. For example, a bulge in a flat surface may signal the presence of a salt dome. Your textbook has a good explanation of how technology assists us in this effort. So I want you to read Chapter 3 before class next time.

Audio	23.	What is the lecture mainly about?
Answer	B	The other points relate to the main topic of the lecture: the major types of oil traps.
Audio	24.	Why does the professor begin by talking about the process that transforms organic material into oil and gas?
Answer	A	He is introducing the main topic by providing background information. When he begins the main topic, he makes a direct transition: "that's what I really want to talk about."
Audio	25.	Listen again to part of the lecture and then answer the following question.
Replay		"Okay, as geologists, we're interested in locating the traps. Now why would that be so? Because that's where we'll find the oil and gas reserves."
Audio		Why does the professor say this:
Replay		"Now why would that be so?"
Answer	D	He plans to answer the question. Professors often use rhetorical questions in their lectures. By posing a question that they plan to answer, they help students follow the main points.
Audio	26.	Select the diagram of the anticline trap that was described in the lecture. Click on the correct diagram.
Answer	B	An anticline trap is shown in diagram B.
Audio	27.	Identify the nonporous rock in the diagram. Click on the correct letter.
Answer	B	In all traps, the oil is collected in the porous rock and trapped underground by the nonporous rock.
Audio	28.	According to the professor, what do geologists look for when they are trying to locate a salt dome?
Answer	A	A bulge in an otherwise flat area

LISTENING 6 "ANTHROPOLOGY CLASS"

Audio Discussion
Narrator: Listen to part of a discussion in an anthropology class.

Professor:
Before we start, does anyone have a question about the reading assignment? Yes, Jim?

Jim:
Just wondering whether I have a good handle on the concept of power. The book said it was the ability to exercise influence . . . and control over others.

Professor:
Right. And this can be observed on every level of society, from, well . . . the relationships within a family to the relationships among nations.

Jim:
Okay. But then the book, it goes on to say that power is usually structured by customs . . . and . . . and social institutions or laws, but then I read that power can be exerted by persuasive arguments . . . or coercion . . . or even brute force.

Professor:
Sounds like you've got it. But is there a question?

Jim:
Well, it sounds like, in general, groups with the greatest, uh, resources . . . it sounds like they always have an advantage in power struggles. So I was thinking that power is not really justified because it could involve resistance. I mean some people may oppose the individuals or groups in power but they could still . . . they could still . . .

Professor:
. . . impose their will?

Jim:
Yes.

Professor:
So you want to know whether power always involves force?

Jim:
Umhum. Exactly. Because there was a sentence or two in there about legitimate power.

Professor.
Okay. Well actually that is a perfect lead-in to today's lecture. You're right, Jim, that sometimes power is not viewed by society as justified, even though those in control are imposing their will. So sometimes power is not legitimate. But what about power that is accepted by members of society as right and just? That is *legitimate* power. Now we're talking about authority. And that's what I want to focus on today. Then we'll come back to your question again at the end of the class.

Okay. When individuals or institutions possess authority, they have a recognized and established right . . . to determine policies, with the acceptance of those over . . . over whom they exercise control. Max Weber, the German classical sociologist, proposed three types of authority in society: traditional, charismatic, and rational or legal authority. In all three types, he acknowledged the right of those in positions of power to lead . . . with the consent of the governed.

Margie:
So, if I get this right, power is the big category, but authority is a kind of power, when the power . . . when it's recognized as the right of the person or the institution.

Professor:
Yes. When those under the authority of a leader or group give their permission. Got it?

Margie:
I think so.

Professor:
But in all three types of authority in society, Weber acknowledged the right of those in positions of power to lead . . . with the consent of the governed. So how did Weber differentiate among the three types of authority? Well, he divided them according to how the right to lead and the duty to follow are interpreted . . . how the power is legitimatized. In traditional authority, for example, power resides in customs and conventions that provide certain people or groups with legitimate power in their societies. Often their origin is found in sacred traditions. The example that most often comes to mind is monarchy in which kings or queens rule by birthright, not because of any

particular quality of leadership or political election, just because they have a claim to authority based on traditional acceptance of their position, and in some cases, their unique relationships with and responsibility in religious practices.

Margie:
You mean like the royal families in Europe or the emperors in Asia.

Professor:
Precisely.

Margie:
Because the queen of England, for example . . . she is the head of the Church of England as well as the monarch. I think that's right.

Professor:
And that claim to authority is traditional.

Jim:
But she really doesn't have much power though, anymore, does she?

Professor:
I see your point, but what is important is not how much power she has but that the power is given to her by the people because of the traditional authority that she claims as the heir to the throne. . . . Now, this contrasts sharply with charismatic authority, which is derived . . . because of personal attributes that inspire admiration, loyalty . . . and even devotion. Leaders who exercise this type of authority may be the founders of religious movements or political parties, but it's not their traditional right to lead. What's important here is that their followers are mobilized more by . . . the force of the leader's personality than by tradition or the law. So when we think of "charismatic" leaders in the United States, who comes to mind?

Jim:
Well, I can't think of anyone who is alive today, but maybe John Kennedy would be an example because he was able to get people behind him.

Professor:
Good example! Kennedy was able to project a youthful and energetic image that people were proud to identify with.

Margie:
Or Ronald Reagan—I prefer Republicans, Dr. Cooper. Reagan had a lot of charismatic appeal and he exercised authority when he was in office.

Professor:
Great. Now we have both parties represented. In any case, going back to Weber, to qualify for charismatic authority, a leader must be able to enlist others in the service of a . . . cause that transforms the social structure in some way, so politics, especially at the highest levels . . . it often attracts charismatic leaders because it offers the opportunity for social change.

   Which leaves us with the third type of authority—legal rational authority, or power that is legitimized by rules, laws, and procedures. In such a system, leaders gain authority not by traditional birthrights or by charismatic appeal but . . . rather because they're elected or appointed in accordance with the law, and power is delegated to layers of officials who owe their allegiance to the principles that are agreed upon rationally, and because they accept the ideal that the law is supreme. In a legal rational society, people accept the legitimacy of authority as a government of laws, not leaders.

Margie:
So that would be a judge then . . . as an example of someone with legal rational authority.

Professor:
Well, it might be a judge, but it could be a bureaucrat in an office or even the president, let's say, like Richard Nixon, who was threatened with impeachment because he was perceived as not governing within the law. Do you see what I mean?

Margie:
I think so.

Professor:
Jim, is the difference between power and authority sorting itself out now?

Jim:
It is.

Professor:
Okay then. Some sociologists have postulated that the three types of authority—the traditional, charismatic, and legal rational—that these types represent stages of evolution in society. That preindustrial societies tend to

respect traditional authority, but as societies move into an industrial age, the importance of tradition . . . wanes . . . in favor of charismatic author-
Q33 ity, with a natural rise of charismatic leaders. Then . . . as the modern era evolves, the legal rational authority, embodied by rules and regulations . . .
Q34 it replaces the loyalty to leaders in favor of a respect for the law. Of course, other sociologists argue that in practice, authority may be represented by a combination of several of these ideal types at any one time.

Audio	29.	What is the main purpose of this discussion?
Answer	**A**	The distinction between power and authority is made in the introduction, but the main purpose of the lecture is to discuss three types of authority.

Audio	30.	Why do the students mention Kennedy and Reagan?
Answer	**B**	They were examples of charismatic leaders.

Audio	31.	According to the professor, what two factors are associated with charismatic authority?
Answer	**B**	An attractive leader
	C	A social cause

Audio	32.	Listen again to part of the discussion and then answer the following question.
Replay		"But what about power that is accepted by members of society as right and just, that is, legitimate power? Now we're talking about authority. And that's what I want to focus on today."
Audio		Why does the professor say this:
Replay		"But what about power that is accepted by members of society as right and just? That is, legitimate power."
Answer	**B**	Professors often ask questions to introduce a topic. After the question, she continues, "And that's what I want to focus on today" [authority].

Audio	33.	In an evolutionary model, how is rational legal authority viewed?
Answer	**A**	The most modern form of authority

Audio   34.   What does the professor imply about the three types of authority?

Answer   **B**   Because the professor presents both an evolutionary model and an argument for an inclusive model that combines several types of authority, it must be concluded that sociologists do not agree about the development of the types of authority.

LISTENING 7 "LIBRARY"

Audio Conversation

Narrator: Listen to part of a conversation between a student and a librarian.

Librarian: Hi, how can I help you?

Student: Hi, I'm looking for some material on reserve for Business 210.   Q35

Librarian: Okay. Well, who's the professor? You see, we keep the files under the professor's name because there are a couple of sections and the requirements are a little different . . .

Student: Oh, okay. It's Dr. Parsons.

Librarian: Umhum. Parsons? I don't see any books . . .

Student: I think it's a DVD.

Librarian: Oh, yes. Here it is . . . Oh, wait, actually, there are two of them. But that's all right. Now all I need is your student ID.

Student: No problem.

Librarian: There you go. Now, these will be due back at the desk in two hours.

Student: Two hours? But that won't even give me time to go home and . . .

Librarian: Oh, you can't leave the library with reserve materials. You have to use them here. But we have some DVD players in the booths behind the reference section. I think there are several free now.

Student: But I have to take notes and, uh, I don't think I can get everything done in two hours.

Librarian: Well, you can't take materials out again until someone else has used them because the professor only left one copy of each. Sorry. Look, maybe two hours will be enough.

Student: I don't think so. These are case studies, and we're supposed to be able to discuss them.   Q36

Librarian: Oh, I see. Well, when do you have class?

Student:	Tomorrow morning. I know I should have come in earlier, but this isn't my only class. I had an exam earlier today, and I was just waiting to get that out of the way.
Librarian:	I see. Well, look, why don't you . . .
Student:	Isn't there any way to get an exception to the policy?
Librarian:	I'm afraid not.
Student:	Oh. Okay then, let me just check out one of the DVDs. That way, if I finish it, I can check out the other one for two hours, right?
[Q37] [Q38] Librarian:	Sure. That's perfectly fine. And, here's a thought. I don't know if it will work for you since you have a morning class, but if you check out reserve material less than two hours before the library closes, then you can have it overnight . . .
Student:	Overnight?
Librarian:	Yes, but you have to have it back when the library opens the next day and . . .
Student:	But I could do that. Oh, I'm sorry, you were going to say . . .
Librarian:	Well, if you don't return the material to the reserve desk when the library opens, then there's a ten-dollar fine for the first hour and a five-dollar fine for every hour after that . . . that it's late, I mean. The usual fee is one dollar for every hour but when it's an overnight . . .
Student:	Ouch.
Librarian:	It's a stiff fine because we need students to take the privilege seriously. Otherwise, other students who need to use the reserve materials wouldn't have access to them.
Student:	Oh, I understand.
Librarian:	And another thing. Sometimes more than one person is trying to use the overnight privilege so . . . so sometimes when you wait until the end of the day . . .
Student:	Oh. And there isn't any way to put your name on a list or anything?
Librarian:	No, not really. It's first come, first served.
Student:	Okay. Okay. Then, I think I'll go ahead and take the one DVD out now because I can still try to get the second one tonight overnight, can't I?
[Q39] Librarian:	Sure. I tell you what. Come back a little before nine.
Student:	Okay. Will you be here? I mean, I'd rather come back to you.
Librarian:	I'll be here until the library closes.
Student:	Well, then.
Librarian:	Do you still want to take out one of the DVDs?

Student:	Yeah. I might as well get one of them out of the way so I'll only have one left to watch.
Librarian:	Wait a minute. Your ID.
Student:	Oh, I'm sorry, I thought I showed it to you.
Librarian:	You did, but I need to keep it here at the desk until you return the materials.

Audio	35.	What does the man need from the librarian?
Answer	**B**	Material for a class—Business 210, taught by Dr. Parsons.

Audio	36.	What is the man's problem?
Answer	**B**	He needs to prepare for a class discussion.

Audio	37.	Listen again to part of a conversation and then answer the following question.
Replay		"I don't know if it will work for you since you have a morning class, but if you check out reserve material less than two hours before the library closes, then you can have it overnight . . . " "Overnight?"
Audio **Replay**		What does the man feel when he says this: "Overnight?"
Answer	**D**	His tone expresses surprise and interest.

Audio	38.	What is the policy for materials on reserve?
Answer	**D**	Materials may be checked out overnight two hours before closing.

Audio	39.	What does the librarian imply when she tells the man to return at nine o'clock?
Answer	**B**	Because reserve materials can be checked out two hours before the library closes, and the librarian tells the man to come back at nine o'clock, she implies that the library will close two hours later, or eleven o'clock.

LISTENING 8 "LITERATURE CLASS"

Audio Lecture

Narrator: Listen to part of a lecture in a literature class.

Professor:

Today we'll discuss Transcendentalism . . .Transcendentalism . . .which is a Q40
philosophical and literary movement that developed in New England in the

early nineteenth century. Transcendentalism began with the formation in 1836 of the Transcendental Club in Boston, Massachusetts, by a group of artists and writers. There's evidence that the group was involved in somewhat of a protest against the intellectual climate of Harvard. Interestingly enough, many of the Transcendentalists were actually Harvard educated, but they never met in Cambridge. Remember, at this time, Harvard had only eleven professors, and at least eleven members could be expected to attend a meeting of the Transcendental Club. So their intellectual community was large enough to rival the Harvard faculty.

Q41   All right then. Their criticism of Harvard was that the professors were too conservative and old fashioned. Which, come to think of it, isn't an unusual attitude for students when they talk about their professors. But, in fairness, the classroom method of recitation that was popular at Harvard required the repetition of a lesson without any operational understanding of it. In contrast, the Transcendentalists considered themselves modern and liberal because they preferred a more operational approach to education. Bronson Alcott translated Transcendentalism into pedagogy by encouraging the students to think, using dialogues and journals to develop and record their ideas. Language was viewed as the connection between the individual and society. In 1834, Alcott established the Temple School near Boston Commons and later founded a form of adult education, which he referred to as *Conversation*. This was really a process whereby the give and take in a conversation became more important than the doctrine that a teacher might have been inclined to pass on to students, an approach that stood in diametric opposition to the tradition at Harvard that encouraged students to memorize their lessons.

Q42   The Transcendental group also advanced a reaction against the rigid Puritanism of the period, especially insofar as it emphasized society at the expense of the individual—the Puritans, I mean. According to the Transcendentalists, the justification of all social organizations is the improvement of the individual. So, in the literature of the time, the Transcendentalists insisted that it was basic human nature to engage in self-expression, and many interpreted this as encouragement for them to write essays and other opinion pieces. One of the most distinguished members of the club was Ralph Waldo Emerson, who served as editor of the Transcendentalist's literary magazine, the *Dial*. His writing stressed the importance of the individual. In one of his best-known essays, "Self-Reliance," he appealed to intuition as a source of ethics, asserting that people should be the judge of their own actions, without the rigid restrictions of society. You can imagine the reaction of the church, in particular, the Unitarian Church, in which many of the intellectuals held membership. If individuals were responsible for their own code of ethics, then the clergy, and the entire church organization was threatened.

Perhaps because they were encouraged to think for themselves, the Transcendentalists came up with several options for living out their philosophies. Many were devoted to the idea of a Utopian society or at least to a pastoral retreat without class distinctions, where everyone would be responsible for tending the gardens and maintaining the buildings, preparing the food, and so forth. And quite a few were involved in some sort of communal living. Brook Farm was probably the most successful of these cooperatives, although it lasted only six years. Brook Farm and some of the other experimental communities brought to the surface the problem that the Transcendentalists faced when they tried to reconcile a cooperative society and individual freedom. Both Emerson and Thoreau declined to participate in Brook Farm because they maintained that improvement had to begin with an individual, not a group.

From 1841 to 1843, Emerson and Thoreau lived and worked together in Emerson's home, exchanging ideas, developing their philosophies, and writing. Upon leaving Emerson's home, Thoreau built a small cabin along the shores of Walden Pond near Concord, Massachusetts, where he lived alone for two years. Devoting himself to the study of nature and to writing, [Q44] he published an account of his experiences in *Walden*, a book that's generally acknowledged as the most original and sincere contribution to literature by the Transcendentalists.

But I'm getting ahead of myself. Transcendentalism didn't change the educational system, and it certainly didn't reform the church in any significant way, but it did, in a sense, change the direction of American social and political culture because Transcendentalism evolved from its initial literary [Q45] roots into a force that shaped the way a democratic society was interpreted on the North American continent.

Audio	40.	What does this lecturer mainly discuss?
Answer	**A**	Transcendentalism

Audio	41.	Listen again to part of the lecture and then answer the following question.
Replay		"All right then. Their criticism of Harvard was that the professors were too conservative and old fashioned. Which, come to think of it, isn't an unusual attitude for students when they talk their professors."
Audio		Why does the professor say this:
Replay		"Which, come to think of it, isn't an unusual attitude for students when they talk about their professors."
Answer	**A**	Her tone implies that she is joking with the students.

Audio   42.   According to the professor, what was true about the Puritans?
Answer   **C**   They believed that society should be respected above persons.

Audio   43.   Why did the church oppose the Transcendental movement?
Answer   **A**   The authority of the church would be challenged by a code of personal ethics.

Audio   44.   Why did the professor mention *Walden*?
Answer   **B**   It is considered an excellent example of Transcendental literature.

Audio   45.   According to the professor, what was the most lasting contribution of Transcendentalism?
Answer   **D**   Political changes

LISTENING 9 "GENERAL SCIENCE CLASS"

Audio Discussion
Narrator: Listen to part of a discussion in a general science class.

Professor:
Q46 Okay. This is a general science course, and as such, the first thing I want you to understand is the scientific method. In your book, the definition of the scientific method is "an organized approach to explaining observed facts, with a model of nature that must be tested, and then modified or discarded if it fails to pass the tests." So let's take that apart and talk about it. What are observed facts? Anyone?

Student 1:   I'll try.

Professor: Okay.

Student 1:   Isn't a fact supposed to be a statement that everyone agrees on?

Professor: So you would say that a fact is objectively true.

Student 1:   Yeah. That's what I mean.

Professor:
Okay. That sounds good, but what about this . . . we consider it a fact that the Sun rises each morning and the Earth rotates. But facts like that are not always agreed upon. Look, when we say that the Sun rises each morning, we assume that it is the same Sun day after day—an idea that might not have been accepted by ancient Egyptians, whose mythology taught them that the Sun died with every sunset and was reborn with every sunrise. Now, let's consider the case of the Earth's rotation. Well, for most of human history, the Earth was assumed to be stationary at the center of the universe. So, as you can see, our interpretations of facts often are based on beliefs about the world that others might not share. Still, facts are the raw material that scientific models seek to explain, so it's important that scientists agree on the facts. How can we do that? | Q47

Student 2:
How about this . . . a fact has to be verified, I mean, that's where the testing comes in, so we have to be able to test a model, but we have to be able to test a fact, too, right?

Professor:
Now you're on the right track. In the context of science, a fact must therefore be something that anyone can verify for himself or herself, at least in principle. So, even though the interpretation may be different, some interpretation of the Sun is there every morning, and that can be verified. Then, a model is proposed to explain the facts. And a model is…

Student 3: . . . an explanation of the facts.

Professor:
Right. Once the facts have been observed, a model can be proposed to explain them and not only explain what is obvious but also make predictions that can be tested through further observations or experiments. Let's go back to Ptolemy's model of the universe, which assumed that the Earth was the center of everything. Okay, that was a useful model because it predicted future locations of the Sun, Moon, and planets in the sky. However, although the Ptolemaic model remained in use for nearly 1500 years, eventually it became clear that its predictions didn't quite match actual observations—a key reason why the Earth-centered model of the universe finally was discarded.

Student 2: So models are discarded when they don't match the observations. | Q50

Professor:
Exactly. And new models are proposed to explain the facts in a better or more inclusive way. Okay, how does a model achieve the status of a theory?

Student 1:
Well, I guess sometimes the model doesn't fail, you know, it gets repeated by many experiments and the, uh, the uh, predictions are verified.

Professor:
So, when a prediction is verified . . . repeated, then we start to assume that the model is a valid representation of nature, and when that happens with many experiments and a number of different researchers, then the model achieves the status of a scientific theory.

Student 2:   But . . .

Professor: Yes? Jerry?

Student 2:   Well, the problem is that theories get discarded, too, don't they?

Professor:
Absolutely. Because it isn't really possible to prove that a theory is true beyond all shadow of a doubt. And that's good because doubt is a cornerstone of science. Even a well-researched and presented theory should undergo continuous challenges from the scientific community, with further observations and experiments.

Student 3:
I'm sorry. Did we mention the term *hypothesis*? Does that fit in with a model or a theory?

Professor:
Glad you brought that up. A proposed model is often called a hypothesis, and that just means that the scientist is making an educated guess that the model's predictions will bear up under testing.

Q48 Student 3:   So a hypothesis is a proposed model.

Professor:
Right. But let's put this all together, shall we? Step 1 is *observation*, the collection of data, that is, observations. Step 2 is *hypothesis* or a model to

explain the facts and to make predictions. Step 3 is *additional observations* and *experiments*. And here's the important part, when the predictions fail, then we recognize that the model is flawed, and we have to revise or discard it, but when the predictions are verified on a consistent basis, then we consider the possibility that we have a true representation of nature and we elevate the model to the status of a theory.

Student: So step 4 is the *theory*?

Professor:
Right. But, even then, the theory must undergo step 5 . . . that's further observations, experiments, and challenges. Okay so far? . . . Okay. Now for a reality check. In the real world of science, discoveries are rarely made by a process as . . . as mechanical as the idealized scientific method outlined in your textbook . . . the one that we just summarized. For example, anyone recognize the name Johannes Kepler?

Student 2:   Sure. Didn't he propose the laws of planetary motion?

Professor:
He did, in about 1600. But instead of verifying new predictions on the basis |Q49| of his model, he tested the model against observations that had been made previously. And . . . and . . . like most scientific discoveries, Kepler's work |Q51| involved intuition, collaboration with others, moments of insight, and luck. And eventually, other scientists made a lot of observations to verify the planetary positions predicted by his model.

Student 1:   Student 2:
So the . . .   . . . Then

Student 2:   Go ahead.

Student 1:   So the scientific method in the book . . . that's not really the way it happens a lot of the time?

Professor:
Okay, let's put it this way . . . the scientific method is a process that we need to keep in mind as we do the work of scientists, but we should also understand that it's an idealized process for making objective judgments about whether a proposed model of nature is close to the truth. And we should also keep in mind that in the work of scientists, other factors are also brought to bear on those ideal steps in the process.

Audio	46.	What is this discussion mainly about?
Answer	**D**	The scientific method

Audio	47.	Why did the professor give the example of the ancient Egyptians?
Answer	**B**	To prove that facts may be interpreted differently

Audio	48.	Listen again to part of the discussion and then answer the following question.
Replay		"So a hypothesis is a proposed model."
		"Right. But let's put this all together, shall we?"
Audio		Why did the professor say this:
Replay		"But let's put this all together, shall we?"
Answer	**B**	He is beginning a review of the process. Professors often use the phrase "put it together" when they are summarizing, restating, and clarifying several parts of a concept.

Audio	49.	According to the professor, what did Kepler do to verify his theory of planetary motion?
Answer	**C**	He used prior observations to test the model.

Audio	50.	What can be concluded from information in this discussion?
Answer	**A**	A model does not always reflect observations.

Audio	51.	What technique does the professor use to explain the practical application of the scientific method?
Answer	**B**	An example of Kepler's work, which included intuition and luck.

➤ Speaking

Model Test 3, Speaking Section, Track 40

INDEPENDENT SPEAKING QUESTION 1 "ADVICE"

Narrator 2: Number 1. Listen for a question about a familiar topic. After you hear the question, you have 15 seconds to prepare and 45 seconds to record your answer.

Narrator 1: The older generation often gives advice to younger family members. Describe a valuable piece of advice that an older person gave you. Why did it help you?

Narrator 2: Please prepare your answer after the beep.

Beep

[Preparation Time: 15 seconds]

Narrator 2: Please begin speaking after the beep.

Beep

[Recording Time: 45 seconds]

Beep

INDEPENDENT SPEAKING QUESTION 2 "CLIMATE"

Narrator 2: Number 2. Listen for a question that asks your opinion about a familiar topic. After you hear the question, you have 15 seconds to prepare and 45 seconds to record your answer.

Narrator 1: Some people enjoy living in a location that has a warm climate all year. Other people like to live in a place where the seasons change. Which type of climate do you prefer and why? Use specific reasons and examples to support your opinion.

Narrator 2: Please prepare your answer after the beep.

Beep

[Preparation Time: 15 seconds]

Narrator 2: Please begin speaking after the beep.

Beep

[Recording Time: 45 seconds]

Beep

INTEGRATED SPEAKING QUESTION 3 "WITHDRAWAL FROM CLASSES"

Narrator 2: Number 3. Read a short passage and listen to a talk on the same topic. Then listen for a question about them. After you hear the question, you have 30 seconds to prepare and 60 seconds to record your answer.

Narrator 1: A new policy for withdrawal from classes at the university has been established. Read the policy in the college catalogue [printed on page 350]. You have 45 seconds to complete it. Please begin reading now.

[Reading Time: 45 seconds]

Narrator 1: Now listen to the students discuss the policy with each other.

Woman:	The difference in this policy from the old policy is . . . now you only have three reasons to request a full refund after the first week . . . illness, death in the family, or military service.
Man:	Right, but that about covers it, don't you think?
Woman:	Not really. In the old policy, you could drop out to help your family. Look, let's say that your mother's sick. She's not dying but she needs care. Then what? If you drop out to help her, you just lose your tuition.
Man:	Oh, I see. So you think that there should be more flexibility.
Woman:	Yeah. I think every case should be decided on its own merits. This policy is too . . . too . . .
Man:	Too narrow?
Woman:	Too rigid. I think at least some students will have other good reasons to withdraw and they'll just have to take a partial reimbursement because they won't be able to document their eligibility. I'd like to see a procedure, you know, a way to petition for eligibility. . . . I'd like to see that added to the policy.

Narrator 1: The student expresses her opinion of the policy for reimbursement. Report her opinion and explain the reasons that she gives for having that opinion.

Narrator 2: Please prepare your answer after the beep.

Beep

[Preparation Time: 30 seconds]

Narrator 2: Please begin speaking after the beep.

Beep

[Recording Time: 60 seconds]

Beep

INTEGRATED SPEAKING QUESTION 4 "BALLADS"

Narrator 2: Number 4. Read a short passage and then listen to part of a lecture on the same topic. Then listen for a question about them. After you hear the question, you have 30 seconds to prepare and 60 seconds to record your answer.

Narrator 1: Now read the passage about ballads [printed on page 351]. You have 45 seconds to complete it. Please begin reading now.

[Reading Time: 45 seconds]

Narrator 1: Now listen to part of a lecture in a music appreciation class. The professor is talking about the ballad of "Barbara Allen."

Professor:
There are countless versions of the ballad of "Barbara Allen," and although it probably originated in the British Isles, versions are found not only in the British colonies but also in many other countries, including Italy and several countries in Scandanavia. In fact, there are almost 100 versions in the United States alone. But the version that I'm going to play for you today is the traditional Child Ballad number 84 from the reference *English and Scottish Popular Ballads*. In it, the narrative tells the story of Barbara Allen and the young man who fell in love with her. After Barbara Allen rejects him, he dies of unrequited love. And the day after his funeral, Barbara Allen dies of regret. They are buried beside each other in the churchyard, and a red rose grows from his grave. A briar grows from her grave . . . uh, that's a thorny bush . . . and as they twine around each other . . . the rose and the thorn . . . they form a lover's knot. So we see that the lovers who were not united in life are together in death. The music is repetitive, like most ballads, and also important to identifying it as a ballad, the second and the fourth lines of each four-line stanza rhyme.

Narrator 1: Define a ballad, and then explain why "Barbara Allen" can be classified as a ballad.

Narrator 2: Please prepare your answer after the beep.

Beep

[Preparation Time: 30 seconds]

Narrator 2: Please begin speaking after the beep.

Beep

[Recording Time: 60 seconds]

Beep

INTEGRATED SPEAKING QUESTION 5 "THE ASSIGNMENT"

Narrator 2: Number 5. Listen to a short conversation. Then listen for a question about it. After you hear the question, you have 20 seconds to prepare and 60 seconds to record your answer.

Narrator 1:	Now listen to a conversation between a student and her friend.
Friend:	I thought you liked your history class.
Student:	I do. I mean, it's a lot of reading and everything, but I enjoy that, even though it takes a lot of time.
Friend:	So what's the deal?
Student:	Okay, last week Dr. Norman assigned a paper.
Friend:	Well, I think that's fairly standard for a history class.
Student:	Sure. It's on the syllabus, but . . . but it isn't very clear what he wants us to do. And he didn't really clarify it when he talked about it in class. So, I don't know how to start.
Friend:	Hmmn. When's the paper due?
Student:	At midterm, so I have time, but still, I'd like to get going on it.
Friend:	Yeah, but like you say, you have time. Just wait until next week and ask about it again in class.
Student:	I could, but won't he be . . . insulted? After all, he already explained it once.
Friend:	Oh, I don't think he'd mind. He'd probably be glad that you want to do it correctly.
Student:	I don't know. Maybe he would.

Friend: But anyway, if you don't want to do that, you could just make an appointment to talk about your ideas for the paper, you know, to get some direction about the topic. That way the conversation will just naturally lead into an explanation of how he wants you to do it.

Narrator 1: Describe the woman's problem and the two suggestions that her friend makes about how to handle it. What do you think the woman should do, and why?

Narrator 2: Please prepare your answer after the beep.

Beep

[Preparation Time: 20 seconds]

Narrator 2: Please begin speaking after the beep.

Beep

[Recording Time: 60 seconds]

Beep

INTEGRATED SPEAKING QUESTION 6 "ULTRASOUND"

Narrator 2: Number 6. Listen to part of a lecture. Then listen for a question about it. After you hear the question, you have 20 seconds to prepare and 60 seconds to record your answer.

Narrator 1: Now listen to part of a lecture in a general science class. The professor is discussing the way that ultrasound works.

Professor:
Okay, let's talk about how ultrasound works, and how it's used in medical diagnosis. To make a long story short, ultrasound is very similar to the sonar devices we discussed last week. Remember the system that emits ultrasonic pulses and listens for reflected pulses from objects in the ocean? Well, ultrasound is really just another type of sonar. The sound waves used in the ultrasound are created by a crystal that moves rapidly back and forth, creating a sound, but you can't hear it because the frequency is so high. The doctor places the device, the transmitter that sends out the sound waves . . . the doctor puts that on the surface of the skin so the sound

waves are transmitted inside the body. And when this high-frequency sound is directed to a particular area, then the tissue and organs reflect the sound. The patterns of sound that are reflected are processed by a computer, and an image appears on the screen. And that tells the doctor whether there is something unusual there or not. This is very important in the diagnosis of cancer . . . to know whether a tumor is present . . . and also as a noninvasive way to monitor the growth of a fetus during pregnancy.

Narrator 1: Using the main points and examples from the lecture, describe the kind of information that ultrasound can provide, and then explain the way that ultrasound is used in medical diagnosis.

Narrator 2: Please prepare your answer after the beep.

Beep

[Preparation Time: 20 seconds]

Narrator 2: Please begin speaking after the beep.

Beep

[Recording Time: 60 seconds]

Beep

➤ Writing

Model Test 3, Writing Section, Track 41

INTEGRATED ESSAY "EMPEROR PENGUINS"

First, read the passage [printed on page 356] and take notes.

Narrator: Now listen to a lecture on the same topic as the passage that you have just read.

Professor:
Although the reading passage about emperor penguins in your textbook was correct for the time that it was written, new data have come to light

since the book was printed. In fact, we now know that all three assumptions in the passage about this interesting species are probably not true.

First, let's consider whether emperor penguins are monogamous. That is, do they mate for life? With greater observation, we find that the answer is yes and no. Yes, they're monogamous for the mating season and the pair is committed and diligent in caring for their chick, but we also now know that if they don't locate their previous mate the following year in a timely way, they'll mate with another penguin. So this means that it would be more correct to consider them serially monogamous, mating with one partner per season. When the pair *can* find each other within a tight time frame, then, yes, they'll continue to mate with the same partner, but it looks like that happens about only 15 percent of the time.

Now let's look at nest loyalty. A new study by the University of Minnesota used satellite images to verify that emperor penguins were returning to the same location to nest every year. Researchers found six instances in which the penguins didn't return to the same rookery and, in addition, found a *new* rookery that appears to confirm the relocation of an entire colony. This could also account for the disappearance of banded birds from previous studies. And, of course, this disproves the previous assumption about penguins returning to the same rookery every year.

Last, let's revisit the issue of whether emperor penguins are endangered. Just a few years ago, they were given endangered status under the Endangered Species Act because models of declining numbers estimated that their population could decline by as much as one-third by the end of the century. Disappearing sea ice and radical changes in the marine life in current feeding habitats have convinced the scientific community that emperor penguins *must* be protected if they're to survive.

Question
Summarize the main points in the lecture and then explain how they cast doubt on the ideas in the reading passage.

➤ Example Answers and Checklists for Speaking and Writing

🎧 **Model Test 3, Example Answers, Track 42**

EXAMPLE ANSWER FOR INDEPENDENT SPEAKING QUESTION 1 "ADVICE"

My grandfather gave me valuable advice about my reputation. He taught me to value it above material things. When I was a child, I was attracted to my grandfather's watch, and he explained that if the watch failed to keep accurate time, he'd get a new watch. Later, I begged to drive my grandfather's car because it was a much better car than my parents had. He let me drive it occasionally, and he always asked me to be careful. He also made me understand that the *car* could be replaced but . . . but *I* could never be replaced. And he told me that his most prized possession was his good reputation and that was why he had good friends and a successful business . . . I'd like to be like my grandfather someday so that's why I need to guard my reputation as my most prized possession.

Checklist 1

✔ The talk answers the topic question.
✔ The point of view or position is clear.
✔ The talk is direct and well organized.
✔ The sentences are logically connected.
✔ Details and examples support the main idea.
✔ The speaker expresses complete thoughts.
✔ The meaning is easy to comprehend.
✔ A wide range of vocabulary is used.
✔ There are only minor errors in grammar.
✔ The talk is within a range of 125–150 words.

EXAMPLE ANSWER FOR INDEPENDENT SPEAKING QUESTION 2 "CLIMATE"

I've lived in a place with a warm climate all year for most of my life, but one year my family moved to England where the seasons change. I thought it was a beautiful place, and I enjoyed the experience, but I was glad to be home again. In the fall, we don't have to rake leaves; in the winter, we don't have to shovel snow; and in the spring, we don't have to drive in the rain. So a warm climate is a lot less work. And I can wear the same clothes all year in a warm climate, but in a place where the seasons change, you can't.

I remember putting my coats and heavy clothes away when the weather got warmer in England. Best of all, I'd like to see the sun shine every day. So, maybe I'm just used to a warm climate, but for now, that's my choice.

Checklist 2

✔ The talk answers the topic question.
✔ The point of view or position is clear.
✔ The talk is direct and well organized.
✔ The sentences are logically connected.
✔ Details and examples support the main idea.
✔ The speaker expresses complete thoughts.
✔ The meaning is easy to comprehend.
✔ A wide range of vocabulary is used.
✔ There are only minor errors in grammar.
✔ The talk is within a range of 125–150 words.

EXAMPLE ANSWER FOR INTEGRATED SPEAKING QUESTION 3 "WITHDRAWAL FROM CLASSES"

The woman thinks that the eligibility requirement for a 100 percent refund after the second week of classes should be changed. Right now, to qualify, you have to show documentation of serious illness, injury, death of a family member, or military duty. She points out that there could be a case when a student's family might need help but, uh, the . . . the circumstances wouldn't be covered by the policy. Um, she suggests that there should be a way to petition for full reimbursement by explaining the situation, and, uh, each case should be decided based on the circumstances, not on such a limited number of possibilities. So . . . her solution to the problem would be to add the option of petitioning for full refund . . . by explaining the reason for requesting an exception.

Checklist 3

✔ The talk summarizes the situation and opinion.
✔ The point of view or position is clear.
✔ The talk is direct and well organized.
✔ The sentences are logically connected.
✔ Details and examples support the opinion.
✔ The speaker expresses complete thoughts.
✔ The meaning is easy to comprehend.
✔ A wide range of vocabulary is used.
✔ Errors in grammar are minor.
✔ The talk is within a range of 125–150 words.

EXAMPLE ANSWER FOR INTEGRATED SPEAKING QUESTION 4 "BALLADS"

A ballad is, and I am quoting here, "a poem that tells a story and is sung to music." Characteristic of most ballads is the rhyming of the second and fourth lines. And usually ballads are part of an oral tradition, which, uh, it means that over the years, the song is revised as it's passed down from one musician to another. Some popular ballads have been written down and assigned a . . . assigned a number in a reference book by . . . Child. Now, "Barbara Allen" is classified as a ballad because it tells a story about lovers who were not united in *life* but are joined symbolically in *death* by the rose and the thorn on their graves. The second and fourth lines of the song rhyme, and many versions of it are found around the world. One version is listed in the Child reference as number 84. So you see, "Barbara Allen" is not only a ballad. It's a very popular one.

Checklist 4

✔ The talk relates an example to a concept.
✔ Inaccuracies in the content are minor.
✔ The talk is direct and well organized.
✔ The sentences are logically connected.
✔ Details and examples support the opinion.
✔ The speaker expresses complete thoughts.
✔ The meaning is easy to comprehend.
✔ A wide range of vocabulary is used.
✔ The speaker paraphrases in his/her own words.
✔ The speaker credits the lecturer with wording.
✔ Errors in grammar are minor.
✔ The talk is within a range of 125–150 words.

EXAMPLE ANSWER FOR INTEGRATED SPEAKING QUESTION 5 "THE ASSIGNMENT"

The woman's problem is that she doesn't understand the assignment in her history class. She knows that she's supposed to write a paper, but she isn't sure what the professor wants her to do. Um . . . her friend suggests that she ask about the requirements for the paper in her class next week, but she's concerned that the professor will be offended because he's already explained it once. His other recommendation is to make an appointment to talk about the topic for her paper because, during the consultation, she could ask questions. I think the woman should make an appointment to see the professor in his office as soon as possible so she'll have more time to work on the paper after she understands the assignment better. I also think it'd be best to be direct about asking how to complete the requirement because most professors are willing to help students who show an interest in the class.

Checklist 5

✔ The talk summarizes the problem and recommendations.
✔ The speaker's point of view or position is clear.
✔ The talk is direct and well organized.
✔ The sentences are logically connected.
✔ Details and examples support the opinion.
✔ The speaker expresses complete thoughts.
✔ The meaning is easy to comprehend.
✔ A wide range of vocabulary is used.
✔ Errors in grammar are minor.
✔ The talk is within a range of 125–150 words.

EXAMPLE ANSWER FOR INTEGRATED SPEAKING QUESTION 6 "ULTRASOUND"

Ultrasound is like sonar because it sends out ultrasonic, uh, ultrasonic pulses, and then it picks up the reflections of the pulses. In the case of ultrasound, a crystal creates sound waves at such a high frequency that you can't hear them, but when the device that transmits the waves is placed on some part of your body, it sends the waves inside to the part that's being tested, and the organs reflect the sound waves. So that informs the doctor if you have anything suspicious there. Um, ultrasound is very useful in locating cancer and other growths, but it's also used in prenatal care to examine the baby in the months before it's born. In fact, it's fairly standard to produce images of babies to check their patterns of growth, using ultrasound. So ultrasound is very useful for medical diagnosis because it can provide accurate information without surgery or surgical procedures.

Checklist 6

✔ The talk summarizes a short lecture.
✔ Inaccuracies in the content are minor.
✔ The talk is direct and well organized.
✔ The sentences are logically connected.
✔ Details and examples support the main idea.
✔ The speaker expresses complete thoughts.
✔ The meaning is easy to comprehend.
✔ A wide range of vocabulary is used.

✔ The speaker paraphrases in his/her own words.
✔ The speaker credits the lecturer with wording.
✔ Errors in grammar are minor.
✔ The talk is within a range of 125–150 words.

EXAMPLE RESPONSE FOR INTEGRATED ESSAY "EMPEROR PENGUINS"

Many writers begin with a chart like those you practiced in Chapter 3. Only the essay will be scored.

Chart

Emperor Penguins
new data

Mate for life	
Faithful, monogamous Vocal calls, frequencies to locate	For mating season only 15% find same mate next yr

Return to rookery	
Nest yrly Different path Males 1st—females day+ later	U Minn satellite 6 diff rook New rook

Not endangered	
Not protected Stable pop 240,000 breeding prs = 600,000	Now endangered status Model 1/3 decline end century ← disappearing sea ice + changes in feeding habitats

Example Essay "Emperor Penguins"

Although all of the information in the reading was true at the time that it was written, new data have emerged that changes our understanding of emperor penguins. The lecturer mentions three behaviors that need to be reconsidered.

First, emperor penguins do not mate for life, as previously believed. New studies have revealed that they mate for the season and remain committed to their mate and their chick, but, if they do not find the same mate the next year, they will mate with another penguin. Although they use vocal calls to try locating their previous mate, statistically, only about 15 percent find the same mate the following season.

Second, emperor penguins do not return to the same rookery every year to mate. Scientists at the University of Minnesota found six instances in which the penguins mated at a different rookery and one instance in which a new rookery was founded in order to relocate a colony.

Third, although emperor penguins were not on the endangered list and their population was considered stable when the passage was published, a current model shows a 33 1/3 percent decline by the end of the century. Taking into consideration the disappearing sea ice and changes in their habitat, emperor penguins have now been included on the endangered species list.

Checklist for Integrated Essay

✔ The essay answers the topic question.
✔ Inaccuracies in the content are minor.
✔ The essay is direct and well organized.
✔ The sentences are logically connected.
✔ Details and examples support the main idea.
✔ The writer expresses complete thoughts.
✔ The meaning is easy to comprehend.
✔ A wide range of vocabulary is used.
✔ The writer paraphrases in his/her own words.
✔ The writer credits the author with wording.
✔ Errors in grammar and idioms are minor.
✔ The essay is within a range of 150–225 words.

EXAMPLE RESPONSE FOR INDEPENDENT ESSAY "COLLEGE YEARS"

Some writers begin with an outline and others begin with a map of their ideas. Only the essay will be scored.

Outline

College years not best

- Stress
    Decisions—career, job, marriage
    Competition
- Dependence
    Family
    Debts

The best is yet to be

Map

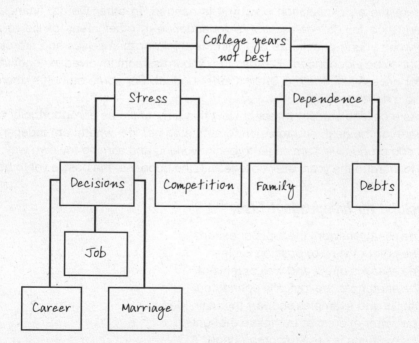

The best is yet to be

Example Essay

I disagree that the college years are the best time in a person's life. Admittedly, college often corresponds with a time when people are young, healthy, and physically strong, and those attributes are highly regarded in Western cultures; however, the college years must also be viewed as a period of high stress and a certain uncomfortable dependence.

Stress converges on college students from many directions. First, there is the pressure to choose a major field of study and, ultimately, to select a career, choices that will affect the rest of their lives. These choices often coincide with another life choice—the selection of a marriage partner. In combination, the stress associated with such important decisions can be very high. Second, there is the daily stress from competition in the classroom, exacerbated by staying up too late studying for tests, preparing papers, and reading assignments. It is well documented that college students tend to gain weight and suffer from many stress-related illnesses.

In addition to the stressful environment, most college students are not financially independent. Many rely on their families for funding, a circumstance that is often uncomfortable for young adults. Asking for money usually requires an explanation of why it is needed. In other words, financial dependence for college results in dependence in other areas of life at a time when young people are beginning to think for themselves and are old enough to be independent. Besides the embarrassment involved in negotiating for necessities, there is often a strict budget. For some students, there is also a debt to repay.

As a college student myself, I view this time of life as an opportunity to prepare for the next, and more important, stage of life, when I am independent and productive. I am eager to begin working and earning my own way. I look forward to the years after college with the hope that the best is yet to be.

Checklist for Independent Essay

✔ The essay answers the topic question.
✔ The point of view or position is clear.
✔ The essay is direct and well organized.
✔ The sentences are logically connected.
✔ Details and examples support the main idea.
✔ The writer expresses complete thoughts.
✔ The meaning is easy to comprehend.
✔ A wide range of vocabulary is used.
✔ Various types of sentences are included.
✔ Errors in grammar and idioms are minor.
✔ The essay is within a range of 300–350 words.

8

SCORE ESTIMATES

IMPORTANT BACKGROUND INFORMATION

It is not possible for you to determine the exact score that you will receive on the TOEFL® iBT. There are three reasons why this is true. First, the testing conditions on the day of your official TOEFL will affect your score. If you are in an uncomfortable room, if there are noisy distractions, if you are upset because you arrived in a rush, or if you are very nervous, then these factors can affect your score. The administration of a model test is more controlled. You will probably not be as stressed when you take one of the tests in this book. Second, the model tests in the book are designed to help you practice the most frequently tested item types on the official TOEFL® iBT. Because they are constructed to teach as well as to test, there is more repetition in TOEFL model tests than there is on official TOEFL® iBT tests. Tests that are not constructed for exactly the same purposes are not exactly comparable. Third, the TOEFL scores received by the same student will vary from one official TOEFL examination to another official TOEFL examination by as many as twenty points, even when the examinations are taken on the same day. In testing and assessment, this is called a standard error of measurement. Therefore, a TOEFL score cannot be predicted precisely, even when two official tests are used. But, of course, you would like to know how close you are to your goal. To do that, you can use the following procedure to estimate your TOEFL® iBT score. An estimate is an approximation.

PROCEDURE FOR SCORING

The official TOEFL® iBT tests have either a longer Reading section or a longer Listening section. The extra part on each test contains experimental questions that will not be graded as part of your score. You will need to do your best on all of the questions because you will not know which questions are experimental. The model tests in this book have either a longer Reading section or a longer Listening section. Use the procedure below with the charts on the following pages to determine your score estimate for each TOEFL® iBT model test.

Test with a short Reading section and a long Listening section

1. Count the total number of correct answers for the Reading section. This is your raw score. Now find the scaled score that corresponds to the raw score on the reference chart. This is your section score for the Reading section.

2. Count the total number of correct answers for the Listening section. Multiply the number by .66 and round to the nearest whole number. This is your raw score. Now find the scaled score that corresponds to the raw score on the reference chart. This is your section score for the Listening section.

3. Rate each of the six questions for the Speaking section on a holistic scale 0—4, add the six scores and divide by 6. This is your raw score. Now find the scaled score that corresponds to the raw score on the reference chart. This is your section score for the Speaking section.

4. Rate each essay for the Writing section on a holistic scale 0—5, add the two scores and divide by 2. This is your raw score. Now find the scaled score that corresponds to the raw score on the reference chart.

5. Add the scaled scores for all four sections. This is your TOEFL estimate.

Test with a long Reading section and a short Listening section

1. Count the total number of correct answers for the Reading section. Multiply the number by .75 and round to the nearest whole number. This is your raw score. Now find the scaled score that corresponds to the raw score on the reference chart. This is your section score for the Reading section.

2. Count the total number of correct answers for the Listening section. This is your raw score. Now find the scaled score that corresponds to the raw score on the reference chart. This is your section score for the Listening section.

3. Rate each of the six questions for the Speaking section on a holistic scale 0—4, add the six scores and divide by 6. This is your raw score. Now find the scaled score that corresponds to the raw score on the reference chart. This is your section score for the Speaking section.

4. Rate each essay for the Writing section on a holistic scale 0—5, add the two scores and divide by 2. This is your raw score. Now find the scaled score that corresponds to the raw score on the reference chart.

5. Add the scaled scores for all four sections. This is your TOEFL estimate.

Note: The scoring of the tests on the CD-ROM that supplements the larger version of this book is more exact because the algorithm accounts for questions that are worth more than 1 point. Nevertheless, your estimates using this procedure will give you a good idea of your progress.

REFERENCE CHARTS

Reading

Raw Score	Scaled Score
39	30
38	29
37	29
36	28
35	27
34	26
33	25
32	24
31	23
30	22
29	21
28	20
27	19
26	18
25	17
24	16
23	15
22	14
21	13
20	12
19	11
18	9
17	8
16	7
15	6
14	5
13	4
12	3
11	2
10	1
9	0
8	0
7	0
6	0
5	0
4	0
3	0
2	0
1	0
0	0

Listening

Raw Score	Scaled Score
34	30
33	29
32	29
31	28
30	27
29	26
28	25
27	23
26	22
25	21
24	19
23	18
22	17
21	15
20	14
19	13
18	11
17	10
16	9
15	8
14	7
13	6
12	5
11	5
10	4
9	3
8	3
7	2
6	2
5	1
4	0
3	0
2	0
1	0
0	0

Speaking

Raw Score	Scaled Score
4.0	30
3.5	27
3.0	23
2.5	19
2.0	15
1.5	11
1.0	8
0	0

Writing

Raw Score	Scaled Score
5.0	30
4.5	28
4.0	25
3.5	22
3.0	20
2.5	17
2.0	14
1.5	11
1.0	8
0	0

EXAMPLES FOR SCORING MODEL TESTS

Example of TOEFL® iBT Model Test with Long Reading Section

Reading Section	Correct Answers		Raw Score	Scaled Score
4 passages 52 questions	46 × .75	=	34.5 = 35	27

Listening Section	Correct Answers	Raw Score	Scaled Score
6 passages 34 questions	30	30	27

Speaking Section	Holistic Rating	Scaled Score
Speaking Question 1	4	
Speaking Question 2	4	
Speaking Question 3	3	
Speaking Question 4	3	
Speaking Question 5	4	
Speaking Question 6	3	
Average number of ratings	3.5	27

Writing Section	Holistic Rating	Scaled Score
Integrated essay	4	
Independent essay	5	
Average number of ratings	4.5	28

TOTAL
Add scaled scores for all sections   109

Example of TOEFL® iBT Model Test with Long Listening Section

Reading Section	Correct Answers	Raw Score	Scaled Score
3 passages 39 questions	36	36	28

Listening Section	Correct Answers		Raw Score	Scaled Score
9 passages 51 questions	44 × .66	=	29.0 = 29	26

Speaking Section	Holistic Rating	Scaled Score
Speaking Question 1	4	
Speaking Question 2	4	
Speaking Question 3	3	
Speaking Question 4	3	
Speaking Question 5	4	
Speaking Question 6	3	
Average number of ratings	3.5	27

Writing Section	Holistic Rating	Scaled Score
Integrated essay	4	
Independent essay	5	
Average number of ratings	4.5	28

TOTAL
Add scaled scores for all sections   109

SCORE COMPARISONS

Common European Framework (CEFR)	Internet TOEFL (iBT)	Institutional TOEFL (ITP)
C1	110-120	627–677
B2	87–109	543–626
B1	57–86	460–542

Note: TOEFL scores are also reported as they relate to the Common European Framework of Reference (CEFR), which is an internationally recognized measure of language proficiency. The equivalency chart above cites equivalencies determined by major research studies; however, they are only estimates of individual scores.

FEEDBACK

A new feature of the TOEFL score report is feedback. A general analysis of your strengths and weaknesses will be included with the numerical score. The computer program on the CD-ROM that supplements the larger version of this book provides feedback along with an automatic score report at the end of each model test.

OPTIONS FOR PERSONAL EVALUATION

Speaking

➤ SpeechRater™
Your Speaking section score on the TOEFL® iBT is determined by human raters. SpeechRater™ is an automated prediction of the score that a human rater would probably assign to your responses. This computer rating includes some, but not all of the features that a human rater considers in evaluations—pronunciation, vocabulary, grammar, and fluency. Although the scoring will provide experience, the actual score may not be the same as your TOEFL score.

Writing

➤ Criterion e-rater®

Your Writing section score on the TOEFL® iBT is a combination of evaluations that include both human and computer raters. The e-rater® in the Criterion® service is an automated prediction of the combined score that a human rater and a computer rater would probably assign to your responses. This computer rating includes some, but not all of the features that a human rater considers in evaluations—organization, style, grammar, vocabulary, complexity, and mechanics. The scoring will provide experience, and is more advanced than the SpeechRater™ however, the actual score may not be exactly the same as your TOEFL score.

For more information about these personal evaluation options, visit *www.ets.org/toefl*. Click on <u>TOEFL Practice Online</u>. Each test costs $45.95, which includes automated scoring for the Speaking and Writing sections.

9

RESOURCES

WEBSITES FOR TOEFL

These websites may include short commercials as well as fee-based media and services, but many free options are also included on the sites. Click on the free material to practice English and help you prepare for the TOEFL.

SHORT AUDIO OR VIDEO CLIPS
These are good resources for the Listening, Speaking, and Writing sections.

www.bbc.com
This site has video and written scripts. Click on *Earth* or *Nature* for content that is most helpful to you as you prepare for the TOEFL.

www.history.com
This site has a large number of short video clips and articles under a variety of academic topics. Click on these categories for TOEFL preparation: *History* or *Science and Technology*. TV programs on the site are not as helpful.

www.openculture.com
This site contains online courses that include lectures in various academic subjects. The lectures are presented by professors from some of the leading colleges and universities. Click on a

subject to see a list of lecture topics. They are delivered as free YouTube audio or video files.

www.ted.com/talks
This site includes thought-provoking talks by experts in various fields of study. Browse the topics and find talks that are of interest to you. Subtitles are available in a limited number of languages.

www.video.nationalgeographic.com
This site is part of the National Geographic Society. Use the following short video categories: *Animals and Nature* (also listed as *Wildlife*), *Environment*, *Science and Space*, *Travel and Culture*. Full feature films are also found on this site, but they are not as useful for TOEFL preparation as the short clips.

Listening Section
Take notes while you listen. Then compare your notes with those of a friend.

Speaking Section
Using your notes, summarize the clip by telling your friend about it.

Writing Section
Referring to your notes, write a summary sentence about the topic.

READING PASSAGES

These are good resources for the Reading section.

www.encyclopedia.com
This site offers unlimited possibilities for short reading passages on academic topics from reliable research sources. To solve the problem of what to choose, click on one of the *Featured Topics*. After a trial period, you may be asked to pay a small fee to continue using the site, but you are not obligated.

en.wikipedia.org
This site is a free encyclopedia that is written in English and edited by the general public. Click on *Featured Articles* to search for interesting topics by academic category. There is no charge to read the articles in Wikipedia.

SPEAKING AND PRONUNCIATION

This is a good resource for the Speaking section.

www.cooldictionary.com
This site is a free talking dictionary sponsored by Webster dictionaries. First click on **Pronunciation Help** and then type in a word or phrase and click on **Generate Sound**. Although it may seem slow at times, the words or phrases are pronounced very well.

TOEFL® iBT RESOURCE CENTERS

Contact a local TOEFL iBT Resource Center for general information about the TOEFL. These centers cannot help you register for the test or provide you with your scores.

Canada
DesignedUX
Email: *dustin@designedux.com*
Phone: **1-647-436-6521**
Website: *www.designedux.com*

Egypt
AMIDEAST
38 Mohie El Din Abou El Ezz Street, Dokki-Giza, Egypt
Phone: **+20-2-19263**
Fax: **+20-2-795-2946**
Email: *egypt@amideast.org*

France
ETS Global B.V.
Email: *mcondette@etsglobal.org*
Phone: **+31 (0)20 880 4166**
Website: *www.etsglobal.org*

Germany
ETS Global B.V.
Email: *tkraninko@etsglobal.org*

India
Learning Links Foundation
1209 Padma Tower 1, 5 Rajendra Place, New Delhi, 110008 INDIA
Email: *toeflinfo@learninglinksindia.org*
Phone: **+91 9 7112 37111**
Website: *http://www.learninglinksindia.org*

Indonesia
International Test Center
Plaza Sentral lt. 17 Jalan Jendral Sudirman Kav. 47 Jakarta
Pusat 12930
Phone: **+6282123237788** (TOEFL® iBT Hotline)
Phone: **+62215711943**
Fax: **+62215711944**
Website: *www.itc-indonesia.com*

Japan
CIEE
Cosmos Aoyama, 5-53-67 Jingumae, Shibuya-ku, Tokyo 150-8355, Japan
Email: *toefl@cieej.or.jp*
Phone: **(81 3) 5467 5477**
Website: *http://www.cieej.or.jp*

Mexico
IIE Mexico
Berlin 18 60 Piso Col. Juarez, Mexico City C.P. 06600
Email: *cmaldonado@iie.org*
Phone: **55925260**

Poland
ETS Global in Poland
ul. Barska 28/30, Block B, 2nd Floor, 02-315 Warszawa
Email: *jwrzesinska@etsglobal.org*
Phone: **+48 22 890 00 17 ext. 13**
Website: *www.etsglobal.org*

Saudi Arabia
AMIDEAST
Al Kindi Plaza #59 Diplomatic Quarters P.O. Box 352,
Riyadh 11411 Kingdom of Saudi Arabia
Phone: **01-483-8800**
Email: *saudiarabia@amideast.org*

Spain
ETS Global B.V.
Email: *jrrufo@etsglobal.org*

Taiwan
Chun Shin
2F, No.45, Sec2, Fu Xing S Rd, Taipei 106 Taiwan, ROC
Email: *service@toefl.com.tw*
Phone: **(88 6) 2 2701 7389**
Website: *www.toefl.com.tw*

Turkey
ETS Global B.V.
Email: *timre@etsglobal.org*

United Arab Emirates
AMIDEAST
CERT Technology Park Higher Colleges of Technology Muroor
Road (4th Street)
PO Box 5464 Abu Dhabi, Abu Dhabi
Phone: **(971-2) 445-6720**
Fax: **(971-2) 443-1489**
Email: *uae.testing@amideast.org*

Vietnam
IIG VIETNAM JSC
Hanoi Head Office No. 75, Giang Van Minh Street Ba Dinh District–
Hanoi City, Vietnam
Email: *info@iigvietnam.com*
Phone: **(84 4) 3773 2411**
Website: *www.toefl.com.vn*
Website: *www.iigvietnam.com*

IIG VIETNAM JSC
Danang Branch Office No. 268 Tran Phu Road Hai Chau District–
Danang City, Vietnam
Email: *danang@iigvietnam.com*
Phone: **(84 511) 3565 888**
Website: *www.toefl.com.vn*
Website: *www.iigvietnam.com*

IIG VIETNAM JSC
No. 3, 3 Thang 2 Road Ward 11 District, 10–HCM City, Vietnam
Email: *saigon@iigvietnam.com*
Phone: **(84 8) 3929 2633/34**
Website: *www.toefl.com.vn*
Website: *www.iigvietnam.com*

GLOSSARY OF CAMPUS VOCABULARY

academic advisor   n.   a person who helps students make
decisions about their academic programs

Example: Dr. Jones is the *academic advisor* for the
engineering students.

Suggestion: You should see your *academic advisor* before
you decide.

Surprise: Dr. Jones is your *academic advisor*?

Problem: I can't see my *academic advisor* until Friday.

ace   v.   to receive a grade of A

Example: I *aced* that exam.

Suggestion: Find someone who *aced* the course to help you.

Surprise: Kathy *aced* her computer science class?

Problem: If I don't *ace* the final, I'll get a B in the class.

admissions office   n.   the administrative office where students
apply for admission to a college or
university

Example: I have an appointment at the *admissions office* to
review my application.

Suggestion: Why don't you go over to the *admissions office*?

Confirmation: Did you say you couldn't find the *admissions
office*?

Problem: I need to get to the *admissions office* before five
o'clock.

all-nighter   n.   a study session that lasts all night

Example: We had to pull an *all-nighter* to get ready for the
final exam.

Suggestion: If I were you, I wouldn't pull another *all-nighter*.

Surprise: So your roommate *did* pull another *all-nighter*.

Problem: I have to pull an *all-nighter* in order to be ready
for the final exam.

article n. a publication about an academic subject

Example: We read six *articles* in addition to the reading in the textbook.

Suggestion: You had better read the *articles* that were assigned.

Surprise: You read the *articles* already?

Problem: I need to read the *articles* again.

assignment n. work that must be done as part of the requirements for a class

Example: The *assignment* was to read two chapters in the textbook.

Suggestion: You had better read the *assignment* before class.

Surprise: So you *do* read the *assignments* after all.

Problem: I can't finish the *assignment* before class.

assistant professor n. a college or university teacher who ranks above a lecturer and below an associate professor

Example: Dr. Green is an *assistant professor*.

Suggestion: Why don't you find out whether he is a lecturer or an *assistant professor*?

Confirmation: Dr. Green is an *assistant professor*, right?

Problem: I need to find out whether Dr. Green is an *assistant professor*.

assistantship n. an opportunity for a graduate student to teach or do research in exchange for a stipend

Example: Terry got an *assistantship* from State University.

Suggestion: If I were you, I would apply for an *assistantship*.

Surprise: So you *did* get an *assistantship* from State University.

Problem: The *assistantship* doesn't pay as much as I thought it would.

associate professor   n.   a college or university teacher who ranks above an assistant professor and below a professor

Example: Dr. Peterson is an *associate professor* now, but she will be promoted to a full professor at the end of the year.

Suggestion: You could ask the secretary if Dr. Peterson is an *associate professor*.

Confirmation: Dr. Peterson isn't an *associate professor*, is she?

Problem: If Dr. Peterson is an *associate professor*, I used the wrong title in my letter to her.

audit   v.   to attend a course without credit

Example: It usually costs as much to *audit* a course as to take it for credit.

Suggestion: You could *audit* the course if you don't need the credit.

Surprise: You mean you are *auditing* the course?

Problem: If I *audit* the course, I won't get credit for it.

bear   n.   a difficult class

Example: That computer science course was a *bear*.

Suggestion: I heard that Dr. Young's class is a real *bear*, so I would advise against it this semester.

Surprise: Your roommate thought this class was a *bear*?

Problem: Two of the classes I am in are real *bears*.

be (get) behind   v.   to be late; to have a lot of work to do

Example: I *am behind* in my physics class.

Suggestion: You *are behind* in your psychology class so you should study.

Surprise: Bill *is behind*?

Problem: I can't go to the party because I *am behind* in my classes.

bike n.   an abbreviation of the word bicycle
   Example: Many students ride their *bikes* on campus.
   Suggestion: You could park your *bike* outside the student union building.
   Confirmation: Did you say your *bike* was locked?
   Problem: I can't ride my *bike* to the pizza parlor because there isn't any parking for it.

bike rack n.   the metal supports where bicycles are parked
   Example: That *bike rack* is full, but there is another one by the library.
   Suggestion: If I were you, I would use the *bike rack* closest to the door.
   Surprise: The *bike rack* was moved from in front of the library?
   Problem: The *bike racks* at my dormitory will not hold all of the students' bikes.

blackboard n.   the (black) writing surface in the front of the classroom
   Example: Dr. Mitchell always writes the important words on the *blackboard*.
   Suggestion: You had better copy everything the instructor writes on the *blackboard*.
   Confirmation: Did you say you copied all of the material that was on the *blackboard*?
   Problem: I can't see what is written on the *blackboard*.

book n.   a written work
   Example: The *books* for this class cost eighty dollars.
   Suggestion: You shouldn't wait too long to buy your *books*.
   Surprise: You didn't buy all of your *books*?
   Problem: I can't buy all of my *books* with only fifty dollars.

book bag   n.   a bag in which to carry books and school supplies
    Example: This *book bag* is very heavy.
    Suggestion: Why don't you buy a sturdy *book bag* so it will last longer?
    Surprise: Your brand new *book bag* fell apart?
    Problem: I can't carry all of my books at one time because my *book bag* is too small.

bookstore   n.   the store on campus where students buy their textbooks
    Example: The *bookstore* opens at seven in the morning.
    Suggestion: You should be at the *bookstore* before it opens so that you can get a used book.
    Surprise: You mean that you were at the *bookstore* early and there were still no used books?
    Problem: The *bookstore* is too far from my apartment for me to walk.

break   n.   a pause in work or study
    Example: Let's take a *break* after we finish our homework.
    Suggestion: If I were you, I would take a *break* before I began a new project.
    Surprise: You mean you're taking a *break* right now?
    Problem: I can't take a *break* until I complete this section of the problem.

bring up   v.   to improve
    Example: If Jack doesn't *bring up* his grades, he won't get into graduate school.
    Suggestion: If you want to *bring up* your grades, you will have to study more.
    Surprise: You *brought up* your grades without studying?
    Problem: If I don't study more, I won't be able to *bring up* my grades.

cafeteria   n.   a restaurant where students can select food from several choices and carry their meals on trays to their tables

Example: Let's order a pizza instead of going to the *cafeteria*.

Suggestion: Why don't we meet in the *cafeteria* before going to see our advisor?

Confirmation: You like the food in the *cafeteria*, right?

Problem: I can't meet you in the *cafeteria* because I have to speak with my professor after class.

call on   v.   to acknowledge in class; to invite to speak

Example: The professor *calls on* students who sit in the front more often than those who sit in back.

Suggestion: If you want the professor to *call on* you frequently, then sit in the front of the room.

Surprise: You sat in the front of the room and weren't *called on*?

Problem: I didn't know the answer when the professor *called on* me.

call the roll   v.   to read the names on a class roster in order to take attendance

Example: Some professors don't *call the roll*, but Dr. Peterson always does.

Suggestion: You should always find out whether or not the professor *calls the roll*.

Confirmation: You weren't there when Dr. Peterson *called the roll*, were you?

Problem: I need to get to class earlier so that I will be there when Dr. Peterson *calls the roll*.

campus   n.   the buildings and grounds of a college or university

Example: State University has a beautiful *campus*.

Suggestion: You should see the *campus* before you decide to apply to school here.

Surprise: You mean you walked the entire *campus* by yourself?

Problem: I can't go with you to see the *campus* if you go this afternoon.

campus security   n.   the police on campus
 Example: In an emergency, call *campus security*.
 Suggestion: You had better call *campus security* to report that your bicycle is missing.
 Confirmation: The *campus security* is understaffed, isn't it?
 Problem: Carol had to call *campus security* to help her get her car started.

carrel   n.   a private study space in the stacks of the library
 Example: There are never enough *carrels* for all of the graduate students.
 Suggestion: You should go to the library early in the evening if you want a *carrel*.
 Surprise: You mean the *carrels* are free?
 Problem: There aren't enough *carrels* in the library.

chapter   n.   a division in a book
 Example: The professor assigned three *chapters* in the textbook.
 Suggestion: If I were you, I would set aside several hours to read all of the *chapters* assigned today.
 Surprise: So you *did* allow enough time to finish the *chapters*.
 Problem: I have to go to the lab, and I am in the middle of a *chapter*.

cheat   v.   to act dishonestly
 Example: Students who *cheat* may be expelled from the university.
 Suggestion: You should not *cheat* because the penalty is serious.
 Confirmation: Gary was expelled because he *cheated*, right?
 Problem: I know that some of my friends *cheated*, but I don't know what to do about it.

cheating n. a dishonest act
    Example: Sharing answers on an exam is *cheating*.
    Suggestion: You could sit alone during the exam so that the professor knows you are not *cheating*.
    Surprise: You consider copying a few sentences from a book *cheating*?
    Problem: Should I report it to the professor if I see someone *cheating*?

check out v. to borrow
    Example: You must have a library card to *check out* books.
    Suggestion: If you want to *check out* books for your research paper, you had better go to the library soon.
    Surprise: So you *didn't* go to the library to *check out* the books you needed.
    Problem: I need a new library card to be able to *check out* books.

class n. the meeting place and the content of a course
    Example: We have three *classes* together this term.
    Suggestion: You could arrange your schedule so that you have three *classes* on the same day.
    Surprise: So you wanted your *classes* to be on Friday?
    Problem: I have to work on Tuesdays and Thursdays, so I can't have *classes* on those days.

class discussion n. an exchange of ideas during a class
    Example: Dr. Green often has *class discussions* instead of lectures.
    Suggestion: If I were you, I would prepare for a *class discussion* in tomorrow's class.
    Confirmation: You prepared for the *class discussion*, didn't you?
    Problem: I am not ready for the *class discussion* today.

closed out   adj.   to be denied access to a class
   Example: Register early so that you aren't *closed out* of the classes you want.
   Suggestion: Why don't you plan to register tomorrow before you are *closed out* of the classes you need to graduate?
   Surprise: Sue registered early to avoid being *closed out* of her classes?
   Problem: I was *closed out* of the English class I needed.

coed   adj.   an abbreviation for *coeducational*, which is a system of education in which both men and women attend the same school or classes
   Example: Most of the schools in the United States are *coed*.
   Suggestion: If I were you, I would live in a *coed* dormitory.
   Confirmation: Did you say you don't attend a *coed* school?
   Problem: My parents don't want me to live in a *coed* dormitory.

college   n.   a school that grants a bachelor's degree; an undergraduate division or a school within a university
   Example: Steve applied to the *college* of business at State University.
   Suggestion: You need to apply to the *college* of nursing early.
   Surprise: So you *did* apply to several *colleges* after all.
   Problem: The *college* of education requires three letters of recommendation.

commencement   n.   a graduation ceremony
   Example: Larger colleges and universities usually have *commencement* more than once each year.
   Suggestion: You had better be early for *commencement* because it starts on time.
   Surprise: So you *did* attend last year's *commencement* exercises.
   Problem: I don't have a cap and gown for *commencement*.

committee   n.   a group of professors who guide a graduate student's program and approve the thesis or dissertation

Example: Bill's *committee* signed his dissertation today.

Suggestion: You should be prepared before you meet with your *committee*.

Surprise: Your *committee* didn't approve your dissertation topic?

Problem: I need to do more research before I meet with my *committee*.

computer   n.   a programmable electronic machine that calculates, processes, and stores information

Example: At some universities, students must bring their own *computers* with them to school.

Suggestion: If I were you, I would purchase a *computer* before going to college.

Surprise: You mean you don't know how to use a *computer*?

Problem: I need to have my *computer* repaired.

computer disk   n.   a magnetic disk on which computer data is stored

Example: It's a good idea to save a copy of your papers and projects on a *computer disk.*

Suggestion: You should always have extra *computer disks.*

Confirmation: You saved your work on a *computer disk*, didn't you?

Problem: I can't print my paper until I find my *computer disk.*

counselor   n.   a person who gives advice, often of a personal nature

Example: See your advisor for academic advice and a *counselor* for personal advice.

Suggestion: Why don't you speak with your *counselor* about the problems with your roommate?

Confirmation: You have to make an appointment before seeing your *counselor*, don't you?

Problem: I can't see my *counselor* until tomorrow.

course   n.   a class
   Example: How many *courses* are you taking this semester?
   Suggestion: If I were you, I would take fewer *courses* this
                semester.
   Surprise: You registered for your *courses* already?
   Problem: I need to take *courses* that apply to my major.

course request (form)   n.   a form used to register for a class
   Example: A student's academic advisor usually signs a
                course request form.
   Suggestion: You should pick up a *course request* form from
                the registrar's office today.
   Surprise: So you *did* pick up your *course request* form.
   Problem: I need to speak with my advisor about my *course*
                request form.

cram   v.   to study at the last minute
   Example: Nancy always *crams* for the quizzes in her math
                class.
   Suggestion: Why don't you study each night instead of *cramming*
                the night before the test?
   Surprise: You mean you *crammed* for the biology final?
   Problem: I need to be more organized so I won't have to
                cram for my tests.

credit   n.   a unit of study
   Example: I have thirty *credits* toward my master's degree.
   Suggestion: Why don't you check your *credits* with your
                advisor?
   Confirmation: You have enough *credits* to graduate, right?
   Problem: I have to take thirty more *credits* in my major
                area.

credit hour n. the number that represents one hour of class per week for one term

    Example: This course is three *credit hours*.

    Suggestion: You could take eighteen *credit hours* this semester.

    Surprise: So you *did* complete fifteen *credit hours* last summer.

    Problem: I can't take enough *credit hours* to graduate this semester.

curve n. a grading system that relies on the normal curve of distribution, resulting in a few A grades, the majority C grades, and a few failing grades

    Example: Grading on the *curve* encourages competition.

    Suggestion: Forget about the *curve*, and just do your best.

    Surprise: Dr. Graham grades his tests on the *curve*?

    Problem: Since the exams were graded on the *curve*, a 95 was a B.

cut class v. to be absent from class, usually without a good excuse

    Example: My roommate *cut class* on Monday because he didn't come back to campus until late Sunday night.

    Suggestion: You had better not *cut class* on Thursday.

    Surprise: You *cut class* to sleep in?

    Problem: I can't *cut class* because I have too many absences.

dean n. an administrator who ranks above a department chair and below a vice president

    Example: The *dean* called a meeting with the department chair.

    Suggestion: You should meet with the *dean* about your problem.

    Surprise: So you *did* speak with the *dean*.

    Problem: Vicki has to prepare a presentation for the *dean*.

dean's list   n.   the honor roll at a college or university

Example: You must maintain a 3.5 grade point average to be on the *dean's list*.

Suggestion: You had better improve your grades if your want to make the *dean's list*.

Confirmation: Jack made the *dean's list* last semester, didn't he?

Problem: I can't make the *dean's list* this semester.

declare   v.   to make an official decision about a major field of study

Example: Most students *declare* their major in their third year at the university.

Suggestion: If I were you, I would *declare* my major before I take any more classes.

Confirmation: You *declared* your major last year, right?

Problem: Joe needs to *declare* his major soon.

degree   n.   an academic title awarded to a student who completes a course of study

Example: The three most common *degrees* are a bachelor's, a master's, and a doctorate.

Suggestion: You should get your *degree* before you get married.

Surprise: So you *did* graduate with a *degree* in music theory.

Problem: I can't get a good job without a *degree*.

department   n.   a division of a college or university organized by subject

Example: The English *department* offers classes for international students.

Suggestion: Why don't you check the *department's* phone number again?

Surprise: So you *did* work in the English *department* office.

Problem: I can't find the list of the *department* offices.

department chair n. a university administrator for a division of a college or university

Example:	The professors in a department report to the *department chair*.
Suggestion:	You could speak to the *department chair* about auditing the class.
Confirmation:	Dr. Carlson is the new *department chair*, isn't he?
Problem:	I can't meet with the *department chair* until after registration.

diploma n. the certificate of completion for a degree

Example:	Students receive their *diplomas* at the graduation ceremony.
Suggestion:	You should get your *diploma* framed.
Surprise:	So you *did* show your family your *diploma*.
Problem:	I need to mail this form and pay my fees before I can get my *diploma*.

dissertation n. a thesis that is written in partial fulfillment of the requirements for a doctorate.

Example:	Dr. Green wrote his *dissertation* on global warming.
Suggestion:	If I were you, I would consider several ideas before selecting a *dissertation* topic.
Surprise:	You mean you already started your *dissertation*?
Problem:	I can't find enough research on my *dissertation* topic.

distance learning n. courses organized so that students can complete the requirements by computer, or other media, often without going to campus

Example:	There are several *distance learning* opportunities for working adults.
Suggestion:	Why don't you sign up for that course through *distance learning*?
Surprise:	So you *did* take that *distance learning* class.
Problem:	I can only take three *distance learning* classes.

division   n.   a group of departments in a college or university

Example: The *division* of modern languages includes both the Spanish department and the French department, as well as the German department.

Suggestion: Why don't you go to the *division* of math and sciences to find more information about biology instructors?

Surprise: You mean you've already spoken to Dr. Conrad about the entrance exam for the *division* of social sciences?

Problem: I need to find out what opportunities the *division* of modern languages offers for foreign study.

doctorate   n.   the degree after a master's degree awarded to an academic doctor

Example: Karen will receive her *doctorate* in the spring.

Suggestion: You should meet with your academic advisor to discuss a *doctorate*.

Surprise: So you *did* receive your *doctorate* from State University.

Problem: I must complete my dissertation before I get my *doctorate*.

dorm   n.   an abbreviation for dormitory

Example: Living on campus in a *dorm* is often cheaper than living off campus.

Suggestion: You should live in a *dorm* for at least one year.

Confirmation: Did you say you have lived in a *dorm* for four years?

Problem: Sue needs to apply now for a room in the *dorm*.

draft   n.   a preliminary copy of a paper or other written document

Example: A good student does not turn in a first *draft* of a paper.

Suggestion: You should edit each *draft* on the computer.

Surprise: You mean you wrote the first *draft* in one night?

Problem: I can't turn in my essay because I have only the first *draft* written.

drop   v.   to withdraw from a course
    Example: If you *drop* a course early in the term, you may get a partial refund.
    Suggestion: If I were you, I would *drop* the class immediately.
    Surprise: You mean you *dropped* the class because it was too hard?
    Problem: Bill needs to *drop* one of his classes because he is taking too many credit hours.

drop out   v.   to withdraw from a college or university
    Example: Mark *dropped out* because he needed to work full-time.
    Suggestion: You could *drop out* and then reenter next semester.
    Confirmation: Did you say Diane *dropped out* after her junior year?
    Problem: I have to *drop out* because I don't have enough money for tuition.

due   adj.   expected on a certain date
    Example: The assignment is *due* on Friday.
    Suggestion: Why don't you turn in the paper before it's *due?*
    Confirmation: The project is *due* this week, isn't it?
    Problem: I can't complete the assignment by the *due* date.

elective (course)   n., adj.   an optional academic course
    Example: In the junior year, most students are taking elective *courses*, as well as requirements.
    Suggestion: Take some *elective* classes in your areas of outside interest.
    Confirmation: You are going to take an *elective* in art appreciation, right?
    Problem: I can't take any *elective* classes this semester.

enroll   v.   to register for a course or a university program
    Example: Only a few students *enroll* in seminars.
    Suggestion: Why don't you *enroll* early before the class fills up?
    Surprise: You mean you didn't *enroll* in the computer class?
    Problem: I can't *enroll* in that class without taking the introductory class first.

essay   n.   a short composition on a single subject, usually presenting the personal opinion of the author

Example: An *essay* is often five paragraphs long.
Suggestion: If I were you, I would make an outline before writing the *essay*.
Surprise: So you *did* get an A on the *essay*.
Problem: I have to write an *essay* for my class on Friday.

exam   n.   an abbreviation for examination

Example: The professor scheduled several quizzes and one *exam*.
Suggestion: You had better prepare for the *exam* in chemistry.
Surprise: You studied for the physics *exam*?
Problem: I have to meet with my study group before the *exam*.

excused absence   n.   absence with the permission of the professor

Example: Dr. Mitchell allows every student one *excused absence* each semester.
Suggestion: You could take an *excused absence* in your Friday class so we could leave early.
Confirmation: You have two *excused absences* in biology, don't you?
Problem: I already have one *excused absence* in Dr. Mitchell's class.

expel   v.   to dismiss from school

Example: Gary was *expelled* because he cheated on an exam.
Suggestion: You should avoid getting *expelled* at all costs.
Surprise: Gary was *expelled* from the university?
Problem: I would be *expelled* if I helped you.

extension n. additional time

Example: We asked Dr. Peterson for an *extension* in order to complete the group project.

Suggestion: You should organize your time so that you will not have to ask for an *extension*.

Surprise: You mean your request for an *extension* was denied?

Problem: I need to meet with my professor to discuss an *extension*.

extra credit n. additional points for doing an optional assignment

Example: *Extra credit* can bring up your grade by one letter.

Suggestion: You could talk to the professor about doing something for *extra credit*.

Confirmation: You signed up for *extra credit*, right?

Problem: Professor Stephens doesn't offer any options for *extra credit*.

faculty member n. a teacher in a college or university

Example: Dr. Baker is a *faculty member* at State University.

Suggestion: Why don't you ask a *faculty member* for directions?

Confirmation: You didn't meet any of the new *faculty members* when you visited the campus, did you?

Problem: I don't know the other *faculty members* in my department very well.

fail v. to receive an unacceptable grade

Example: If Mary gets another low grade, she will *fail* the course.

Suggestion: You had better complete the project or you will *fail* the class.

Surprise: You mean you *failed* the exam?

Problem: I have to study tonight, or I will *fail* the test tomorrow.

fee n. a charge for services
Example:	You must pay a *fee* to park your car on campus.
Suggestion:	If I were you, I would pay my *fees* before the late penalty applies.
Confirmation:	Did you say there are *fees* for using the recreational facilities?
Problem:	I need to go to the business office to pay my *fees*.

field trip n. a trip for observation and education
Example:	The geology class usually takes several *field trips* to the museum.
Suggestion:	You should wear sturdy shoes on the *field trip*.
Surprise:	You didn't sign up for the *field trip* to the art gallery?
Problem:	I have to go on a *field trip* Saturday morning, but my boss won't let me off work.

fill-in-the-blank(s) (test) n., adj. an objective test in which the student completes sentences by writing in the missing words
Example:	Dr. Stephens always gives *fill-in-the-blank* tests during the semester, but he gives short-essay finals.
Suggestion:	You had better study the definitions for the *fill-in-the-blank* portion of the test.
Confirmation:	The test was all *fill-in-the-blanks*, right?
Problem:	Kathy needs to do better on the *fill-in-the-blank* questions.

final (exam) n. the last examination of an academic course
Example:	The *final* will include questions from the notes, as well as from the textbook.
Suggestion:	You should use both your notes and the text to review for the *final exam*.
Surprise:	You finished your *final* in an hour?
Problem:	I have to prepare for two *final exams* on the same day.

fine n. a sum of money paid for violation of a rule

Example: The *fine* for keeping a library book after the due date is one dollar per day.

Suggestion: You should move your car to avoid a *fine*.

Confirmation: Did you say you were charged a *fine* for parking there?

Problem: I need to pay my *fines* before the end of the semester.

flunk v. to fail

Example: I would have *flunked* the course without my study group.

Suggestion: You could make an appointment with the professor before he *flunks* you.

Confirmation: Did you say you might have flunked the test?

Problem: We are going to *flunk* this quiz if we don't study for it.

flunk out v. to be dismissed from school for failure

Example: Tim *flunked out* of State University before he enrolled here.

Suggestion: You had better start working harder or you are going to *flunk out*.

Confirmation: Your roommate *flunked out*, right?

Problem: If I don't get good grades on my finals, I am going to *flunk out*.

fraternity n. a social organization for male college students

Example: Bill is going to join a *fraternity*.

Suggestion: You could join a professional *fraternity*.

Surprise: You were invited to join three *fraternities*?

Problem: I can't afford to join a *fraternity*.

fraternity row n. a street where many fraternity houses are located

Example: I live on Fifth Street, near *fraternity row*.

Suggestion: Why don't you walk down *fraternity row* to look at the homecoming decorations?

Surprise: Ken isn't going to live on *fraternity row* next year?

Problem: I can't find a place to park on *fraternity row*.

freshman   n.   a first-year college student
    Example: Most of the students in Manchester Hall are *freshmen*.
    Suggestion: You should establish good study habits while you are a *freshman*.
    Surprise: You didn't live in a dorm when you were a *freshman*?
    Problem: The *freshmen* have to take requirements.

full-time   adj.   the number of hours for standard tuition at a college or university, usually 9 hours for a graduate student and 12–15 hours for an undergraduate student
    Example: Tom is a *full-time* student this semester.
    Suggestion: If I were you, I would register as a *full-time* student this semester.
    Confirmation: The scholarship is only available to *full-time* students, right?
    Problem: I need to register as a *full-time* student to be eligible for a loan.

get (be) behind   v.   to be late or off schedule
    Example: I am *getting behind* in my math class.
    Suggestion: You had better study this weekend or you will *get behind* in English.
    Confirmation: Ken *got behind* in his classes, didn't he?
    Problem: I *got behind* in French, and now my class is really confusing.

get caught up   v.   to bring up-to-date
    Example: We are going to *get caught up* in our classes this weekend.
    Suggestion: Why don't you *get caught up* in English before you start your next project?
    Confirmation: Sue *got caught up* over vacation, didn't she?
    Problem: I need to *get caught up* before final exams.

G.P.A.   n.   abbreviation for grade point average

Example:	Kathy's *G.P.A.* as an undergraduate was 4.0, but she isn't doing as well in graduate school.
Suggestion:	You should be concerned about your *G.P.A.*
Surprise:	Laura's *G.P.A.* dropped last semester?
Problem:	I can't raise my *G.P.A.* if I take calculus.

grade point average   n.   a scale, usually 0–4, on which grades are calculated

Example:	If students' *grade point averages* fall below 2.0, they will be placed on probation.
Suggestion:	If I were you, I would speak to my academic advisor about your *grade point average.*
Surprise:	You mean an applicant's *grade point average* is more important than work experience?
Problem:	I need to improve my *grade point average.*

grades   n.   a standard number or letter indicating a student's level of performance

Example:	We will get our *grades* in the mail a week after the semester is over.
Suggestion:	You should check the *grades* that the professor posted.
Surprise:	Our *grades* are already in the mail?
Problem:	I have to have better *grades* to get into the college of business.

graduate school   n.   a division of a college or university to serve students who are pursuing masters or doctoral degrees

Example:	I would like to apply to *graduate school* after I complete my bachelor's degree.
Suggestion:	Why don't you work a year before applying to *graduate school*?
Surprise:	So Tracy *did* get accepted to *graduate school.*
Problem:	I have to get letters of recommendation to apply to *graduate school.*

graduate student   n.   a student who is pursuing a master's or doctorate

Example: *Graduate students* must maintain higher grades than undergraduate students.

Suggestion: You had better work with the other *graduate students* on this project.

Confirmation: Only *graduate students* are allowed to take this class, right?

Problem: All of the students in the class are *graduate students* except me.

grant   n.   funds for research or study

Example: Carol received a *grant* for her research in psychology.

Suggestion: You should apply for a summer *grant*.

Surprise: You mean there are *grants* available for undergraduate students?

Problem: Bill needs to write a proposal before Tuesday if he wants to be considered for a *grant*.

group project   n.   an assignment to be completed by three or more students

Example: I prefer to work on *group projects* instead of on assignments by myself.

Suggestion: You should select your *group project* before midterm.

Surprise: You've chosen your *group project* already?

Problem: The *group project* will take more time than I thought.

hand back   v.   return an assignment

Example: Dr. Graham always *hands back* our assignments the next day.

Suggestion: You had better be there when Dr. Mitchell *hands back* your exam.

Confirmation: Dr. Mitchell hasn't *handed back* your exam yet, has he?

Problem: I can't find the exam that he *handed back.*

handout   n.   prepared notes that a teacher provides to the class
 Example: Dr. Stephen's *handouts* are always very helpful.
 Suggestion: You had better save all of your *handouts*.
 Surprise: You lost the *handouts*?
 Problem: I need to organize all of my *handouts* before I
       start to study for the final.

head resident   n.   the advisor for a dormitory
 Example: The *head resident* can help you resolve problems
       with your roommate.
 Suggestion: If I were you, I would introduce myself to the
       head resident.
 Surprise: So you *did* speak with the *head resident*.
 Problem: I can't find the *head resident*.

health center   n.   the clinic on campus to provide basic health
         care for students
 Example: We are going to the *health center* for a free eye
       examination.
 Suggestion: You had better go to the *health center* for that
       cough.
 Surprise: You mean the *health center* is closed?
 Problem: I am too sick to go to the *health center.*

health insurance   n.   protection for students who may need
          medical attention
 Example: *Health insurance* is required on most campuses.
 Suggestion: You need to purchase *health insurance* through
       the university.
 Confirmation: You don't have *health insurance*, do you?
 Problem: I have to earn some more money to pay for my
       health insurance.

hit the books v.   to study very hard
 Example: I have to *hit the books* tonight and tomorrow to get ready for the midterm.
 Suggestion: You had better *hit the books* for Dr. Sheridan's exam.
 Surprise: You mean you didn't *hit the books* for the psychology exam?
 Problem: My friends have to *hit the books* this weekend so they can't go to the party with me.

homework n.   schoolwork done at home
 Example: If I do my *homework* every day, I understand the lectures better.
 Suggestion: Why don't you do your *homework* before dinner?
 Confirmation: There wasn't any *homework* last night, was there?
 Problem: I have to do my *homework* in order to be prepared for the class discussion.

honors adj.   special recognition for exceptional students
 Example: Jane is an *honors* graduate.
 Suggestion: You could live in an *honors* dorm.
 Surprise: So you *did* enroll in the *honors* program.
 Problem: The courses in the *honors* program are much harder than the regular courses.

housing office n.   an administrative office for residence halls and off-campus rentals
 Example: Let's go over to the *housing office* to ask about apartments near the campus.
 Suggestion: If I were you, I would check at the *housing office* for a dorm application.
 Confirmation: The *housing office* closed early, right?
 Problem: I need to speak with someone in the *housing office* about my application.

incomplete n. a grade in a course that allows students to complete requirements the following term

Example: I asked Dr. Young for an *incomplete* in his class.

Suggestion: You should request an *incomplete* at least two weeks before the end of the term.

Confirmation: Bill took an *incomplete* in sociology last semester, didn't he?

Problem: I can't ask Dr. Young for another *incomplete*.

instructor n. a college or university teacher who ranks below an assistant professor

Example: My *instructor* for math is from Hawaii.

Suggestion: You should check with the *instructor* to see if there is room in the class.

Confirmation: Did you say the *instructor* was absent?

Problem: I can't seem to get along with my *instructor*.

interactive television (course) n. a distance learning course that is taught on two-way television connections

Example: The instructor for our *interactive television course* is on a campus about fifty miles away.

Suggestion: You could take that course on the *interactive television*.

Surprise: Dr. Stephen's course is offered on *interactive television*?

Problem: *Interactive television courses* make me uncomfortable.

interlibrary loan n. a system that allows students on one campus to borrow books from other libraries on other campuses

Example: It takes at least a week to receive a book by *interlibrary loan*.

Suggestion: You could see if the book is available through *interlibrary loan*.

Confirmation: Your *interlibrary loan* books arrived in time, right?

Problem: I can't seem to find the desk for *interlibrary loans*.

internship n. a training opportunity for an advanced student or a recent graduate

Example: Bill got an *internship* at the University Hospital.
Suggestion: You should apply for an *internship* very early.
Surprise: You are getting paid for your *internship*?
Problem: I need to serve a two-year *internship*.

junior n., adj. a third-year college student

Example: When I am a *junior*, I plan to study abroad for a semester.
Suggestion: You could concentrate on your major your *junior* year.
Surprise: A *junior* can study abroad?
Problem: I need to carry eighteen credit hours both semesters of my *junior* year.

keep grades up v. to maintain a good grade point average

Example: If Joanne doesn't *keep her grades up*, she will lose her scholarship.
Suggestion: You need to study harder if you want to *keep your grades up*.
Surprise: Kathy didn't *keep her grades up* this semester?
Problem: I can't *keep my grades up* and work full-time.

lab n., adj. abbreviation for laboratory

Example: The course includes a five-hour *lab*.
Suggestion: You had better allow sufficient time for your biology *lab*.
Confirmation: You missed the last *lab* session, right?
Problem: I need to find a partner for my psychology *lab*.

lab assistant n. a graduate student who helps in the lab

Example: Bill is Dr. Peterson's *lab assistant*.
Suggestion: You could ask the *lab assistant* for help.
Confirmation: You are the *lab assistant*, aren't you?
Problem: I need to speak with the *lab assistant* before class.

laboratory   n.   a classroom equipped for experiments and research

Example: The physics *laboratory* at State University is very old.

Suggestion: You could meet your biology study group in the *laboratory*.

Confirmation: The *laboratory* isn't closed Saturday, is it?

Problem: I have to get directions to the *laboratory*.

lab report   n.   a written description of the laboratory activities

Example: Our *lab reports* are due every Friday.

Suggestion: If I were you, I wouldn't wait to start my *lab report*.

Surprise: You mean the *lab reports* have to be typed?

Problem: I have to turn in my *lab report* tomorrow.

laptop   n.   a compact, portable computer that you can use on your lap

Example: Mary's *laptop* goes with her everywhere.

Suggestion: If I were you, I would buy a new *laptop*.

Surprise: Your laptop *crashed*?

Problem: I forgot to bring my *laptop* with me to class.

learning assistance center   n.   an area used for tutoring and special programs to help students with their classes

Example: I have to meet my tutor at the *learning assistance center* at four o'clock.

Suggestion: You should go to the *learning assistance center* for help in the morning.

Surprise: So Nancy *did* go to the *learning assistance center* for tutoring.

Problem: The tutors at the *learning assistance center* are all juniors and seniors, so I don't qualify.

lecture n.   a presentation for a class, delivered by the professor
    Example: The *lectures* are really interesting, but I don't
                        enjoy the labs as much.
    Suggestion: You should take more notes during Dr. Mitchell's
                        lectures.
    Confirmation: Did you say say the *lecture* is canceled for
                        today?
    Problem: I can't keep up with the *lectures*.

lecturer n.   a college or university teacher, usually without rank
    Example: Mr. Lewis is only a *lecturer*, but his classes are
                        very good.
    Suggestion: If I were you, I would speak with the *lecturer*
                        about your questions.
    Surprise: The *lecturer* isn't here?
    Problem: I can't take notes because the *lecturer* speaks
                        too fast.

library n.   the building on campus where books and other
                 research materials are kept
    Example: Vicki has a job in the *library*.
    Suggestion: Your study group could reserve a study room in
                        the *library*.
    Surprise: You mean the *library* is within walking distance?
    Problem: I need to return my books to the *library*.

library card n.   an identification card that permits the holder to
                     borrow books and materials from the library
    Example: Without a *library card*, you can't borrow books
                        here.
    Suggestion: You should get a *library card* right away.
    Surprise: So you *did* bring your *library card* with you.
    Problem: I can't use my *library card* because I owe a fine.

library fine   n.   a payment for returning books and materials after the due date

Example: You can't get your grade report unless you pay your *library fines.*

Suggestion: You should pay your *library fines* immediately.

Confirmation: You owe ten dollars in *library fines*, don't you?

Problem: Nancy needs to pay her *library fines* before she checks out any more books.

lost and found   n.   an area on campus where items are kept for their owners to reclaim

Example: Maybe someone picked up your book and took it to the *lost and found*.

Suggestion: Why don't you check at the *lost and found* for your backpack?

Surprise: You mean Sue's wallet wasn't at the *lost and found*?

Problem: Sue needs to fill out a report at the *lost and found*.

lower-division (course)   adj.   introductory-level courses for first- and second-year students

Example: Seniors don't usually take *lower-division* courses.

Suggestion: You should take *lower-division* classes your first year.

Surprise: You mean all of the *lower-division* classes are full?

Problem: I have to take a *lower-division* class before I can take the advanced course.

major   n.   a field of study chosen as an academic specialty

Example: My *major* is environmental studies.

Suggestion: You should declare your *major* by your junior year.

Confirmation: You have to declare a *major* to graduate, don't you?

Problem: I have to tell my advisor my *major* tomorrow.

makeup test n. a test taken after the date of the original administration

Example: Dr. Stephens usually allows her students to take a *makeup test* if there is a good reason for being absent.

Suggestion: You could speak with Dr. Stephens about taking a *makeup test*.

Surprise: So Dr. Peterson *did* let you take a *makeup test*.

Problem: Dana needs to take a *makeup test* before spring break.

married student housing n. apartments on or near campus for married students

Example: There is usually a waiting list to be assigned to *married student housing*.

Suggestion: If I were you, I would get an application for *married student housing* today.

Confirmation: Did you say there are no vacancies in *married student housing*?

Problem: We need to pick up an application for *married student housing*.

Mickey Mouse course n. a very easy course

Example: This is a *Mickey Mouse course*, but it is on my program of study.

Suggestion: Why don't you take one *Mickey Mouse course* this semester just for fun?

Surprise: You thought physics was a *Mickey Mouse course*?

Problem: I have to take this *Mickey Mouse course* to fulfill my physical education requirement.

midterm n. an exam that is given in the middle of the term

Example: I got an A on my *midterm* in accounting.

Suggestion: Why don't you study with your study group for the music theory *midterm*?

Surprise: You mean Sue failed her economics *midterm*?

Problem: I have three *midterms* in one day.

minor   n.   a secondary area of study
Example: With a major in international business, I decided to do my *minor* in English.
Suggestion: You should *minor* in economics since you're studying prelaw.
Confirmation: You've completed all of your *minor* classes, right?
Problem: I need one more class to complete my *minor*.

miss (class)   v.   to be absent
Example: My roommate is missing a lot of classes lately.
Suggestion: If I were you I wouldn't *miss* Dr. Mitchell's class today.
Surprise: So you *did miss* class last Friday.
Problem: I can't *miss* any more of Dr. Mitchell's classes, or my grade will be lowered by one letter.

multiple-choice test   n.   an objective test with questions that provide several possible answer choices
Example: We usually have *multiple-choice tests* in Dr. Graham's classes.
Suggestion: You had better study very carefully for Dr. Graham's *multiple-choice test*.
Confirmation: It was a *multiple-choice test*, wasn't it?
Problem: I don't usually do well on *multiple-choice tests*.

notebook   n.   a bound book with blank pages in it for notes
Example: I lost the *notebook* with my biology notes in it.
Suggestion: You should make sure that your *notebook* is well organized.
Surprise: You lost your *notebook*?
Problem: I need to organize my *notebook* this weekend.

notebook computer   n.   a computer the size of a notebook

    Example: Joe has a *notebook computer* that he uses in
                       class.

    Suggestion: Why don't you use my *notebook computer* to see
                       whether you like it?

    Surprise: So you *did* purchase a *notebook computer*.

    Problem: I can't possibly afford a *notebook computer* right
                       now.

notes   n.   a brief record of a lecture to help students recall the
              important points

    Example: We didn't take *notes* in class today because most
                       of the lecture was from the book.

    Suggestion: You should copy Tracy's *notes* before the next
                       test.

    Surprise: You mean you lent your *notes* to someone?

    Problem: I need to recopy my *notes* this evening.

objective test   n.   a test with questions that have one possible
                 answer, usually presented in a multiple-choice,
                 matching, or true-false format

    Example: The final exam will be an *objective test*, not an
                       essay test.

    Suggestion: You should probably prepare for an *objective test*
                       in math.

    Confirmation: The final exam was an *objective test*, right?

    Problem: I have to study harder for *objective tests*.

off campus   adj.   not on university property

    Example: There are some very nice apartments just *off
                       campus* on State Street.

    Suggestion: You should come to campus early unless you
                       want to park *off campus*.

    Surprise: You mean Carol doesn't want to live *off campus*?

    Problem: I need to live *off campus* to save money.

office   n.   a place for university faculty and staff to meet with students and do their work

Example: Mr. Lewis has an *office* in Madison Hall.

Suggestion: Most of the advisors' *offices* are in Sycamore Hall.

Surprise: So you *did* find Mr. Lewis's *office* before he left for the day.

Problem: I have to go to the business *office* tomorrow to ask about my bill.

office hours   n.   a schedule when faculty are in their offices to meet with students

Example: *Office hours* are usually posted on the door of the professor's office.

Suggestion: You should write down the instructor's *office hours* in your notebook.

Confirmation: You don't know Dr. Miller's *office hours*, do you?

Problem: I can't find my copy of Dr. Miller's *office hours*.

online course   n.   a course taught on the Internet

Example: There is a separate list of *online courses* this semester.

Suggestion: Why don't you consider an *online course* in economics?

Confirmation: Joe took an *online course* last year, right?

Problem: I need a computer to take an *online course*.

on probation   prep. phrase   experiencing a trial period to improve grades before disciplinary action

Example: Kathy is *on probation*, so she will probably be studying this weekend.

Suggestion: You had better keep up your grades or you will end up *on probation*.

Surprise: Sue is *on probation* again?

Problem: I can't let my parents find out that I am *on probation*.

on reserve   prep. phrase   retained in a special place in the library, usually for use only in the library

Example: Dr. Young always puts a lot of books *on reserve* for his classes.

Suggestion: You could check to see if the book is *on reserve*.

Surprise: You mean the articles are *on reserve*?

Problem: I have to find out which books are *on reserve*.

open-book test   n.   a test during which students may consult their books and notes

Example: *Open-book tests* are often longer than other tests.

Suggestion: You should still prepare even though it is an *open-book test.*

Surprise: You mean you didn't know it was an *open-book test*?

Problem: I can't find my notes for the *open-book test.*

orientation   n.   a program for new students at a college or university during which they receive information about the school

Example: I missed the first day of *orientation*, so I didn't get a map.

Suggestion: You should sit near the front during *orientation.*

Surprise: So you *did* go to freshman *orientation.*

Problem: I have to go to *orientation* tomorrow evening.

override   n.   permission to enter a class for which the student does not qualify

Example: Dr. Stephens will usually give you an *override* if you need the class.

Suggestion: You should speak to the professor about getting an *override* for that class.

Confirmation: Did you say your request for an *override* was denied?

Problem: I need to get an *override* so that I can take that class.

paper   n.   a research report

Example:	The *papers* for this class should be at least ten pages long.
Suggestion:	You had better follow Dr. Carlyle's guidelines for this *paper*.
Surprise:	Laura turned in her *paper* late?
Problem:	I can't print my *paper* because I need an ink cartridge for my printer.

parking garage   n.   a structure for parking, usually requiring payment

Example:	The *parking garages* are too far away from the classrooms.
Suggestion:	You had better get a parking permit for the *parking garage*.
Surprise:	You mean you don't know which *parking garage* you used?
Problem:	I have to find a *parking garage* with a vacancy.

parking lot   n.   an area for parking

Example:	This *parking lot* is for students only.
Suggestion:	You should avoid leaving your car in the *parking lot* overnight.
Surprise:	You mean your car was towed from the *parking lot*?
Problem:	I have to leave early to get a spot in the *parking lot* beside the dorm.

parking permit   n.   permission to park in certain parking lots or garages

Example:	Your *parking permit* expires at the end of the month.
Suggestion:	If I were you, I would get a *parking permit* when you register.
Confirmation:	My *parking permit* hasn't expired, has it?
Problem:	I need to pay my fines before they will issue me another *parking permit*.

parking space   n.   a designated area for one car
   Example: There is a car in my *parking space*.
   Suggestion: You should not use a reserved *parking space*.
   Surprise: So you *did* park in someone else's *parking space*.
   Problem: I can't find a *parking space*.

parking ticket   n.   notice of a fine due for parking in a restricted
                          area
   Example: If you don't take care of your *parking tickets*,
                  you won't be able to register for classes next
                  semester.
   Suggestion: You could avoid getting *parking tickets* by using
                  the student parking lots.
   Surprise: You mean Carol got a *parking ticket* because she
                  didn't have a permit?
   Problem: I have to save money to pay my *parking tickets*.

part-time   adj.   less than the full work day or school day
   Example: Laura has a *part-time* job after school.
   Suggestion: Why don't you get a *part-time* job to pay for your
                  books?
   Confirmation: You applied for a *part-time* job on campus, right?
   Problem: I need to find a *part-time* job this summer.

pass back   v.   to return tests and assignments to the owner
   Example: Dr. Young is going to *pass back* our quizzes
                  today.
   Suggestion: You should ask Dr. Young for an appointment
                  after he *passes back* the tests.
   Surprise: Dr. Young didn't *pass back* the papers?
   Problem: I have to get my paper from Dr. Young because I
                  wasn't there when he *passed them back*.

placement office n. the office where students receive assistance in locating employment

Example: Several companies are interviewing students at the *placement office* this week.

Suggestion: Why don't you check the interview listing in the *placement office* on Monday?

Confirmation: Joe got his job through the *placement office*, didn't he?

Problem: I need to schedule an interview in the *placement office*.

plagiarize v. to use someone else's written work without giving that person credit

plagiarizing n. the use of someone else's work without giving that person credit

Example: To avoid *plagiarizing*, always cite the source.

Suggestion: If you change this sentence, it will keep you from *plagiarizing*.

Surprise: You mean you know someone who *plagiarized*?

Problem: The professor thought that I had *plagiarized* a report.

pop quiz n. a quiz that is given without notice

Example: We had a *pop quiz* in our sociology class today.

Suggestion: You should always be prepared for a *pop quiz*.

Confirmation: Did you say you passed all of the *pop quizzes*?

Problem: I have to be on time to class in case there is a *pop quiz* at the beginning of class.

post (grade) v. to publish a list and display it in a public place

Example: The grades for the exams are *posted* on Dr. Graham's door.

Suggestion: You should see if the grades have been *posted* yet.

Confirmation: The assignments aren't *posted* yet, are they?

Problem: I can't get to campus to see if the grades are *posted*.

PowerPoint (presentation)   n.   a series of slides created on the computer, which can be viewed using a projector

Example: Most of the professors use *PowerPoint* presentations in class.

Suggestion: You could do a *PowerPoint* presentation for your project.

Confirmation: *A PowerPoint* presentation will fulfill the requirement, won't it?

Problem: I am not very happy with my *PowerPoint* presentation.

prerequisite   n.   a course required before a student is eligible to take a higher-level course

Example: This English class has two *prerequisites*.

Suggestion: You should check the *prerequisites* before seeing your advisor.

Surprise: You took the *prerequisites* last year?

Problem: I have to pass the *prerequisites* before I can register for the next class.

presentation   n.   a lecture, speech, or demonstration in front of the class

Example: Your *presentation* in our anthropology class was very interesting.

Suggestion: You could use more pictures in your *presentation*.

Surprise: You mean your *presentation* is fifty minutes long?

Problem: I need to get over my fear of public speaking before I give my *presentation*.

probation   n.   a period of time to improve grades

Example: Jane is on *probation* this term.

Suggestion: You should hire a tutor before you are put on *probation*.

Confirmation: Did you say you are on *probation*?

Problem: I have to pass this class, or I'll get put on *probation*.

professor   n.   a college or university teacher who ranks above an associate professor
    Example: Dr. Baker is a *professor* of English.
    Suggestion: Why don't you speak with your *professor* about the project?
    Confirmation: The *professor's* office hours are posted, aren't they?
    Problem: I need to speak to my *professor* before class on Friday.

program of study   n.   a list of the courses that a student must take to fulfill the requirements for graduation
    Example: If you want to change your *program of study*, you must see your advisor.
    Suggestion: Why don't you review your *program of study* in your catalog?
    Confirmation: The *program of study* is a four-year plan, isn't it?
    Problem: I need to become familiar with my *program of study*.

project   n.   an assignment that often involves the application of knowledge
    Example: We can do the *project* by ourselves or in a group.
    Suggestion: Why don't you and your study group do the *project* together?
    Surprise: You did the *project* that everyone is talking about?
    Problem: I have to present my *project* to the class.

quarter   n.   a school term that is usually ten to twelve weeks in length
    Example: This *quarter* has gone by very quickly.
    Suggestion: You could take fewer classes next *quarter*.
    Surprise: You mean you have to finish your thesis this *quarter*?
    Problem: I need to study harder next *quarter*.

quiz   n.   an evaluation that is usually shorter and worth fewer
points than a test
  Example: We have a *quiz* in our algebra class every week.
  Suggestion: You should always be prepared for a *quiz*.
  Confirmation: The *quiz* doesn't include last night's reading,
                   does it?
  Problem: We have a *quiz* in chemistry this week.

registrar   n.   a university official in charge of keeping records
  Example: You need to see the *registrar* about your grade
                   change.
  Suggestion: If I were you, I would check with the *registrar*
                   about your transcript.
  Surprise: So you *did* file a change of address with the
                   registrar.
  Problem: The *registrar* is unavailable until next week.

registration   n.   the process for enrolling in courses at a college
or university
  Example: *Registration* always takes longer than I think it
                   will.
  Suggestion: You should meet with your advisor before
                   registration.
  Surprise: You mean that early *registration* is available for
                   graduate students?
  Problem: I can't get to *registration* before noon.

report   n.   a written or oral presentation of results, either of
research or experimentation
  Example: Ken gave an excellent *report* in our management
                   class today.
  Suggestion: If I were you, I would allow more time for my next
                   report.
  Surprise: So you *did* listen to Ken's *report*.
  Problem: I have to do five oral *reports* for speech class.

research   n.   investigation or study

    Example: Dr. Peterson is going to give a lecture about her *research* on cross-cultural interaction.

    Suggestion: You could use my class for your *research*.

    Confirmation: Your *research* is complete, isn't it?

    Problem: I need more sources for my *research*.

research assistant   n.   a research position under the supervision of a faculty member

    Example: The *research assistants* get to know the faculty better than the other graduate students do.

    Suggestion: You could apply to be a *research assistant* next year.

    Surprise: You mean Don's a *research assistant*?

    Problem: I need to speak to the *research assistant* who works in the psychology lab.

research paper   n.   a written report based on research

    Example: Use at least ten references for your *research papers*.

    Suggestion: You had better go to the library soon if you want that book for your *research paper*.

    Confirmation: We have to present our *research paper* to the class, don't we?

    Problem: I can't get started on my *research paper*.

residence hall   n.   a dormitory on campus

    Example: All freshmen have to live in a *residence hall*.

    Suggestion: You could move to another *residence hall*.

    Confirmation: You have a single room in a *residence hall*, right?

    Problem: All of the *residence halls* are full.

resident advisor n.   an advisor who lives in a dormitory in order to provide supervision and counseling for the students

Example:	We call our *resident advisor* the "head resident."
Suggestion:	Why don't you speak to the *resident advisor* about your problem?
Surprise:	You live next door to the *resident advisor*?
Problem:	I need to speak with the *resident advisor* regarding the desk in my room.

review session n.   a study meeting to review material before a test, often led by the professor

Example:	I'm on my way to a *review session* for my art appreciation class.
Suggestion:	You could schedule a *review session* with your study group.
Surprise:	The *review session* was productive?
Problem:	I can't meet Thursday afternoon for the *review session.*

room and board n.   fees for room rent and meals

Example:	*Room and board* goes up every year.
Suggestion:	You should plan to include the price of *room and board* in your budget.
Confirmation:	Did you say your scholarship covers *room and board*?
Problem:	I need to find a part-time job to pay for *room and board*.

roommate n.   a person who shares a room or rooms

Example:	I think Diane is looking for a *roommate*.
Suggestion:	Why don't you and Diane get another *roommate*?
Surprise:	You mean you're looking for another *roommate*?
Problem:	I need a *roommate* to share my rent.

schedule   n.   a list of courses with days, times, and locations
    Example: My *schedule* this semester allows me to work in the afternoons.
    Suggestion: With your *schedule*, you could get a job at school.
    Confirmation: Your *schedule* doesn't include evening classes, does it?
    Problem: I can't fit that class into my *schedule*.

scholarship   n.   a grant awarded to a student
    Example: Tracy got a *scholarship* to attend a special summer course abroad.
    Suggestion: Why don't you apply for a *scholarship*?
    Confirmation: There aren't any *scholarships* available for international students, are there?
    Problem: I have to turn the application in tomorrow to be eligible for the *scholarship*.

section   n.   one of several options for the same course
    Example: Everyone wants to take the *section* that Mrs. McNiel teaches.
    Suggestion: You could ask Mrs. McNiel to let you into her *section*.
    Surprise: You mean there are no *sections* open in the morning?
    Problem: I can't get into that *section* because it is closed.

semester   n.   a school term that is usually fifteen to eighteen weeks in length
    Example: When the *semester* is over, I am going to visit my family.
    Suggestion: You could sign up for more classes this *semester*.
    Confirmation: This *semester* ends before winter break, doesn't it?
    Problem: I need to take eighteen credit hours next *semester*.

senior   n.   a fourth-year student
    Example: Laura will be a *senior* next semester.
    Suggestion: If I were you, I would take that class as a *senior*.
    Surprise: You mean Dana is a *senior*?
    Problem: I have to take five classes when I'm a *senior*.

short-essay test   n.   a test with questions that require a written response of one sentence to one paragraph in length
    Example: I would rather take a *short-essay test* than an objective test.
    Suggestion: You had better study your notes for Dr. Mitchell's *short-essay test*.
    Surprise: You think a *short-essay test* is easier than an objective test?
    Problem: I have three *short-essay tests* in that class.

shuttle   n.   a bus that has a short route around the campus area
    Example: Carol has a car, but she still uses the campus *shuttle* most of the time.
    Suggestion: If I were you, I would take the *shuttle* at night.
    Confirmation: Did you say there's no *shuttle* on Sundays?
    Problem: I need to leave early to catch the *shuttle*.

sign up (for a class)   v.   to enroll (in a class)
    Example: Let's *sign up* for the same geology class.
    Suggestion: You should *sign up* for Dr. Brown's music theory class.
    Surprise: So you *did sign up* for the field trip.
    Problem: I can't *sign up* for that class because it conflicts with my schedule.

skip class   v.   to be absent
    Example: Nancy has been *skipping class* again.
    Suggestion: If I were you, I wouldn't *skip class* this week.
    Surprise: Ron *skipped class* yesterday?
    Problem: Bill *skipped class* on the day of the test.

snack bar   n.   a small restaurant area where a limited menu is available
Example: We usually meet at the *snack bar* for a quick lunch.
Suggestion: You could meet me at the *snack bar*.
Surprise: So you *are* going to the *snack bar* after class.
Problem: I need to go to the *snack bar* between classes because I don't have a break for lunch.

social security number   n.   a nine-digit number that is often used for student identification, as well as for employment purposes
Example: What is your *social security number*?
Suggestion: You should memorize your *social security number*.
Confirmation: Your *social security number* is on your license, isn't it?
Problem: Anna doesn't have a *social security number*.

sophomore   n.   a second-year college student
Example: A full-time student is usually a *sophomore* by the third semester.
Suggestion: You had better complete your general education classes by the end of your *sophomore* year.
Surprise: You mean Bill is only a *sophomore*?
Problem: I can't take advanced psychology because I am only a *sophomore*.

sorority   n.   a social organization for female college students
Example: About a dozen *sororities* are on campus.
Suggestion: You should consider joining a *sorority*.
Surprise: So you *did* join a *sorority*.
Problem: *Sororities* require a lot of time.

spring break   n.   a short vacation in the middle of the spring semester

Example: Some of my friends are going to Florida for *spring break*.

Suggestion: Why don't you visit your family over *spring break*?

Confirmation: You got your research paper done over *spring break*, right?

Problem: I have to work during *spring break*.

stacks   n.   the area of the library where most of the books are shelved

Example: At a small college, the *stacks* are usually open to all of the students.

Suggestion: You should look in the *stacks* for that book.

Surprise: The librarian let you go up in the *stacks* to look for your own book?

Problem: I need to find a carrel in the *stacks*.

student   n.   one who attends a school

Example: State University has more than fifty-thousand *students* enrolled on the main campus.

Suggestion: If you tell them that you are a *student*, maybe you will get a discount.

Surprise: You mean you aren't a *student*?

Problem: I need to find five *students* to complete my study.

student I.D. number   n.   a number used for identification at a college or university, often a social security number

Example: Your social security number is your *student I.D. number*.

Suggestion: You should write your *student I.D. number* on all of your papers.

Confirmation: Pat has a *student I.D. number*, doesn't she?

Problem: I can't seem to remember my *student I.D. number*.

student services   n.   an administrative branch of a college or university that provides noninstructional support services for students

Example: I have to go over to *student services* to meet with a financial aid advisor.

Suggestion: You had better go to *student services* to check on your dorm application.

Confirmation: The *student services* office is open during registration, isn't it?

Problem: I have to go to the *student services* office before the end of the day.

student union   n.   a building on campus where students can relax

Example: There is a movie at the *student union* tonight.

Suggestion: You could meet Ken in the *student union* before the concert.

Surprise: You mean the *student union* is closed over the holidays?

Problem: The *student union* closes at 10:00 P.M.

studies   n.   research investigations

Example: Many *studies* have been conducted here at State University.

Suggestion: Why don't you speak with Dr. Mason about her *studies*?

Surprise: So Jane is beginning her *studies*?

Problem: I have to complete my *studies* by the end of the semester.

study   v.   to acquire knowledge or understanding of a subject

Example: I have to *study* if I want to get a good grade in this class.

Suggestion: Why don't you plan to *study* at my house this weekend?

Confirmation: You *studied* for that test, didn't you?

Problem: I need to allow more time to *study*.

study date   n.   a date in which the activity is studying

Example: Joe and Diane have *study dates* most of the time.

Suggestion: You could arrange a *study date* with Jack before the test.

Surprise: You mean you don't have a *study date* tonight?

Problem: I have to meet Jack at the library for our *study date*.

study lounge   n.   a quiet area of a dormitory where students can go to study

Example: Even the *study lounge* is noisy in this dorm.

Suggestion: Why don't you meet me in the *study lounge* this evening?

Confirmation: Did you say that the *study lounge* is quiet?

Problem: I can't concentrate in the *study lounge*.

subject   n.   an area of study

Example: Math is my favorite *subject*.

Suggestion: Why don't you ask Tracy for help with the *subjects* she tutors?

Confirmation: You can get tutoring in all of the *subjects* taught at the university, can't you?

Problem: I have to take a lot of classes in *subjects* that I don't really like.

summer school   n.   the summer sessions, which are usually June through August

Example: *Summer school* starts the second week of June this year.

Suggestion: Why don't you take the art appreciation course in *summer school*?

Surprise: You mean you've gone to *summer school* every summer?

Problem: I can't go to *summer school* this year.

T.A.   n.   an abbreviation for teaching assistant
    Example: Laura has applied to be Dr. Graham's *T.A.*
    Suggestion: You should see the *T.A.* if you have questions
                  about the lecture.
    Surprise: So Bill *did* apply to be a *T.A.*
    Problem: I have to find Dr. Graham's *T.A.* before class
                  tomorrow.

teaching assistant   n.   a graduate student whose teaching duties
                              are supervised by a faculty member
    Example: We have a *teaching assistant* for the discussion
                  session of this class.
    Suggestion: You had better speak with the *teaching assistant*
                  before the next lab session.
    Confirmation: Did you say you haven't spoken with the *teaching
                  assistant*?
    Problem: The *teaching assistant* is really difficult to
                  understand.

tenure   n.   an academic rank that guarantees permanent status
    Example: Professor Peterson has *tenure*, but Mr. Lewis
                  doesn't.
    Suggestion: Why don't you request the requirements for
                  tenure?
    Surprise: You mean Dr. Peterson has *tenure*?
    Problem: Mr. Lewis will have to get his Ph.D. to qualify for
                  tenure.

term   n.   a time period when school is in session, usually a
             quarter or a semester
    Example: Dana needs two more *terms* to graduate.
    Suggestion: Dana had better take statistics next *term*.
    Confirmation: Nancy passed all of her classes last *term*, right?
    Problem: I have to complete my dissertation in three *terms*.

test n. an evaluation that is usually longer and worth more points than a quiz, but shorter and worth fewer points than an exam
Example: You will have a *test* every week in this class.
Suggestion: If I were you, I would work with my study group before the *test*.
Surprise: You mean you forgot about the *test*?
Problem: I have to study for two *tests* next week.

textbook n. a book that is used for a course
Example: The *textbooks* can be purchased at the bookstore or ordered over the Internet.
Suggestion: You could purchase used *textbooks* for some of your classes.
Surprise: You mean you had to buy new *textbooks*?
Problem: I can't find good used *textbooks* anywhere.

thesis n. a written research report in partial fulfillment of a graduate degree
Example: Tracy isn't taking any courses this semester because she is writing her *thesis*.
Suggestion: You should get the handbook at the graduate school before starting your *thesis*.
Confirmation: Tracy isn't writing her *thesis* this semester, is she?
Problem: I need to allow at least one semester to write my *thesis*.

transcript n. a printed copy of a student's grades
Example: The admissions office requires two *transcripts* with every application.
Suggestion: Why don't you request an extra copy of your *transcript*?
Confirmation: You got your *transcript*, didn't you?
Problem: I have to have those *transcripts* by next Monday.

transfer   v.   to change schools
Example: It is better to *transfer* at the beginning of the third year.
Suggestion: If I were you, I would *transfer* as soon as possible.
Confirmation: Dana *transferred* to State University, right?
Problem: I can't *transfer* colleges because I would lose credits.

tuition   n.   fees for instruction at a school
Example: The *tuition* is different from school to school.
Suggestion: You should check the *tuition* before deciding on a college.
Surprise: *Tuition* at private colleges is more?
Problem: I need a scholarship to pay my *tuition*.

tuition hike   n.   an increase in the fees for instruction
Example: There is a *tuition* hike every year at State University.
Suggestion: You should sign the petition protesting the *tuition* hike.
Confirmation: Did you say you graduated before the *tuition* hike?
Problem: I can't afford another *tuition* hike.

turn in   v.   to submit an assignment
Example: Please *turn in* your homework before you leave.
Suggestion: You had better *turn in* your paper before the end of the day.
Surprise: You mean I could have *turned in* my paper tomorrow?
Problem: I have to *turn in* the paper by Friday or I will get an F.

tutor   n.   a private instructor, often another student
Example: I have to meet my *tutor* at the library.
Suggestion: Why don't you get a *tutor* for your accounting class?
Surprise: You mean Jack is your *tutor*?
Problem: I can't afford to hire a *tutor*.

tutoring   n.   private instruction
    Example: Nancy needs some *tutoring* in this class.
    Suggestion: You could earn extra money *tutoring* for math.
    Surprise: So you *did* get the *tutoring* job.
    Problem: *Tutoring* takes a lot of time.

undergrad   n., adj.   abbreviation for undergraduate
    Example: I think that Dana is an *undergrad*.
    Suggestion: You could still enroll for *undergrad* classes while you are waiting to hear from the graduate school admissions office.
    Confirmation: You're an *undergrad*, right?
    Problem: I need to apply for an *undergrad* scholarship.

undergraduate (student)   n., adj.   a student pursuing a bachelor's degree
    Example: Some *undergraduates* require five years to complete a four-year program.
    Suggestion: You should look at more than one *undergraduate* program.
    Surprise: You mean you completed your *undergraduate* courses in three years?
    Problem: I can't complete my *undergraduate* degree before we move.

upper-division (course)   adj.   advanced courses for third- and fourth-year students
    Example: Most of the *upper-division* courses are numbered 400 or above.
    Suggestion: Why don't you take an *upper-division* music class?
    Surprise: You mean grammar is an *upper-division* course?
    Problem: Dana needs to take an *upper-division* math class.

whiteboard   n.   the (white) writing surface in the front of the classroom

Example: Professor Jones always writes the discussion topics on the *whiteboard* at the beginning of class.

Suggestion: You had better sit in front if you want to be able to read the notes on the *whiteboard*.

Confirmation: We will have a *whiteboard* in the room, won't we?

Problem: The *whiteboard* is too small.

withdraw   v.   to leave school

Example: My roommate *withdrew* from school.

Suggestion: You should *withdraw* so that you won't have failing grades on your transcript.

Surprise: You mean your parents want you to *withdraw* from school?

Problem: I have to *withdraw* from school at the end of the semester.

work-study   adj.   a special program that allows study time when there is nothing to do on the job

Example: There are several *work-study* positions open in the finance office.

Suggestion: Dana should apply for the *work-study* program next semester.

Confirmation: Vicki's library job is a *work-study* position, isn't it?

Problem: The *work-study* students couldn't answer my questions.

Xerox (machine)   n.   a copy machine

Example: There is a long line at the *Xerox* machine.

Suggestion: You could use the *Xerox* machine in the library.

Surprise: You mean there are only three *Xerox* machines on campus?

Problem: I need to find a *Xerox* machine.

NOTES

division n.   a group of departments in a college or university
    Example: The *division* of modern languages includes both the Spanish department and the French department, as well as the German department.
    Suggestion: Why don't you go to the *division* of math and sciences to find more information about biology instructors?
    Surprise: You mean you've already spoken to Dr. Conrad about the entrance exam for the *division* of social sciences?
    Problem: I need to find out what opportunities the *division* of modern languages offers for foreign study.

doctorate n.   the degree after a master's degree awarded to an academic doctor
    Example: Karen will receive her *doctorate* in the spring.
    Suggestion: You should meet with your academic advisor to discuss a *doctorate*.
    Surprise: So you *did* receive your *doctorate* from State University.
    Problem: I must complete my dissertation before I get my *doctorate*.

dorm n.   an abbreviation for dormitory
    Example: Living on campus in a *dorm* is often cheaper than living off campus.
    Suggestion: You should live in a *dorm* for at least one year.
    Confirmation: Did you say you have lived in a *dorm* for four years?
    Problem: Sue needs to apply now for a room in the *dorm*.

draft n.   a preliminary copy of a paper or other written document
    Example: A good student does not turn in a first *draft* of a paper.
    Suggestion: You should edit each *draft* on the computer.
    Surprise: You mean you wrote the first *draft* in one night?
    Problem: I can't turn in my essay because I have only the first *draft* written.